Education and Development:
Tradition and Innovation   Volume One

Education and Development: Tradition and Innovation

Introductory Volume: A Human Rights Analysis
Volume One: Concepts, Approaches and Assumptions
Volume Two: Equity and Excellence in Education for Development
Volume Three: Innovations in Delivering Primary Education
Volume Four: Non-formal and Non-governmental Approaches

This book is to be returned on
or before the date stamped below

UNIVERSITY OF PLYMOUTH

EXMOUTH LIBRARY

Tel: (01395) 255331
This book is subject to recall if required by another reader
Books may be renewed by phone
CHARGES WILL BE MADE FOR OVERDUE BOOKS

Education and Development:
Tradition and Innovation Volume One

Concepts,
Approaches and
Assumptions

Edited by
James Lynch, Celia Modgil
and Sohan Modgil

CASSELL

Cassell
Wellington House
125 Strand
London WC2R 0BB

PO Box 605
Herndon
VA 20172

First published 1997

British Library Cataloguing-in-Publication Data
A catalogue record for this book is available from the British
Library.

ISBN 0-304-32889-8 ✓

Typeset by York House Typographic Ltd, London
Printed and bound in Great Britain by The Bath Press

Contents

Contributors

Jean Anderson International Education Centre, The College of St Mark and St John, Plymouth

Mark A. Burch International consultant in environmental and sustainable development, based in Manitoba, Canada

Barry Cooper Graduate Research Centre in Education, University of Sussex

Fred Chambers Centre for International Education and Management, Chichester Institute of Higher Education

Lynn Davies School of Education, University of Birmingham

Phillip Hughes Australian National University, Canberra

Kenneth King Centre of African Studies, University of Edinburgh

Carol A. Kochhar George Washington University, Washington, DC

Colin Lacey Professor Emeritus, University of Sussex

Léo Laroche International Consultant in Data Processing and Statistical Analysis, Québec Department of Education

James Lynch International consultant and retired staff member of the World Bank

Stephen May Sociology Department, University of Bristol

Celia Modgil Goldsmiths College, University of London

Sohan Modgil School of Education, University of Brighton

Audrey Osler School of Education, University of Birmingham

Fernando Reimers Institute for International Development, Harvard University

Micheline C. Rey-von Allmen Faculty of Psychology and Educational Sciences, University of Geneva

Robert Smith Centre for International Studies in Education, University of Bristol

Clem Tisdell Department of Economics, University of Queensland

Harry Torrance Graduate Research Centre in Education, University of Sussex

Introduction:
The Purpose, Context and
Structure of the Series[1]

JAMES LYNCH

The purpose of the series

This book series is intended to make a seminal contribution to the debate about a key area of public policy for developing countries: the achievement of universal primary education – its form, content, process and financing. The agenda of the series can be stated briefly: to encourage the urgent achievement of basic and primary education for all, and to explore ways in which this can be achieved expeditiously, cost-effectively and with personal and social outcomes of high quality. The point of departure of the series is the right to education of every individual enshrined in the 1948 Universal Declaration of Human Rights and reaffirmed at the 1990 World Conference on Education for All (WCEFA). Education for All (EFA) is thus seen as an entitlement based in human rights and not as a privilege. The series is committed to the view that at least at the primary level, education must be free, and 'all' must include girls, and children with special educational needs, as proclaimed in the 1994 Salamanca Statement and Framework for Action on Special Needs Education (UNESCO and Ministry of Education and Science, Spain, 1994), as well as the children of minorities and indigenous peoples.

The series arises not only from the necessity to achieve this goal, but also from the urgency of achieving it for social, economic and political reasons. Moreover, the series is expressive of a number of fundamental concerns and issues, currently neglected or subject only to partial observance by governments and aid agencies:

* inadequate attention to the human rights dimension in the provision of universal primary education, including the right to participation;
* restriction of the goals of primary education and its contribution to human development, economic progress and democratic nation-building;
* inappropriate financial and budgetary strategies, including burdening the poor with fees for services which should be free according to international human rights declarations;
* unhelpful economic assistance for social-sector development and especially education, in the form of credits, often with multiple strings, rather than loans, a strategy which only further burdens with foreign debt countries already bitterly poor;
* naive utilization or misunderstanding of the meaning and accuracy of statistical indicators of progress towards universal primary education and its outcomes;
* the utilization of 'flags of convenience' which inaccurately portray the aims and objectives of projects and programmes;
* and the lack of reflexivity and sensitivity of many development educators and agencies to the often inappropriate industrialized paradigms and models which they seek to impose on developing countries.

The preparation of this series coincides with and takes strength from the 1995 UN Year for Tolerance and the launching of the United Nations Decade for Human Rights Education in December 1994.[2] Education for all is seen not only as a human right and a goal in itself, but also as contributing to overall human resource development, to poverty alleviation and to broader economic growth for developing countries, across dimensions of knowledge, skills, attitudes and values, both personal and social. To put this another way, the series takes as its point of departure the three classic, major goals of education: personal and social development; wealth creation, consistent with environmental sustainability; and democratic nation-building. The series does not accept that the goals of primary education can be restricted solely to literacy and numeracy, as goals in their own right, and it regrets the lack of attention to the third of the above goals, often referred to as the civic purposes of education, by many national governments, bilateral agencies and international organizations. Open, democratic government is indispensable to a free-market approach to development, and the school is the major socializing agency where learning about democratic citizenship, human rights and market economies has to take place.[3] Lack of attention to this third important educational goal, concerned with democracy, human rights, economic literacy and active citizenship according to the rule of law, may well have contributed at least in part to a number of political legitimation problems and crises which have been suffered by many developing countries in the period since independence, not least *vis-à-vis* their cultural diversity.

If the series is based on the case that education, at least at the primary level, is a basic and inalienable human right, it also contends that human right is linked to collateral fundamental human rights to basic health care and adequate nutrition,[4] which are indispensable to maximizing the exercise of the right to education.[5] Contributors to the series oppose the exclusion or limitation of the 'package' of entitlements in education, health and nutrition for reasons of ethnicity, gender, language or other cultural characteristics, social or economic position, religion or political persuasion. For it is the case that some governments, considering and seeking to use this right to education as a privilege to be allocated to their religious or political adherents, restrict the right to this package of entitlements or even, under the

banner of positive discrimination, restrict educational opportunities for some ethnic groups in their country. This series unequivocally condemns such practices as infringements of human rights, and also as economically craven. Equally, some cultures, misinterpreting religious tenets, seek to exclude and limit the right to or quality of educational provision for girls, practices and arrangements which the series also unequivocally condemns as breaches of international human rights instruments and covenants to which, in most cases, the governments of these countries are signatory. Consequently, the practice of some international funding agencies in failing to call the projects which they finance in developing countries to the bar of a human rights accountability, which could prevent such abuses, is also deprecated and should be corrected.

Financial and budgetary strategies and the assistance policies of aid agencies can influence the ability of the poor to enjoy their human rights. Thus, while recognizing the need for a stable political, institutional and macro-economic setting for sustainable development, as well as for financial integrity, the series is committed to the need for safety nets and checks and balances, including the attachment of 'social covenants' to all adjustment programmes, in order to protect specified essential social expenditures. It supports an updating of the United Nations' 20/20 initiative, without which major social targets, such as universal free primary education, cannot be achieved.[6] Moreover, the series shares the view that all international, bilateral and multilateral aid for primary education, and indeed social-sector investment in general for the least developed countries, should be in the form of grants and not loans, and that debts incurred by these countries for social sector investments should be 'forgiven', so as to support and not undermine the development of an appropriate social and political, as well as economic, policy environment and climate.[7] But it is important to approach the task of development with humility, realizing that international development can only support social and economic development in poor countries; it cannot replace that commitment and the political will on the part of the country itself. As a corollary, therefore, to the measures proposed above, the fight against the debilitating effects of corruption on the development of the poorest nations has to be pursued more vigorously and successfully. It should be seen for what it is: treason against one's own people; and the efforts of bilateral and multilateral agencies must be directed to making it culturally unacceptable.

Ownership and self-determination are clearly critical factors in fundamental development, but involvement of local communities in the provision of primary education has often been little more than a cynical means to move the burden of financing on to the backs of the poor, where such approaches have not included the allocation to those communities of the resources needed to fulfil the devolved functions. Such strategies may make the entitlement to free primary education less rather than more accessible for many families and children. The series advocates, therefore, the local, national and international responsibility of communities, governments and agencies to secure the means for all children to enjoy their human rights, not at some point in the distant future, but with an urgency which reflects the fact that children who do not have an opportunity for a quality primary education are being denied a full human entitlement and development, at the same time as richer governments are expending billions on armaments and profligate luxuries.

The resources for such fiscal goals and financing strategies can readily be provided in grant form, if the political will is generated and the right policy decisions made in industrialized countries and international organizations, but only if developing countries take their responsibility seriously and also make the right financial allocations that are necessary and indeed promised.[8] The series, for example, condemns the widespread practice of demanding cost contributions and recovery from the parents of primary students and impoverished local communities, at the same time as the same developing countries massively subsidize the higher education of students predominantly from among the élites. Such practices are unjust, and economically and politically purblind. The financial burden being thrust on local communities by the current vogue for non-financed devolution has, thus, to be seen in a holistic and cumulative

context, which also includes consideration of the demands being simultaneously made by other subsectors, such as health, water and sanitation, infrastructure and nutrition.

The series also arises from a concern at the misuse of statistics to express the extent of achievement of educational development and at the implicit cultural baggage of many projects. For example, governments and aid agencies often refer to the gross enrolment ratio, as though this were some reliable indicator of progress towards universal primary education. In reality it may be a truer indicator of how inefficient the system is, because the ratio is inflated by repetition and under- and over-age pupils. Similarly, staff : student ratio cannot be taken an indicator of either class size or the efficiency of teacher deployment or utilization, and of course in so far as a specialist as opposed to a class teacher approach is adopted in primary education, it is not even a useful tool alone for calculating teacher supply and demand. Again, most project indicators include enrolment rather than attendance or completion of a particular stage of education, or, more importantly, the learning and human development which has been achieved. Further, disbursement as a major indicator of project performance in education is extremely unreliable.

Equally, many projects may sail under false flags of convenience, such as poverty alleviation or equity enhancement. Yet when the 'deep structure' of the project is examined the bulk of resources is allocated to other objectives. Some projects, for example, trumpet their commitment to girls' education, but allocate much more funding to prestigious building works in cities than to any direct incentives for the enrolment of girls, such as the remission of school fees or textbook and other costs, the provision of scholarships for girls, the recruitment of women teachers and administrators, or the provision of adequate water and sanitation in schools.

Many development educators are often unaware of the underlying values and epistemologies which silently guide their judgements and decisions about education in developing countries. Addressing this problem, the series seeks to make explicit and critically evaluate current assumptions and ideologies of development and to review the role of 'Northern' paradigms and knowledge monopolies on the aims, structure, functions and effectiveness of education in developing nations. It is not the contention of this series that the only unsuccessful transfer is from industrialized to developing countries. Quite the reverse: there are examples of unsuccessful transfer between and among developing countries (Jennings, 1993). The series is arguing against two things: the costly neglect of indigenous culture, knowledge systems and informal social networks, and the monolithic or, rather, monist expectations of culture. For it is inadequate knowledge of such local cultural and social conditions and the neglect of cultural diversity which weaken and make less effective so many projects.[9] Projects should be accounted according to criteria of both social and economic capital growth.

To this end, the series includes contributions where projects have sought to draw on local knowledge resources, as well as descriptions and critical analyses of policy and practice in the field from different perspectives. It offers descriptions of promising innovations in project design, implementation and evaluation. Contributions describe and appraise the work of international and regional organizations, including the major development banks, national and bilateral agencies and non-governmental organizations. The series includes contributions from project workers, aid specialists, academics and scholars, practitioners and workers in the aid field, and politicians and educators from both industrialized and developing countries. Thus, although the overall coherence of the series derives from its concern with education and development, contributors are from a number of different sectors, disciplines and walks of life, and the series as a whole adopts an intersectoral and interprofessional approach – one which it, in turn, advocates.

Contributors to this series have been encouraged to ground their chapters in human rights, to adopt novel, exploratory and even speculative approaches, to critically review current policy and practice, and to expose the underlying theories, assumptions and paradigms which have sustained strategies of development in the field of education

in developing countries for some fifty years with such very mixed results. Authors were asked to base their accounts, wherever possible, on first-hand experience and practice, in so far as that was possible. Their contributions include accounts of approaches and projects which have manifested thinking and action 'outside the box', as well as critiques of existing strategies and tactics. Particular attention is given to activities fostering local capacity development and community participation with appropriate resource support, and to strategies which encourage self-determination as a means towards development, as well as the involvement of women and girls and other groups currently under-represented or discriminated against in receiving, offering, managing and administering essential social services.

In addition to making a contribution to the debate about education for all and how to achieve it, the series also has a broader purpose: to contribute to the debate about present and future relations between industrialized and developing countries, which will provide an essential context to their partnership in pursuit of education for all. It aims to respond to the need for a more critical appraisal of those relationships, and to stimulate fresh thinking on how to replace the growth and 'dependence paradigms' of development dominant during the 1960s, 1970s and 1980s with a new 'covenant of interdependence'. In particular, the horrific impact of current growth paradigms on natural resource depletion, the environment and social structures indicates the need to draw economic policies to the bar of a rigorous environmental and social accountability.

In an interdisciplinary and cross-sectoral way, the series thus seeks to raise fundamental issues concerning the contribution of education to economic and broader social and political development. In questioning old-established assumptions and orthodoxies in the field of education in developing countries, with their underlying values, presuppositions, aims and strategies, the series also includes critiques of the costs (including the processes of costing), the benefits (and the way those benefits are conceptualized), as well as the financial constraints surrounding improved educational provision in developing countries. These latter are seen within the pathology which includes the international 'helping' organizations and agencies themselves. Through this critique, the series seeks to establish new parameters and theoretical insights, and to indicate both strategic and tactical initiatives. Above all, the series seeks to highlight the shared responsibility of industrialized countries for the poverty and deprivation of developing countries and for the restricted life chances of their populations through the economic and cultural dominance–submission relationship inherent in the industrialized countries' interactions with the 'South'. The development of an appropriate universal primary and basic education of high quality, seen as both process and product, and linked to both basic health care and adequate nutrition entitlements, can be a major means to change that relationship and, at the same time, as a means for the construction of new and healthier, non-exploitative relationships to the benefit of all humanity, where interests above self-interest are seen as valid and desirable.

The context of the series

With the disappearance in the 1990s of the old bifocal superpower conflict and military competition, the opportunity, unimaginable only a few short years ago, seemed to have presented itself for the first time for a redirection of huge resources from armaments to infrastructural, human resource and other investments in the developing world. Not without continuing tensions and conflicts, the ideological conflict which was the Cold War has been replaced by a broad, and (it is true) sometimes too cosy, convergence of view with regard to development and, in many cases, the denationalization and liberalization of both political and economic sectors. But the ideological and other changes are not all going in the same direction. Rather, if we consider political, economic, environmental and social spheres, this latter in a human rights perspective, it is evident that we are faced by a complex and changing series of patterns, with both positive and negative aspects and

effects. In other words, the current scene is very uneven, with contradictory indications in all spheres.

Fundamental political changes have occurred, for example, in Eastern Europe, but can also be seen in the establishment of an increasing number of democratic governments to replace former military dictatorships in Latin America, the relaxation of previously authoritarian rule in some parts of Asia, and the introduction of multi-party systems in parts of Africa. Again, not without continued criticism from a number of nations, there has been an increase of confidence in the United Nations and its ability to solve some world problems successfully, even if only by keeping warring factions apart and providing succour to the sick and famished, and those displaced by war and natural disaster. Further, in many countries with very different cultures and political systems, there has been widespread although not universal recession in the role of government in citizens' lives, which has brought into sharper relief the contrast between the progress of these latter countries on the one hand, and on the other the continuing authoritarianism and lack of economic, political and broader social progress in many, but not all, developing countries.

Increasingly, developed countries or groups within those countries, such as the 'Déclaration de Berne' in Switzerland, are identifying their own responsibility for monitoring their own capitalism and its effects on developing countries. They are seeking to support developments towards a much more open trading system, assisting developing countries to manage their debt burden, encouraging investment and facilitating access to capital markets. Moreover, as the world's economies have become much more integrated, driven by such factors as reduced barriers to trade, wider access to technology and falling costs of transport and communication, international agencies have concentrated increased attention on the growing economic gap between North and South and the problems of delivering basic services to the two-thirds of humankind who live in underdeveloped countries. So acute has this problem of development inertia become that the 1980s is being referred to as the lost decade for Africa. But there is little doubt that poverty increased in most Latin American countries during the 1980s as well. Moreover, the gap between the rich and the poor in many developed countries also widened.

To address many of these development problems, the view has been repeatedly advanced that the peace dividend from disengagement in Europe may be used to alleviate the deadening poverty of most of the underdeveloped world's population. In similar vein, others argue that, with the 'liberation' of Eastern Europe, attention should now be turned to liberating the developing countries from dictatorship, war and civil strife, corruption, exploitation and poverty, which have been their lot since independence. Yet the reality is that the demise of the old order has resulted in greater, not less, disorder, conflict and instability. Some contend that the most valuable progress for the world's poorest nations would be further liberalization of trade and of restrictive agricultural policies in the industrialized countries, although many observers point with resigned pessimism to the static state of development indicators in many countries, such as enrolments in education, infant mortality and life expectancy, and the continuing existence of runaway population explosion, starvation, corruption and grinding poverty in many developing countries.

In the environmental sphere too, in spite of the fact that the so-called green revolution is now well established, the pace of depletion of irreplaceable human resources is accelerating. The Jomtien Conference emphasized the importance of education as a precondition for balanced development, and the United Nations Conference on Environment and Development (UNCED), convened in Rio de Janeiro in June 1992, drew governments together on the need to reconcile the demands of development with the preservation of the environment. Sustainable development rose higher on the agenda of action. The importance of increasing and improving environmental education and broadening awareness was indeed one of the few major points on which all participants agreed. The October 1992 World Congress for Education and Communication on Environment and Development (ECO-ED) in Toronto, Canada, was also aimed at strengthening the delivery of environ-

mental education and the development of new networks and partnerships involving the general public, industry and commerce, international and bilateral agencies, governments and non-governmental organizations (NGOs). The World Development Report for 1992 points to the clear feasibility of combining improved environmental conditions, rapid economic development and eradication of widespread poverty if the right policy choices are made (World Bank, 1992). But the challenge still remains to devise and implement effective action which will go beyond the declarations.

The art of matching human need and ecological realities to achieve sustainable development is still very immature. Some argue, for example, that the world's non-renewable resources are still being exhausted with a rapidity that spells disaster for all, unless there can be global agreement on the utilization of the world's natural resources for the good of all humankind. Also associated with an ever harsher competitive surge is the rising recognition of the many world environmental crises, ranging from the depredation of the rain forests in Asia, South and North America, deliberate or accidental nuclear contamination (sometimes with international consequences, as in the case of Five Mile Island, Chernobyl, and many places in Russia), pollution of the air, crowding of the skies, local and international noise pollution, the extinction and near-extinction of animal and plant species to the depletion of the ozone layer and global warming.

It is in this economic, political and environmental context that human rights has become a major international issue, with some major aid agencies requiring conformity with international conventions and norms as part of their quid pro quo for aid. The charter of the European Bank for Reconstruction and Development includes a commitment to 'the fundamental principles of multiparty democracy, the rule of law, respect for human rights and market economics' (Sonenshine, 1990). Moreover, with the increased ease of international communication and the greater visibility of human rights violations, major initiatives have been taken in order to call states to international accountability. But in spite of such commendable progress, the continuing abuse of human rights, and especially those of women and children, the tendency to one-party states and military coups and dictatorships, and continued ethnic and religious bigotry, conflict and genocide, starkly profile the continuing lack of social, economic and political progress in large areas of the earth and for a majority of its population.

Further, some development banks have been accused of bolstering authoritarian regimes, supporting governments practising ethnic, religious and gender discrimination (which are thus in breach of United Nations covenants and resolutions), conniving at human rights abuses, and of favouring in their practice, if not in their rhetoric, the rich over the poor. Nor, it has been argued, do processes for the appointment of top officials to these institutions inspire confidence in democracy and transparent and open procedures. Accusations that the Bretton Woods institutions are a tool of American foreign policy appear from time to time, as well as the presence of North American cultural hegemony of the paradigms which the institutions seek to broadcast to the developing world. Moreover, major aid agencies are criticized for failing to take into account sufficiently the human right to participation in major infrastructural decisions of the people most closely affected, and regularly neglecting the social resettlement dimension of such projects from barrages to hydroelectric schemes and road-building. Such projects are often subjected to a unidimensional appraisal, rather than being considered within their ecosystemic and social context.

Worldwide prevailing and countervailing tendencies are vying with each other, with policy-making resting far too often, even exclusively, on preponderantly economic grounds. On the one hand, there is clearly an increased level of awareness, with international declarations and conventions beginning to set an agenda for progress; on the other hand, not least in the human rights sphere, these are paralleled by continued, even accelerated, abuse. Moreover, accompanying whatever positive developments have taken place have been three further concomitants which have brought with them their own problems. The first of these has been the rediscovery of 'ethnicity',

sometimes long submerged in authoritarian harmony, leading to tensions, bigotry, a re-emergence of extreme right-wing sentiments and parties in Europe and, in its extreme form, to economic blockade, civil war, the disintegration of nations and genocide. Linked to this in some cases has been the growth of militant forms of Islam. The second has been a growing consciousness that the military confrontation between East and West is gradually being replaced by a surge in global competition for the world's economic resources, of which Iraq's attack on Kuwait was only one manifestation. Third, and not unrelated to the 'celebrations' of the fiftieth birthday of the Bretton Woods institutions, there has been a gradual awakening to the fact that the current international world order is in need of a fundamental reform, if the problems of developing nations are ever to be resolved. The highly successful financial order established by the Bretton Woods Conference in the 1940s and the institutions then established are being subjected to increasingly critical appraisal for their contemporary role in what is now seen as the pathology of underdevelopment.

The World Development Report for 1990 states: 'a substantial increase in the resources for fighting poverty appears entirely affordable. It is a matter of political commitment and the reassessment of donors' priorities' (World Bank, 1990a, p. 136). The subsequent volume in the series picks up the relay baton, identifying the 'challenge of development' as the most important challenge facing the human race (World Bank, 1991a, p. 1). But, as the 1990 World Development Report expresses it, 'effective action to help the poor, involves some costs for the nonpoor in both developed and developing countries' (World Bank, 1990a, p. 143). Yet at the moment, industrial nations spend about twenty times as much on military purposes as they do on aid to developing countries. Further, although over a billion people, more than 20 per cent of the world's population, are existing on less than $1 a day, the West is still extracting more in interest payments and capital than it is donating in aid and lending in credits. In spite of increased allocations to basic and primary education, the vast majority of industrialized countries are far from achieving the UN target of 0.7 per cent of the gross domestic product allocated to aid (International Council of Voluntary Agencies, 1994).

International reports continue to draw attention to the widespread malnutrition, abuse and premature death which are the lot of women and children in the developing world (United Nations Children's Fund, 1990). Eight million children die each year from preventable diseases and one-third of all children in developing countries are either mentally or physically impaired by malnutrition (United Nations Children's Fund, 1994), at the same time as industrialized countries continue their profligate use of the world's material resources. Industrialized countries seem blithely unaware of the subsidized development aid which they receive from the developing world, to which they act as magnets, drawing away its best and most scarce human capital, sometimes as a by-product of aid projects and other donor investments. If the developed world is in earnest in its pursuit of development, then it has to be more aware of the need for 'cost downside analysis' of its aid for recipients.

In order to begin to reverse at least the developmental and educational deficits, international gatherings, such as the 1990 Jomtien Conference on Education for All have highlighted the central importance of human resource development and especially basic education for the creation of the human capital indispensable to productive social development and economic growth. They have begun to forge an international consensus on a framework for action to meet basic learning needs, highlighting particularly the special needs of women and girls, but also those of the impaired and disadvantaged. For example, the action framework agreed by more than 150 nations which participated in the Jomtien Conference states that education for women and girls 'should be designed to eliminate the social and cultural barriers which have discouraged or even excluded women and girls from the benefits of regular education programmes, as well as to promote equal opportunities in all aspects of their lives' (World Conference on Education for All, 1990, p. 62). The Salamanca Statement and Framework for Action further strengthened the need to address and include those with special educational needs, if a

real universal primary education were to be achieved (UNESCO and Ministry of Education and Science, Spain, 1994).

One of the major aims of the controversy-ridden World Summit for Social Development, held in Copenhagen in March 1995, was to seek to divert to the world's very poor some part of the 'peace dividend' arising from the end of the Cold War. Although some of the summit's aims were thwarted by conflicts about child labour and controversial ideas such as an international tax on currency transactions, it did focus attention once again firmly not only on the need to tackle poverty, but also on the success with which it can be and has been tackled in some of the nations of East Asia. The World Bank, in documents provided for the summit, admitted that although sound economic policies and a well-functioning labour market are essential for economic growth, they remain insufficient without investments in human capital (World Bank, 1995b, p. xi). Human capital was defined as knowledge, skills and good health, seen as prerequisites for productive employment, informed and active citizenship and a better quality of life (ibid.). Investments in universal primary education in particular were seen as instrumental in bringing about the East Asian 'miracles' and were advocated in order to boost the economic growth of the poorest countries. Four priorities for investment were seen as crucial for development: basic education; girls' education; cost-effective health services; and early childhood development (ibid., p. 45).

The fact remains, however, that declarations and good intentions are unlikely to suffice unless attitudes and underlying assumptions, financing priorities and strategies, and models of project design, implementation and evaluation also change. That means allocating a higher priority and greater resources to human resource development, not just in rhetoric, but also in practice and in action. For human capital development affords the poor in developing countries perhaps the only kind of negotiable capital they are ever likely to accumulate for their future and that of their children, community and country. It also means that criteria for project success and sustainability must include social as well as economic indicators

(Cernea, 1993). Supply-side economic inputs and technology transfer will not alone suffice to achieve development if they ignore essential cultural and social preconditions and the need for participation on the part of the beneficiaries, who also have expertise.

Yet a great weakness of many projects is that, in spite of considerable talk of beneficiary participation and putting people first, they neglect, or have inadequate understanding of, local culture, knowledge and informal institutions (see, however, Davis, 1995). Moreover, they tend to expect a single reality, rather than the diversity of views and constructions of reality which is the norm in most societies. The assumptions underlying the knowledge base of some projects are thus monist, monolithic and exclusive, rather than diverse and inclusive. Indeed, knowledge internationally and within nations sometimes tends to be used to undermine and disparage the practical experience, knowledge reality and values of those in need, with consequent and continued knowledge-poverty, economic decline, environmental degradation, disease and starvation.[10] Lack of knowledge of local culture and local informal systems of information and communication can be a major cause of project underperformance or failure. Poverty increases and human injustice seem to prevail (Watson, 1992).

But that need not be so. Local knowledge, culture and social structures can be used to enhance the efficiency and effectiveness of projects. Technology transfer can team up with rather than ignore indigenous knowledge systems. Specialist know-how and technical knowledge can also be disseminated more widely for the social and economic reconstruction of those material conditions and ideological and political coalitions which can liberate the human spirit from material and intellectual bondage, rather than enslave and subjugate it. Policy distortions, particularly in project design and technical assistance strategies which militate against this process of exchange can be eliminated. In this process of democratizing knowledge, education has a fundamental, powerful and heretical role to play in human capital development and social structural regeneration, so crucial to an improved, accelerated and sustainable development. But a more inclusive consciousness, such as that required for sustainable development, presupposes a new education, putting people first, oriented to intuition and imagination and to the experience, values and perceptions and ways of knowing of groups and nations traditionally excluded from a positivist, scientific rationalist approach to development.

Even from an economic point of view, and compared with bald rates of return on other investments, the yield on educational investment is princely. The economic returns on educational investment, for example, have been well catalogued over a number of years (Schultz, 1961; Bowman, 1980). Although there are other 'yields' to investment in primary education, a synthesis of the wealth of 'rate of return on education' studies from different countries would appear to indicate that the estimated rates of return are typically more than 10 per cent and that the highest rates of return are on investment on the lowest level of formal education (Psacharopoulos, 1985). Primary education, it appears, has a direct and positive effect not only on economic development, but also on productivity, as well as on life chances, health, nutrition and the rate of population increase. There is also some evidence to support the argument that in addition to the greater economic returns which investments in primary education yield, they also contribute to greater equity (United Nations Children's Fund, 1991), as well as to social development and nation-building (Lockheed and Verspoor, 1992). Yet in practice primary education continues to receive a low priority and status. Many nations in the developing world continue to invest many thousand times more per capita on higher education of the already privileged than they invest in primary and basic education, and military spending in many developing countries still exceeds expenditure on health, nutrition and education combined.

Nor can the pattern of provision for the future be just more of the same for all. As in developed countries, there are many patterns of educational organization and schooling provision which may be effective in developing countries: some centralized, some decentralized; some with a pragmatic curriculum, some with an encyclopedist;

some with teacher training at higher-education level, some with higher secondary schools; and so on. The question has to be asked: what educational approaches can be developed which are more efficient and cost-effective, more relevant and tailor-made for the problems of each nation, rather than mass-produced 'hand-me-down' panaceas, produced in the dominant intellectual and social powerhouses of the West? What is the best cultural and economic fit? What are the real costs to the countries receiving aid and what are the benefits of particular approaches to them and their peoples? Above all, what are the major priorities?

After all, most developed countries have survived the first century of mass basic and primary education without a national assessment system; why is it such a high priority for developing countries to have one? Similarly, the effective schools movement in the United States and analogous developments elsewhere may have indicated the educational inputs which are likely to be most influential in stimulating learning, but common sense indicates that there are many different patterns and models of 'good school'. Common sense also seems to counsel against trying to clone failed North American or European models of effective schools on to the backs of developing nations. Not all children in the developed world are offered exactly the same curriculum, so how can it be appropriate for children in the developing world to be offered a uniform, homogenized curriculum? Why are poor children in developing countries required to pay fees for primary schooling and, in some cases, their texts and materials, when children in many rich countries do not do so?

Of course, much has taken place in the first half of the new decade, especially as a consequence of the influential Jomtien Conference. Important progress has been made at the conceptual level, offering new criteria for judgement. Internationally, new, more comprehensive conceptualizations of what constitutes deprivation and development have been proposed to replace predominantly economic criteria.[11] The human service delivery paradigm for primary education has begun to change, promising improvements in the lot of millions of children currently excluded from school because of impairments. Bilateral and multilateral organizations have alike increased their funding to basic and primary education, in some cases very substantially. Networks and organizational focal points for mutual assistance have been established. Multilateral organizations, such as the World Bank, have agreed to give priority for investment credits to six major areas, among which is increasing the participation in education of those who comprise the majority of the unschooled: women and girls (World Bank, 1990b). International organizations, national governments, regional meetings and NGOs have provided guidelines for action, accounts of pertinent research, rosters of what seems to work and what the most potent and influential inputs may be, case studies of successful innovations, critical appraisals of national strategies, and plans of action. International analyses are now resulting in the construction of catalogues of evaluated approaches indicating what may be effective in overcoming cultural, ideological and material barriers and facilitating enrolment and learning in certain cultural and social contexts (King and Hill, 1990).

In the field of the education of women and girls, too, the benefits, constraints and strategies are beginning to be better understood and documented (Herz *et al.*, 1991). *The World Development Report 1990* (World Bank, 1990a) draws attention to a twofold strategy which is necessary if world poverty is to be reduced. Education features prominently in that strategy of efficient labour-intensive growth, combined with the adequate provision of social services, including primary education, basic health care and family planning (World Bank, 1990a). But it is the focus on the achievement of education for all which has reasserted the basic right of all the world's citizens, contained in the International Declaration of Human Rights, to education at least at the primary level. That right must include a right to a quality education appropriate to particular national, local and personal needs or it is meaningless.

In both industrialized and developing countries, the role of education in broader human resource development for its own sake and to support efficiency-based sustainable policies for economic and social development is undeniable.

In the North, education must evolve a concept of an environmentally and economically sustainable development, responsible world economic and political co-citizenship, and an appreciation of the North's responsibility for 'shaping and sharing a new global community'. It must facilitate that ceding of resources from the non-poor to the poor of which the World Development Report spoke (World Bank, 1990a, p. 143). For that goal, education in the North will need to sensitize students to the consequences for the South of their unbridled 'greed'. In the South, education must provide the human resource development to pull the majority out of the slough of poverty and ignorance. It must provide for the generation of income-earning opportunities, the encouragement of entrepreneurship and wealth creation, a balance between the role of government and the private sector and for nation-building and democratic institutions. It must seek to create a more communal and cohesive society, to maintain or construct the social capital implicit in communitarian traditions as a basis for economic development[12] and to nurture a national stature to participate fully in the shaping of the new world community. For both North and South, the message is that nations must encourage a new, more inclusive and human-rights-based social consciousness for innovation and competitiveness, coupled with a long-term commitment to technical training, capital investment, new technologies and education (Porter, 1990).

For new strategies and new human relationships to develop, innovation at the conceptual and operational levels is also required. No one intellectual methodology is adequate to the task. There has to be an understanding and acceptance of responsibility for the costs to the many of the waste of the few, for the immorality of claiming human rights for oneself and directly or indirectly infringing those same rights of others, for the detrimental effects of cultural neocolonialism and educational hegemony for the donor and the recipient alike,[13] for the drain of human capital from developing to developed countries and the role of 'aid' in this process. It is this concern for partnership and participation, for mutuality and reciprocity, for social as well as economic development,[14] for the recognition of the crucial role of education in

human resource development and sustainable development within a context, where human rights are recognized and respected by governments, groups and individuals, which is the central focus of this series. Its aim is to contribute to the forging of a fundamental paradigm change in values and a new course of action in the field of education congruent with human rights, in order to achieve a new and more financially equitable and humanly just relationship between developed and developing countries for the benefit of all.

The structure of the series

This series of books comprises five volumes, including a specially written composite introductory volume. Several major themes run through all volumes:
* gender equity;
* inclusive schooling;
* a universal package of entitlements for all children based on fundamental human rights;
* economic, social and cultural mutuality between developed and developing countries;
* environmental sustainability;
* financial equity;
* community involvement, democratic participation and educational development seen as fundamental human resource development for economic progress.

Each volume has, in addition, its own organizing focus.

In Volume One, *Concepts, Approaches and Assumptions*, it is the basic economic values, epistemologies and paradigms of bilateral and multilateral agencies which form the focal points. These domains are scrutinized for their functionality in assisting the achievement of universal primary education and a package of 'social entitlements' in education, health and nutrition. Values, epistemologies and paradigms are seen by contributors not as taken-for-granteds, but as the problematic purveyors of structures and practices which often inhibit rather than facilitate development. The export of home-base epistemologies by both bilateral and multilateral agencies may be seen as a latter-day cultural imperialism which frequently makes the process of development longer and more difficult, because it represents a foreign cultural graft that is often rejected by the receiving nation. Moreover, it complicates cognitive processes, excludes local culture, knowledge systems and informal social structures, is often accompanied by the neglect of cultural diversity in the developing country and makes projects less effective than they would otherwise have been. If beneficiary participation is seen as really important, then it must embrace both social and cultural participation.

Thus, contributors to the volume see the need for an urgent reappraisal of current paradigms of development in order to fit them to the philosophy of client centredness and beneficiary participation. The introduction of environmentally sustainable, economically realistic, socially and culturally more sensitive paradigms provides a backcloth to a revised role for education in the creation of a new, more inclusive consciousness which can better align greater human justice and equity with human need and durable development, at the same time as making investments more effective and productive. The volume critiques some of the major theoretical and practical assumptions and frameworks underlying current concepts of development aid to the developing world. To assist practitioners and policy-makers as much as possible, this volume draws on actual projects in order to exemplify the issues and policy dilemmas in making educational development in the developing countries more attentive to human rights considerations. The values operationalized and projected by both multilateral and bilateral agencies are considered in the context of the international cultural hegemony of Western intellectual styles. Several authors argue the need for a change of paradigm towards the human rights point of view.

The case is argued for a movement away from inputs, such as enrolments, to a deeper consideration of processes and outputs, such as time-on-task, attendance, completion and functional learning achievement. Innovative and successful experiences are described and specific examples of promising approaches are given at interna-

tional, national and project levels, with a critical commentary of the criteria used to judge the effectiveness of such work. Amended criteria are proposed for use by policy-makers, including the need for more integrated formative monitoring, in-depth research and evaluation during programme implementation.

In the economic domain, the assumptions underlying the policies of major multilateral agencies, such as structural adjustment, are considered, and their backwash effects on the education sector and human rights are highlighted. The negative flow of investment between developing and developed countries is appraised in the light of both human capital and primary resource implications. The right of developing countries to receive equitable recompense for both forms of resource when they are exported is situated in the context of a human rights entitlement (presaging the major concern of Volume Two) envisaged in terms of both individual and national rights, as well as in the context of the current international economic, political and environmental framework for the implementation and securing of those rights. The necessity of local capacity enhancement as a major goal of development within compact and uncomplicated design is argued and illustrated. The issue of the massive 'reverse transfer' of technical assistance by developing countries to developed through the recruitment of many of the best brains to the West after the home-base country has invested heavily in their education and training forms part of the case for a new approach to international resource allocation and models of technical assistance. The need to improve the information base, its quality and reliability, not least in the monitoring of allocations, is seen as a basic step towards any improvement of either quality or quantity.[15]

In Volume Two, *Equity and Excellence in Education for Development*, two overlapping populations of children form the main focus: those with special educational needs, and girls. The volume picks up some of the human rights issues raised in Volume One from a different perspective, and seeks to expose the manifold infringements of the human rights of these special populations, and the connivance of many international agencies at those infringements. Supported by international human rights conventions and declarations, which form a *de jure* foundation for the education of all children of primary school age, the leitmotif of this volume is the need for a fundamental universal entitlement, including basic and primary education, basic health care and adequate nutrition. Nations and international agencies alike are bound by this human rights entitlement. They cannot pick and choose, to recognize or not. It is these rights which determine the entitlement of children to life chances, not international financial orders and decisions, or the whim of project designers. The contributions seek to address the entitlement within a context broader than the educational sector alone, including health and nutritional dimensions, and to see it in both intersectoral and interprofessional contexts.

The neglect of cultural and social diversity in the dominant epistemologies of development education is critiqued, and the powerful, complex and intertwined constraints to the education of the two populations, referred to above, is argued to demand more effective intersectoral and interprofessional approaches. The weakness of criteria for project design attentive to the needs of these two groups is discussed. A case for affirmative action, including targeted subsidies, is advanced in view of the greater gains that society reaps from the education of girls and women. The continued efficacy of outdated service delivery paradigms is considered as a major inhibitor of more equitable and inclusive schooling. Examples of programme or project strategies which have been discriminatory or neglectful of the needs and rights of women are given, as are examples of positive approaches which have been successful. In particular, teacher education and curricular and materials reforms are seen as necessary, although not sufficient alone, to encourage the enrolment and retention of girls in primary education. Consideration is also given to the determining role of physical facilities in attracting and retaining girls in school. The relationship between educational level attained and total period fertility rate, birth spacing and social and economic status of women, as well as the economic benefits to society, are considered. The volume also contains several examples of innovatory approaches which take into account the issues of diversity and gender equity.

As in the other books of this series, Volume Three, *Innovations in Delivering Primary Education*, shares a number of common themes and values with the preceding volume: basic and primary education as a human right; the concept of a package of entitlements; the necessity of critiquing underlying values and assumptions; and the need to develop new, more equal forms of partnership. The volume commences with a discussion of some of the major inputs to basic and primary education which have a determining effect on the quality of the processes and outcomes of that education. The need to look inside the 'boxes' to see what is behind the label is emphasized, so that, for example, it is not just the question of textbooks being available that is important, but the quality of their production and content, the timeliness of their availability and the skill of their utilization. Again the underlying values and assumptions of much that passes as development education are considered problematic. The need for new forms of collaboration and partnership within a peer relationship is emphasized, as is the role of in-country research. Against a backcloth of the form, content and process of initial and in-service teacher education, and the need for enhanced funding through such strategies as virement of funding from other educational subsectors to primary education; issues of access, enrolment, attendance, repetition and drop-out are considered.

The volume includes examples of innovatory projects and developments and it highlights the importance of curriculum development in the improvement of the quality of primary education. The values underpinning the curriculum are seen as a field of competition among ideological perspectives and beliefs, and the volume considers the basic alternative educational paradigms of human learning which might underpin the work of international agencies, both multilateral and bilateral. Issues of quality and quantity of provision are seen as interconnected rather than as bipolar dilemmas, and the need for a redefinition of outcomes is advanced at the same time as the case is advanced for the inclusion of both extrinsic and intrinsic incentives and measures of success. The linear and restricted current paradigm of human learning and achievement and the over-emphasis on hardware and on Western concepts of education and success are considered, as well as the role of the dominant international groups and that of leading urban élite groups in-country. The need for principles for project construction, implementation and evaluation that are attentive to Freire's concept of conscientization is underlined.

Volume Four, *Non-Formal and Non-Governmental Approaches*, continues the 'cross-cutting' themes introduced in the previous volumes and retrieves many of the issues and principles enunciated in those volumes: education as a human rights entitlement, linked to similar entitlements in health and nutrition; the need to re-examine underlying values, definitions and assumptions; the need for new forms of collaboration and partnership. It highlights the distinctive role of NGOs in development education and identifies some of the tensions inherent in their relationships with governments, particularly in the context of efforts at coordination and innovation. Examples are given of the pioneering role and function of NGOs, and characteristics of successful models are described. A typology of NGOs is proposed across several dimensions and the proven role of NGOs in educational innovation is highlighted through a consideration of the pressures which force NGOs to be innovative and cost-effective. None the less, a case is made for greater self-evaluation and research into the technology of implementation of these organizations. A particular focus is placed on the experience of NGOs in delivering the kind of intersectoral package of entitlements advocated by this series.

The commonly encountered conflicts between governmental provision of education services and those provided by international or especially national voluntary agencies sets the scene for the volume. The reasons for the customary success of such agencies in comparison with government across a range of criteria and kinds and modes of provision are identified, and the case is advanced for more, not less, involvement of such agencies and the adoption of the approaches and values of

those agencies by government systems, with greater interrelationship and learning between the two sectors. A set of principles for such cooperative approaches, which incorporates the reasons for the relative success of NGO activities in education, is developed in concert with the overarching human-rights-attentive principles.

Community empowerment and mobilization are seen as a means to secure greater equity and access to the human right to education, health and nutrition. Non-formal education is seen as different but not necessarily worse or second-best. Indeed, some projects and programmes appear to be better than formal programmes, with the cultural 'fit' being better in content, delivery and timing. The need for close community involvement, the devolution of responsibility and greater participation are seen as essential prerequisites if the rigidity of the formal education system is not to contaminate and inhibit the non-formal sector as well. Arguments are developed for a lighter hand of government in education to develop greater ownership of education and associated services by the community. Examples of good practice in the provision of educational services are given and ideas generated for a more genuine and effective partnership among central and regional governments and communities. Emphasis is placed not only on likely improved outcomes, but also on the intrinsic values of the process itself in generating commitment and economic and environmental responsibility.

The political role of community involvement is related to the encouragement of civic values and responsibility, as well as to the securing of democracy and political consensus to provide a stable seedbed for any development. The role of the mass media in the delivery of education and associated services is discussed and the results evaluated. The advantages of structural, curricular and organizational deviation from central frameworks are elucidated from practice. The issue of cultural diversity is seen as requiring a particular contribution from non-formal educational approaches. The volume also focuses on the crucial role of non-formal educational in expanding opportunities and encouraging greater urban–rural equity, as well as a vehicle for delivering such areas as mother-tongue instruction. The volume concludes with a rationale for greater interpenetration of formal and non-formal educational modalities, leading to economies of scale and utilization and thus efficiency gains for wider and higher-quality coverage to make actual the charter of entitlements introduced in Volume One.

The agenda for this volume

The agenda for this volume is to identify the implicit and explicit factors which impede the provision of universal primary education, seen as a package of entitlements based on fundamental human rights, and to propose policies and practices which will facilitate its early, efficient and qualitative introduction. Factors inhibiting such a development are seen as part of a wider pathology of induced dependence and 'underdevelopment' of developing nations, of which the aid agencies form a part. For this reason, the entitlement to primary education as part of a broader package of entitlements in health and nutrition is seen within the context of the need for a new economic, social, political and cultural covenant to govern the relations between rich nations and poor.

At the macro level, mistaken or sometimes craven policies, induced dependence, economic and cultural, as well as international and personal 'convenience' connivance by agencies and developed nations at corruption and breaches of human rights, are seen as major constraints to the full coming of age of developing countries. International agencies which, by their own admission, have neglected the social cost of policies such as structural adjustment are seen as in need of urgent reform and more democratic control. Structural adjustment is seen as just one of the many constraints inherent within the current macroeconomic and political context, within which developing countries have to work under the threat of *force majeure*, in a labelling and stigmatizing process of continued enforced underdevelopment. The functions and effects of the 'reverse thrust' of financial and technical assistance are considered, which not only drain countries of their human capital, but encourage its flight in the name of development.

Similar flaws can be seen at the micro level, where communities are excluded from the education of their children, where the human rights of minorities, girls and those with impairments are infringed, where the models of teaching and teacher education are those of yesteryear, where the paradigm of human learning is one addressed to a 'convenience food' teachability, with all receiving the same regardless of their needs, where the outcomes are seen as numerical rather than human, and where the input–output model neglects the processes as ends in themselves. These current weaknesses are contrasted with the framework of international conventions and agreements on human political, social and cultural rights and agreements concerning the environment. The volume argues the need for conceptualizing alternative, holistic strategies for the provision of a primary educational entitlement to all children, integrated as a package of entitlements with nutritional and health benefits – the whole package grounded in human rights. Contributors see the need to cocoon that entitlement within a broader realignment of international relations between developed and developing countries – a new international covenant for financial and cultural relations between the 'North' and the 'South'. A series of 'least demands' to be levied against individuals and agencies involved in education in and for developing countries is proposed, and alternative criteria of both need and effectiveness are suggested.

Free and universal primary education is considered as an integral part of a package of entitlements, deriving from basic human rights for all populations of children everywhere. Contributions analyse the basic components for a future financial and social world order and the economic, cultural and environmental relationships between developed and developing countries which could positively influence the education sector: the financial and cultural paradigms, financing patterns and modes; investment flows to the education sector as a whole and its subsectoral distribution; implicit and explicit customs and ground rules set by the international agencies and developed world; operational concepts, modalities and practical approaches; and the underlying value assumptions.

Alternative bases are proposed for a 'Charter of Relationships' at both macro and micro levels and based on a more mutual and reciprocal relationship, and principles of procedure are identified for a new international order for the delivery of educational services as a right, rather than as the privilege of the few. At the micro level, a new, more child-centred and culturally responsive model of the education 'enterprise' is advanced. New definitions of what constitutes good and effective education and how it is monitored and evaluated are suggested, and the implications for the education system of all countries, both developed and developing, are drawn out. The volume concludes with a reflexive overview of the content and argument of the volume and an invitation to the reader to further dialogue. It introduces and critically assesses some of the major intellectual paradigms and practical frameworks adopted in education and development. Using education as a focal point, the volume is concerned with both interdisciplinary and intersectoral approaches, particularly those linking education, population and environmental issues, health and nutrition.

Notes

1 This introduction draws on some of the material in my book *Education and Development: A Human Rights Analysis* (Cassell, 1997).
2 The decade for Human Rights Education was formally proposed by the Director-General of UNESCO, Federico Mayor, at the 1993 World Conference on Human Rights in Vienna. In October 1994 the UNESCO International Conference on Education adopted a framework recommending learning for peace, human rights and anti-racism.
3 For a more extensive treatment of the interrelationship between economic success and liberal democracy, see *The Economist* (27 August 1994), especially pp. 9 and 15–17.

4 Ill-health and malnourishment have adverse effects on children's learning and thus on the efficiency of utilization of resources invested. See Pollitt (1990).
5 In one of its publications prepared for the 1995 Summit on Social Development, the World Bank committed itself to assist in the attainment within the next generation of universal quality primary education, universal access to cost-effective health care and the elimination of malnutrition. See World Bank (1995a, p. v).
6 The United Nations' 20/20 initiative proposes that at least 20 per cent of government budgets and at least 20 per cent of aid agencies' programmes be devoted to basic social services.
7 There are indications that the volume of tied aid is increasing as a proportion of the total, at the same time as the total aid budget is being eroded by the inclusion of relief spending (approximately 7 per cent in 1993). See International Council of Voluntary Agencies (1994).
8 The current target is 0.7 per cent of gross national product (GNP) to be allocated to development assistance by the industrialized countries.
9 There are some signs that major agencies are beginning to appreciate the importance of local culture. See Davis (1995).
10 For a more detailed exposition of this case, see Gran (1986).
11 See United Nations Development Programme (1993, pp. 10, 100–1, 135–7). The Human Development Index (HDI) is an indicator of development that includes three key components: longevity, knowledge and income. The combination of these to arrive at an average deprivation index is considered to be a more comprehensive measure of development than GNP alone.
12 A recent treatment of the importance of the relation between this social capital and economic success is given by Fukuyama (1995).
13 There is some disturbing evidence of the continued political involvement of France and French politicians in former colonies. See the series of so-called 'Black Books', for example 'Coalition pour ramener à la raison démocratique la politique africaine de la France' (1995).
14 A recent influential publication emphasizes the interrelationship between social structures which generate trust and economic success. See Fukuyama (1995).
15 See, in this respect, the interesting policy proposals in World Bank (1991b).

References

Bowman, M. J. (1980) Education and economic growth: an overview, in T. King (ed.), *Education and Income: A Background Study for the World Development Report, 1980*. World Bank Working Paper 402. Washington, DC: World Bank, pp. 1–71.

Cernea, M. (1993) The sociologist's approach to sustainable development, *Finance and Development*, **30**(4), 11–13.

Coalition pour ramener à la raison démocratique la politique africaine de la France (1995) *2ème Dossier noir de la politique africaine de la France*. Paris: Agir Ici.

Davis, S. H. (1995) Recovering indigenous knowledge systems in Southern Africa, *Bank's World*, **14**(1), 6–9.

The Economist (1994) Democracy works best, *The Economist*, 332(7878).

Fukuyama, F. (1995) *Trust: The Social Virtues and the Creation of Prosperity*. New York: The Free Press of Glencoe.

Gran, G. (1986) Beyond African famines: whose knowledge matters? *Alternatives*, **11**(2), 275–96.

Herz, B., Subbarao, K., Habib, M. and Raney, L. (1991) *Letting Girls Learn: Promising Approaches in Primary and Secondary Education*. World Bank Discussion Paper 133. Washington, DC: World Bank.

International Council of Voluntary Agencies (1994) *The Reality of Aid*. Geneva: ICVA/Eurostep/Actionaid.

Jennings, Z. (1993) The non-institutionalisation of the use of self-instructional materials in primary schools in Jamaica: the case of Project Primer, *Journal of Curriculum Studies*, **25**(6), 527–42.

King, E. M. and Hill, M. A. (eds) (1990) *Women's Education in Developing Countries*. Washington, DC: World Bank.

Lockheed, M. and Verspoor, A. (1992) *Improving Primary Education in Developing Countries*. New York: Oxford University Press.

Pollitt, E. (1990) *Malnutrition and Infection in the Classroom*. Paris: UNESCO.

Porter, M. H. (1990) *The Competitive Advantage of Nations*. New York: The Free Press of Glencoe.

Psacharopoulos, G. (1985) Returns to education: a further international update and implications, *Journal of Human Resources*, **20**, 584–604.

Schultz, G. W. (1961) Investment in human capital, *American Economic Review*, **51**, 1–17.

Sonenshine, M. (1990) Time for a profitable advance on human rights, *Financial Times*, 21 August, p. 15.

UNESCO and Ministry of Education and Science, Spain (1994) *The Salamanca Statement and Framework for Action on Special Needs Education*. Paris: UNESCO.

United Nations Children's Fund (1990) *The State of the World's Children*. New York: UNICEF.

United Nations Children's Fund (1991) *The State of the World's Children*. New York: UNICEF.

United Nations Children's Fund (1994) *The State of the World's Children*. New York: UNICEF.

United Nations Development Programme (1993) *Human Development Report 1993*. New York: Oxford University Press.

Watson, K. (1992) Language, education and political power: some reflections on North–South relationships, *Language and Education*, **6**(2–4), 99–121.

World Bank (1990a) *Poverty: The World Development Report 1990*. Oxford: Oxford University Press.

World Bank (1990b) *The Dividends of Learning*. Washington, DC: World Bank.

World Bank (1991a) *The Challenge of Development: The World Development Report 1991*. Oxford: Oxford University Press.

World Bank (1991b) *Assistance Strategies to Reduce Poverty*. Washington, DC: World Bank.

World Bank (1992) *Development and the Environment: World Development Report 1992*. Oxford: Oxford University Press.

World Bank (1995a) *Investing in People: The World Bank in Action*. Washington, DC: World Bank.

World Bank (1995b) *Advancing Social Development*. Washington, DC: World Bank.

World Conference on Education for All (1990) *Meeting Basic Learning Needs: Final Report*. New York: WCEFA.

Abbreviations and Acronyms

AAU	Academic Audit Unit
ABE	adult basic education
ACEP	Australian Co-operative Assessment Programme
AI	annual inspection
AIMAV	Association Internationale pour le Développement de la Communication Interculturelle
ALBSU	Adult Literacy and Basic Skills Unit
ANC	African National Congress
APEL	accreditation of prior learning from experience
APPEP	Andhra Pradesh Primary Education Project
APU	Assessment of Performance Unit
ASQC	American Society for Quality Control
BC	British Council
BD	Education Committee of the Board of Deputies of British Jews
CAI	computer-aided instruction
CAPS	Central American Peace Scholarship
CARE	Co-operation for American Relief Elsewhere
CATS	credit accumulation and transfer system
CES	Centre for Educational Sociology
CHETNA	Centre for Health Education, Training and Nutrition Awareness
CIFEDHOP	International Training Centre on Human Rights and Peace Teaching
CIIP	context/impact/process/product
CNAA	Council for National Academic Awards
COSC	Cambridge Overseas School Certificate
COTU	Central Organization of Trade Unions
CPD	continuing professional development
CVCP	Committee of Vice Chancellors and Principals
DDEP	District Primary Education Programme (India)
DES	Department of Education and Science
DFE	Department for Education
DIET	District Institutes of Educational Training (India)
EC	European Community
ECO-ED	Education and Communication on Environment and Development
EDSAC	Education Sector Adjustment Credit
EFA	Education For All
EHE	Enterprise in Higher Education
EP	educational psychologist
EPF	education production function
EPLF	Eritrean People's Liberation Front
EPRDF	Ethiopian People's Revolutionary Democratic Front
EQUIP	education quality improvement programme
ERA	Education Reform Act
ERASMUS	European Action Scheme for the Mobility of University Students
ERIC	Educational Resources Information Center
ERS	Education Resource Service
ESOL	English as a second or other language
FE	further education
FEFC	Further Education Funding Council

FEPADE	Business Foundation for Educational Development
FEU	Further Education Unit
GCE	General Certificate of Education
GCSE	General Certificate of Secondary Education
GDP	gross domestic product
GNP	gross national product
GOI	Government of India
GOK	Government of Kenya
HDI	Human Development Index
HE	higher education
HEFCE	Higher Education Funding Council of England
HEI	higher education institute
HEQC	Higher Education Quality Council
HIID	Harvard Institute for International Development
HMI	Her Majesty's Inspectors/Inspectorate
IAEA	International Association for Educational Assessment
IDA	International Development Association
IEA	International Association for the Evaluation of Educational Achievement
IFM	international faculty mobility
IIEP	International Institute for Educational Planning
IIP	Investors in People
ILEA	Inner London Education Authority
ILO	International Labour Office
IMF	International Monetary Fund
INSEE	Institut National de la Statistique et des Etudes Economiques
INSET	in-service training
IQE	ideal quality of education
ISR	Institute for Social Research
IT	information technology
ITE	initial teacher education
JEDT	Jewish Educational Development Trust
JFS	Jewish Free Schools
KAL	knowledge about language
KBSR	New Primary School Syllabus (Malaysia)

KCPE	Kenya Certificate for Primary Education
KNUT	Kenya National Union of Teachers
LEA	local education authority
LINC	language in the National Curriculum
LMS	local management of schools
MDI	measure-driven instruction
MINED	Ministry of Education (Mozambique)
MNC	multinational corporation
NATO	North Atlantic Treaty Organization
NC	National Curriculum
NCC	National Curriculum Council
NESIC	National Education Standards and Improvement Council
NFE	non-formal education
NFER	National Foundation for Educationl Research
NGO	non-governmental organization
NIER	National Institute for Educational Research
NQT	newly qualified teacher
NTA	non-teaching assistant
NUT	National Union of Teachers
NVQ	National Vocational Qualification
ODA	Overseas Development Administration
OECD	Organization for Economic Co-operation and Development
OFSTED	Office for Standards in Education
OISE	Ontario Institute for Studies in Education
OLF	Oromo People's Liberation Front
OSCE	Objective Structured Clinical Examinations
PGCE	Postgraduate Certificate of Education
PRP	performance-related pay
PVO	private and voluntary organization
QAD	Quality Assessment Division
REDIC	Red Latinoamericana de Información y Documentación
RE/I	religious education/instruction
RFP	Request for Proposals
SACRE	Standing Advisory Council for Religious Education
SALs	Structural Adjustment Loans

SAT	Standard Assessment Test	UN	United Nations
SCAA	School Curriculum and Assessment Authority	UNCED	United Nations Conference on Environment and Development
SCE	School Certificate of Education [Scotland]	UNCHR	United Nations Centre for Human Rights
SECALs	Sectoral Adjustment Loans	UNDP	United Nations Development Programme
SEN	special educational needs		
SENCO	special needs co-ordinator	UNESCO	United Nations Educational, Scientific, and Cultural Organization
SLD	severe learning difficulties		
SNO	supranational organization		
SOED	Scottish Office Education Department	UNICEF	United Nations (International) Children's (Emergency) Fund
SYPS	Strathclyde Young People's Survey	UPE	Universal Primary Education
TA	teacher assessment	US AID	United States Agency for International Development
TAFE	technical and further education		
TEC	Training and Enterprise Council	WCEFA	World Conference on Education for All
TGAT	Task Group on Assessment and Training		
		WHO	World Health Organization
TQA	Teacher Quality Assessment	WSSD	World Summit for Social Development
TSC	Teachers Service Commission		
TVEI	Technical and Vocational Education Initiative	ZFET	Zionist Federation Educational Trust
UDACE	Unit for the Development of Adult Continuing Education	ZIMFEP	Zimbabwe Foundation for Education with Production
UFC	Universities Funding Council		
ULIE	University of London Institute of Education		

Part One

Economic Interdependence, Education and Development

1 Education and Structural Adjustment: Unmet Needs and Missed Opportunities

FERNANDO REIMERS

Background

For many countries around the world, and particularly those in Latin America and sub-Saharan Africa, the 1980s were characterized by two consistent lines of policy discourse in the areas of economic and education reform. The education discourse gave growing emphasis to education and training as a cornerstone of economic, social and political development. At the international level, the decade culminated with the World Conference on Education for All in Jomtien, Thailand (after a number of regional preparatory conferences), which stated the need to strengthen education systems, to overcome the deficiencies of the past and to ensure the right of all to educational opportunity. The economic discourse emphasized the need to restructure economies, to face growing trade and fiscal imbalances, and to restore the conditions that would stimulate growth and set countries on the course to sustainable development. Much of the emphasis of the economic discourse was a response to the realization, early in the 1980s, that many countries had been pursuing economic policies which were unsustainable in the long term, replacing fiscal discipline with access to easy credit in international markets. When Mexico announced in 1982 that it could no longer service its debt obligations, international financial institutions and many other countries recognized the need to restructure their economies to achieve first stabilization and next economic growth.

This desire for restructuring was thwarted, however, by the conditions prevailing in school systems around the world. This conflict between rhetoric and reality in terms of educational opportunity stems, I will argue, from the failure of adjustment programmes in practice to give education a central role as part of the transformations needed to restore growth.

The World Bank and the International Monetary Fund were prime actors in supporting these reforms, through structural adjustment loans and sector adjustment loans:

> [World] Bank adjustment lending is usually undertaken in parallel with IMF programs – almost always for SALs [structural adjustment loans] and in most cases for SECALs [sectoral adjustment loans]. The Fund has primary responsibility for supporting policy changes to tackle the immediate sources of inflation or balance of payments difficulty and the Bank for supporting measures that get a new pattern of growth going. Macroeconomic and structural reform are intimately linked, however, and their effects cannot be sensibly separated. (World Bank, 1992a, p. 7)

In theory one could reasonably expect that the education and economic policy discourses of the 1980s would have worked in tandem, complementing and supporting each other, particularly since a central aspect of the education argument was that the development of human capacities was a necessary condition to enable countries to increase productivity. This argument was developed and supported by a number of national and international agencies, including those which supported efforts towards economic reform and restructuring. The World Bank was one of the key sponsors of the World Conference on Education for All, and one of the institutions, along with several regional banks, which increased their commitments to education in their lending portfolio. Education was also a central element of a number of World Bank policy documents on the subjects of poverty and economic restructuring (World Bank, 1988, 1990).

In practice, however, the actions which followed from education and economic policies were less than mutually reinforcing. In particular, many adjustment policies neglected the domains of education and training, with the consequence that the educational aspirations of the 1980s were not met.

This chapter will review the changes in key aspects of the education systems of all countries of the world, and will compare the performance of countries which adjusted and those that did not. The purpose of the analysis is to test the hypothesis that countries which adjusted were better able, as was their intent, to improve the performance of their education systems.

This hypothesis differs from other approaches to the education adjustment debate. Some parts of this debate have centred on whether adjustment 'worsened' education conditions in many countries, and a good part of it has focused on whether it is possible to attribute the decline in education and social conditions to adjustment efforts, since it is hard to know how things would have turned out in the absence of adjustment. From the point of view of education policy, these arguments are ill-founded. Adjustment was not attempting to 'worsen' education conditions, nor was it trying simply to mitigate the deterioration in economic conditions which preceded adjustment in most countries. The purpose of adjustment was to restore the conditions that would enable countries to recover rates of economic growth that would allow them to increase the quality of life of their populations, to reduce poverty and to sustain development. Since all accounts give education and training a central role in promoting economic productivity and growth, sound processes of economic adjustment, aimed at restoring the conditions to sustain growth, should have given education and training systems an equally central role in the process of adjustment. The question of whether education systems, after more than a decade of adjustment experience, are not performing

as poorly as the education systems of countries which did not adjust, or not as poorly as they were before adjustment, is not an appropriate test of the explicit aims of the adjustment process. The key question, and the one to be addressed by this chapter, is: Are the education systems of countries which followed policies to reform economic systems adequately addressing the education and training needs of the population? Are they doing this better than they were prior to adjustment? Are they doing it better than the education systems of countries that did not adjust?

The empirical evidence to answer these questions will be obtained by analysing data on a number of educational indicators presented in the latest *World Education Report* of UNESCO (1993). For some purposes countries have been grouped by region of the world, using the same regional groupings as those offered by UNESCO. For purposes of comparing countries with different adjustment experience, countries have been grouped following the classification developed and used in the latest World Bank report assessing adjustment lending (World Bank, 1992a). This World Bank report is based on comparisons between (a) 27 countries which underwent intensive adjustment experience (those that received two structural adjustment loans or three or more adjustment operations effective by June 1990, with the first adjustment operation effective in June 1986 or before), (b) 30 countries which underwent other adjustment experience (those that received at least one adjustment loan effective by June 1990), and (c) 20 non-adjustment countries (those that did not receive adjustment lending by June 1990). In addition, the analysis will occasionally compare these three groups of countries with a fourth group of 'other non-adjusters', comprising countries included in the adjustment lending report of the World Bank (World Bank, 1992a). The analysis will be based on examining how educational indicators compared in countries in the four groups described, as a group or by region of the world, emphasizing sub-Saharan Africa, Latin America and Asia.[1]

Table 1.1 shows the four groupings of countries which will be used for analysis.

Table 1.1 Countries compared in the analysis by adjustment experience

Intensive adjustment lending countries (27)
Bolivia, Brazil, Chile, Colombia, Costa Rica, Côte d'Ivoire, Ghana, Guinea-Bissau, Jamaica, Kenya, Korea (South), Madagascar, Malawi, Mauritania, Mauritius, Mexico, Morocco, Nigeria, Pakistan, Philippines, Senegal, Tanzania, Thailand, Togo, Turkey, Uruguay, Zambia

Other adjustment lending countries (30)
Algeria, Argentina, Bangladesh, Benin, Burkina Faso, Burundi, Cameroon, Central African Republic, China, Congo, Ecuador, Former Yugoslavia, Gabon, Gambia, Guyana, Honduras, Hungary, Indonesia, Mali, Niger, Panama, Sierra Leone, Somalia, Sri Lanka, Sudan, Trinidad and Tobago, Tunisia, Venezuela, Zaïre, Zimbabwe

Non-adjustment lending countries (20)
Botswana, Dominican Republic, Egypt, El Salvador, Ethiopia, Greece, Guatemala, Haiti, India, Lesotho, Liberia, Malaysia, Myanmar, Nicaragua, Papua New Guinea, Paraguay, Peru, Portugal, Rwanda, Syrian Arab Republic

Other non-adjustment lending countries (103)
Gaza Strip, Afghanistan, Albania, Angola, Antigua and Barbuda, Armenia, Australia, Austria, Azerbaijan, Bahamas, Bahrain, Barbados, Belarus, Belgium, Belize, Bhutan, British Virgin Islands, Brunei Darussalam, Bulgaria, Cambodia, Canada, Cape Verde, Chad, Comoros, Cuba, Cyprus, Former Czechoslovakia, Denmark, Djibouti, Dominica, Equatorial Guinea, Estonia, Fiji, Finland, France, Georgia, Germany, Grenada, Guinea, Hong Kong, Iceland, Iran, Iraq, Ireland, Israel, Italy, Japan, Jordan, Kazakhstan, Kiribati, Korea (North), Kuwait, Kyrgyzstan, Laos, Latvia, Lebanon, Libya, Lithuania, Luxembourg, Maldives, Malta, Moldova, Monaco, Mongolia, Mozambique, Namibia, Nepal, Netherlands, Netherlands Antilles, New Zealand, Norway, Oman, Poland, Qatar, Romania, Russian Federation, Samoa, San Marino, St Christopher and St Kitts, St Lucia, St Vincent and Grenadines, São Tomé and Principe, Saudi Arabia, Seychelles, Singapore, South Africa, Spain, Suriname, Swaziland, Sweden, Switzerland, Tajikistan, Tonga, Turkmenistan, Tuvalu, Uganda, Ukraine, United Arab Emirates, United Kingdom, United States, Uzbekistan, Vietnam, Yemen

Source: Countries are classified in the first three groups as suggested in World Bank (1992a, Table 1.1, p. 15).

Growing challenges to education systems around the world

In 1990 there were at least 1.6 billion adults in the world who could not read and 190 million children of primary school age out of school.[2] Most of these persons live in Asia or sub-Saharan Africa.

There has been greater recent effort in Asia to educate the population, as indicated by lower shares of children out of school in the world totals (67 per cent) than of illiterates (71 per cent). The shares for sub-Saharan Africa are 17 per cent of the world's illiterates and 21 per cent of its children out of school. During the 1980s many opportunities were lost to make a significant dent in these figures.

In spite of the huge challenge represented by the large number of people who cannot read and of children of school age who are not enrolled in school, countries in the world were making about the same level of effort, in terms of spending per student as a share of per capita gross national product (GNP), at the end of the decade as they were at the beginning. There were marginal gains for primary education, particularly in Asia and Europe. Sub-Saharan countries were making less effort in all levels of education.

Between 1980 and 1990, relative to per capita GNP, education expenditures per pupil around the world increased slightly for primary education, and decreased for secondary and tertiary education. In primary education Asian countries were spending 7 per cent more at the end of the decade, whereas countries in Europe were spending 16 per cent more. In contrast, in 1990 countries in sub-Saharan African were spending only 88 per cent per pupil of what they spent in 1980, relative to per capita income.

In secondary education, in 1990, on average countries around the world spent 98 per cent of the level per student in 1980, but countries in sub-Saharan Africa were spending only 70 per cent of what they spent at the beginning of the decade.

In tertiary education, in 1990, on average countries in the world were spending 91 per cent of the spending levels of 1980, whereas in sub-Saharan Africa they were spending 69 per cent of spending levels at the beginning of the decade.

Considering that in a number of countries per capita income did not grow during the decade, the impact of unchanged or declining levels of effort in actual levels of spending per pupil is more significant. There are also large income disparities between regions, as summarized in Table 1.2. On average, countries in Asia have a per capita in-

Table 1.2   Average income per capita in different regions in 1990

Region	GNP per capita	Standard deviation	Countries
Other Africa	1,896	1,687	7
Sub-Saharan Africa	659	889	41
Latin America	1,512	780	18
Caribbean and other	3,378	2,904	13
USA and Canada	21,075	884	2
Asia	5,425	6,876	29
Europe	13,942	9,624	24
Oceania	5,693	7,259	6

Source: Derived from UNESCO (1993).

come eight times higher than those in sub-Saharan Africa, countries in Europe twenty times higher, in the USA and Canada thirty-two times higher.

Because efforts to finance education did not increase during the 1980s, around the world one out of every five children of school-going age remained out of primary school (net enrolment rates averaged 80 per cent) at the end of the decade, but there were great regional disparities: net enrolment rates exceed 90 per cent in Asia, Europe, Oceania, the USA and Canada and the Caribbean, but are only 55 per cent in sub-Saharan Africa and 84 per cent in Latin America. The lack of opportunity to enrol and stay in primary school is more pronounced for girls: net enrolment rates for primary education are 51 per cent in sub-Saharan Africa and 81 per cent in Latin America.

On average, net enrolment rates around the world increased by less than 4 per cent during the 1980s. In sub-Saharan Africa and Latin America, where they could have increased the most since starting levels were the lowest, they increased only by 5 per cent – that is, less than an additional student per 100 every two years; in Asia they increased by 8 per cent. This indicates that the educational efforts of the 1980s, despite all the new rhetoric on the importance of education, were barely sufficient to keep up with population growth. The landscape of educational opportunity did not widen during the decade and, as will be discussed later, for many people opportunity shrank.

Educational opportunity is constrained not only for the children who do not have access to school, but also for those whose schools do not help them

learn. Many of the children who enter first grade never reach the minimum of a fourth-grade education which would allow them to acquire basic reading and numeracy skills. Whereas in the USA and Canada 96 per cent of the children reach grade 4, and in Europe 98 per cent of the children do, in sub-Saharan Africa only 75 per cent of a cohort reaches grade 4, and in Latin America the figure is 71 per cent. An even smaller percentage of children complete primary education: 63 per cent in sub-Saharan Africa and 54 per cent in Latin America, in contrast to 82 per cent in Asia, 93 per cent in the USA and Canada, and 96 per cent in Europe.

As the educational pyramid shrinks towards the end of the primary cycle and as there are limited spaces at the secondary level, only some of the students receive a high school education. At the secondary level, only Europe, the USA and Canada, and Oceania have net enrolment rates exceeding 80 per cent. Asia has enrolment rates of 52 per cent, Latin America 34 per cent and sub-Saharan Africa 12 per cent. Secondary education has remained a largely neglected level in education policy and efforts in many countries around the world for many years, and the 1980s were no different. Very few students have access to this level and there is substantial ambiguity regarding the goals and objectives which the level can achieve.

There was almost no progress with secondary enrolment during the decade: on average net enrolment rates increased by one student, in the age group, every two years. Education efforts in secondary education barely kept up with population growth.

The number of university students per 100,000 population – of which a certain percentage are already university graduates – increased from 1,000 to 1,300 around the world. In sub-Saharan Africa this figure increased from 131 students per 100,000 in 1980 to 188 in 1990, in Latin America it increased from 1,404 to 1,929, in Asia from 992 to 1,317, in the USA and Canada from 4,673 to 5,347, and in Europe from 1,273 to 2,000 students per 100,000 persons.

The slow dynamism of education systems around the world, which was insufficient to outpace population growth, left the educational endowment of the world unchanged. As with financial endowments, when there is inflation, the failure to grow amounts to a loss. In a world increasingly reliant on talent, creativity and education the failure to progress amounts to a big loss – a loss of opportunities. The countries with high illiteracy rates made little progress during the 1980s. In sub-Saharan Africa, where one in two persons is illiterate, literacy rates increased between 1980 and 1990 by only 5 per cent.

In sum, large challenges faced by the education systems of many countries in 1980 remained unmet at the end of the decade. Among these challenges were the large number of children who remained unreached by the education system, and the inequitable provision of educational opportunity to children from different socio-economic backgrounds, to boys and girls, to children living in cities and in rural areas, to children of different religious groups or ethnic backgrounds. Another challenge was the low efficiency of education systems.

How could so many problems remain in spite of the growing awareness of the importance of education, in spite of the Jomtien conference and the preparatory and follow-up activities, in spite of the commitments made by donors and governments at these conferences? This gap between education policy discourse during the 1980s and the poor education conditions faced by many countries in the world represents a paradox. I will argue that this paradox is the result of the conflict between educational aspirations on the one hand and the practice of adjustment programmes on the other, and in particular of the omission to address explicitly in the practice of adjustment the educational and social conditions.

The rest of this chapter will examine the role of home and school-related conditions as they influenced educational opportunity and as they changed under adjustment programmes. These account for the influence of adjustment in educational opportunity via demand and supply factors. Demand factors refer to the support which families can contribute to the education of their children. Supply factors refer to the quality of education offered in schools as influenced by conditions such as the level and structure of government budgets.

The changes in home conditions

To examine educational opportunity one has to begin at home, for not only are home conditions the first to influence a child's ability to learn, but they are also the conditions which will mediate the impact of school factors in providing educational opportunity. Although the contribution of home factors to educational opportunity is poorly understood and more research and evidence are necessary to explain the dynamics of household decision-making regarding participation in school, it is possible to derive some plausible hypotheses out of the available evidence.

Availability of schools is a step to providing access to school, but only if parents send their children to the schools. Policies and legislation mandating basic education send a signal to communities which may encourage enrolment, but in the end it is parents who decide how to respond to these norms and laws. A number of factors influence parental decisions and the role of home conditions in fostering school-based learning: culture, tradition, education of the parents are all factors which play a role in how parents think about whether a particular daughter or son should enrol in school and how much time they should devote to their school work. One set of factors influencing these decisions are the economic conditions facing households; where the labour of children yields a greater marginal contribution to the well-being of the family the costs of going to school are higher for that family. For families living in poverty the costs of sending children to school may be higher. In 1985 there were 1.1 billion people in the world living in poverty, of whom more than half lived in extreme poverty.[3]

> On the cost side, a critical factor is the real incomes of the poor, since the lower the income, the greater the costs appear. There is evidence that the direct costs of education alone can be quite high in relation to incomes of poor households: for example, in three West African countries, parental costs of primary education amounted to from 7 to 14 per cent of average per capita GNP. This would be equivalent to 30 per cent or more of the income of low-income households. Thus any reduction in incomes of the poor can be expected to reduce demand for education. (Stewart, 1993, pp. 4–5)

We do know that poverty increased in many countries in the 1980s[4], particularly as, because rates of economic growth did not pick up, it was harder to address distributional issues. Economic growth has been sluggish particularly in sub-Saharan Africa, where per capita income declined in most countries, adjusters or non-adjusters alike. In Latin America the only countries which have experienced growth are intensively adjusting countries. In Asia income has increased in most countries, whether adjusters or non-adjusters.[5] The World Bank assessment of adjustment lending concludes that growth declined in the early part of the 1980s and recovered at the end of the decade to the level of 1970; the rates of growth were 5 per cent a year for middle-income countries, but only 3.5 per cent a year for low-income countries. Per capita private consumption followed these trends, but the higher population growth rate in the low-income group almost multiplied the effect of growth: the annual growth of per capita consumption was only 0.7 per cent in low-income countries (World Bank, 1992a). The same report concludes that it is hard to assess empirically the incidence of adjustment on poverty, since data are lacking, but suggests that in the long run adjustment probably helps to reduce poverty and that the poor suffered most in countries which did not adjust; the report also concludes that poverty increased or did not improve in most low-income countries. 'Once population growth is taken into account, however, the consumption increases may not have been large enough to reduce the number of poor in the low-income countries' (World Bank, 1992a, p. 20).

Reductions in per capita income may mean higher reductions for the poorest groups. UNICEF has estimated that a 2 to 3 per cent decline in average income in Africa means quintupling such a drop for the poorest (Jolly and Cornia, 1984). In Latin America some have argued that a 5 to 10 per cent reduction in GNP would translate into a reduction three to four times larger for low-income families because of the fact

> that minimum wages drop faster than do average wages, that the prices of essentials are subject to greater increases than is the Consumer Price Index, that the newly unemployed frequently also suffer the loss of health coverage and that cuts in public expenditures are typically asymmetrical. In terms of child welfare, these biases are further aggravated by the fact that poorer families generally have a larger than average number of children. (Albanez *et al.*, 1989, p. 1)

Reductions in household income influence educational opportunity in two ways: they increase the need to pull children out of school and send them to work, and they increase the costs of items normally financed by families (notebooks, transportation, uniforms). A study of the impact of adjustment in Costa Rica, for instance, documents that in this country enrolment in secondary education decreased substantially during the adjustment process:

> [T]he reason for attrition most given was the high direct cost of secondary schooling in the forms of uniforms, books (not provided at the secondary level), notebooks and other supplies, transportation, and assessments by the schools for teacher supplies. Transportation costs per pupil were especially important since they were often estimated to be about 8,000–10,000 colones per year. When uniforms, books, and other expenses are added to this, it is not unusual to find 15,000–20,000 colones in direct costs for each child in secondary school, when that school is not in walking distance. Even without transportation costs, it is likely that a family has to spend, with books, almost as much as the public spending per pupil in academic secondary education. Thus, the private direct costs of academic secondary education may be between one-third and two-thirds of the total costs, excluding income foregone. (Carnoy and Torres, 1994, p. 81)

Evidence from Côte d'Ivoire shows how the educational opportunity of the poor may suffer more than that of other groups, even while education seems to be protected in national expenditure figures. Côte d'Ivoire undertook one of the first structural adjustment programmes in Africa, and sustained it during the 1980s while maintaining the share of government expenditures in education. Between 1985 and 1988 net enrolment rates for the non-poor increased (from 66 to 74 per cent for males and from 54 to 58 per cent for females); however, they declined for the very poor, particularly for females (from 22 to 17 per cent). Net enrolment rates declined even more in secondary education for the very poor (from 9.7 to 3.5 per cent for males and from 5.3 to 1.2 per cent for females), whereas they remained stable for the non-poor (from 37 to 34 per cent for males and from 19 to 21 per cent for females). Primary school repetition rates (as inferred from mismatches between age and grade in which students are enrolled) also increased particularly for the very poor (from 38 to 64 per cent for males between 1985 and 1988, and from 28 to 53 per cent for females in the same period), whereas they increased substantially less for the non-poor (from 29 to 37 per cent for males and from 33 to 38 per cent for females) (Grootaert, 1994).

In sum, the poverty faced by many households around the world during the 1980s constitutes a factor that did not support educational opportunity. In effect, when poor parents can contribute less to the education of their children, or have greater need for their labour, one should expect state policies to compensate these conditions. Since educational opportunity results from both public and private efforts, or from the contributions of public schools and home conditions, greater public effort can in part counteract the net effect of reduced private contributions. Unfortunately, education policy in countries suffering economic hardship did not follow this approach. Facing a new scenario resulting from economic adjustment, education systems continued trying to do 'more of the same', with fewer resources. The net effect was a decline in educational opportunity.

Changes in public financing of education

A good indicator of the effort a society makes in education is the percentage of GNP devoted to financing public education. This is influenced by the share of education in government expenditures and by the share of government expenditures in GNP. It is possible to maintain the priority of education relative to GNP while pursuing policies to reduce public expenditures by increasing the share of education in the total budget. Failure to do

that suggests that education is not valued more than any other activity publicly funded.

Table 1.3(a) shows that proportionately more adjusting countries reduced the share of education in GNP than non-adjusting countries in sub-Saharan Africa, where 50 per cent of the countries which underwent intensive adjustment reduced the national effort in education and 25 per cent showed no growth, whereas 75 per cent of the non-adjusting countries and 100 per cent of all the other non-adjusting increased education as a percentage of GNP.

The pattern is very different in Latin America and in Asia (Table 1.3(b) and c)). In Latin America education expenditures as a share of GNP declined in 50 per cent of the intensively adjusting and other adjusting countries; among non-adjusters and other non-adjusters it declined in most of them, so education effort was somewhat greater among adjusting countries in Latin America. In Asia it increased in most countries, both adjusting and non-adjusting.

In all groups of countries the magnitude of declines in education effort outweighed the magnitude of the cases where it increased. On average, therefore, intensively adjusting countries had reductions in education expenditures as a share of GNP while other countries showed increases. This is particularly the case for sub-Saharan Africa. In Asia, in contrast, adjusting countries averaged increases in education expenditures which exceeded those of non-adjusting countries. In Latin America, expenditures declined on average in all categories of countries. These figures are summarized in Table 1.4.

It is important to point out, however, that these changes in educational effort during the decade do not stem from reduced government effort. In sub-Saharan Africa the share of education of total public expenditures increased in most intensively adjusting countries (86 per cent), whereas in most other countries it declined. In Latin America effort increased in about half of the countries, independently of adjustment. In Asia effort decreased in most intensively adjusting countries, increasing in all others. In 1990 there was no difference between regions of the world in how much government effort was made in education (countries average 15

Table 1.3 Changes in education as a percentage of GNP between 1980 and 1990

(a) In sub-Saharan Africa

Country	1980	1990
Intensive adjustment lending countries		
Declines		
Mauritania	5.0	4.7
Mauritius	5.3	3.7
Senegal	4.5	3.7
Zambia	4.5	2.9
No growth		
Kenya	6.8	6.8
Malawi	3.4	3.4
Increases		
Ghana	3.1	3.3
Tanzania	4.4	5.8
Other adjustment lending countries		
Declines		
Central African Republic	3.8	2.8
Congo	7.0	5.6
Mali	3.8	3.2
Sierra Leone	3.8	1.4
Zaïre	2.6	0.9
Increases		
Burkina Faso	2.2	2.3
Burundi	3.0	3.5
Cameroon	3.2	3.4
Gabon	2.7	5.7
Gambia	3.3	3.8
Zimbabwe	6.6	10.6
Non-adjustment lending countries		
Decline		
Lesotho	5.1	3.8
Increases		
Botswana	7.1	8.4
Ethiopia	3.3	4.8
Rwanda	2.7	4.2
Other non-adjustment lending countries		
Increases		
Mozambique	3.8	6.3
Seychelles	5.8	8.5
Swaziland	6.1	6.4
Uganda	1.2	2.9

(b) In Latin America

Country	1980	1990
Intensive adjustment lending countries		
Declines		
Bolivia	4.4	3.0
Chile	4.6	3.7
Costa Rica	7.8	4.6
Mexico	4.7	4.1
Increases		
Brazil	3.6	4.6
Colombia	1.9	2.9
Uruguay	2.3	3.1

Other adjustment lending countries

	1980	1990
Declines		
Ecuador	5.6	2.8
Venezuela	4.4	4.1
Increases		
Honduras	3.2	4.6
Panama	4.9	5.5
Non-adjustment lending countries		
Declines		
El Salvador	3.9	1.8
Guatemala	1.9	1.4
Increase		
Haiti	1.5	1.8
Other non-adjustment lending countries		
Decline		
Cuba	7.2	6.6

(c) In Asia

Country	1980	1990
Intensive adjustment lending countries		
Decline		
Korea (South)	3.7	3.6
Increases		
Pakistan	2.0	3.4
Philippines	1.7	2.9
Thailand	3.4	3.8
Other adjustment lending countries		
Decline		
China	2.5	2.3
No growth		
Sri Lanka	2.7	2.7
Increase		
Bangladesh	1.5	2.0
Non-adjustment lending countries		
Decline		
Syria	4.6	4.1
Increases		
India	2.8	3.5
Malaysia	6.0	6.9
Other non-adjustment lending countries		
Declines		
Iran	7.5	4.1
Israel	7.9	6.0
Japan	5.8	4.7
Increases		
Cyprus	3.5	3.6
Hong Kong	2.5	3.0
Kuwait	2.4	5.0
Oman	2.1	3.5
Qatar	2.6	3.4
Saudi Arabia	5.5	6.2
Singapore	2.8	3.4
United Arab Emirates	1.3	1.9

Source: Derived from UNESCO (1993). Countries are classified in adjustment groups as indicated in Table 1.1.

Table 1.4 Average (unweighted) change in education expenditures as a percentage of GNP between 1980 and 1990 by intensity of adjustment and by region

	Mean	Standard deviation	Countries
All countries	0.1525	1.4079	101
Intensive adjustment	−0.2045	1.1483	22
Other adjustment	0.0125	1.8553	24
Non-adjusters	0.3308	1.1138	13
Other non-adjusters	0.3643	1.3152	42
Sub-Saharan Africa	0.3222	1.6049	27
Intensive adjustment	−0.3375	0.9956	8
Other adjustment	0.1091	1.9336	11
Non-adjusters	0.7500	1.3699	4
Other non-adjusters	1.8000	1.0893	4
Asia	0.2476	1.2516	21
Intensive adjustment	0.7250	0.6994	4
Other adjustment	0.1000	0.3606	3
Non-adjusters	0.3667	0.7572	3
Other non-adjusters	0.0818	1.6473	11
Latin America	−0.4867	1.4096	15
Intensive adjustment	−0.4714	1.5521	7
Other-adjustment	−0.2750	1.8209	4
Non-adjusters	−0.7667	1.2220	3
Other non-adjusters	−0.6000	0.0000	1

Source: Derived from UNESCO (1993). Countries are classified in adjustment groups as indicated in Table 3.1
Note: The standard deviations should simply be interpreted as an indicator of variability within every category of countries, as documented in Table 1.3. Since this analysis is concerned with the population of countries, and not with a sample of them, it would not be accurate to use the standard deviations to estimate errors of inference of parameters for an unknown population.

per cent of government expenditures for education).

Similarly, changes in education expenditures in real terms did not relate to whether countries were adjusting or not. Education expenditures increased in two-thirds of the countries of sub-Saharan Africa, in about half the countries of Latin America and in 85 per cent of the countries of Asia. These increases, however, barely kept with increases in the size of the school population, as will be discussed later.

The changes documented in Table 1.3 and 1.4, therefore, stem from the changes in macroeconomic conditions, particularly in levels of economic growth during the decade. In most countries government effort was maintained at previous levels, hence failing to adjust to new circumstances. This is an example of how governments facing changing economic conditions continued to do 'more of the same', with the exception of some intensively adjusting countries in sub-Saharan Africa. The fact that governments failed to respond strategically to give education a central role amid the process of adjustment should come as no surprise as the process of budgeting is more responsive to routine and history: that is, new years' budgets generally reflect across-the-board increases or decreases to historical figures; budget offices are typically poorly equipped to alter drastically the structure of government spending. Ministries of education find it especially difficult to present an economic rationale for their programmes and to engage the finance ministry effectively in the different steps of the budget cycle.

However, even if not surprising, the failure of strategic change points to missed opportunities in the adjustment process as the low levels of education of the population have been highlighted as one of the obstacles to successful adjustment by several documents including the recent World Bank assessment of adjustment policies:

> What is missing is a group of stars from the low-income or Sub-Saharan African group ... The explanation for weaker policy change and greater fragility appears to lie in long-term conditions: a weaker human resource base, inadequate and sometimes declining economic infrastructure, less diversified economic structures, and poorly functioning institutions. (World Bank, 1992a, p. 25)

At least the first and fourth of these conditions are the result of the education and training systems of the countries. A shift from *ex post* explanation to proactive change will require the strengthening of these systems to the point where the region can have a stronger human resource base and well-functioning institutions. There is no evidence that the adjustment process supported the development of that vision or that it captured these opportunities.

The opportunities missed by the adjustment process also include a restructuring of education expenditures. Most public education budgets (90 per cent on average) are devoted to recurrent expenditures; that is, expenditures on routine ongoing categories, such as salaries, as opposed to investments in physical infrastructure. Recurrent expenditures are indeed very important, as there is no education system that functions without teachers, the primary item which uses up recurrent expenditures. It is hard to assess, in abstract, the significance of the changes in the share of recurrent expenditures, but generally increases in this share are interpreted as a reduction in the ability of ministries to launch large initiatives which require investments in education. In practice, however, many governments can fund such investments out of other sources (social investment funds, for instance), and therefore public expenditures on education are, by definition, primarily expenditures in routine recurrent items.

In sub-Saharan Africa, the percentage going to recurrent expenditures declined in most intensely adjusting countries, whereas in all other countries it increased. In Latin America, the percentage in recurrent expenditures declined in half of the intensively adjusting countries; in most other countries it increased. In Asia, the percentage of recurrent expenditures increased in most countries.

Most of these resources are spent on salaries. On average the world devotes only 3.5 per cent of recurrent expenditures to teaching materials, though this share is higher in the USA and Canada (7.2 per cent) or Europe (5.4 per cent) than in sub-Saharan Africa (4 per cent), Asia (2.3 per cent) or Latin America (0.94 per cent).

Even though the largest share of education budgets went to salaries, these declined in real terms in many countries. This simply shows that the stagnant or barely growing education budgets did not keep up with the growth in teacher appointments, and with the ageing of the teaching population accompanied by increases in rank and salary levels. In addition, the mechanisms established by ministries of finance to discourage public spending and the inabilities of ministries of education translated into increased delays in the disbursement of salaries. As a result teachers were paid less and irregularly. Irregular payments further diminished the value of the pay cheque as teachers often borrowed from local stores and elsewhere at higher than bank interest rates to meet

Table 1.5 Evolution of teacher salaries (average) in seven countries (constant prices)

Country	Primary				Secondary				Higher			
	1970	1975	1980	1985	1970	1975	1980	1985	1970	1975	1980	1985
Colombia	100	123	92	103	100	123	92	103	100	—	—	—
Congo	100	76	43	29	100	75	44	28	100	75	45	41
Côte d'Ivoire	100	124	88	57	100	42	25	39	100	108	81	53
Indonesia	100	42	26	41	100	42	25	39	100	42	22	3
Mexico	—	100	63	47	—	100	71	35	—	—	—	—
Togo	100	80	66	50	100	80	66	50	100	80	66	50
Zambia	100	103	80	55	100	94	77	41	100	92	74	40

Source: Tibi (1989, p. 1).

daily expenses. Table 1.5 shows how teacher salaries fell in real terms in a sample of adjusting countries during the 1980s.

Stewart has emphasized the decline in teacher salaries in adjusting countries, but also highlighted the fact that there is variability in the specific measures adopted by different countries:

> In Tanzania, the 1987 level of a starting teacher was just 29 per cent of the 1977; that of someone at the top of the scale was only 23 per cent of the 1977 level. In Kenya, teacher salaries fell by 30 per cent, and in Zimbabwe by 40 per cent, but the falls were much smaller in Malawi and Zambia. In Costa Rica, between 1980 and 1987, the salary level of a primary school teacher fell by 30 per cent and a secondary school teacher by 35 per cent. Data for real recurrent expenditures per teacher (a broad indicator of teacher wage-levels) show declines in forty countries, especially concentrated in African and Latin American countries. (Stewart, 1993, p. 18)

Declines in teacher salaries lowered teacher morale and increased confrontations between teachers – who are the persons who provide educational opportunity in real schools – and policy reformers; this was a hostile environment to entertain proposals for educational innovation and improvement of education conditions. Declines in salaries also increased the need for teachers to supplement their incomes by moonlighting, thereby reducing the time available to prepare, and sometimes attend, classes. Some teachers, particularly those trained in fields with higher demand in other occupations such as mathematics and sciences, left the teaching profession. The most serious impact of declines in teacher salaries will be long term, because salaries serve as signals to prospective applicants to the teaching profession. There is evidence that the teaching profession has become a less attractive field for secondary school graduates, who are in turn declining in number. Data from UNESCO show that there has been a decline in the proportion of students enrolled in teacher training at the secondary level. Between 1980 and 1989, enrolment in teacher training as a percentage of total enrolment declined from 7.2 to 6.6 per cent in Africa and from 4.1 to 3.2 per cent in Latin America (UNESCO, 1991). Under pressure to reduce the public wage bill many countries have begun to favour recruitment of candidates with lower levels of training, who command lower salaries. Though research on school effectiveness suggests that the relationship between formal teacher training and teaching effectiveness is mixed, most countries are making these replacements without regard to their impact on the quality of schools.

To add to the direct frustrations faced by teachers from the decline in their incomes, their job became more difficult as a result of the shortages of other inputs in the teaching process (textbooks, notebooks or even chalk) and as a result of the increased burdens faced by students. Teaching became a more difficult job during the 1980s.

The low levels in non-salary items in a context of growing scarcity in homes and communities also had important consequences for the quality of education. A teacher cannot teach effectively if she runs out of chalk, if students have no textbooks or notebooks, if schools crumble:

> In a set of country briefs on adjustment lending countries in Sub-Saharan Africa, Bank staff cited inadequate non-wage O&M as a key problem in the allocation of public expenditures in seventeen of nineteen countries ... Some countries have experienced a collapse of effective service delivery – schools without teaching materials. (World Bank, 1992a, p. 57)

How did ministries of education allocate resources between levels during the 1980s? In sub-Saharan Africa 86 per cent of the intensively adjusting countries reduced the share of the budget for primary education, whereas about half of all other countries did so. In the other regions of the world no difference is seen in the change in the share of the budget going for primary education between countries having different adjustment ex-

periences. Nor are there any differences by adjustment experience between regions in the changes in the share going for secondary education.

The share of the budget going to higher education increased the most among adjusting countries in sub-Saharan Africa, though not in other adjusting countries. In most adjusting countries in sub-Saharan Africa and Latin America this share increased; in Asia the share declined in most adjusting countries.

Another way to examine the priorities of education systems between different levels is to examine the change in per pupil expenditures per level as a percentage of per capita GNP. This ratio declined for the primary level, on average, in adjusting countries in sub-Saharan Africa, but increased in countries which did not adjust. At the end of the decade, adjusting countries in sub-Saharan Africa were investing only the equivalent of 9 per cent of per capita GNP per primary school pupil; by contrast, non-adjusters in the region were investing 19 per cent. In Latin America this share increased slightly during the decade, but increased more in countries which did not adjust. In Asia this share increased by 20 per cent in intensively adjusting countries and in countries which did not adjust.

Expenditures per pupil in secondary education, relative to per capita GNP, declined in sub-Saharan Africa throughout the decade. In Latin America the share increased in all but intensively adjusting countries. In Asia the share increased significantly in adjusting countries.

The ratio of per pupil expenditures to per capita GNP for tertiary education declined in sub-Saharan Africa, though more in countries which did not adjust. In Latin America this share declined only in intensively adjusting countries. In Asia this share declined in all countries.

The failure of the adjustment process to address head-on the role of education as part of the process of restoring growth meant that after more than a decade of adjustment there are severe distortions which remain, for instance, in education spending. There is no evidence that the adjustment process has contributed at all to addressing these distortions. For example, in 1990, intensively adjusting countries were spending 36 times as much per pupil in tertiary education as per pupil in primary education, and non-adjusters were spending 17 times as much. In sub-Saharan Africa intensively adjusting countries were spending 77 times as much per tertiary pupil as per primary pupil, whereas countries with less intensive adjustment experience were spending 54 times as much, and countries which had not adjusted were spending 38 times as much. In Latin America and Asia, where tertiary students cost only 7 times as much as primary school students, there were no differences in this ratio by adjustment experience.

The disparities in sub-Saharan Africa worsened during the 1980s, particularly for countries which adjusted; at the beginning of the decade, the countries which later adjusted intensively were spending 70 times per tertiary student as they were per primary school student; non-adjusters were spending 65 times as much.

How could adjustment processes have had so little impact in a sector which is considered central to promoting productivity and restoring economic growth? An important policy instrument of adjustment loans was the conditionalities agreed upon by donors and borrowers. An analysis of the conditionalities of loan agreements shows that social-sector conditionality was relatively unimportant during the decade. Until 1988 only 3 per cent of the conditionalities referred to social policy reforms (including education and health); between 1989 and 1991 this figure had risen only to 7 per cent (World Bank, 1992a, Table A.2.1, p. 82). This shows that whereas the rhetoric of adjustment may have emphasized the importance of education, in practice the concern for education conditions was not a central consideration in the adjustment process.

From 'more of the same' in expenditures to reduced educational opportunity

If one looked only at the evidence presented in the previous section there would be little of significance to discuss, for education systems did not act in a radically different way from the beginning to the end of the 1980s. Governments devoted about the same share to education; expenditures in real terms stayed about the same, most of them going to teacher salaries; and the disparities between spending per pupil in different levels stayed about the same, or worsened slightly. What could be wrong if so little changed? The problem is precisely that so little changed when there were such large unmet needs at the beginning of the decade, when policy discourse recognized and promised to address those needs, when there were radical changes affecting the economies and societies in which people work and live. The failure of education systems to adjust to these changes meant that the educational needs of many were not met. The problems included omission and neglect on the part of the élite groups responsible for policy formulation as well as international donors. Both failed to expand educational opportunity in a changing world.

The opportunity to enter primary school declined in sub-Saharan Africa by 5 per cent on average; that is, the number of children enrolled in the first grade did not keep up with the growth in the number of children of school age. Since on average one in three children never enrol in school in this region this is a good example of a missed chance to expand educational opportunity. Declines in intake rates were more prevalent in countries which adjusted, although there is a wide range of variability among countries in the region.

In some adjusting countries the declines in intake rates were much higher, as for example in Ghana, where they declined from 97 per cent in 1980 to 83 per cent in 1990, or Cameroon, where they went from 96 to 86 per cent in the same period. Other declines were more modest. In Côte d'Ivoire, for instance, the percentage of children entering first grade declined from 67 to 60 per cent in the decade, in Tanzania from 83 to 78 per cent, in Benin from 79 to 75 per cent, in the Central African Republic from 70 to 66 per cent and in Niger from 30 to 27 per cent. It should be pointed out that not all adjusting countries had declines in their intake rates: for instance, Zambia increased these rates from 91 to 97 per cent in the decade, Senegal increased them from 45 to 55 per cent and Burkina Faso from 22 to 36 per cent (UNESCO, 1993).

Primary net enrolment ratios increased on average more in countries which did not adjust. In sub-Saharan Africa, for instance, net enrolment ratios did not increase in intensively adjusting countries, while they increased on average by 11 per cent during the decade in non-adjusting countries. In Latin America, whereas intensively adjusting countries increased net enrolment ratios by 1 per cent during the decade, these increased by 8 per cent in countries which did not adjust.

The percentage of children who repeat grade in primary school decreased in all regions except sub-Saharan Africa, where the increase was larger, on average, in countries which adjusted. This is consistent with the evidence cited from household data in Côte d'Ivoire. The worsening of repetition rates suggests that learning conditions deteriorated. Even for those children who stayed in school, educational opportunity diminished.

In contrast to these changes in educational opportunity at the basic level, there were no differences between adjusting and non-adjusting countries in the opportunity to enrol in secondary school and in higher education. Since relatively few students have access to these levels, as discussed earlier, it is likely that these are students from the most advantaged home backgrounds, and therefore the contribution of home factors is less vulnerable to influences in the changing economic circumstances or to changes in per pupil expenditures. As we have seen, however, there are individual countries such as Costa Rica where enrolments in secondary schools declined.

Conclusions

The evidence examined in this chapter is consistent with that yielded by other studies of the same subject, including some conducted at institutions which have played a central role in supporting the adjustment process of many countries, such as the World Bank.

One of the earliest studies was supported by UNICEF, and examined the effects of adjustment on various educational indicators in ten countries between 1979 and 1983; this study showed that out of seven countries three showed decline in enrolment ratios, two did not change and two showed improvements through targeted programs. All six countries with indicators of educational attainment showed declines (Cornia *et al.*, 1987, pp. 24–6).

A World Bank study of the impact of adjustment identified reductions in education expenditures and in net enrolment ratios in twenty-five intensely adjusting countries between 1980 and 1985, in contrast with the trends in the same countries prior to adjustment and with the changes in non-adjusting countries (Kakwani *et al.*, 1990, p. 44). This study concluded:

> Expenditures on health and education have increased in non-adjusting countries. Most of the intensely adjusting countries ... show a decline in per capita expenditures for health and education ... [these] are cause for concern, especially for those countries that, by any account, need significant improvement in their social sector infrastructure. In Brazil and Mexico these declines took place against the background of a growing government sector, relative to GDP. Greater emphasis needs to be given to the protection of the social sectors during the course of adjustment to avoid a further slideback. Because providing health and education services is an *investment* in human capital, such greater emphasis can be fully comparable with adjustment policies that aim at long-term sustainable growth. (ibid.)

The evidence examined confirms that economic adjustment programmes failed to address the growing educational needs or to develop a strategy that would make human capital central to restoring productivity and economic growth, and to reducing poverty. These outcomes are contrary to the policy discourse of education and even to the policy discourse of economic adjustment.

Economic recession and adjustment influenced the conditions facing households, and particularly the poor, thereby reducing a source of support to educational opportunity. Rather than responding to these adjustments with greater efforts, governments also reduced their contributions to opportunity, if not by what they did then by what they failed to do. Governments continued doing 'more of the same' as countries and communities experienced drastic changes in their economy and living conditions. As countries reduced the priority given to education relative to resources per capita, the quality of education deteriorated and teacher salaries fell in real terms in many places, reducing the time available for teaching and for preparation. The declining and minuscule shares for teaching materials and for school repairs made teaching more difficult.

In the absence of an open exploration of alternatives and of public discussion of the educational costs of the choices which could be made, the politics of adjustment favoured the groups with greater lobbying power, namely urban dwellers and those from higher income groups. This explains why the disparities in allocation between education levels remained, or in some cases worsened, in spite of adjustment. The politics of adjustment at a micro level also had consequences that constrained equity. Urban schools closer to the centres of distribution of supplies and teaching materials were better able to maintain their absolute level of resources (and therefore to increase their share of a declining total pie) than rural schools. There is no alternative explanation for why most intensely adjusting countries in sub-Saharan Africa reduced the share of the education budget going for primary education while increasing the share for higher education, with the consequent deterioration in per pupil spending per capita at the primary level. The fact that this pattern was the opposite to what non-adjusters were doing in the same region defies the rationality of education adjustment.

As a result of these changes, which represent choices, educational opportunity diminished, particularly for the most disadvantaged children; that is, those who remained out of school or who could only access the lower levels of primary education. Net enrolment ratios declined in a good number of countries in sub-Saharan Africa. Though data are scanty, limited evidence shows

that the declines in net enrolment ratios were particularly acute for the poorest children. Also in sub-Saharan Africa, intake rates barely increased. In contrast, there is no evidence of adverse impact at the secondary and tertiary levels, though here too conditions failed to improve during the decade.

But the evidence examined also documents the fact that countries have choices, that there is nothing automatic in how the education sector is to fare under adjustment. These choices are made in concert between national policy-making élites and international agencies. The fact that so many countries seem to have made such poor choices for the education system reflects unfavourably on the competence of both national policy-making élites and international organizations.[6] It is notable that so much of the discussion of the adjustment process is silent about the real persons who made these choices. But recognizing that there is freedom to choose is a first step in establishing much-needed accountability both in governments and in development organizations.

During the 1980s many countries chose to neglect education, thereby constraining educational opportunity. Behind this choice is a short-term focus of the adjustment process which led many to a passive attempt to 'react' to reductions in funds, rather than to a proactive exploration of alternatives. The weak institutional capacity of many ministries of education to generate these alternatives, and to effectively engage in dialogue with ministries of finance and others who were instrumental in designing the adjustment process, is another factor explaining the choices which were made. But behind these choices are also real individuals both in government and in international organizations who designed education plans and who negotiated structural and sector adjustment loans. An appropriate question which emerges from the mixed results of adjustment is whether the differences in educational opportunity yielded by different choices have had any differential impact on the careers of those who made these choices.

A major step towards improving the quality of the choices to be made in the future will be to establish mechanisms of accountability and open systems of evaluation and discussion of the options for reforming education systems. Democratic processes where different stakeholders can assess the impact that proposed reforms will have on their educational opportunities, or those of their children, will increase the chances that the choices made reflect the preferences of those societies that have to live with the consequences. It may be necessary in this democratic exploration of alternatives to think about educational opportunity in the broadest possible sense, and to consider options with maximum freedom. For it may be that in some countries it is time to reinvent education systems; it may be that doing 'more of the same' is not the best way to respond to the challenges of the future.

Proactive consideration of a wide range of options for change and democratic dialogue and mobilization in support of reform – these were the opportunities missed by adjustment during the 1980s, and they remain the challenges which can capture the imagination of the education leaders of the future.

Notes

1 The methodology used for analysis is based on comparisons of unweighted means for countries in different categories and on comparisons of the likelihood that an indicator for a country in a given adjustment category has positive or negative growth rates. I developed this methodology in research reported earlier (Reimers, 1994).

2 I have estimated these figures on the basis of 97 countries which reported 831 million adult illiterates and of 48 countries which reported 39 million children out of school to UNESCO. Estimates for countries which did not report these figures were based on population and dependency ratios using average ratios for illiterates and children out of school in the rest of the countries in the region. These estimates are conservative, as it is likely that countries with better statistics also have better education conditions, therefore the estimates represent a lower bound of true figures.

3 The poor are those living below an income of $370 a year, and the extremely poor are those living below $275 a year (World Bank, 1990, Table 2.1, p. 29).

4 It should be pointed out that there is great variation in how countries fared under adjustment regarding poverty. In some countries the poorest groups were protected by an increase of the rural–urban terms of trade, in other cases the urban poor were very hard hit by the economic recession ensuing the immediate phases of adjustment. By most accounts poverty increased during the 1980s in sub-Saharan Africa and Latin America (World Bank, 1992b).

5 These conclusions are drawn from analysing the figures of per capita GNP provided by UNESCO (1993).

6 I use 'competence' in a broad sense; whether the poor results for education of adjustment programmes result from inadequate skills on the part of the staff involved or inadequate organizational procedures or structures is irrelevant for the purposes of this chapter.

References

Albanez, T., Bustelo, E., Cornia, G. and Jepersen, E. (1989) *Economic Decline and Child Survival: The Plight of Latin American in the Eighties.* Innocenti Occasional Papers. Florence: UNICEF.

Carnoy, M. and Torres, C. (1994) Educational change and structural adjustment: a case study of Costa Rica, in J. Samoff (ed.), *Coping with Crisis: Austerity, Adjustment and Human Resources.* Paris: UNESCO.

Cornia, G., Jolly, R. and Stewart, F. (1987) *Adjustment with a Human Face.* Oxford: Oxford University Press.

Grootaert, C. (1994) Education, poverty, and structural change in Africa: lessons from Côte d'Ivoire, *International Journal of Educational Development*, **14**(2), 130–45.

Jolly, R. and Cornia, G. A. (eds) (1984) *The Impact of World Recession on Children.* Oxford: Pergamon Press.

Kakwani, N., Makonnen, E. and Van Der Gaag, J. (1990) *Structural Adjustment and Living Conditions in Developing Countries.* Working Paper PRE 467. Washington, DC: World Bank, Welfare and Human Resources Department.

Reimers, F. (1994) Education and structural adjustment in Latin America and sub-Saharan Africa, *International Journal of Educational Development*, **14**(2), 119–29.

Stewart, F. (1993) Education and adjustment: the experience of the 1980s and lessons for the 1990s. Mimeo, Oxford University.

Tibi, C. (1989) Conditions in the teaching profession: a current problem, *IIEP Newsletter* (Paris), **7**(4).

UNESCO (1991) *World Education Report*. Paris: UNESCO.

UNESCO (1993) *World Education Report*. Paris: UNESCO.

World Bank (1988) *Adjustment Lending: An Evaluation of Ten Years of Experience*. Washington, DC: World Bank.

World Bank (1990) *Poverty: The World Development Report*. Washington, DC: World Bank.

World Bank (1992a) *Adjustment Lending and Mobilization of Private and Public Resources for Growth*. Washington, DC: World Bank.

World Bank (1992b) *Development and the Environment: World Development Report 1992*. Washington, DC: World Bank.

2 World Bank Educational Policy: From Technicism to Close Proximity?

ROBERT SMITH

Introduction

This chapter seeks to raise a number of issues about the educational policies of the World Bank. The Bank is an important actor in international education, and its staff, consultants and experts influence and even determine educational policy-making and implementation in the developing world. In what follows, the concept of policy is defined and a number of approaches to policy analysis are examined. The major characteristics of World Bank policy formulation are identified, particularly the main principles underlying the methodology the Bank uses to identify policy options. The Bank's style of development assistance is shown to be positivistic, non-participatory and intellectually restricted in its choice of paradigms and use of research. In conclusion, more effective and appropriate means of policy formulation are suggested.

What is policy and how is it formulated?

Policy can be variously defined. As Jenkins (1978) points out, there is little in the way of a consistent conceptualization of the term 'policy' itself, and pages could be, and have been, filled with competing definitions. This does not discourage Jenkins himself from offering the following definition of public policy, adapted from a 1971 definition by G. K. Rogers:

> [Policy is] a set of inter-related decisions taken by a political actor or group of actors concerning the selection of goals and the means of achieving them within a specified situation where these decisions should, in principle, be within the powers of these actors to achieve. (Jenkins, 1978, p. 15)

Anderson argued in 1975 that 'policy making typically involves a pattern of action extending over time and involving many decisions' (cited in Jenkins, 1978, p. 17). Educational policy may be conceived as a subset of public policy and it is certainly true to say that it also carries concepts of goals, action and use of resources. However, the distinction between policy-making and decision-making is not always clearly made even by recognized experts in the field. In the vast literature on international education, policy is often rather simplistically identified with action. Torsten Husen in his introduction to Simmons (1980) says:

> A decade ago we were far less aware than we are now of the role of politics in educational planning. The expert was perceived as a technician who presented policy makers with unequivocal 'solutions' to problems posed by the latter. There are, however, no mechanical linkages between research and knowledge on the one hand and *policy action* on the other. (emphasis added)

Unfortunately, as this chapter makes clear, the period between Husen's remarks and the present day has not brought about a noticeable change in this state of affairs. This view of 'policy as action' is reflected in the Bank's 1980 *Education Sector Policy Paper*, which is introduced with the words:

'The policy of lending by the World Bank for education has evolved gradually since 1962 when the first education project was approved.' In other words, policy begets projects and is best understood as the rationale for intervention. As a working definition for the purposes of this chapter we can state that policy, in international educational terms, means the explicit set of investment choices and subsequent decisions which provide a government or agency with an agenda for achieving those educational goals which are thought to be desirable.

There could of course be an enlightening and fruitful exploration of the implicit set of choices which many governments make, either deliberately or through neglect, and which equally influence goals. A case in point would be the relative neglect, by successive Pakistani governments, of female education in spite of the compelling evidence of the high rates of economic return to such investments. It is probably true to say that there is always a hidden agenda in the set of investment choices governments make or fail to make.

The definition offered above would certainly fit the interpretation of policy used by the World Bank. The Bank's literature does not evince much difficulty in identifying policy options, be they investment in technical or vocational education or investment in universal primary education. As with many textbooks on educational research in which the identification of research problems is regarded as unproblematic, so with the Bank, for whom the 'policy option' is equally unproblematic. Policy options are à la carte, almost preselected or self-evident. What the Bank likes is 'choice-making'. This syndrome of the self-evident policy option, a key weakness in the Bank's approach, is made even more dangerous by reliance on dubious approaches to and interpretations of research. These weaknesses form the fundamental argument of the chapter.

The analysis of policy

Before the weaknesses in the Bank's approach to policy formulation can be addressed directly, it would be useful to review the tools available to the policy analyst. Policy analysis as applied to education relies heavily on borrowings from political policy analysis. The work of Dale (1986) gives a breakdown of what happens when educational policy is analysed. In brief, Dale proposes that there are three main approaches or 'projects' in educational policy analysis:

1 *Social administration*, which derives from perceptions of a client's needs and is intended to 'mend the world' or improve the client's lot. The purpose of the social administration project is to come up with an answer which will ameliorate some practical problem.
2 *Policy analysis*, which derives from a client's requirements and seeks technical ways of improving decision-making; the classical 'hired gun' policy analyst focuses on better methods rather than better answers.
3 *Social science* projects, which are academic, derive from theory and seek to improve or extend theoretical understanding.

This taxonomy is useful, but the projects should not be seen as mutually exclusive, and analysis of the Bank's activities in policy analysis, formulation and implementation sees the institution moving from one mode to another – which leads to the proposition that a fourth project exists, namely the *technicist–empiricist*, for those who believe that all problems are simply challenges and are amenable to technical solutions; the challenge merely lies in finding that solution. To this end the Bank gathers, commissions or generates extensive research data, filters them and draws conclusions for action – that is, policy. In one sense the technicist–empiricist combines the social administration approach with the policy analysis and social science projects. He or she seeks to mend the world by improving decision-making, basing evidence on particular research. Bowers (1982) describes technicism as the belief that all problems can be overcome if only the right technology is applied. This is reminiscent of Elmore's (1989) concept of forward mapping with its 'implicit and unquestioned assumption that policy makers control the organizational, political and technological processes that affect implementation [of policy choices]' (p. 246).

Turning to technicism–empiricism in practice, we can see this project applied in a variety of influential sources. Simmons and Alexander (1980) review research on factors which promote school achievement in developing countries. Their review lists a large number of research studies and allocates to each an 'educational production function' (EPF), a statistical technique which purports to measure the impact of school inputs such as teacher quality and school facilities on cognitive achievement. Simmons and Alexander provide a brief technical description of the strengths and limitations of the EPF. In a revealing statement the authors admit that the deficiencies in the procedure prohibit automatic policy recommendations based on EPFs. However, this technical procedure may 'still be a useful analytical tool for improving rather than optimizing the allocation of educational resources, if the improvements are first tested experimentally before being adopted as a policy' (Simmons and Alexander, 1980, p. 80).

Simmons wrote in 1980 as a policy analyst and adviser for the World Bank. He also chose to preface his book with the dedication, 'To those adults and children who can benefit from more humane education policies', yet his book is a hymn to technicism. In the same publication a chapter by Selowsky is entitled 'Preschool age investment in human capital' (Selowsky, 1980). It is in fact an argument premised on the statement that 'the character of a school's output depends largely on a single input, namely the characteristics of the entering children. Everything else – the school budget, its policies, the characteristics of the teachers – is either secondary or completely irrelevant' (ibid., p. 97). The chapter is illustrated with a bizarre figure which shows the relationship between the hours per year a child spends exposed to the environment matched with Bloom's development curve. A figure like a triumphal arch is the result – in a chapter devoted to the argument that pre-school pays off in terms of children's later learning.

The preoccupation of the Bank and its employees with technicizing educational debate is clearly illustrated elsewhere in the literature. The *Education Sector Policy Paper* of 1980 has over a third of its pages devoted to tables and figures. Backing policy decisions with hard data is always desirable but the Bank uses technical material like a bazooka; its presentations lack subtlety. For example, p. 121 of the 1980 Sector Policy Paper provides a histogram showing results of studies relating primary schooling to net social rates of return in selected countries – twenty countries in all. The bar chart indicates that net rates of return to primary education are very high (33 per cent or more) in countries like Venezuela, Colombia, Thailand and Uganda. Yet the context is not explained. Measurement is purely numerical and never qualitative. Other tables are accompanied by cryptic statements like 'weighted by reciprocal of the standard error'. Harassed permanent secretaries in the ministries of education of developing countries are unlikely to call up a statistician for an explanation of the technicalities. In the recent Bank review paper *Priorities and Strategies for Education*, a histogram shows unproblematically that school libraries have the most positive effect on pupil learning at the primary level (World Bank, 1995, p. 82). In McLuhan's phrase, 'the medium is the message', and a bar chart with a prominent profile speaks loudly, drowning the still, small voice which says, 'However, in certain countries and at certain times ...'

The Bank's influential document *Education in Sub-Saharan Africa* (World Bank, 1988) follows firmly in the technicist–empiricist tradition. It promotes a policy framework for the sub-Saharan countries of 'adjustment, revitalization and selective expansion' in education. The *Education in Sub-Saharan Africa* report summarizes educational progress since the 1960s, characterizing it as 'massive' and as having 'improved the human capital stock' (World Bank 1988, p. 1). However, the policy document goes on to state that the advances of the previous twenty years are now seriously threatened, partly by circumstances outside the educational environment. High population growth rates combined with economic stagnation have led to severe qualitative problems. There is an irony here: the case for low quality is made out in largely quantitative terms and these quantitative terms are almost exclusively concerned with pupil cognitive achievement, although measurement of 'inputs' is included as an additional set of criteria for quality. The policy recommendations put forward by the Bank to address the shortcomings of Africa's over-extended and substandard educational provision are prefaced by an appeal for the African nations to formulate and implement 'an internally coherent set of policies that reflect[s] the nations' unique history and aspirations and that effectively address[es] ... recently exacerbated problems in the education and training sector' (World Bank, 1988, p. 2).

In more concrete terms, the Bank goes on to suggest that this internally coherent set of policies will be characterized by adjustment, revitalization and selective expansion. Adjustment will entail diversifying sources of finance (to include cost recovery from the participants in education) and 'containment' of unit costs. Strategies for achieving the latter include reduction of repetition and drop-out, more effective utilization of teachers and adopting more realistic construction standards for school buildings. Revitalization represents a return to 'fundamentals': commitment to academic standards, provision of an effective package of learning materials, and improved investment in and utilization of physical plant and equipment. Finally, the Bank recommends selective expansion of certain sectors of education: universal primary education, distance teaching, skill training for both in-school and out-of-school youth and the building up of research and post-graduate education (World Bank, 1988, pp. 2ff).

Another important Bank document, *Education for Development: Evidence for New Priorities* (1990a), states that 'Detailed data on the major areas of educational policy and practices are available to produce a new analysis ... and to recommend coherent, practical policies for the future' (World Bank, 1990a, p. 1). In other words, we know the answers so here are the strategies for solving the problems of education in developing countries. This particular document presents the familiar argument that a schooled population will be the one best prepared for a period of rapid social and economic change; that a knowledge gap is already developing between the richer and the poorer countries; and that a detailed mass of data has been accrued over the past twenty-five years by the Bank and other agencies which will provide firm evidence for qualitative improvement and quantitative expansion of schooling. Hundreds of research studies on various aspects of policy are now available to guide decision-makers.

As Samoff (1993) indicates, the Bank's use of phrases like 'There is strong evidence that ... ' (World Bank, 1988, p. 42) gives a dubious, even spurious, endorsement to its policy generalizations. 'Research shows ... ' prefaces many Bank pronouncements, begging many questions. In *Education for Development* (World Bank, 1990a) the statement is made that three decades of analysis now provides a 'solid base' for understanding the relationship between education and development, analysing the contributions to be made by different levels of education, evaluating qualitative measures, assessing success and failure, and suggesting alternatives. This positivistic stance characterizes much Bank discourse and is reflected again in the 1995 review paper:

> Education produces knowledge, skills, values and attitudes; it is essential for civic order and citizenship and for sustained economic growth and the reduction of poverty. Education is also about culture; it is the main instrument for disseminating the accomplishments of human civilization. (World Bank, 1995, p. xi)

'If you're so smart, how come you ain't rich?' was the title of an otherwise forgettable rock and roll song some years ago. Applied to the Bank and its policy publications this title could be adapted to, 'If you know so much, how come you ain't more successful?' The Bank's pursuit of answers, and its methods, are illustrated in further publications.

The juggernaut of Bank policy

In 1991 Marlaine Lockheed and Adriaan Verspoor, supported by a considerable team of World Bank staff writers, produced the Bank's *Improving Primary Education in Developing Countries* (Lockheed and Verspoor, 1991). The foreword to the book states, 'A nation's children are its greatest resource' (Lockheed and Verspoor, 1991, p. xiii), and this technicist statement sets the tone for an almost wholly instrumental view of education and its role in developing countries. The authors' preface does begin with the words, 'This book is about children, learning and primary schools' (Lockheed and Verspoor, 1991, p. xv). Unfortunately, the book is not about those things. It is solely about the uses to which primary education can be put to bring about 'national development'. Lip service is paid to primary education serving other purposes, such as helping children 'function effectively in society'. But again the language is revealing. Children do not live happily, enjoy their childhood, have fun; they 'function effectively'. The neglect of arguments for the intrinsic and social value of schooling characterizes much Bank discourse.

Lockheed and Verspoor take as their agenda the role of primary education in national development and the current problems with this vital sector in developing countries. Their argument develops along a purely technicist–empiricist line; situational analysis, major problems or challenges, probable points of intervention, solutions available, strategies to be adopted and policies to be embraced. About half of their substantial book is text (pp. 1–232) and the remainder (pp. 235–415) is tables and references. The textual section is richly illuminated with boxes, diagrams and figures, ninety-four in all, or one every two or three pages. There is no doubt that the book – a formal statement of Bank thinking – is intended as a handbook for problem-solving. The answers are presented unproblematically.

There is something endearingly Deweyan about the authors' approach. Education is just another frontier to be conquered, and identifying the right tools will enable us to carry out the task effectively – the 'covered wagon' school of policy formulation. But in this more enlightened age the covered wagon must also be looked at from the Native American viewpoint. The juggernaut marked 'policy initiatives' is rolling across the prairies, which will never look the same again. Indeed, it can be argued that the covered wagon school as represented by Lockheed and Verspoor is positively dangerous.

Similar criticisms could be made of *Higher Education: The Lesson of Experience* (World Bank, 1994). This publication, again produced by a Bank team of experts, starts with a conventional statement that universities are essential in all countries for the education of future leaders and the provision of high-level manpower. Governments invest heavily; the Bank has assisted in the development of higher education throughout the world. In the past twenty years, enrolments in lower- and middle-income countries have increased by an average of 6.2 per cent per annum. However, quality is perceived to be deteriorating.

Public subsidies are too high and more equitable income distribution suffers as graduates earn more and more. The need for reform is 'widely acknowledged' – a generalization akin to the 'research shows ...' arguments beloved of the Bank. Proposed solutions to the 'crisis' include more privatization, diversified sources of funding, redefinition of the state's role in higher education and more emphasis on quality and equity – all echoes of Coombs's analysis of a decade ago (Coombs, 1985). The document is fraught with contradictions. Cost recovery is proposed, but student loan schemes are characterized as largely unworkable. Higher education's contribution to economic growth and poverty alleviation is alluded to while the soaking up of valuable resources and the growing scale of graduate unemployment are also noted. Equity is promoted as a goal for higher education through positive discrimination, yet privatization is also recommended, presumably to provide places for those who can afford to pay. Income-generating activities for universities, such as research and consultancy services, are recommended.

At the same time, note is taken of the poor quality of staff in many universities in developing countries. Underpinning the whole analysis is the unexamined assumption that higher education's contribution to economic growth and development is unproblematic. Worse, for a statement of World Bank policy towards higher education, no radical or robust alternatives to the standard model are offered, except for a brief discussion of diversifying tertiary-level institutions. Little or no research on innovatory practices is offered. Exemplars of good practice are drawn almost exclusively from countries where the Bank is most active. Just as the 'covered wagon' school of policy formulation of Lockheed and Verspoor is dangerous, so the conventional wisdom of *Higher Education: The Lesson of Experience* presents other dangers: there are no new ways of doing things; we must continue to operate with a blunt instrument; we can readily transfer politically neutral solutions across cultures.

The long-awaited review paper *Priorities and Strategies for Education* (World Bank, 1995) is full of examples of the Bank's unwillingness to learn from the experience of its own past or that of others. The fundamental premise of the document is that basic formal education remains the key to economic advancement for poor countries. Lip-service is paid in various places to the socializing or cultural aspects of education – usually in terms of how these elements affect the earning power and productive capacity of the educated. Throughout the document, the language is that of the technicist. Effective education is dependent on five 'inputs', which include 'tools for teaching and learning' (World Bank, 1995, p. 6). Attention to the outcomes of schooling is restricted to economic analysis and standard measures of achievement. The key priority for education is that 'it must meet economies' growing demands for adaptable workers who can readily acquire new skills and it must support the continued expansion of knowledge' (World Bank, 1995, p. 1). This is put forward as a prescription for countries where there are no jobs and where the days of mass semi-skilled employment have gone for ever, if they even existed. Most disturbingly of all, the Bank persists in transferring economic evidence from the United States to the developing countries of Africa. Evidence of rises in wage premiums in the USA associated with mastery of elementary mathematics is advanced as a justification for investment in basic education in countries which have little or no industrial employment capacity (World Bank, 1995, p. 97). Like most industrialized countries the United States has huge opportunities for part-time, casual, informal employment from job-sharing to dish-washing and clerical work. Countries like Kenya and Tanzania do not have these opportunities, and designing universal primary education on the premise that they do is at best misleading. Lewin (1993) offers an interesting and alternative interpretation of data from these countries.

The Bank's insistence on its sectoral approach (World Bank, 1995, p. 13) is also a cause for concern. As its prescriptions show, the emphasis is on making the education sector more efficient and effective. But unless change in education is accompanied by other changes in the economy which lead to job creation, basing educational policy on fitting primary school leavers for employment is doomed to failure. The Bank's structural readjustment programmes have rarely led to greater employment opportunities; rather the reverse.

It has been said earlier that the Bank is a bank and that it takes an economist's view of the role and purpose of education. This is a legitimate enough stance, although it has the obvious weaknesses of any one-dimensional view of social phenomena. Unfortunately, questions must also be raised about the legitimacy of the Bank's economics, particularly its enthusiastic embracing of cost–benefit analysis as a reliable tool (World Bank, 1995, p. 21). The section of the Bank's review paper devoted to a discussion of education and development (ibid., pp. 17–31) is at best controversial, particularly as the Bank's whole policy position is based on the premises laid out in this section. Apart from the elision of human capital theory into rates-of-return analysis (ibid., p. 21), no cognizance is taken of the very strong arguments put forward to contest the conventional wisdom of cost–benefit analysis (see, for example, Hough, 1992). An arguably faulty view of the relationship between schooling and economic development leaves one with deep concerns regarding the Bank's self-proclaimed advisory role: 'Bank financing will generally be designed to leverage spending and policy change by national authorities' (World Bank, 1995, p. 14). Purists will cringe at the use of the word 'leverage' as a verb, less for its technicist overtones and crass use of language than for the inherent danger of exerting leverage at the wrong place and in the wrong way.

Where does policy come from?

To explore these dangers more fully we return to the earlier question, 'Where does the received wisdom of policy come from?' The regular output of World Bank policy documents is firmly based on an unproblematic and positivist view of the world – that is, what is broken can be fixed – and appears to be equally firmly based on a broad network of research findings. Enough has probably been said already about the inherent dangers of the positivist–technicist view. Fägerlind and Saha have this to say about the positivistic style of much discourse on education and development: 'What we felt was lacking in the field ... was a broader and more coherent view of how the economic, social and political aspects of societies as a whole affected and were affected by education' (Fägerlind and Saha, 1983, p. vi). They go on to state: 'Our conviction that efforts to use education to promote change in particular directions could be both highly successful or doomed to failure motivated us to think more carefully about the complexity of the relationship and how it works' (ibid., p. vi). This understanding of the complexities of policy formulation appears to be lacking in the Bank's approach to finding answers and solving problems. As noted earlier, the relatively unproblematic critical path analysis which the Bank adopts tends to oversimplify what Fägerlind and Saha use as the rationale for their argument: the complexity of the relationship between education and national development. The formula the Bank appears to adopt is that clearly defined problem areas can be identified, equally clear research findings can tell us how to resolve the problems, and by dint of rational strategies the mismatch between education and national development can be bridged (and the covered wagons roll on).

The research dimension is an important one in all Bank publications. The quoting of research findings lends an air of legitimacy to otherwise shaky or unclear arguments. Weiss (1979), in an article entitled 'The many meanings of research utilization', presents seven models of how research can influence policy-making, ranging from the linear model of fundamental applied research through to the enlightenment and 'intellectual enterprise' models. The Bank appears to use research from a number of the categories identified by Weiss. Lockheed and Verspoor (1991) provide examples of utilizing research for advocacy, for problem-solving and as a linear model. They present many policy statements as unproblematic yet often quote only one research study in support of their position (see Lockheed and Verspoor, 1991, p. 67, for an example). The book is dotted with broad generalizations under the heading either of 'blind alley' as an unworkable policy choice or 'promising avenue' for something 'proved' to be effective.

Samoff (1993) has some tough words to say about the Bank's use, or abuse, of research. Not only does he criticize the Bank's generalizations concerning what the research actually says but he takes issue with the notion that research actually does influence policy-making in the way the Bank assumes it does or should. Writing of the World Conference on Education for All, Samoff states, 'The Jomtien resolutions are but a single example of the privileged position of research or, more accurately, of claims about research and its findings in the discourse on educational policy' (Samoff, 1993, p. 185). Samoff also identifies a convergence in aid agency approaches which prevents nation states from shopping around for support for policies not reflected in Bank priorities. Britain's Overseas Development Administration (ODA) makes no bones about linking its aid policies to those of the Bank and a shift can be detected in the agency's willingness to support larger Bank initiatives by taking on components of Bank projects rather than identifying and pursuing its own interventions. In Samoff's words, 'The World Bank has come to be the lead agency in setting the education and development agenda' (Samoff, 1993, p. 187). Samoff's analysis of the rise of the Bank as the lead player shows clearly the inherent contradiction in using a bank as the main development agency. As a bank it requires quick and obvious returns. Its staff are dependent on short-term successful outcomes to their activities if preferment and advancement are to follow. The dominant perspective is economic: what works must be expressed in explicit and quantitative terms. As Samoff expresses it:

> The greater the role in the [project] approval process played by individuals who consider themselves 'hard' scientists (a self-description that is common among, but not limited to, economists) the greater the pressure for explicit and unambiguous research findings expressed in quantitative terms. (Samoff, 1993, p. 190)

Research is expensive and complex to undertake. Small wonder that the agency itself does it — commissioning, undertaking and managing the research enterprise. But this incestuous procedure merely serves to reinforce the weakness of Bank policy formulation. In-house experts, working within an organizational climate which, though not monolithic, has a style of its own, are almost bound to find the answers they are supposed to be looking for. The notion that there may in fact be no answers cannot be entertained. This is clearly illustrated by a leading Bank expert, George Psacharopoulos, who presents an analysis of the 'problem' of policy in African education as a story of failure because policies have not been implemented fully or properly and have not been clearly stated nor financed adequately. Therefore:

> Perhaps the safest course of action for the policy maker would be to abstain from educational policy fireworks and concentrate on the documentation of cause and effect relationships – the only activity, in my opinion, that can lead to successful school improvement. (Psacharopoulos, 1990, p. 21)

Once again we see the Bank's search for definitive answers, through research or exemplars, presented in a technicist–empiricist mode. Answers are 'out there', like nuggets in a reef, and the wagons have to roll on to find them as efficiently as possible.

The picture drawn so far has been one of a hugely influential and even dominant force in world educational development which promotes policy decisions and choices with great authority. Yet from the Bank's own literature it is clear that the research dimension of the Bank's pronouncements is seriously flawed, both on the grounds of its reliability and validity and in terms of its uncritical acceptance of findings which are at the least equivocal, and data which are often highly inaccurate and unreliable but which are taken for granted. A specific example of this is found in Lockheed and Verspoor's (1991) espousal of providing school snacks instead of lunches (as a contributor to improved cognitive performance). The work of one researcher, Pollitt, is quoted to support this policy recommendation. Nothing is said of the cultures in which a snack is an unknown concept. Incidentally, school lunches are written off as a 'blind alley' because there are few statistically sound studies which have examined the effect of school lunch on academic achievement; by the same token the Bank has not 'proved' that they have no effect.

In fact, Lockheed and Verspoor (1991, p. 85) go on to suggest that no scientific studies exist because of all the variables which intervene in such studies. Yet still they persist in the snack idea as a better policy option. Similarly, they promote the idea of pre-schools as a 'promising avenue' despite their own admission that most of the publicized results are from exemplary programmes conducted under ideal conditions in the United States. Head Start is quoted, 'although the resources for Head Start are more abundant than would be the case in developing countries' (Lockheed and Verspoor, 1991, p. 81). The more deeply this influential survey, published with an introduction from Barber Conable, president of the World Bank, is studied, the more dubious its uses of research appear to be. It would be no exaggeration to conclude that certain policy choices have been selected by the Bank and its positivist technicians after which supportive research findings have been culled and presented. This, in the case of the Bank, is where policy comes from, and this is the received wisdom that harassed permanent secretaries and national commissions grasp at in the hope of getting to grips with the complexities of their educational systems.

An alternative approach to policy formulation

Perhaps there is a sense in which organizations like the World Bank can never be changed. They are banks after all, and as such they have their own priorities, which are largely fiscal and economic, what Samoff (1993) refers to as the 'financial–intellectual complex', chillingly reminiscent of 'military–industrial complex'. Education is bound to be viewed by a bank through an economic lens. It is also true to say that the World Bank is not the only source of policy advice and that a number of countries are resisting the glib and unexamined assumptions which underlie much of what the Bank promotes, although, as noted above, it is becoming increasingly difficult to do so.

Yet the question remains: how should policy be formulated and on what evidence should we base decision-making? Surely the vast resources of great international bodies with their high-powered teams of economists, educators, sociologists, political scientists, evaluators and statisticians should be our best option? Jenkins (1978, p. 3) notes that policy formulation normally derives from the interaction of three sources: rational choice-making; internal and external political influences; and the influence of 'a network of organizations pursuing different goals'. The World Bank has become the major player among the external political forces and its network of hired guns, deputy sheriffs and wagon trains populates the landscape of international education. Jenkins's analysis indicates that in fact policy formulation is a complex activity without clear and predictable methods or outcomes. In discussing policy-making it is easy to conceive of it as an event. As Weiss puts it:

> A group of authorized decision makers assemble at particular times and places, they review a problem (or opportunity), they consider a number of alternative courses of action with more or less explicit calculation of the advantages and disadvantages of each option, they weight the alternatives against their goals or preferences and then select an alternative that seems well suited for achieving their purposes. (Weiss, 1982, p. 292)

This description of rational policy-making is subjected by Weiss to a closer analysis. She suggests that the characteristics of the model are boundedness (of time, actors and space), purposiveness and calculation. In addition, constructs such as perceived significance and sequential order play important roles in the process of rational decision-making and policy formulation. However, in the real world decisions are arrived at through widely different procedures, or 'undirected strategies' as Weiss calls them (Weiss, 1982, p. 296). It is useful to use Weiss's typology as a framework for examining the policy formulation process of the World Bank.

Undirected strategies

First among the undirected strategies is reliance on *custom* and *implicit rules*. This phenomenon can be recognized in the workings of the Bank. Whether applied to setting up a new university or designing a new examination system, similar policy questions are likely to be asked and are likely to be based on our understanding of what has always been done and what other people are currently doing. The solecism of 'new innovation' is not so ridiculous when we see how few innovations are actually new. The analysis presented in the Bank's *Higher Education: The Lesson of Experience* (World Bank, 1994) has already been alluded to in terms of its resonances with Coombs's earlier work. Alison Girdwood suggests that within this Bank publication, 'the diagnosis is largely familiar, as are many of the proposed solutions' (Girdwood, 1994). Reliance on custom and past solutions is alive and well in this Bank offering. Weiss goes on to identify *improvization* as a further tactic in policy formulation. What she calls 'impromptu accommodation' features in much policy development. If this analysis is correct, even more fears must be expressed over approaches to policy which attempt total control, leaving little to the exigencies of everyday change or even crises.

Elmore (1989) refers to the 'implicit and unquestioned assumption that policy makers control the organizational, political and technological processes that affect implementation' and defines this as 'forward mapping'. His paper goes on to argue that such approaches are based on a 'noble lie' – life simply is not like this. Weiss supports this with her notions of improvization and *mutual adjustment*. The latter term describes the ways in which groups or individuals in organizations make decisions by reacting to other decisions made around them within the organization. Despite the protestations of writers like Samoff (1993) that the Bank is not monolithic, it must be argued that shared confidences, departmental meetings regarding new projects, and preferred approaches to problem-solving are the everyday topics of conversation within the organization.

Reacting to decisions being made in the surrounding environment must be an influential source of policy formulation. Weiss's concept of *accretion*, whereby procedures are repeated when similar – or not so similar situations recur, might have been derived from analysis of recent policy developments in the Bank. Given a commitment to market economics and a New Right value system, the accretion of decisions based on concepts like added value, value for money and 'limited resource' should come as no surprise. The absence of statements reflecting a more humanistic view of the purposes of education should be included in Weiss's taxonomy under the heading of *erosion* as a negative route to policy.

To return to Weiss, she lists *negotiation* and *move and counter move* as additional policy formulation strategies. Horse-trading, claim-jumping and log-rolling are metaphors borrowed from Hollywood's greatest mythology but ones which describe with some accuracy what happens as part of 'rational' policy-making. Jones (1992, p. 197) reports on 'Tunisia III' as a key project learning experience for the Bank. He goes so far as to say that the Tunisian government did not want the project for which it was to borrow $8.9 million. In renegotiations Bank staff 'displayed a commendable degree of flexibility'; in other words, horse-trading became essential.

A particularly fascinating aspect of Weiss's analysis is her concept of *a window for solutions*. Weiss remarks, 'Officials often become wedded to pet remedies and they seek opportunities to implement them ... These are cases where the solution is in hand, and partisans seek a "window" that will provide an opening for their ready made nostrum' (Weiss, 1982, p. 297). Transfer of solutions in this manner is noted by Jones (1992, p. 200) in his comments on the Bank's influential 1990b publication *Primary Education: A World Bank Policy Paper*. Worst-case scenarios were transferred from low-income African countries to form the policy basis for all countries.

Finally, Weiss suggests that *indirection* is a potent source of policy making. Decisions emerge as a by-product of other decisions and unintended outcomes become policy. By these and many other routes, Weiss suggests, policy can 'happen' without a set piece of formal decision-making. Weiss's analysis is helpful and it would be naive to think that all Bank policy was planned, rational and purposive.

In sharp contrast, Elmore (1989) has developed a concept which he confesses to borrowing from Mark Moore of the Kennedy School of Government at Harvard: that of 'backward mapping' as a means to policy implementation. The remainder of this chapter is devoted to arguments in favour of a more human and culturally sensitive approach to the business of external political influence – a 'green' wagon train.

Backward mapping as the way forward

Elmore introduces his discussion of implementation research and policy decisions with some charmingly naive statements: 'Better policies would result ... if policy makers would think about whether their decisions could be implemented before they settle on a course of action' (Elmore, 1989, p. 244). He goes on to argue that very little advice is actually available for people to make implementation choices wisely. The importance of clarity over the consequences of adopting one framework rather than another is more dominant than arguments over which framework to adopt. The normal procedure when analysing policy choices and their implementation is that of 'forward mapping'. Objectives are set (from the top), expectations are specified, action initiatives are described and implementation begins. Monitoring and evaluation may also be specified. The ODA follows this approach in its so-called 'logical framework' for project preparation in which wider objectives, immediate objectives, outputs and inputs are laid down along with procedures for measuring achievement of the objectives. Elmore rightly criticizes the weaknesses of this logical approach on the basis of the assumption that policy-makers can control the organizational, political and technological processes which will affect implementation – what he calls the 'noble lie' (Elmore, 1989, p. 246). In what was described earlier in the chapter 'as the empiricist–technicist role of the World Bank, this set of assumptions, or noble lie, is explicit in many of the Bank's statements. For example, in the education sector paper of 1980 we read: 'The Bank's involvement has encouraged educational improvements, modified traditional methods, helped raise local management capacity, and provided a strong source of funding for buildings and equipment' (World Bank, 1980, p. 7). Again, in the 1995 Review paper it is stated:

> Bank programmes will encourage governments to give a higher priority to education and educational reform, particularly as economic reform takes hold as a permanent process. Projects will take more account of outcomes and their relation to inputs, making explicit use of cost–benefit analysis, participatory methods, learning assessments and improved monitoring and evaluation. (World Bank, 1995, p. 15)

Returning to Elmore, we find that 'backward mapping' takes an entirely different approach from the positivist, logical framework strategy. According to Elmore:

> It begins not at the top of the implementation process but at the last possible stage, the point at which administrative actions intersect private choices ... Having established a relatively precise target at the lowest level of the system, the analysis backs up through the structure of implementing agencies,

asking at each level two questions: What is the ability of this unit to affect the behaviour that is the target of the policy? And what resources does this unit require in order to have that effect? (Elmore, 1989, p. 246)

This approach is in sharp contrast to that described above as typical of the World Bank. Instead of perpetuating the noble lie that policy-makers can control the environment in which their policies will operate, backward mapping as a strategy would allow the dispersal of control and a concentration on the factors which can only indirectly be influenced by policy-makers anyway. The most difficult part of backward mapping for organizations like the Bank to accept would be the substitution of formal devices of command and control for 'informal devices of delegation and discretion that disperse authority' (Elmore, 1989, p. 248).

Elmore neatly summarizes what he means by backward mapping in the following way:

> begin with a concrete statement of the behaviour that creates the occasion for a policy intervention, describe a set of organizational operations that can be expected to affect that behaviour, describe the expected effect of those operations, and then describe for each level of the implementation process what effect one would expect that level to have on the target behaviour and what resources are required for the effect to occur ... [This] emphasises, in other words, that it is not the policy or the policymaker that solves the problem, but someone with immediate proximity. (Elmore, 1989, p. 254)

It must be noted that Elmore is writing specifically about implementation, the implication being that the policy decisions are already made and more effective implementation is the sole objective. But there is no reason why Elmore's model could not be transferred to policy formulation too. It has already been made clear that policy formulation is not simply a matter of rational choice-making. It is far more complex an activity than can be answered by Psacharopoulos's plea for 'cause and effect' to be documented and replicated.

The implications for research-based policy formulation – the ostensible approach of the Bank – are profound. Instead of the caricature of the high-powered researcher combing the libraries and resource centres of the world for materials to support Bank policy initiatives we see something developing on a more human scale. If we followed Elmore's 'critical path' as outlined above and developed a concrete statement, say from the Chief Inspector of Schools of Zambia, to the effect that secondary teachers do not know enough to teach O-level classes effectively and that, in the time-honoured phrase, 'something must be done' as a policy imperative, then we can begin to construct the set of operations that might affect this behaviour. We might then go further and describe the expected outcomes of these operations and so on, building from the base up. Contrast this with the peddling of received wisdom from questionable research findings ...

If the Bank is to overcome its present image as the purveyor of ready-made policy solutions it will need to shift to a more human scale and type of activity. The human resources are available throughout the developing countries for the 'someone with immediate proximity' to play a crucial role in policy formulation and implementation. This might be a new form of empiricism-technicism but it will carry the advantage of authenticity. Philip Jones suggests that:

> It is on its own terms as an international financial institution that the World Bank should primarily be assessed and its work in education interpreted ... Conversely, in their rhetoric and organizational behaviour, the Bank and its staff would do well to reflect the limits of the Bank's charter and the constraints on its thinking imposed by its banking character. (Jones, 1992, p. 265)

This may be taken to mean that the World Bank can be weaned away from its narrow econometric view of what is wrong with education in the developing world and what needs to be done to put it right. Noel McGinn (1994) has suggested that organizations like the Bank have focused too much on calling for education to improve the global competitiveness of national economies, a strategy feasible only for states which are already economically powerful. But what else can a Bank promote? McGinn's case for redesigning education to contribute to integration at a transnational level is a strong one, but unlikely to be well received by a powerful supranational organization, which in McGinn's words is 'weakening the ability of a state to be the major influence on every-

thing that takes place within its borders' (McGinn, 1994, p. 291). In stark contrast to a backward mapping orientation, the Bank provides loans only for its own, specified programmes, establishes conditionalities which must be met before money is advanced, produces 'guidelines' concerning the hire of consultants and the selection of overseas training institutions, coordinates policy-making among various countries and, as has been demonstrated, uses in-house research to justify its recommendations (McGinn, 1994, p. 293).

From ideology to close proximity

The argument developed so far has tried to show that the World Bank is the most powerful actor in the international education development enterprise. In Jones's (1992, p. xiv) words, it 'lies at the centre of the major changes in global education of our time'. The Bank promotes certain policies which it claims derive from sound research evidence. This is arguable, if not demonstrably exaggerated. The Bank views education as a subject for investment and the project as the main (although not the sole) mode of delivery. Out of its experience of projects comes much of its current ideology. As a bank it emphasizes the economic role of education and tends to see education as subject to realities imposed by the economy of a recipient country rather than by cultural or political realities. Frequently the Bank's prescriptions for the economic restructuring of developing countries include, as a condition, the restructuring of the education system. As a source of international expertise the Bank has grown over the past thirty years to the point where it claims to have developed a set of solutions to educational problems. It is able to point to the 'success' of various initiatives in various countries and to press for their adoption transnationally. Trends or cycles in solution offering can be detected, starting with an early concern for physical infrastructure, the curriculum, textbook development and manpower requirements through to reform of management, raising quality and efficiency, and the human resource development emphasis of today. Yet there is an overwhelming sense of the externality of Bank policy initiatives as they are culled from published sources. The story is of hired guns and deputy sheriffs moving into disputed territory to bring order, rather than of enabling those in close proximity to work out their own salvation. However, it must be remembered that the Bank is a bank and like all banks it expects to supervise the use of its lending. How can backward mapping become a preferred and effective mode for the Bank?

Project design offers itself as an obvious target for a revised approach by the Bank. But project design is usually based on some kind of needs analysis or research, and project implementation is normally accompanied by project evaluation. It is in these three related areas that Elmore's principles might best be worked out. It would be encouraging to see the Bank commissioning more research from in-country experts. Where there is limited capacity, let the Bank build this up first. The organization uses research findings as the rationale for many of its interventions. Close proximity research is a prerequisite for successful project design.

But the partnership element in project design does not characterize Bank approaches despite changes introduced since the recent Wapenhans Report. Even in the 1995 review paper, 'household involvement' as a policy is restricted to co-opting parents into school governing bodies and encouraging choice of schools in a caricature of the New Right policy developments of metropolitan countries (World Bank, 1995, p. 11). The concept of consultation is not prominent in the Bank's policy recommendations. Jones (1992, p. 210) discusses 'Singapore 1', a project through which the Singapore government planned to relocate its university campus. The Bank thought the existing campus adequate and it took four missions over three years plus two related United Nations Development Programme (UNDP) missions before the Bank agreed on an appraisal mission. When the Singapore government stood firm over its plan the Bank agreed to a loan, insisting on a number of conditions which over time proved irrelevant and which were eventually abandoned. Jones (1992, p. 203) notes that

'Very frequently, Bank thinking for project content differed not only from the borrowing government's, but also public and student opinion, reflected in enrolment preferences.' More recent Bank policy documents have promoted the issue of quality in education but have in reality been more concerned with doing more with less. What most countries and their communities are looking for is better quality and better opportunities, not reduced cycles of schooling, double shifts or less well-qualified teachers. Developing true partnership with borrowers is perhaps the greatest difficulty facing the Bank, especially as the methods it uses to develop policy are so divorced from the daily reality of the actual pupils, teachers and managers of schools in low-income countries. There is perhaps an inevitable paradox between the Bank's 'macro' approach and the manifest need for participation and involvement at the local level. This more human dimension is a huge challenge for technically oriented Bank staff and is reflected in the 1995 review paper (World Bank, 1995, p. 15). However, as Jones puts it:

> The subjective, the interpretive, the aesthetic, the normative and the ideological all play their part in the resolution of economic problems, and in that prior questioning leading to the posing of economic questions ... A starting point could involve fresh consideration of the humanistic and spiritual dimensions of development ... The complex and costly arrangements embodied in the work of the World Bank ... might well enjoy invigoration and technical revitalization through fresh consideration of their underlying purposes – the promotion of peace, human dignity, well-being and happiness. (Jones, 1992, p. 267)

But if the Bank is to change there must be some reciprocity. Borrowing governments are committing their children and grandchildren to the repayment of huge IDA loans, 'soft' though they may be. This presents them with the responsibility for resisting what they know will never work and for seeking ways of exercising leverage to ensure that more viable projects result from their negotiations with the Bank. That governments need skills, training and expertise to subject Bank proposals to more rigorous analysis is a precondition for successful negotiation. McGinn's plea for transnational cooperation finds resonance here, as does his fear that organizations like the World Bank and the agencies that simply follow its lead reduce the chances of this happening. There is a role for the social scientist, in Dale's terms 'seeking to improve or extend theoretical understanding' (Dale, 1986, p. 58), in helping governments play a fuller role, or even defend themselves, in negotiating with the Bank.

Subjecting the Bank's activities to more rigorous analysis, evaluating its projects and drawing attention to the strategies neglected by the Bank will help bring policy decision-making into much closer proximity. It has been emphasized by many commentators that the Bank is a bank and should be judged accordingly. But the Bank has become more than a bank. Its advice, its policy imperatives and its interventions go far beyond the purely financial. It is insufficient for the Bank to premise its lending policies purely on the kinds of positivistic, value-for-money, intellectually restricted approaches which this paper has identified. As Jon Lauglo, one of the 'referees' quoted in the 1995 review paper puts it in commenting on Bank policy:

> like governments, the Bank performs a political role and it has an institutional culture which is more hospitable to some kinds of research and some kinds of conclusions than to others. It will be predisposed to assimilate those findings which do not contradict its overall policies of markets, modern sector development and a leaner state. In education it will pay special attention to quantitative studies that see education within a production function paradigm. (Lauglo, 1996, p. 13)

Education is fundamentally a human and cultural activity. Ways must be found by the Bank to engage more fully and more humanly with this reality. By the same token, governments, staff of ministries of education and others in close proximity to the tens of thousands of children whose educational opportunities may be blighted or blessed by Bank-funded projects have to find ways of contesting the worst excesses of the Bank's technicist–empiricists and of supporting and extending its more human activities. Perhaps most importantly, all those engaged in the process of working out what education and development

mean need to understand and accept the discontinuities, ambiguities and plain dilemmas of what we are trying to do rather than seeking the Holy Grail of the one best solution.

This chapter has shown that the World Bank is a powerful actor in the formulation of educational policy in the developing world. Its interpretation of policy-making has, however, been from within a technicist paradigm. Its uses of commissioned and other research lead to positivistic conclusions regarding the use of schooling as a means to economic development in the world's poorer countries. As an institution it has maintained a distance between itself and the end users of the education system: the pupils, the teachers, the communities. Attempts are being made to bridge these gaps but the dominant rhetoric of the Bank is modernist and technicist, couched in the language of the economist. Even wider gaps are opening up between the authoritative pronouncements of the Bank and the recipient governments negotiating loans for educational development. An argument for debate and discussion in closer proximity to the classroom realities of the developing world is made. The growth of a deeper and more effective partnership is called for if Bank interventions are to bring about policy changes which are within the powers of the actors to achieve. At the same time there is a profound need for more rigorous and critical analysis of the Bank's success rate in bringing about change, particularly as its voice becomes more insistent and its strength as a policy-maker grows.

References

Bowers, C. A. (1979) Ideological continuities in technicism, liberalism and education. Mimeo, Center for Educational Policy Management, University of Oregon.

Coombs, P. (1985) *The World Crisis in Education: The View from the 80s.* New York: Oxford University Press.

Dale, R. (1986) *Introducing Education Policy.* Milton Keynes: Open University Press.

Elmore, R. (1989) Backward mapping: implementation research and policy decisions, in B. Moon, P. Murphy and J. Raynor (eds), *Policies for the Curriculum*. London: Hodder & Stoughton.

Fägerlind, I. and Saha, L. (1983) *Education and National Development: A Comparative Perspective*. Oxford: Pergamon.

Girdwood, A. (1994) Don't bank on this solution, *Times Higher Education Supplement*, 22 July, p. 12.

Hough, J. (1992) *Educational Cost-Benefit Analysis*. Overseas Development Administration Research Report. London: ODA.

Jenkins, W. I. (1978) *Policy Analysis: A Political and Organizational Perspective*. London: Martin Robertson.

Jones, P. W. (1992) *World Bank Financing of Education*. London: Routledge.

Lauglo, J. (1996) Banking on education and the uses of research, *International Journal of Education and Development* (forthcoming World Bank review issue).

Lewin, K. (1993) *Education and Development: The Issues and the Evidence*. London: Overseas Development Administration.

Lockheed, M. and Verspoor, A. (1991) *Improving Primary Education in Developing Countries*. Washington, DC: World Bank.

McGinn, N. F. (1994) The impact of supranational organizations on public education, *International Journal of Educational Development*, **14**(3), 289–99.

Psacharopoulos, G. (1990) *Why Education Policies Can Fail: An Overview of Selected African Experiences*. Discussion Paper 82, Africa Technical Department Series. Washington, DC: World Bank.

Samoff, J. (1993) The reconstruction of schooling in Africa, *Comparative Education Review*, **37**(2), 181–222.

Selowsky, M. (1980) Preschool investment in human capital, in J. Simmons (ed.), *The Education Dilemma*. Oxford: Pergamon, pp. 97–112.

Simmons, J. (ed.) (1980) *The Education Dilemma*. Oxford: Pergamon.

Simmons, J. and Alexander, L. (1980) Factors which promote school achievement in developing countries: a review of the research, in J. Simmons (ed.), *The Education Dilemma*. Oxford: Pergamon, pp. 77–96.

Weiss, C. (1982) Policy research in the context of diffuse decision making, in D. Kallen, G. B. Kosse, H. C. Wagenaar, J. J. J. Kloprogge and M. Vorbeck (eds), *Social Science and Public Policy Making*. Windsor: NFER.

Weiss, C. (1979) The many meanings of research utilization, *Public Administration Review*, **5**, 426–31.

World Bank (1980) *Education Sector Policy Paper*. Washington, DC: World Bank.

World Bank (1988) *Education in Sub-Saharan Africa*. Washington, DC: World Bank.

World Bank (1990a) *Education for Development: Evidence for New Priorities*. Washington, DC: World Bank.

World Bank (1990b) *Primary Education: A World Bank Policy Paper*. Washington, DC: World Bank.

World Bank (1994) *Higher Education: The Lessons of Experience*, Washington, DC: World Bank.

World Bank (1995) *Priorities and Strategies for Education: A World Bank Review*. Washington, DC: World Bank.

3 The Economics of Universal Primary Education: The Balance of Investment and Yield

CLEM TISDELL

Introduction

According to numerous economic studies (see, for example, Psacharopoulos, 1994), high rates of return or yield continue to be earned from investment in primary education. Investment in such education is profitable both from an individual's private point of view and socially. Primary education is the foundation of virtually all formal educational systems and a prerequisite for many types of non-formal training; it is the main source of literacy and numeracy in most societies and a powerful force in transmitting social skills and values. Individuals lacking primary education are likely to find it difficult or impossible to cope in modern societies and may lose their dignity and ability to protect their own interests. It is therefore not surprising that access to primary education has been accepted as a human right.

Nevertheless, as Christopher Colclough and Keith Lewin (1993, p. 1) point out, despite the fact that primary schooling has been accepted as a human right for around fifty years, a quarter of the children eligible to attend primary school in developing countries do not do so and for the most part remain illiterate. Furthermore, in sub-Saharan Africa the situation has deteriorated. The proportion of those eligible to attend primary schooling declined in the 1980s and this trend continued into the 1990s. Nevertheless, mainly as a result of increased access to primary education in East Asia, access to education in this period increased slightly for developing countries as a whole.

As discussed below, investment in primary education is a sound investment both in terms of private and social rates of economic returns and compared to the level of returns on higher education and other forms of investment. Maintaining or even increasing investment in primary education should be given a high priority as a means of improving the efficiency of resource use and as a means of stimulating economic growth and development. It is rational from an economic viewpoint, particularly for less developed countries, to give a high priority to investment in primary education. However, in sub-Saharan Africa investment in primary education has been insufficient to maintain relative access of eligible students. In many developing countries, government investment per student enrolled tends to increase with the level of education. This means that overall economic returns to investment in education are not maximized. In discussing these and related matters, this chapter considers general issues involved in determining economic returns to primary education, reports empirical findings about these returns and discusses the balance of investment in education in relation to level of education, regional distribution and gender before considering some special issues.

Economic returns to investment in primary education: general issues

Although many people support the desirability of universal primary education on moral grounds, it can also be assessed from an economic point of view. The most widely used approach of economists is to regard expenditure on education as an investment in human capital. Outlays on education, like outlays on other forms of capital, can add to future economic benefits or income. In order to assess the economic value of such outlays or investment, we need to consider the added income or economic benefits received (as a result of extra education) in relation to the extra outlays involved; that is, the rate of return on the investment involved.

Generally, rates of return on education are estimated on two bases: the *private* return (that is, the return on investment by individuals); and the *social* return (that is, the return on investment in education by the government and by individuals combined). The latter level of investment is usually much higher than the former because in most countries education is heavily subsidized by the government. For example, school fees may be absent in government schools and private schools may receive state subsidies.

The investment by individuals in education includes not only any school fees paid and the schooling expenses incurred but also any income forgone while pursuing education. In the case of primary school children, income forgone may be low. However, rural families in developing countries may experience some reduction in family income as a result of sending their children to primary school. Economic benefits are usually estimated in terms of extra income received by individuals as a result of their increased investment in education, such as an increase in the number of years of their schooling. The social rate of return is usually estimated also by taking this as the benefit, but the total investment to which it is related is private investment in education *plus* that of the government. Consequently, because most governments subsidize education to varying degrees, the social rate of return on investment in education is usually lower than the private rate of return because of the government subsidy for education.

A number of alternative methods have been used to estimate the rate of return on education, and these are discussed for example by Psacharopoulos and Ng (1994). The two basic methods are the age–earnings profile method and the earnings function approach, as originally suggested by Min-

cer (1974) and subsequently extended. The first method takes the economic benefits of those achieving a particular level of education to be their extra earnings compared to the earnings of a control group with a lower level of education. These extra earnings when compared with the extra investment required for the additional education enable the rate of return on education to be estimated. However, the comparative age–earnings profile method requires a considerable amount of data and so the earnings function approach is often used.

Both approaches concentrate on estimating differences in private earnings of different groups and relating these to years of education finished or to stages of education successfully completed. These are used to estimate both private and social returns. Although this may give a reasonable approximation to private returns, one can have some doubts about its value for estimating social returns. In general, this method is liable to understate social returns.

First, this is so because increases in education may raise total factor productivity so that the income of the less well educated rises along with income of the more educated. Therefore, a complementarity in income exists and this will not be detected by examining differences in earnings between better- and less-educated groups. We may also say that this is an externality effect. Furthermore, provision of education reduces the *transaction* costs involved in organizing society and carrying out economic activity. These benefits are not always group specific and so will not all be captured by cross-sectional comparisons of earnings. Furthermore, it should be noted that the concept of social return to education is much narrower than the concept of social return as used in welfare economics. This is clear from Pigou (1932), for example. As pointed out by Jimenez (1987, Ch. 2, esp. p. 24) and Tisdell (1982, section 14.7), social returns to education do not take into account market failures, for example due to externalities, merit goods, shortcomings of the private financial sector in supplying finance for education and so on. Consequently, social returns from investment in education are liable to be underestimated from the perspective of welfare economics (cf. Weisbrod, 1964).

The above discussion of returns is based upon the human capital approach (Hansen, 1970) as originally proposed by Becker (1964), and assumes that the most important contribution of education is to raising the productivity of those who receive more education. However, some economists have suggested that education's primary role is to act as a sorting or screening device separating the clever from the less clever and selecting those with traits such as greater persistence, application and so on which may be valuable in the workforce. This role is believed by some supporters of the screening hypothesis to be more important than the productivity-enhancing effects of education (Taubman and Wales, 1974). Much recent discussion has centred on the efficiency of formal educational systems as screening devices (Varian, 1992, Ch. 25). In practice, most educational systems perform dual roles of productivity enhancement and screening even though argument persists about the relative importance of each (Colclough and Lewin, 1993, p. 29).

Neo-Marxists are critical of established economic analysis of education because in their view it does not bring attention to the role of the education system in perpetuating inequalities in the social system (Fägerlind and Saha, 1983, pp. 54–7). Educational systems can add to social inequality or cause it to persist in a number of ways. For example, the richer members of society may find it easy to finance the education of their offspring and do so for longer, thus purchasing higher-quality education for them. They may also transmit to their offspring values embedded in the educational system. Therefore, their offspring may not be easily 'screened out' by the educational system. This may also be the case for dominant élites in socialist countries. This process *may* result in social return on investment in education not being maximized because, for example, the gifted offspring of the poorer members of society cannot easily remain in the educational system. Neo-Marxists and others suggest additional social mechanisms that can result in educational systems supporting social inequality (Fägerlind and Saha, 1983, pp. 54–7).

The importance of these mechanisms is probably greatest at higher levels of education. Universal primary education is likely if anything to reduce social inequality. Furthermore, screening is unlikely to be an important factor at the primary level of education.

Returns to investment in education: empirical findings

Numerous empirical studies have been undertaken of returns on education, the findings of which have been summarized on different occasions during the last few decades by Psacharopoulos, most recently in Psacharopoulos (1994) and earlier, for example, in Psacharopoulos (1973). In general these empirical findings support the following propositions:

1   Returns on primary education are higher than for higher levels of education. This is true for both private and social rates of return.
2   The rates of return on investment in primary education appear to be favourable in comparison to rates of return on physical capital.
3   Computed rates of return on education tend to decline with economic development and are higher for low-income countries than for high-income countries. Psacharopoulos (1994) is of the view that this indicates diminishing returns on investment in education.
4   By regions, returns on investment in education are estimated to be highest for sub-Saharan Africa, next highest for Asian countries (excluding their OECD members) and least for OECD countries.
5   Returns to investment in education appear to have declined over the past decade or so.
6   The evidence about differences in economic returns to investment in education by gender is inconclusive.

Let us consider the above points bearing in mind that differences in the rate of return affect the optimal economic allocation of investment. For example, investment is education should be increased in areas where marginal returns exceed those elsewhere. If, for instance, primary education gives a higher marginal rate of return than investment in education at higher levels, overall returns on investment in education will be raised by diverting funds from higher levels of education to primary education.

Taking the latest available studies for countries throughout the world, Psacharopoulos (1994) estimates for the world as a whole that the private rate of return on investment in primary education is 29.1 per cent, on investment in secondary education 18.1 per cent and on higher education 20.3 per cent. Social rates of return are lower because of government support for education. They are 18.4, 13.1 and 10.9 per cent respectively for primary, secondary and higher education. The private rate of return for primary education exceeds the social rate of return by about 50 per cent, by slightly more for secondary education and by almost 100 per cent for higher education. This reflects the fact that in the world as a whole, the proportionate subsidy for higher education is higher than for lower levels of education.

For most countries the social rate of return on investment in primary education is in excess of returns from investment in physical capital. Comparatively, therefore, it is a worthwhile investment.

Estimated rates of return to education are higher for low-income countries than for higher-income countries. For example, in a comparison of rates of return from investment in primary education for low-income countries and middle-income countries, social rates of return are estimated to be 23.4 and 14.3 per cent respectively and private rates of return 35.2 and 21.3 per cent respectively (Psacharopoulos, 1994, p. 1328). However, one can debate whether the differences are as great as the estimates indicates. The (social and economic) costs of pockets of illiteracy and of lack of basic education can be very high in developed countries. Furthermore, it is possible that the economic benefits from education are more highly diffused in higher-income countries than in low-income ones. The consequences would be smaller marginal economic benefits in relation to the individual from extra investment in educa-

tion, with significant benefits flowing to others. Or alternatively, in higher-income countries, shifts in the productivity function may be more important than changes in its slope as a result of greater investment in education. Account should also be taken of redistribution of income through taxation and other fiscal measures. For example, higher incomes earned by the educated may be partially redistributed to the poor or the needy through the fiscal system.

Estimated regional returns to investment in education appear to be negatively correlated with levels of income in the world's major regions. Lower-income regions are estimated to have higher returns on investment in education than higher-incomes regions but at the same time have the least investment in education and, because of their low incomes, the greatest inability to increase this investment. This situation can be illustrated for example by comparing sub-Saharan Africa with the OECD group of countries. Private rates of return to education in sub-Saharan Africa are estimated by Psacharopoulos (1994) to be 41.3 per cent for primary, 26.6 per cent for secondary and 27.8 per cent for high levels of education with the corresponding social rates of return being 24.3, 18.2 and 11.2 per cent. By comparison, the estimates of Psacharopoulos (1994) for OECD countries are private rates of return to primary education of 21.7 per cent, for secondary education 12.4 per cent and for higher education 12.8 per cent. The corresponding estimated social rates of return are 14.4, 10.2 and 8.7 per cent. After sub-Saharan Africa, rates of return to investment in education are highest in Asia, excluding its OECD members.

Psacharopoulos (1994) found after examining the literature that rates of return on investment in education for the world as a whole appear to have declined in recent decades. The reason for this trend is unclear.

Evidence about comparative rates of return on investment in education of males and females is inconclusive. For primary education, the estimates of Psacharopoulos (1994) indicate a much lower private rate of return for females (12.8 per cent) than for males (20.1 per cent), but at higher levels of education this rate of return is higher for education of females than males. From a social point of view, it is possible that the returns on investment in education of females are considerably higher than suggested by these income-level estimates. For example, family size tends to decline with education of females and this may be a positive social influence in developing countries experiencing 'excessive' rates of population growth (Clark and Clark, 1994). Also, females tend to be the principal carers in families. Better education can enable females to improve their own health and that of their family. This provides economic benefits in terms of averted costs for treatment of illness and in terms of productivity increases, and reduces mortality rates of mothers and infants (World Bank, 1995, pp. 9–10). Furthermore, in many developing countries (especially in sub-Saharan Africa) women play a major role in subsistence production and non-wage employment (Roy *et al.*, 1996). Education can add substantially to the productivity of such activities, which are often ignored in economic assessments of the value of education.

The balance of investment in education

As pointed out in the previous section, estimated rates of return from investment in primary education considerably exceed those for higher levels of education. Furthermore, according to available evidence, rates of return to education in lower-income countries are greater than in higher-income countries.

The first relationship suggests that in countries not achieving universal primary education, priority should be given to investing in primary education. In order to increase returns on total funds used for education, it seems that funds should be diverted from higher levels of education to primary education. This is certainly the view of the World Bank, which recommends low- and lower-middle-income countries with low net primary enrolment ratios (say, below 75 per cent) to give priority in public policy and spending to increasing access to and the quality of primary schools

(World Bank, 1995, p. ix). Many countries in sub-Saharan Africa and South Asia fall into this category. For countries with medium net primary enrolment ratios (90–95 per cent), such as many in Latin America, the Middle East and North Africa, focus on increasing access to primary schools and in raising their quality is still in order but compared to the first set of countries more emphasis should, according to the World Bank (1995, p. xx), be placed on increasing access to and quality of secondary education. Countries with higher net primary enrolment ratios, such as those in East Asia, are recommended by the World Bank (1995, pp. xx) to raise the quality of primary education and to concentrate on increasing access to and the quality of secondary education. For levels of education above primary level, the World Bank appears to favour increasing reliance on private provision of education and private funding, for example via fees, a matter which will be discussed below.

The second inequality mentioned, namely greater returns on investment in education in lower-income countries than in higher-income ones, suggests that global returns from education would be increased if funds for investment in education were diverted from high-income to low-income countries. However, it is most likely that such a diversion without a concomitant increase in investment in physical capital would quickly result in diminishing marginal returns to investment in education in developing countries. Furthermore, one cannot be at all confident that estimates of returns based upon differences in the earnings of individuals with different amounts of education account fully for the economic value of education. Positive spillovers or externalities of various kinds imply that such an approach underestimates full social returns. Furthermore, complementarities between education and returns on other factors of production such as physical capital mean that the educated do not necessarily capture the full value of their education. This implies that returns on education for the economy as a whole may be greater than those attributed to education by economists on this basis of estimates of the earnings of individuals from education. Thus, in this case the whole may be greater than the sum of its parts.

In the world as a whole, there has been a considerable increase in investment in education in recent decades. As a result, the ratio of primary education enrolments to the primary school age population has increased in every region of the world except in sub-Saharan Africa. Africa remains a major problem because during the 1980s its gross primary enrolment ratio fell from an already low level of 80 per cent to around 70 per cent. In all major regions of the world, except sub-Saharan Africa, the expected number of years in schooling of a 6-year-old rose. In sub-Saharan Africa, which already had the lowest expected years of schooling in 1980, it fell.

Despite the fact that globally there have been significant improvements in access to education (but with sub-Saharan Africa moving against the trend), a number of major problems, as pointed out by the World Bank (1995, p. 15), remain:

1 The absolute number of children without any education in the world as a whole is expected to increase until at least 2015.
2 Only half of primary school children complete the primary school cycle.
3 Illiteracy of adults remains a major problem.
4 Partly because of greater worldwide access to primary education (Africa excepted), demand for secondary and tertiary education is growing at a rate faster than can be financially accommodated by many educational systems. Public funds for expansion of education at these levels remains short in many developing countries.

In addition,

5 The gap between educational spending per capita in developed countries and less developed countries remains high, and on the whole the quality of education is superior in more developed countries. Furthermore, the gap between per capita expenditure on education in high-income countries and the lowest-income countries is increasing.

The proportionate out-of-school population is highest in Africa, South Asia and the Middle East. In 1990, 50 per cent of all primary age children were not in school in sub-Saharan Africa, 27 per cent were not in school in South Asia and 24 per cent in the Middle East. These regions have the lowest enrolment ratios for girls and the highest fertility levels. Whereas access to education in South Asia and the Middle East is growing slowly, in sub-Saharan Africa it has declined.

In sub-Saharan Africa, increases in primary enrolments in the 1980s failed to keep pace with population growth and consequently not only the absolute number of individuals without primary education rose but also the relative number. On the other hand, gross enrolment ratios in secondary and higher-level education in Africa rose between 1980 and 1990. This changing pattern has been the subject of criticism by the World Bank because rates-of-return analysis suggests that in Africa's case priority should be given to investing available funds in primary rather than higher levels of education. In addition, because the level of government subsidy for education is higher per student at higher levels of education and because it is usually the children of richer members of society who proceed to this level, emphasis on expanding higher education adds to social inequality. Nevertheless, even if Africa were to divert all its funds from higher education to primary education, this would not substantially increase access to education.

Africa experienced severe economic and social difficulties during the 1980s, falling levels of per capita income, and in many of its countries disruptive wars, civil unrest and high levels of international debt. Problems of sustaining economic growth and of growing international debt were not confined, however, to Africa. The 'solution' proposed by the International Monetary Fund (IMF) and the World Bank was the adoption of structural adjustment policies involving a reduction in the size of the public sector and a greater reliance on free markets and private enterprise. As Jones (1992, p. 162) points out, this general trend influenced the policy recommendations of the World Bank about education. According to Jones (1992, p. 162), the education staff of the Bank needed to ensure that their approach to education 'was in line with Bank and IMF austerity measures and structural adjustment policies'. During the 1980s and the early 1990s many publications of the World Bank and its officers stressed the possibilities of gains in economic efficiency from greater privatization of education at higher levels and from the charging of user fees. It was further argued that this could increase access to higher levels of education, especially in countries which forbid or restrict private supply of education.

In any case, in most countries, but especially in developing countries, great pressure is being placed on government budgets by increasing public demands for educational facilities, especially at higher levels. At the same time there has been increased political resistance to the raising of taxes. In the least developed economies, several of which have experienced falling per capita incomes (especially in Africa), capacity to pay for public provision of education has been reduced. In such circumstances there appear to be few practical alternatives to greater privatization of the supply of education and use of fees at higher levels of education. Certainly, increased efficiency in provision of education would make for more effective use of scarce resources. For the same expenditure on education, increased efficiency could result in greater access to or improved quality of education, or both. There are significant differences in per unit costs of delivering education between countries, and the World Bank has marshalled some transnational evidence to suggest that access to education and its economic efficiency increase up to a point with the charging of fees for education and with its private supply (Tan and Mingat, 1992).

In line with the above, the World Bank supports a stylized policy package for education. This involves free primary education and free lower secondary education but increased charging of fees at higher levels of education, with fees being charged 'for all public higher education, combined with loan, tax and other schemes' to enable needy students to defer payment until they have sufficient income to afford repayments (World Bank, 1995, p. xvii). Scholarships based on academic merit and educational allowances, for example stipends, for the poor also form a part of the package. Furthermore, it is recommended that top priority be given in public spending in all countries to

primary education, moving up the educational ladder to secondary education when access to and quality of primary education becomes high.

Even if these measures are adopted by the poorest countries, the capacity of their people to pay will still leave all with an educational system significantly inferior to that in high-income countries.

As a percentage of GNP, public expenditure on education in high-income countries is almost twice that in low-income countries (World Bank, 1990, p. 63), and of course the absolute public contribution per student is much greater in high-income countries because of their higher per capita incomes. The disparity in educational expenditure per student is very great between low-income and high-income countries. In 1985, for example, the median recurrent expenditure per primary pupil in high-income countries compared to that in low-income countries was 50 : 1. This relative discrepancy increased from 1965 onwards (World Bank, 1990, p. 63) and undoubtedly has continued to do so in recent years. On the grounds of equity, a case seems to exist for developed countries to provide greater aid to less developed countries for education. Furthermore, rates-of-return analysis indicates that some diversion of funds for education from high-income countries to low-income ones would increase global returns on investment in education even though there are qualifications to consider, as mentioned above.

This is not to suggest that there really is a case for reducing investment in education in high-income countries. Rates of return from education compare well with the alternative rates of return from investment in physical capital, which are believed on average be in the region of 10–12 per cent. Furthermore, as suggested above, rates of return on investment in education may be underestimated. This is especially evident for estimates of rates of return on investment in the education of women. When account is taken of the impact of education on fertility and health and in reducing poverty the comprehensive social returns from education of females are much increased. Although access of girls and women to education has greatly improved globally, they still remain a disadvantaged group in terms of access to education, particularly in the Middle East, South Asia and Africa. The situation is improving only slowly in these regions.

From the fact that the social rate of return on primary education is high, one would expect investment in education to be a significant contributor to economic growth. Studies of the sources of economic growth such as that of Denison (1967) indicate that, along with technological progress and economies of scale, this is so. New economic growth theories, such as those of Romer (1986), give a central role to education as a vehicle for economic growth. Even if education is not a prime mover of economic growth, it (particularly primary education) is a vital complementary ingredient. Without necessary supporting investment in education, economic growth generated by sources other than increased education is unlikely to be sustained and the quality of life may leave much to be desired.

Some general issues

Returns on education have most frequently been evaluated by economists by comparing the earnings of those with more education with those with less. The resulting estimates are often the basis for policy advice about the efficient allocation of investment in education. However, economic efficiency is not the only factor to be considered in educational policy. Equity is also important. Furthermore, the earnings approach does not capture the full yields from investment in education. For example, it may not capture the total productivity benefit of education and features such as the value of improved health and reduced rates of fertility in countries experiencing excessive population growth. Also, not all averted costs are taken into account. For example, consider the education of handicapped people. Education of handicapped people may add little or nothing to the earnings of many of them but may still confer an economic advantage. For example, it may reduce the costs imposed on those caring for them by enabling

handicapped people to take greater care of themselves.

Efficiency arguments suggest that, ideally, investment in each individual's education should proceed until the (discounted) social marginal return equals the (discounted) marginal cost of the investment. Ideally, social benefit should be interpreted in its widest sense and ought to include, for example, external benefits and allowances for averted costs. Such a rule is likely to favour meritocracy in education – greater investment in the education of individuals who show greater productivity from education (cf. Tisdell, 1982, section 14.7) – but with this being modified for averted costs considerations to ensure greater allocation of education to the handicapped and less gifted than otherwise. Such an approach will result in inequality in distribution of educational investment in favour of the intellectually gifted but with some modification to allow for averted cost elements in the case of the handicapped and less gifted.

Two alternatives to the above approach can be considered: equal allocation of educational resources to all, and greater investment in the education of the handicapped, less gifted or disadvantaged than in the education of intellectually more gifted individuals. There is no economic case for such equality from the point of view of maximizing yields from investment in education (Tisdell, 1982, section 14.7). Nevertheless, relative equality in primary education for individuals may be justifiable because one is likely to be uncertain which children of primary school age are intellectually gifted and which are not. Not that this can always be resolved for all with absolute certainty.

As for compensatory equality, this is liable to reduce the overall yield on investment in education even further. This is not to deny that compensatory investment in education for groups discriminated against may assist in raising their social status and could in the longer term increase the contribution of the group to total productivity. The use of educational inequality for social engineering in this way involves an immediate efficiency cost and may, but need not, involve a long-term one.

Rawls (1971) has argued that economic inequality is justified only if it is to the advantage of all. It is possible that some inequality in education could be to the advantage of all, as for example extra support for the intellectually gifted because the spillover to the rest of society from their education may be high. This aspect is, however, probably less important at lower levels of education than at higher ones.

The above arguments support the desirability of all groups in society having access to primary education. The question also needs to be considered whether extra educational support should be available to those students who are likely to be disadvantaged for economic reasons or by their social status. There are some grounds for such support: for example, to enable children from disadvantaged backgrounds to remain in the educational system long enough for the more intellectually gifted to be selected and provided with support to move up the educational ladder.

Concluding comments

The socio-economic case for universal primary education is very strong. This is true not merely because of the high comparative rates of return (based on enhanced earnings) from investment in such education; it is likely to be more so taking into account averted costs to society, externalities and impacts on total productivity. Furthermore, such access may also be considered to be just from the point of view of reducing inequality of opportunity.

Despite the above position, the global situation of primary education is unsatisfactory. In the world as a whole, the absolute number of children without primary education is increasing. More than half of primary school children do not complete the primary school cycle, and some groups, such as women and girls, continue to be disadvantaged not because of lack of intellectual merit, but because of social prejudice. Furthermore, gross inequality exists between investment in primary education in high-income countries and that in low-income countries. This gap is increasing, and

is reflected in differences in access to primary education and its quality between high- and low-income countries.

All educational systems are experiencing constraints on growth in expenditure because public funding has not expanded in line with perceived or actual needs. In the case of low-income countries, this constraint has tightened because their income per capita has not increased or has even declined (for example, in several African countries), so reducing the capacity of governments to raise funds by means of taxation for public finance. In the case of developed countries, a broad change in social philosophy has occurred involving greater resistance to increased taxation and to government involvement in the economy. How permanent this change of attitude will be remains to be seen. These trends have resulted in pressure for greater economic efficiency in the delivery of education, growing emphasis on the user-pays principle and support for greater private provision of educational services. Nevertheless, there continues fortunately to be general support for the view that primary education should be universal and free to the individual, even though globally there is a long way to go in translating this into reality.

References

Becker, G. S. (1964) *Human Capital.* New York: National Bureau of Economic Research.

Clark, C. and Clark, J. (1994) The status of women and the provision of basic human needs in developing societies, in K. C. Roy and C. Clark (eds), *Technological Change and Rural Development in Poor Countries.* Oxford: Oxford University Press, pp. 81–108.

Colclough, C. and Lewin, K. (1993) *Educating All the Children: Strategies for Primary Schooling in the South.* Oxford: Oxford University Press.

Denison, E. F. (1967) *Why Growth Rates Differ: Post-war Experience in Nine Western Countries.* Washington, DC: Brookings Institute.

Fägerlind, I. and Saha, L. J. (1983) *Education and National Development: A Comparative Perspective.* Oxford: Pergamon.

Hansen, W. L. (ed.) (1970) *Education, Income and Human Capital*. New York: National Bureau of Economic Research.

Jimenez, E. (1987) *Pricing Policy in the Social Sectors*. Baltimore: Johns Hopkins University Press.

Jones, P. W. (1992) *World Bank Financing of Education: Lending, Learning and Development*. London: Routledge.

Mincer, J. (1974) *Schooling Experience and Earnings*. New York: Columbia University Press.

Pigou, A. C. (1932) *The Economics of Welfare*, 4th edn. London: Macmillan.

Psacharopoulos, G. (1973) *Returns to Education: An International Comparison*. Amsterdam: Elsevier.

Psacharopoulos, G. (1994) Returns to investment in education: a global update, *World Development*, **22**(9), 1325–43.

Psacharopoulos, G. and Ng, Y. C. (1994) Earnings and education in Latin America: assessing priorities for schooling investments, *Education Economics*, **2**(2), 187–207.

Rawls, J. R. (1971) *The Theory of Justice*. Cambridge, MA: Harvard University Press.

Romer, P. M. (1986) Increasing returns and long-run growth, *Journal of Political Economy*, **94**, 1002–37.

Roy, K. C., Tisdell, C. A. and Blomquist, H. C. (1996) *Economic Development and Women in the World Community*. New York: Praeger.

Tan, J. and Mingat, A. (1992) *Education in Asia: A Comparative Study of Cost and Financing*. Washington, DC: World Bank.

Taubman, P. and Wales, T. (1974) *Higher Education and Earnings*. New York: McGraw-Hill.

Tisdell, C. A. (1982) *Microeconomics of Markets*. Brisbane: Wiley.

Varian, H. (1992) *Microeconomic Analysis*, 3rd edn. New York: W. W. Norton.

Weisbrod, B. A. (1964) *External Benefits of Public Education: An Economic Analysis*. Industrial Relations Section, Department of Economics, Princeton University, NJ.

World Bank (1990) *Primary Education: A World Bank Policy Paper*. Washington, DC: World Bank.

World Bank (1995) *Priorities and Strategies for Education* (draft). Washington, DC: World Bank, Education and Social Policy Department.

4 Education for Sustainable Livelihood

MARK A. BURCH

The past four decades have seen repeated warnings (Carson, 1962; Erlich, 1969; Meadows *et al.*, 1972; World Commission on Environment and Development, 1987) regarding the environmental impact of economic activities. Awareness of the relationship between economic development and environmental degradation has a long history and has often been brought to the attention of politicians and business leaders (Groves, 1992). Some dire predictions have failed to materialize, partly from benefit of technical innovation, and partly from luck. Many predictions have materialized, and continue to materialize, along with unimagined surprises, so that the work of more contemporary writers aims less at predicting future emergencies than at mapping their expanding proportions in the present (Brown *et al.*, 1990, 1991; Brown and Kane, 1994; Erlich and Erlich, 1990, 1991; Ponting, 1991; Meadows *et al.*, 1992). Some people now believe that the approaches used to promote economic development in Southern Hemisphere countries since World War II have been largely ineffective. The same development assumptions and technologies applied in Northern countries have left a legacy of environmental degradation the remediation of which is only barely started. Moreover, in both Northern and Southern societies, the record of development efforts in creating conditions which foster the overall social good is equivocal at best. Our experience with social and economic development since 1950 suggests that doing more of the same will prove inherently unsustainable, both politically and environmentally. The concepts and assumptions which guide development must be refashioned from basic values upwards. The role of education in this process is critical.

To understand how development efforts have taken an unsustainable turn, and how we might fashion more sustainable approaches to improving our lot in the world, it will be helpful to adopt ideas introduced by Thomas Kuhn (1962) in *The Structure of Scientific Revolutions*. Although talk of 'paradigms' and 'paradigm shifts' is not new, Kuhn has nevertheless provided an eminently useful set of metaphors for understanding how we organize our thinking about the world as well as our activities in it.

Paradigms

Thomas Kuhn introduced the concept of a *paradigm* in natural science as a theoretical construct which helps to organize our understanding of natural phenomena. Once articulated, paradigms attract adherents who share a belief in the theory. Paradigms provide coherent direction, and sometimes even methods, for future efforts to elaborate the scientific and technical implications of the theory.

Whereas a scientific theory aims to explain natural phenomena, Fritjof Capra (1982) extended the idea of a paradigm by making it a synonym for *world-view*, or that constellation of shared beliefs and non-rational responses which characterizes a particular way of being in the world, i.e. a pattern of livelihood. Gregory Bateson (1979) hypothesized that paradigms, when viewed as information-organizing systems in living things, influence far more than our intellectual opinions about the nature of things. They can also shape the dynamics of sensation and perception at preconscious and unconscious levels.

Education as socialization to a paradigm

The persistence of a paradigm requires that its tenets and methods be communicated from one individual to another, and from one generation to the next. This occurs through both cognitive and emotional messages. Together with the hypothetical propositions the paradigm offers concerning the nature of things comes the conviction that the propositions are factual, that they are important, that they somehow stand out from a background of all other considerations which can be (or must be) omitted from discussion as irrelevant, superstitious, or simply beyond the 'proper' boundaries of the discipline. The influence of paradigms extends beyond their intellectual function into the realm of psychology and sociology as groups sharing the same belief distinguish themselves on this basis from others who do not share the paradigm. Adherence to the orthodox paradigm thus constitutes the foundation of personal and group identity, of social esteem and of strong political allegiances. Some may hold to these systems so strongly that they will die rather than exchange a familiar paradigm for an alternative world-view.

Among the many things which education can claim to be, it is pre-eminently a process of shaping, through communication, every level of individual thought and behaviour to conform to established paradigms. Its content may be symbols, affective experience or non-verbal behaviour. But it is inherently patterned, value-laden and prescriptive. Put more simply, education is the process whereby we acquire the paradigm (or the set of paradigms) which define the 'good life' prescribed by our civilization as well as the recommended methods for achieving it.

Every paradigm is an abstract 'map' based on selected information which configures the perceptual and cognitive processes of consciousness.

Because paradigms are abstractions concerning the nature of things, they necessarily *omit* some of the data of experience. A paradigm may 'work' well in spite of its omissions provided that the factors omitted are not determinative of the future survival of the civilization subcribing to the paradigm. When important facts not represented in a dominant paradigm become determinative, however, paradigm change becomes a matter of survival. For this reason, both that which is included and that which is excluded from our traditional development paradigm are 'deep causes' of our environmental and social crisis. The work of education for sustainable livelihood thus involves reconfiguring human consciousness through the formation of a new intuitive context (paradigm) for making development decisions.

The Northern development paradigm

The modern concept of 'development', and international development in particular, originated in North America as an outgrowth of the Marshall Plan to rebuild Europe following World War II. Development was equated with economic growth, defined as expansion in the scale and number of economic activities, increasing consumption of resources and energy, and increasing levels of personal and national income. Development defined as qualitative improvement in the conditions of human life was never wholly absent from this model, but qualitative improvement was believed to follow more or less necessarily from economic growth.

The achievements of science and technology during and after World War II established the expectation that continued technological development would confer increasing control over the forces of nature. This control in turn would generate more material wealth from nature, promising for human beings ever-increasing affluence. The 'good life' was thus defined as material wealth gained through the manipulation of nature for human benefit by means of the Cartesian–Baconian scientific paradigm.

Traditional societies whose development trajectories had taken them in directions other than those of Northern countries were viewed as 'underdeveloped' or, more recently and more charitably, simply 'developing'. Implicit was the assumption (and the value judgement) that all societies should 'develop' an industrialized, consumption-oriented economy and that they should do so using the concepts, values, technologies and economic and social instruments which define the Northern development paradigm.

Development, education and communication of the first kind

As the Northern development paradigm has become more entrenched, education has become ever more entrained to the requirements of economic growth fuelled by technological development. Science is concerned with the observable, quantifiable dimensions of the material universe. It is concerned with public knowledge which is replicable and objective. Technology, as applied science, is the vehicle which fuses knowledge of *how* nature works with human values concerning *what* we want to achieve with this knowledge. The spectacular success of science and technology, however, has tended to focus educational resources and pedagogical practice increasingly on the 'how' of development, with diminishing attention being paid to everything else, everything omitted or disparaged by the scientific paradigm. The results of this trend are written on the face of the Earth.

Education which prepares people to participate in a development process configured according to the thought forms of the scientific paradigm requires what I have called *communication of the first kind*. Communication of the first kind relies on a narrow band of mostly visual and auditory sensation. Messages consist of strings of verbal or numeric symbols devoid of emotional content and sensuous richness. The symbols represent bits of a depersonalized 'objective' reality, a world of quantities and forces which have been discovered in artificially simplified laboratory situations. Communication of the first kind relies on electronic devices, print and pictures. Because its messages and contents can be highly specialized and technical, communication of the first kind tends to become the domain of experts and specially trained élites. It is impersonal, outer-directed, analytical, reductionistic and instrumental. It is, in fact, the perfectly congruent outgrowth of a world-view which sees human beings as subjects observing from a distance the behaviour of an 'outside world' which they seek to predict and control through manipulation of natural forces – not as participants but as detached, uninvolved observers.

This orientation to experience is more characteristic of the traditional Cartesian–Newtonian world-view than it is a fair description of the most recent work in theoretical physics and mathematics, which now wholly eschews the idea of human objectivity in scientific observation. Nevertheless, it is precisely this antiquated paradigm which still permeates the attitudes and behaviour of economists and politicians in many countries. It is certainly the world-view which underpins much of the economic development thinking of the past four decades.

Omissions from the Northern development paradigm

Every paradigm is a map claiming to represent the nature of things. Every paradigm includes some information at the cost of excluding other information. No map can contain all the information about the territory of experience without itself becoming the territory it represents and thereby losing much of its utility as a map. The critical question concerning any paradigm is an instrumental one: does the map provide the information necessary to achieving the goals of the journey for which the map is intended? A map designed for hiking which fails to include accurate information about rivers, gorges and mountain ranges is useless and perhaps dangerous, even though it might be accurate with respect to political boundaries, rights of way and property lines.

The value of a *scientific* paradigm lies in its simplicity, its formal elegance, the number of observations which it can organize and explain, its consistency with other, complementary paradigms, and its ability to generate publicly verifiable predictions of phenomena. The value of a *development* paradigm – that is, a map of the facts and directions necessary for people to secure and improve their livelihood in the world, and to do this so as not to undermine the chances for continuous improvement in the future – must be assessed in terms of its performance in achieving its basic purposes. If data begin to accumulate suggesting that decisions based on the paradigm actually undermine the prospects for a high quality of life in the future, or undermine the present quality of life, then the paradigm must be reassessed to determine whether false information has been mistakenly included or true information mistakenly omitted.

So far, no one has proposed a detailed, coherent, plausible and verifiable paradigm for sustainable livelihood. It is possible, however, to identify some omissions from the traditional development paradigm which guides decision-making in our society. It is also at least plausible to suggest that information and values which have been omitted from the dominant paradigm may include the information needed to compensate its self-defeating excesses. In fact, a very great deal has been omitted or else relegated to a category of 'scientific irrelevance'.

Scientific rationalism mostly omits consideration of non-rational experience such as intuition, emotion, aesthetics, sensuality, values, and any phenomena which are not publicly observable. Preference for analytic and reductive approaches to problem-solving marginalizes synthetic and holistic approaches to decisions. Emphasizing abstract, symbolic, formal and objective forms of communication tends to overlook personalized, subjective, concrete and immanent forms of communication such as touch, taste, odour and movement. The technical and economic élites within Northern societies, which are largely male-dominated, limit the participation of women in

particular and members of traditional and non-European cultures in general. Both the cult of the heroic scientific discoverer and its economic counterpart in the self-made business entrepreneur marginalize communitarian and collective values rooted in family, community and geographical identity. Finally, the ascendancy of an 'economic anthropology', a model of human nature based on the biases inherent in economic thinking, marginalizes practically every value other than individual economic self-interest.

This pattern of inclusions/exclusions comprising the traditional Northern development paradigm has produced historically unprecedented levels of individual wealth at the same time as unprecedented levels of inequality in the distribution of that wealth. Control over some of the forces of nature is purchased at the price of environmental damage, loss of irreplaceable species and habitats, creation of highly persistent and toxic waste products, depletion of natural resource stocks, alterations of atmospheric chemistry, pollution of fresh water supplies both above and below ground, measurable and significant changes to the Earth's ozone layer, increasingly unsustainable levels of population growth, and increasingly unattainable expectations regarding consumption of material goods and services. Many people have experienced significant improvement in general education, nutrition, reduced infant mortality, and extended life span, but even these gains are threatened by the limiting conditions created by the very development process intended to achieve them.

Education for sustainable livelihood and communication of the second kind

Calls for more sustainable approaches to development (International Union of Concerned Scientists *et al.*, 1990; World Commission on Environment and Development, 1987; United Nations Conference on Environment and Development, 1992) have arisen largely because the way Northern technical societies approach development is causing changes in the ecosphere which make long-term human survival doubtful. Sustainable development thus refers to that as yet unspecified complex of values, attitudes, behaviours, technical artefacts, intellectual instruments, institutional forms and spiritual intuitions which situate human development harmoniously *within* the ecosphere rather than in *opposition* to it.

Now if education includes communication transactions which establish and maintain paradigms, and, moreover, if paradigms guide human decisions and activities in synergy (more or less) with the ecosphere, then education toward more sustainable paradigms of livelihood requires forms of communication which compensate for the omissions of the established development paradigm. I have called such transactions *communication of the second kind.*

Communication of the second kind names communication transactions which are qualitative, holistic, aesthetic, intuitive, imaginative, concrete, immediate, visceral, sensory, personal, subjective, non-linear, and often related to the 'depth' dimension of human experience. Communication of the second kind can thus be described as a continuous, multi-sensory communion among all living things and their surroundings. In human beings, this process occurs at three levels, each nested within the other.

The first level subsists *within* individuals and includes communication between the conscious and unconscious domains of personal experience. C. G. Jung (1959) described a continuous 'dialogue' between the unconscious and consciousness consisting of a ceaseless flow of imagery which is driven ultimately by the somatic life of the person. Progoff (1958) characterized this imagery as representing the totality of individual awareness, both conscious and unconscious, and also as expressing individual developmental goals. Consciousness is not merely the passive recipient of imagery from the unconscious but also presents to the unconscious a continuous flow of sensory, perceptual and cognitive experience from the individual's social, physical and biological contact with the extra-personal world.

The transactions occurring precisely in the domain defined by the *relationships* between individuals and their societies constitute the second level of communication of the second kind. Individual subjective experience has little relevance to society until it finds expression in overt behaviour. It is through the overt behaviour of individuals and their complex interactions, through the collective shaping and reshaping of physical environments, and through the creation of 'artefacts' that society communicates its prescribed paradigms to individual members. Conversely, it is also through these transactions that individuals make both material and behavioural contributions to that great assembly of activities and artefacts which we call 'society'.

Not only do individuals experience within themselves the innate, spontaneous imagery which draws forward the process of personal development, individuals are party to relationships in society which are capable of forming *shared images* of development; that is, collective development goals. Such imagery can entrain the imaginations of individuals in the formation of collective purposes and projects which transcend the abilities of individuals. A whole range of little studied and less understood group dynamic processes evoke, select and synthesize the imaginative products of individuals to form group goals.

Finally, a third domain of communication subsists between the *human species*, taken collectively, and the *ecosphere*. The ecosphere *embeds* organisms within a 'supra-organismic' context. Like every other species, human beings are in continuous 'dialogue' with the ecosphere whether they are conscious of it or not. Humans send 'messages' to the ecosphere through production and consumption behaviours. And it may be that the ecosphere is responding to these activities through climate change, immune system suppression, changes in fertility rates and perhaps even the subliminal and intuitive perceptions symbolized in dreams, visions and fantasies.

A pedagogy which evokes as much of this capacity as possible *may* provide sufficiently rich data and a sufficiently holistic perspective to compensate for the limitations of the Cartesian worldview. I am not suggesting the abandonment of science and technology, the insights of economics, or the lessons of history any more than Newtonian physics has been abandoned in the age of relativity. On the contrary, what is required is a pedagogy that situates these achievements in a more holistic paradigm of livelihood informed by a wisdom deeper than human reason and supported by more information than can be gathered by physical measurements.

In a classic but little-quoted work written close to the end of his life, *A Guide for the Perplexed*, E. F. Schumacher (1977) addresses directly this problem. The world-view of science, he argues, is one which concerns the physical level of being. When it confines itself strictly to this level and attends to convergent problems, problems which can be solved with increasing precision and clarity the more attention they receive, it is brilliantly successful.

When, however, the 'paradigms' of science are applied to higher levels of being characterized by life processes, consciousness and self-awareness, and to divergent problems, problems the solutions of which can never be finally established but only transcended through personal development, then the results are disastrous. There can *never* be a solution to the question of how the laws of physics can be applied to improve human welfare with the same finality and convergence of results as how the laws of physics can be applied to predict the movement of a projectile. Yet education for sustainable livelihood must concern itself precisely with questions of the former sort as much as with the latter.

Compensating omissions through education for sustainable livelihood

The development and adoption of new technologies and institutional policies can be accomplished as a matter of conscious decision. Perhaps this alone will achieve sustainability. Perhaps this is all that Northern cultures are capable of, given their long history of devaluing any experience other than the reports of 'objective' science. Yet such technical and policy adjustments would then continue to be based on the same suppositions as have led us to the present crisis, namely that living well in the world is simply a matter of scientific rationality directing the will. We press on this way despite daily evidence that scientific rationality and will-power are aspects of consciousness, limited aspects of our being, and manifestly only occasionally and sporadically in control of our behaviour.

That living sustainably within Earth's ecosystems may be more a matter of *wisdom* which properly directs our behaviour is an idea seriously entertained by relatively few people. Wisdom is broader and deeper than reason alone, that is to say, more holistic. Being more holistic, it must necessarily embrace and respect more varieties of information and experience than does science. Wisdom attends to both the seen and the unseen, the measurable and the measureless, the qualitative and the quantitative, the outer and the inner, the subjective and personal as well as the objective and collective. Wisdom respects the reasons of the heart as well as the head, messages from the body as well as financial markets, the lessons of history as well as the projections of futurists.

Wisdom must direct its attention to human *behaviour* more than to human *intentions*. It is all well and good to have a rightly directed will since this is what quiets subjective guilt. But the ecosphere is little concerned with what human beings intend, what we wish, or how much guilt we feel or avoid. The ecosphere is not even concerned with whether or not our intentions and choices are based on good science. What matters is how we *behave*. What matters is our capacity to manage our own behaviour based on a deeply grounded, holistic wisdom as well as accurate, objective knowledge concerning how our behaviour affects other people and species. Science tells us how our behaviour affects the world. Wisdom guides us in applying science so as to sustain that world. Wisdom is not a scientific theory. Science can inform right livelihood, but it can never be the source of it.

If these arguments are sound, then development of sustainable societies requires educational activities that meet a number of criteria:

First, education for more sustainable livelihood will involve deepening and expanding human consciousness; that is, opening people's awareness to different kinds of information from within themselves, from their social relationships, and from the biophysical environment. This is not a luxury we can attend to after establishing successful businesses and becoming very rich. It is prerequisite to sustainable livelihood in any form.

Second, there is not only a need for expanded awareness, but also for a redirection of that awareness and its correlative development activities. Part of this might be achieved by a change in how we approach the ecosphere to meet our needs. Customarily we modify the environment to satisfy our needs and aspirations. The only limits we place on this activity are whatever limits our imaginations face in creating new 'needs'. It may be time now to *modify our needs and aspirations* in order to satisfy environmental constraints, or, at a minimum, to move further along the continuum of possibilities leading in this general direction.

Third, if the development goals of individuals are to be sustainable within their respective societies, and if broader social goals are to have the power to engage the creative involvement of individuals, then the two must emerge in synergy. Furthermore, if the development activities of human beings are to be sustainable within the ecosphere, human development as a whole must proceed *in synergy with the ecosphere.* Progress in both areas can be made by setting the appropriate context and process for educational activities and development decisions. This will be achieved at the same time as our paradigms of the 'good life' become more inclusive of previously omitted experiences and information.

If individual consciousness can become dangerously narrowed by adopting certain prejudices toward the unconscious and toward bodily experience, so too can societies dangerously narrow synergy among their own members simply by excluding some people from participating in setting development goals. Development agendas which are not 'socially sustainable' — for example, agendas which promote war, poverty, deep personal alienation, systematic discrimination or sexism — are not likely to be environmentally sustainable either. This is the case because any society which maintains discriminatory patterns of public participation in decision-making thinks, as it were, with only half of its head. Social inclusion must be seen as a high road toward cognitive and emotional inclusion which should, in principle, contribute to a more inclusive, and hence more *accurate*, development paradigm.

Part of the context-setting process also calls for more intensive questioning of basic beliefs about the nature of things such as the notion that development always requires 'trade-offs' and 'compromises'. Both ideas assume that improvement in one aspect of the human condition cannot be attained without tolerating deterioration somewhere else. Whenever development decisions are framed this way, more thought and creativity should be given to the issues. The *only* patterns of development which can be sustained are those based on synergy; that is, those specifying that configuration of activity which *simultaneously and mutually* benefits the individual, society and the ecosphere.

To attain this goal requires a process of both education and development that evokes the visions of individuals within an *inclusive* social context. Education must include a repeating cycle of group process intended specifically to nurture more holistic awareness in individuals while drawing forth the imagery of personal, social and planetary wellness and then allowing these images to interact so that the whole group moves toward a deeper consensus on how development of the community can proceed. Disciplines already exist which achieve similar results, examples being group meditation practices, healthy community 'visioning' processes, 'focusing' training and others.

Finally, the education of both individuals and societies towards more sustainable patterns of livelihood must be given an ecological context. This can be achieved by communicating many times in many different ways what is the current state of our relationship with the ecosphere. This goal relates closely to the traditional goals of 'environmental education'. It is not enough merely to devise educational practices which expand and deepen human consciousness, nor even enough to foster socially inclusive systems for setting development goals. Neither of these taken separately or together ensures a reference to the ecosphere which supports and sustains *all* human activities, goals and achievements. If human civilizations are to be sustained on Earth beyond the next century, the ecosphere must form the context *within* which all other human decisions are taken, not the stage *upon* which human fantasies of greed and power are enacted.

What can we expect from such an undertaking? We are accustomed to educational proposals which attempt to specify their outcomes ahead of time. After all, how shall we decide to begin unless we think we know beforehand that the whole process will 'pay off'? Yet dare we trust our fate solely to the paradigms which have been so instrumental in bringing humanity to its current crisis?

Whether the educational process outlined above will produce simple answers to specific environmental problems is impossible to tell. What the process *will* do is gradually shift our conscious frame of reference, because our world-view will be restructured by additional information not available to us from a purely scientific or economic perspective. The problems we face will still be there, but the *problem solver* will have been changed, and from this changed perspective the problems themselves may find new solutions.

References

Bateson, G. (1979) *Mind and Nature: A Necessary Unity.* New York: Bantam Books.

Brown, L. R., Durning, A., Flavin, C., French, H., Jacobson, J., Lowe, M., Postel, S., Renner, M., Starke, L. and Young, J. (1990) *The State of the World 1990: A Worldwatch Institute Report on Progress toward a Sustainable Society.* New York: W. W. Norton.

Brown, L. R., Durning, A., Flavin, C., French, H., Jacobson, J., Lenssen, N., Lowe, M., Postel, S., Renner, M., Ryan, J., Starke, L. and Young, J. (1991) *The State of the World 1991: A Worldwatch Institute Report on Progress toward a Sustainable Society.* New York: W. W. Norton.

Brown, L. R. and Kane, H. (1994) *Full House: Reassessing the Earth's Population Carrying Capacity.* Washington, DC: Worldwatch Institute.

Capra, F. (1982) *The Turning Point: Science, Society, and the Rising Culture.* New York: Bantam Books.

Carson, R. (1962) *Silent Spring.* Boston: Houghton Mifflin.

Erlich, P. (1969) *The Population Bomb.* New York: Ballantine Books.

Erlich, P. and Erlich, A. (1990) *The Population Explosion.* New York: Simon & Schuster.

Erlich, P. and Erlich, A. (1991) *Healing the Planet.* New York: Addison-Wesley.

Grove, R. H. (1992) Origins of Western environmentalism, *Scientific American*, **267**, 42–7.

International Union of Concerned Scientists, World Wide Fund for Nature and United Nations Environment Programme (1990) *Caring for the World: A World Conservation Strategy.*

Jung, C. G. (1959) *Archetypes and the Collective Unconscious.* New York: Pantheon Books (Bollingen Series XX).

Kuhn, T. (1962) *The Structure of Scientific Revolutions.* Chicago: University of Chicago Press.

Meadows, D. H. *et al.* (1972) *The Limits to Growth.* Rome: The Club of Rome.

Meadows, D. H., Meadows, D. L. and Randers, J. (1992) *Beyond the Limits: Confronting Global Collapse, Envisioning a Sustainable Future.* Post Mills, VT: Chelsea Green.

Ponting, C. (1991) *A Green History of the World.* London: Sinclair Stevenson.

Progoff, I. (1958) *The Death and Rebirth of Psychology.* New York: McGraw-Hill.

Schumacher, E. F. (1977) *A Guide for the Perplexed.* London: Harper & Row.

United Nations Conference on Environment and Development (1992) *Agenda 21.* New York: United Nations.

World Commission on Environment and Development (1987) *Our Common Future.* Oxford and New York: Oxford University Press.

5 Building National Capacity for Educational Development: A Mozambique Initiative

JEAN ANDERSON

Capacity-building

The term 'capacity-building' seems to have found its way into the aid jargon since the 1990 Jomtien Conference. (WCEFA, 1990) Indeed, it is in danger of becoming a 'spray-on' phrase as 'community' was in earlier decades, to be included in all projects and initiatives. Intervention in communities, however defined, was seen as being acceptable, but grassroots community initiatives tended to be treated warily, especially by leaders, whether in the developed or developing world, who did not really want a status quo to be too heavily disturbed. This resulted in a loss of impact, and eventually a degree of cynicism. The meaning of 'community' became obscure and the significance of community involvement in initiatives was not really recognized, as claims were made by nearly all projects that the community was involved.

So will the term 'capacity-building' suffer a similar treatment? Is this to be another catch-all phrase of little tangible substance? Like 'community', capacity-building should be a powerful and challenging force for change.

The monographs based on the round tables organized at the 1990 Jomtien Conference (Haggis, 1991; Fordham, 1992) identified a fourth requirement. The initial discussions were concerned with the purpose and content of basic education, the need for equity and international commitment in any expanded vision, and the requirements for providing 'education for all'. These 'requirements' were initially identified as: developing a supportive policy context, mobilizing resources, and strengthening international solidarity (Wyndham, 1992). However, a fourth requirement, 'building national technical capacity', was added as a result of discussions among participants and was identified as the development of 'existing technical capacity, a critical need in many countries, developing or developed in their economic or educational status' (Wyndham, 1992, p. 1). This third monograph explores further what this might entail: establishing or reinforcing technical services for collecting or analysing data, and the human resource implications of data-based decision-making; the need to relate more effectively the inputs and processes of educational management to the outputs of the learning process; and the necessity for improved management and professional development, not only to enhance cost-effectiveness but to improve the quality of life for both the recipients and the providers.

These are ambitious goals and embrace all the focuses identified at Jomtien. Currently, a wide range of projects, operating in many countries, are addressing the priorities and problems identified. Many of these projects pre-date the 1990 conference; others have been initiated since. Examples of large-scale international aid programmes include the Andhra Pradesh Primary Education Project (see Little *et al.*, 1994), designed to improve access to and raise the quality of primary education, and the system for the improvement of education in Guatemala (SIMAC), a nationwide initiative to improve curriculum relevance. Both can report successes, but both identify a lack of appropriate administrative personnel at central and regional level as a barrier to implementation (see Carney *et al.*, 1994). On a smaller scale, the use of interactive radio to raise primary school quality, especially in literacy and mathematics, has had considerable success in a number of countries (for example in the Dominican Republic), which highlights the importance of strong political support and commitment in order to maintain sustainability. Kenya too had a highly successful radio pilot project, but then the Ministry of Education downgraded its priority rating in its budget planning, and early enthusiasm and success were lost. There are many successful NGO initiatives (for example, the Minds Across project in Uganda – see Namaddu, 1991) whose ideas might be adapted and related to capacity-building in other regions if they were more widely circulated. Similarly, the strengths and weaknesses of a good textbook policy in the Philippines, as outlined by Colclough and Lewin (1990), indicate a weakness in administrative efficiency and a lack of coordination on the part of some donor agencies which have affected the content of the curriculum and training strategies needed to respond to and support a textbook improvement project.

What many of these projects reveal is that however imaginative and successful in the short term they prove to be, whether large-scale or pilot project, whether World Bank or multilateral agency initiated, or small-scale NGO sponsored, they all ultimately depend on the political and professional commitment of national decision-makers in educational development, and an increased management competence to implement new strategies if sustainability on a large scale is to be maintained.

It is these two areas, a central professional and political commitment and a capacity to implement via a diffused administrative management structure, that form the foundations for successful capacity building in order to develop coherent, good-quality basic education programmes that are supported by the recipients: parents, children, teachers, and other relevant professionals, and local leaders whose work depends on effective basic education programmes.

Responding to this challenge in part is the aim of most aid and loan-giving agencies, whether in the compilation of data to enable ministry of educa-

tion officials to make choices (for example, the World Bank *Social Sector Strategy Review for Nepal*, 1989), targeting poor areas to raise overall literacy levels (for example, Chile's 900 Schools Programme for the Underprivileged, launched in 1990 after the return to democracy – see Guttman, 1993), or the production of training and support programmes for practising school heads by the Commonwealth Secretariat education programme in order to 'improve the capacity and performance of schools' (Commonwealth Secretariat, 1993, p. iii, Preface). All such programmes are clearly responding to the challenge of capacity-building as defined by the Jomtien Conference (WCEFA, 1990).

Capacity-building in Mozambique

Capacity-building in Mozambique poses an exceptional challenge. As a result of nearly twenty years of war there is a huge problem of reconstruction and rehabilitation of the infrastructure. Sixty per cent of the nation's schools were either damaged or destroyed. The return of $1\frac{1}{2}$ million refugees and the internal displacement of 4 million has resulted in a 25 per cent increase in those eligible for basic primary education. In addition, there are the problems encountered in so many developing countries: low educational quality, a high proportion of untrained teachers, and a shortage of high-level personnel, which is a legacy of the Portuguese educational system. Research by the World University Service (1994) has revealed that catering for a massive increase in demand for educational provision, even if only maintaining current enrolment ratios, would require a 30 per cent increase in recurrent spending (1993–5). Quality enhancement would require an additional 80 per cent on recurrent education budgets!

This was the post-Jomtien task confronting the interim peacetime government and prior to the country's first general elections for almost two decades. The purpose of this chapter is to focus on one initiative and, it is hoped, to demonstrate how the initiative has responded to the need for capacity-building within the Ministry of Education (MINED).

The development of the programme

From early in 1992 and bearing the recommendations of the Jomtien Conference in mind, a series of conferences and seminars was held during which policies, strategies and priorities were discussed. Participants in these meetings included key personnel from MINED, provincial directors, donor agencies, NGOs and religious groups. Recognizing its 'own inadequacies and incapacity to introduce and manage radical changes with its limited resources of expertise' (Minister of Education's foreword to the *Master Plan for Basic Education*, 1994) MINED conceived an interesting and innovative plan, with the support of UNICEF. The 'expanded vision' of basic education as outlined at Jomtien was a concept that needed to be disseminated in Mozambique, and the meetings referred to above did help to carry the 'education for all' message to many areas of the country, to both professionals and parents. The implementation of such a vision is another matter, and clearly those who would be responsible for directing and shaping policy needed to understand what they would be trying to achieve. As in many other developing nations, many of those who now found themselves in positions of responsibility for basic education within MINED had originally been educated to take up positions in the secondary field. In Mozambique the situation was even more desperate. Not only was the country trying to recover from a devastating war, but it had inherited a colonial legacy which had provided very limited access to education for local Mozambicans. In addition, the language of communication was Portuguese and few people had a working knowledge of English, the language of much of the literature on basic or primary education. Nevertheless, with the encouragement and support of donors, especially UNICEF, discussions on basic education were held with practitioners and academics in other countries, and visits were made by members of MINED to other countries, as well as reciprocal visits by experts from several countries who came to address seminars and participate in discussions about how to implement an 'education for all' policy.

During a comparative lull between the peace accord of 1992 and the impending elections, one of the plans which came to fruition was to identify and select a cadre of personnel, mostly from within the ministry, who would come together to work on a programme which would enable them to deepen their knowledge and understanding of basic education so that as planners and administrators they would have the capacity to work sensitively in order to bring about change. In 1992, therefore, officials from MINED subsequently visited a number of countries (the Netherlands, Portugal, the UK) in order to explore the possibilities of establishing a programme for ministry officials, who would be the key agents for change in Mozambique's strategy to provide basic education to be delivered mainly through a reformed primary school curriculum. As a result the College of St Mark and St John, Plymouth, England, a voluntary college which had both a long-standing reputation for innovative work with overseas students and a good reputation for primary teacher education, became the third member of the partnership, along with MINED and UNICEF. The aim was to provide a programme which would enable its participants to 'make informed judgements on policy and practice in basic/primary education in line with EFA [Education for All] goals' (1993 Course Student Handbook).

Clearly any programme in which considerable sums were to be invested by UNICEF, as part of its role as a donor agency focusing on the welfare of children, had to be conceived as part of Mozambique's overall planning to expand and improve the quality of basic education. There was also an increased sense of urgency after the signing of the peace accord in October 1992, which naturally raised hopes in the country for a return to peaceful educational development. In addition, MINED, in deciding to release a number of its key officers from their normal duties to undertake such a programme, expected results, as it recognized that the day-to-day running of the ministry would be affected while such a programme was being mounted. At the same time, however, it was also recognized that in order to ensure motivation and commitment from the participants, opportunities for personal development needed to be provided too.

Identifying the participants

In identifying and selecting the participants for the programme a number of considerations had to be borne in mind. Originally the programme was seen as the first of three phases, and it was therefore thought appropriate that the majority of the participants would be key post-holders within the central ministry. A second factor which had to be taken into account was that the programme would be delivered in English, and indeed at one level this was perceived to be an asset, given that the new Mozambique was now surrounded by countries that had adopted English as an official language and as a medium of instruction in many of their schools. So a secondary bonus was perceived, in that these officials would be afforded an opportunity to develop their own competence in English. At the same time, however, it was recognized that a requirement to speak and learn in English might inhibit some potential participants, given that the decision to pursue a degree-awarding course demanded a recognized level of competence in the language. Within these parameters, nineteen students were identified (nine men and ten women), all of whom had the academic credentials to embark on the course, and preference was given to those who held posts within the ministry. All of them were perceived to have the potential to contribute to the planning and implementation of a basic education strategy, even though some were not located in the emerging basic education unit which was in process of being established within the ministry. They included the head of education planning, three members of the inspectorate team which had the responsibility for ZIPs (zones of pedagogical influence, for advisory and in-service work), the head of assessment and examinations, the head of primary teacher education, and personnel involved in curriculum development, welfare, special educational needs, technical and vocational education, distance learning programmes, and private-sector development. In addition, three students were recruited from outside the MINED headquarters: the principal of a leading teacher training college, a senior member of a provincial education team, and a senior member of the language institute, who in fact was the English-language tutor for the pre-sessional course. It is interesting to record that some two and a half years on from the inception of the programme these students are still in the same or similar posts. As Prawda (1993) noted in a paper on educational decentralization in Latin America, programmes where personnel remain in post for a considerable period have a better chance of a successful outcome than ones in which personnel are constantly being changed. This has all too often been a problem in developing nations where expertise is in short supply, and the temptation has been to relocate personnel to different posts, perhaps to respond to a newly perceived crisis or direction of policy. It is to MINED's credit that it has, on the whole, enabled its key personnel to grow and develop within the areas to which they were appointed at the outset of the programme. The final section of this chapter, which attempts to evaluate the success of this policy in terms of the inputs currently being made by the participants to their particular professional areas as well as the implementation of a coherent basic education strategy, will explore this aspect further.

The course

The decision having been taken to offer the programme through an award-bearing course, this then had to be designed and validated so that it met the needs of MINED, the funding agency (UNICEF) and the validating body (the University of Exeter, which at that time was the validator for most of the college's degree-awarding courses). The result was a new course in terms of content which reflected the philosophy of basic education delivered mainly via primary schooling and took account of the needs of the participants as key agents for change in Mozambique's basic education, but with a structure that was compatible with other part-time B.Phil./M.Ed. courses operating at the college. The course title was B.Phil./M.Ed. in Professional Development (Basic/Primary Education) for Developing Countries.

Staffing the course

A small core team of staff from the college was designated to design and mount the course modules, within both Mozambique and the UK. Its members' expertise encompassed primary education, experience in managing programmes and teaching in developing countries, and experience in setting up and monitoring research projects. They were supported by inputs from other specialist agencies and personnel, in both the UK and Mozambique, the aim being to provide opportunities for participants to explore issues relevant to the group as a whole and to their own specific professional interests. In addition, a local tutor was appointed to act as a liaison officer and provide student support. It was fortunate that a well-respected Mozambican, trained in the UK and therefore familiar with the demands of British universities, was available from within MINED to take on this role.

The course structure

The structure, five taught modules plus a dissertation, is typical of many part-time degree programmes. The decision to operate the programme on a home-and-away basis is worth justifying, however. Given current global initiatives to run programmes in-country wherever possible, on the grounds of both cost and relevance, the decision to bring participants to the UK after the first two modules for five months needs to be explained. It is important to remember that all the participants were key professionals and consequently, even with ministerial blessing for their release from duties, demands on them were high as long as they were in the ministry and in post. Also, although all participants underwent a pre-sessional programme in English, the opportunity to live in an English-speaking environment was seen as having very positive advantages. Indeed, when the participants came to the college their college accommodation was deliberately organized so that they lived alongside both British and other international students, and not as a separate Mozambican group. But most importantly, it was hoped that the opportunity to live and work as a group away from everyday pressures would enable communication, debate and dialogue to develop within the group and so facilitate the emergence of a common platform from which educational strategies could develop within MINED in Mozambique. This hope has been more than fulfilled, and any future evaluation of the programmes would recognize the value of enabling this first group to come together away from their normal work pressures to explore appropriate strategies for their country.

What happened, therefore, was that the first two modules, each of three weeks' duration, were taught within the MINED, in an area which was intended to provide a focal point for the development and resourcing of basic education. A three-week gap between these modules was set aside for the writing up of the first assignment, and satisfactory completion of both modules and their accompanying assignments had to be accomplished before the UK part of the programme could be undertaken. Of the original nineteen students identified, two selected themselves out after Module 1, one having decided to pursue a career outside education and one for reasons unknown. The rest have remained 'on board'. Three further modules were then mounted in the UK before the participants returned to Mozambique to undertake research and write up their theses. This was originally expected to take a year, but, for reasons to be discussed later, this period was extended for some participants.

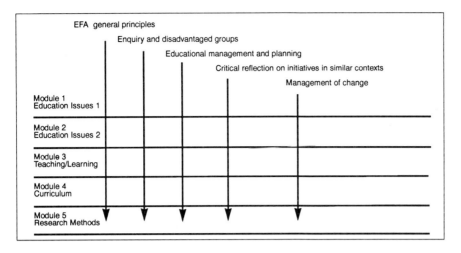

Figure 5.1 Themes running through the modules. *Source:* Course Handbook (1993).

Course content and methodology

Figure 5.1 indicates the recurring themes which were interwoven within all the taught modules. In terms of sequence, the course commenced in Mozambique with an examination of current issues in educational development in order to develop a conceptual framework in relation to policies which might be implemented in order to respond to the Jomtien goals in basic education, and then considered in some detail the role of initial training and teacher support systems in the development of high-quality primary education. Because of the adoption of a problem-oriented approach to the teaching methodology employed, each participant was able to bring to the group as a whole their experience, knowledge and professional priorities, and share ideas about future policy initiatives. The preparation of teaching materials and the delivery of them to the group enabled many participants to be involved in direct team teaching situations, an experience which for many had not been possible previously as a result of their current professional responsibilities. In addition, the writing of two 4,000-word assignments meant that these initial modules made considerable new demands. Their response was impressive; the work rate was high and the incentive to succeed and go overseas for the next part of the course proved to be a strong motivating factor.

The second part of the course took place in the UK and consisted of two further taught modules, which explored approaches to teaching and learning in primary schools, curriculum development, initiatives to revitalize basic education in developing countries, and strategies to decentralize educational management structures. These modules were complemented by visits to primary institutions, including multicultural and second-language initiatives in the East End of London, and the time spent in the UK also afforded opportunities for personal exploration related to the participants' own professional focus, for example time spent with inspectors and advisers responsible for assessment, a conference on refugees and rehabilitation, means of providing for children with special needs in pre-school situations, and examination of strategies to promote environmental education programmes. But perhaps the most valuable outcome of this part of the course was the time it afforded the participants to develop a group identity and empathy with each other's problems and professional responsibilities, which would be carried back to Mozambique. As a result of their performance in further written assignments all qualified to enter the M.Ed. programme. The final UK module, on research methods, aimed to prepare participants as 'education policy-makers and practitioners, to be effective researchers, committed to theory in practice as a means to educational development' (1993 Research Methods teaching file). This approach had been negotiated and agreed upon by all members of the partnership: MINED, the sponsoring agency (UNICEF), the college design team and the participants. This meant that the focus of each individual study was to be on the realities faced by the participants in their own professional settings in Mozambique, helping, it was hoped, to set the stage for enlightened initiatives in the reform of basic education in schools. This approach proved to be successful, and although the focus of certain studies shifted as the research proceeded in Mozambique, all are grounded in the participants' professional roles and are intended to contribute directly to current initiatives.

The research process

The participants returned to Mozambique in August 1994 and were then required to resume their normal duties, even though they had to undertake fieldwork and write up their studies during the ensuing year. The situation was complicated by the postponement of the country's first general elections after the war, and consequently opportunities for fieldwork were initially limited. Schools closed during the run-up to the elections, many participants were involved in election preparations (one even campaigned and subsequently became an MP), and the general atmosphere was tense and uncertain. Consequently, much of the intended fieldwork was put back. The college tutors made regular visits to monitor, support and supervise progress and it was possible to discern certain outcomes even as the studies were still taking shape. For example, the participant from Nampula province immediately mounted in-service courses to disseminate his new ideas and is currently translating teaching materials on management into Portuguese to support in-service programmes for primary headteachers. Two members of the inspectorate clearly incorporated knowledge and ideas developed on the course into their recommendations for the future role and structure of the inspectorate and the ZIPs (the zones which are likely become more significant as focal points for advisory and in-service activities), and reports from educational planning reflect a heightened awareness of a community-oriented approach to schooling. The determination to maintain a strong welfare perspective within MINED is another indicator as a result of the work of the participant responsible for this area within the ministry itself, and also in Parliament.

It would be misleading, however, to suggest that the research proceeded with no problems. For some participants their work-demands, under a newly elected government, have proved to be incompatible with the research process, particularly those whose roles have taken them overseas to represent MINED. For others, the distances from the fieldwork location have caused delays in undertaking interviews and classroom observation, and as communication networks are often slow and unreliable, information from questionnaires and local data has been difficult to obtain. Sustaining momentum under such circumstances is challenging. Regular visits by UK staff have undoubtedly been regarded as supportive and motivating, and the bonds of mutual support among participants, established during the earlier part of the course, have been maintained. A little example, like helping a colleague to come to terms with the word-processor and spreadsheets, indicates much deeper support. One has the impression that the group identity which emerged during the taught part of the course has resulted in a common understanding and determination to come to terms with issues. Everyone has wanted everyone else to succeed.

Outcomes

At the time of writing, more than two-thirds of the studies have been finished and the remaining studies are in process of being written up, the fieldwork having been completed. At this stage it is not possible to predict what the long-term outcomes will be, but a survey of the research undertaken and how each study relates to the writer's professional role indicates the potential value of the research. The Head of the Inspectorate has reviewed the role of inspectors and advisers in order to produce strategies to improve in-service support systems for primary teachers, and this is further supported by a member of the inspectorate team who has investigated the ZIP programmes in order to provide guidelines for the in-service roles of these centres. The Head of Planning has used his research time to bring together much of the data on planning in order to provide a coherent strategy. Such an overview will be supported by a study undertaken by the MINED staff member responsible for the development and monitoring of private-sector initiatives and the research by the Head of Assessment and Examinations, who has investigated the problem of repetition in Mozambique's primary schools. A further study, by the student who is now an MP, though she has also retained her brief for welfare within MINED, has resulted in a policy paper which tries to demonstrate how schools can be the appropriate basis for the welfare of disadvantaged children. In addition, the Head of Technical and Vocational Education, as a result of her research, has sought to produce a clear policy on the role of technology and what it should mean for Mozambican primary education. In terms of curriculum development, two interesting studies from members of the science and geography areas in MINED, based on case study investigation, have produced work which they hope will improve the methodology in the science curriculum and develop a more appropriate environmental focus. Two further studies on language, one which is in process of evaluating the current bilingual language project in Gaza province, and one which examines community attitudes to learning in local languages in Pemba, should contribute to the current ongoing language policy debate in Mozambique. Studies on the effect of local cultures on drop-out rates in Nampula and the cultural factors which affect community participation in Cabo del Gado also highlight the importance of the community when developing and implementing new policies. The special experience of one participant, as a former teacher in a refugee camp in Malawi, has been drawn upon to produce guidelines for in-service work in order to provide more effective learning situations for traumatized children. Finally, in the field of teacher education there is a study by the Head of Primary Teacher Education which draws together a number of aid-sponsored initiatives in Mozambique in order to try to provide a more coherent teacher training strategy, and one which looks specifically at training strategies for the untrained teachers already in the field.

Theses are often destined to linger on dusty shelves in spite of the original high hopes of their authors. There are two aspects of this project which it is hoped will result in their being of real value both for the participants and for the ongoing development of basic education in Mozambique. In personal terms the participants have stated, in informal feedback discussions with tutors, that the work they have undertaken on the modules and the research process, while at the same time grappling with internal policy initiatives and donor proposals, has enabled them to address such problems with greater understanding and clarity. Also, the fact that they know that many of their colleagues who have experienced the same learning programme also have the responsibility of making significant decisions and implementing important strategies has enabled them to move forward with some confidence that there is an increasing consensus of opinion about what needs to be done to implement a successful and equitable basic education programme. There is also an intention, supported strongly by MINED, that the studies' findings should be published so that the thinking behind the participants' research will reach a wider audience, particularly in Mozambique but also for other interested nations too. The funding for the project enables such an enterprise to be undertaken, and the college tutors who have had the responsibility for the running of the course see this as part of their evaluative task, and as a way of supporting sustainability.

Evaluation

An evaluation made by a tutor does lay itself open to criticism, but I shall do my best to offer an impartial interpretation.

Structure

The home-and-away structure adopted for this particular group of senior personnel, which entailed a five-month stay in the UK, though not providing a blueprint for any future programmes, nevertheless proved to be very productive. All the participants were senior post-holders and consequently the opportunity to distance themselves from their positions and explore different perspectives on education as a group was seen by all the partners as being a key feature of this first programme, and so it proved to be. The latter part of the programme, the research process and the writing up of findings at the same time as resuming normal duties, has been more difficult to sustain, as indicated in a previous section ('The research process'). Support from UK tutors needed to be enhanced, and for some participants the combination of their professional post demands and the demands of fieldwork and the compilation of a 20,000-word study have proved to be difficult to sustain, even when participants have been released from duties to coincide with tutorial visits. An alternative structure could have demanded more time back in Mozambique for participants to undertake their studies, but given the professional responsibilities of these participants that was never going to be feasible. Given the fact that their ongoing research has clearly permeated their thinking as they grapple with the demands of their MINED roles, perhaps the structure has proved to be the most appropriate one for this group, particularly as the completion rate is high.

Content

The principal objective of this initial programme was to 'introduce a higher level of professionalism and specialization ... and to build a vanguard cadre of senior and middle ranking planners committed to basic education' (1993 UNICEF Master Plan of Operations, Mozambique, 1994–98). Consequently the course content tried to reflect these needs by raising issues about both the nature of

basic and primary education and the challenges of administering and managing programmes. To some extent the philosophy and practice of basic education dominated the interests of participants in spite of a strong extra input on decentralized management strategies as part of the UK-based programme. However, the raising of awareness about the goals and targets of Education for All (EFA) was achieved and can be seen in the approaches taken in the research studies. Secondary benefits have been an increased confidence in communicating and writing in English and the acquisition of technical skills in information technology, especially word-processing, which have been demonstrated by the fact that the majority of the participants have processed their own studies. Would the senior management teams of other ministries be able to boast the same level of competence?

Sustainability

The issue of sustainability has been the expressed concern of donor agencies in a number of EFA projects. It has been argued that if donor agencies give too much, in terms of resources and expertise, this can undermine self-reliance and motivation for projects to continue. It has also been noted that projects need to be accepted by their recipients if they are to have any real chance of continuity (for example, see Chelu and Mbuluwe, 1994, writing on the SHAPE project in Zambia). Hoppers (1994) argues that institutions and practices are kept alive by people, and that it is their attitudes and commitment that are crucial for the maintenance of momentum. He also goes on to emphasize the significance of the quality of leadership and management at all levels of the system. Elsewhere in this chapter I have suggested that one of the features of this programme has been the continuity in post of most of the student participants.

So how does this programme stand up? Has the question of sustainability been addressed as an issue by those who initiated, planned and implemented this programme?

The initial intention was that this would be the first of three phases, and that subsequent programmes would be increasingly located in Mozambique in conjunction with a local institution. Certain events have overtaken this original plan and it is worth looking at them in terms of the future sustainability of this particular initiative. There have been significant changes in the staffing of the donor agency, and around the time of the general election some changes took place within MINED, including a change of minister and a change in the directorate of the Basic Education unit. There has also been the upgrading of the main local teacher training institution to university status, and MINED is keen to promote the teacher training capacity of this institution.

Staff changes can result in changes in priorities and it is possible to argue that some of the changes indicated above have retarded the commencement of a second phase. On the other hand, there is now a local institution, backed by MINED, eager to participate in this kind of capacity-building and this kind of future partnership. At the outset of the programme it was not possible to identify a suitable local partner institution. Therefore, if donor funds are forthcoming it is likely that a second phase, albeit somewhat delayed, will be mounted in Mozambique with a focus on teacher training needs, and delivered by staff from the local and UK institutions. This will mean that the original partnership between a donor agency, MINED and an overseas institution will be strengthened by a link with the local educational institution, and that the resources and learning of both participants and tutors involved in the first phase will be put to good use. This is a positive move in terms of longer-term sustainability, but it does depend on donor support, albeit reduced, in order to promote the continuation of the programme.

Capacity-building: the contribution of the programme

The idea of capacity-building for educational planning and administration is not new, and indeed it has almost a colonial, paternalistic ring to it. 'Experts' from elsewhere were expected to bring new principles of 'modern' management into the newly independent education systems of the 1960s as they struggled to expand and provide more relevant education (Carron, 1991). Most of these projects were related to the paradigm which saw a relationship between education and economic growth, and were developed on the assumption that this kind of capacity-building required a top-down approach: get the management structures right and designs for successful educational development can successfully follow. But capacity-building also means enhancing abilities at the grassroots level to express and respond to needs, and here is where the notions of 'community' and 'empowerment' are linked to those of capacity-building. The danger is, as indicated in the opening section of this chapter, that the idea of capacity-building will lose its impact if it is treated merely as an easily formulated, generic answer to managerial needs without reference to the requirements of developing education for all.

Countries like Mozambique face problems today for which there is no ready-made capacity solution. They have to contend with population growth, extreme poverty which exacerbates health and environmental problems, and a demand, emanating from the expanding urban centres in particular, for more and better education. In the case of Mozambique, there is also a need to rebuild infrastructure and replace teachers as a result of the war. Yet at the same time some countries face disillusion among communities, as earlier education promises have often not been fulfilled.

The International Institute for Educational Planning (IIEP) stresses that training, research and dissemination activities can support planning and administrative capacities in both industrialized and developing countries (Carron, 1991, p. 7). Carron suggests that although planning and management is an important component of capacity-building it is not the only one, and that institution-building and creating a supportive environment are also necessary components in any capacity-building project.

Within this context, then, it can be suggested that the kind of capacity-building programme discussed in this chapter has a contribution to make.

In working with a group of personnel from an institution, in this case MINED, it has helped to establish a supportive environment in which, it is hoped, future developments may flourish. The programme now needs to build on this foundation. The proposed link with a local institution widens and strengthens this cooperation and should help to facilitate networking and teamwork. The research studies point to the importance of such cooperation and the necessity of taking on board the needs and aspirations of communities in order to put into practice ideas and strategies of educational planners. The need for investigation and ongoing research to respond to issues is also emphasized. It will be interesting to see if this approach to capacity-building bears fruitful, longer-term results.

Acknowledgement

The author would like to acknowledge the assistance of Ian Collingwood, the course leader of the project, and John Anderson, who was the Principal of the College of St Mark and St John at the time of the college initiative, for their helpful suggestions when this chapter was being compiled.

References

The following list does not include documents produced in connection with the setting up and implementation of the programme described in the text.

Carney, M. *et al.* (1994) in A. Little, W. Hoppers and R. Gardner (eds), *Beyond Jomtien: Implementing Primary Education for All.* London: Macmillan.

Carron, G. (1991) *Capacity Building for Educational Planning and Administration: IIEP's Experience.* Paris: International Institute for Educational Planning.

Chelu, F. and Mbuluwe, F. (1994) The Self Help Action Plan for Primary Education (Shape) in Zambia, in A. Little, W. Hoppers and R. Gardner (eds), *Beyond Jomtien: Implementing Primary Education for All.* London: Macmillan.

Colclough, C. and Lewin, K. (1991) *Educating All the Children: The Educational Challenge for the 90s.* Oxford: Clarendon Press.

Commonwealth Secretariat (1993) *Better Schools: Resource Materials for Heads.* London: Commonwealth Secretariat Human Resource Development Group.

Fordham, P. (ed.) (1992) *Education for All: An Expanded Vision.* Round Table Discussion, Theme 2. Paris: UNESCO.

Guttman, C. (1993) *All Children Can Learn: Chile's 900 Schools Programme for the Underprivileged.* Paris: UNESCO.

Haggis, S. (ed.) (1991) *Education for All: Purpose and Context.* Round Table Discussion, Theme 1. Paris: UNESCO.

Hoppers, W. (1994) Learning the lessons: a thematic review of projects and experiences, in A. Little, W. Hoppers and R. Gardner (eds), *Beyond Jomtien: Implementing Primary Education for All.* London: Macmillan.

Little, A., Hoppers, W. and Gardner, R. (eds) (1994) *Beyond Jomtien: Implementing Primary Education for All.* London: Macmillan.

Master Plan for Basic Education in Mozambique (1994). Ministry of Education, Mozambique.

Namuddu, K. (1991) *Collaboration for Educational Change: Improvement of Basic Education through Minds Across.* Paris: International Institute for Educational Planning.

Prawda, J. (1993) Educational decentralization in Latin America: lessons learned, *International Journal of Educational Development*, **13**(3).

WCEFA (World Conference on Education for All) (1990) *Meeting Basic Learning Needs: A Vision for the 90s.* New York: Inter Agency Commission.

World Bank (1989) *Social Security Strategy Review for Nepal*, vol. 2. Report no. 7498 NEP. Washington, DC: World Bank.

World University Service (1994) *Education in Mozambique: Addressing the Approaching Crisis.* London: WUS.

Part Two

Concepts, Parameters and Paradigms for Practical Approaches

6 Participation, Policy Dialogue and Education Sector Analysis

FERNANDO REIMERS

Background

During the 1960s, development specialists began to recognize that education of the population was at the core of a country's ability to increase levels of production; the notion that education could also contribute more broadly to social development also took hold in the field. From that realization the next logical question was: how could the education and training systems of a given country be transformed so as to maximize the contributions of education to development? The field of development education has been answering this question during the past thirty years.

One of the answers that emerged during these three decades was that a country's education system could be improved by bringing a series of tools and methods to the analysis of education constraints and to the exploration of options for change. These methodologies have been varied and have received different names: educational planning, policy analysis, manpower planning, rate-of-return analysis, policy-based education research and school effectiveness research, among others. In spite of the differences among various approaches, implicit in all of them is the recognition that educational decision-makers can make better choices if the consideration of alternatives is informed by the use of highly specialized methods of rational enquiry.

How have these specialized methods come to be used in practice? In fact, the dissemination of these methodologies has followed several channels, among which three are most prominent. The first channel has consisted of training professionals from each country in these skills so they can be

called upon by decision-makers when necessary. A second channel has been supplying these skills in the form of foreign technical advisers who bring their specialized knowledge to assist the process of educational decision-making. A third channel, which has acquired prominence most recently, consists of the use of the results which have been obtained by the application of these specialized methods elsewhere by international organizations in various forms of advocacy and social marketing.

This chapter will discuss the second of these approaches to informing education choices, namely the use of technical assistance to bring in specialized expertise to analyse options for change. I will argue that the non-participatory nature of traditional technical assistance makes it ineffective in promoting meaningful change in education systems. The chapter will then present a case in which a participatory process was followed in order to provide technical assistance to study educational problems. I will conclude by drawing several lessons from this experience.

Education technical assistance in practice

Education technical assistance – that is, the process by which a foreign country or donor brings specialized services to bear in the education system of a recipient country – can focus on the decision-making stage or on the stage of implementing change. Often these are but two stages in the ongoing process of collaboration between donor and recipient countries. Donors assist host governments in the stages of identifying needs and problems, considering alternatives, and designing options and strategies, and also in the consecutive stage of implementing these options and strategies.

This chapter focuses on technical assistance in the analysis and identification of educational needs and the exploration of options. Assistance in the implementation of projects will not be discussed here, although when necessary the links between these two will be addressed. There is often an implicit understanding in the relationship between donors and host countries that technical assistance in analysing and designing options will be followed by assistance in implementing reform. Commonly, the final objective is a project of education reform, and thus assistance in analysis and identification of needs becomes assistance in project design.

In practice, much technical assistance in education decision-making takes the form of specialists from the donor agencies, or of consultants or contractor institutions providing services to these agencies, who arrive in the host country to provide advice. Indeed, foreign advisers have much to offer; many of them bring the lessons learned in long careers providing advice in a wide range of contexts, a valuable input in the process of examining educational constraints and of identifying opportunities for change. Much technical assistance, however, is structured in ways that limit the contacts between foreign advisers and the host government to just a few high-level officials, hence limiting the possibilities of the education systems to 'learn' from this exchange, and also limiting the range of options explored by the advisers.

Specialists in development agencies are often ready to point out the weaknesses of other organizations while they highlight their own strengths. The executive director of an education and health agency in the United Nations has pointed out to me that within the UN system theirs is the best agency, because 80 per cent of their staff are based in the field. A senior official in another UN agency has mentioned that, although his agency does not have the most finan-

cial resources within the system, it has the greatest capacity for analysis. A vice-president in a major international financial institution has boasted that, in comparison with a regional financial institution, his organization has a greater advantage in the quality of its projects because it recruits staff who are technically more proficient. The director of strategic studies of a regional financial institution has been equally proud, saying that it is less ideological than its counterparts in an international financial organization. Several mission directors of a bilateral donor agency have pointed out that their agency has a definite comparative advantage in understanding local conditions over missions from financial institutions, whose people fly in and out of the countries without sufficient time even to read the local newspapers. The list goes on and on. It illustrates that development practitioners are proud of the organizations they work in.

In my experience as a consultant to a good many of these agencies, I find that the commonalities in how technical assistance for policy analysis is offered are greater than the differences. I will illustrate this briefly with four cases from my experience; all took place during the late 1980s or early 1990s.

In the first case, I arrived in a small low-income country as part of an eight-person team of consultants. Our task was to design a basic education project, which would be financed by the United States Agency for International Development (US AID). The team of consultants had been organized by a contractor who provided technical services to the Education Office of the Bureau for Latin America at US AID's headquarters in Washington. The contractor recruited these consultants from university faculties and from people whose primary employment was in consultancy work for international organizations. The members of the team were to spend from two to six weeks in-country, the team leader would spend eight weeks. Most of us overlapped for some time in the country. A set of offices was arranged for the team of consultants in the hotel where we were staying, and the consultants visited offices of the Ministry of Education to collect information and the office of the local mission of US AID as needed. Most of the time of the consultants was spent on reading reports and writing our section of the design document. There was substantial exchange among the members of the team of consultants. There were two meetings with the Minister of Education, but these were primarily ceremonial. Though the mandate of this team was to assess the educational needs of the country and to propose options to address these needs, most of this task was done by the foreign consultants. Ministry staff were interviewed to obtain information.

At the end of the eight weeks the team leader assembled all the different pieces produced by the consultants into a coherent document, with assistance from the project development officer of US AID. Eventually this document evolved into a Request for Proposals (RFP), which was offered for public bid to provide technical assistance and educational services worth several million dollars of grant assistance.

In the second case, a regional bank (the Inter-American Development Bank) was preparing a multi-million dollar loan to support education reform efforts in a small middle-income country. A senior education specialist in this bank was charged with heading a team that would define the basic orientation of this loan. To do this, he assembled a five-person team, two of whom worked for the bank, the other three being consultants who had prior experience working in this country. We spent two weeks in this country drafting the project document. All members of the team had worked previously in the country, which meant we had not only certain prior knowledge of the education sector, but also contacts among colleagues in the Ministry of Education and other relevant organizations. Most of the time in the country was spent in discussions among the members of the team, but there were some field visits to collect information or to fill some information gaps that became apparent in the group discussions. There was one meeting of the group with the Minister of Education and her staff to present a draft of the project document and obtain their reactions. Although this meet-

ing was less ceremonial and addressed more issues of substance than the meeting in case 1, the basic orientation of the loan was provided by the team of advisers. We were of course informed by our prior knowledge and contacts with host country counterparts, but no host country representative formally participated in the group discussions.

This project never reached maturity because of political instability in the country, which halted the negotiations with the bank.

In the third case, I was invited to be a consultant for an international financing agency (the World Bank) to assist in the design of an education project in one of the poorest countries in a developing region. This project had been in preparation for about a year. A group of host country nationals was formally in charge of the preparation of the project. The task manager from the World Bank had a formal counterpart in the country.

She in turn had a staff of about ten persons working on the preparation of this project. This staff included consultants who had been recruited in neighbouring countries.

The preparation of the project was funded by a grant from a major donor, through the World Bank, which meant that the host country counterparts were paid by this grant. Periodically the task manager would organize 'appraisal missions', in which a number of consultants would come in and review the work, providing feedback and leaving indications of work to be completed by the host country counterparts. Again there were extensive exchanges among members of the appraisal missions, both while in the host country and between missions.

Among the cases presented in this section, this one exhibits the most national participation. Ironically, though, in this case the host country team was working completely in isolation from Ministry of Education staff. The team had rented a set of offices on the outskirts of the city and spent more than a year writing papers, discussing problems and preparing the project, and received feedback and suggestions from periodic appraisal and supervisory missions. Yet this local team seemed to have no significant ties to any of the critical actors in the education system. Most important, it lacked basic information for planning and evaluating proposals, because it had very poor links with the Ministry of Education. As a result, the team did not even have access to basic enrolment figures. Coincidentally, I knew of an NGO doing very effective work in basic education in this country because of research I had conducted for other purposes, yet this NGO (the largest providing education services in the country) had not been contacted by the team preparing the project, even though the team had brought in a consultant from a neighbouring country to provide advice on the role of NGOs on education reform.

Perhaps because of the short duration of the appraisal team's visits, or because of the way the relationship was structured between foreign consultants and the host country team, the relationship did not feel truly collegial. It had the feeling of a team of experts who came to validate the choices proposed by the host country team, or to suggest that they be abandoned. Consequently, though the project evolved as a series of iterations between productions from local participants and from teams of supervisory missions, it seemed that the task manager and her consultants were really in the driving seat of this process. At times, consultants were asked to re-write and redesign sections of the project if the production of the national team was considered deficient.

This project was eventually approved as a loan, although there were numerous problems of implementation. During the first year, government officials travelled three times to the Bank's headquarters in Washington, DC, to request expansion in the levels of the loan because original needs had been underestimated. The problems were so serious that a Bank vice-president threatened to cancel the loan 'unless the government can get its act together'.

The last case involved an 'expert mission' requested by the Minister of Education of a middle-income country. This Minister of Education had had a distinguished career in UNESCO, and

upon his appointment he tapped into the UN system for advice. He assembled a mission that included specialists from UNESCO and UNICEF, other consultants who were hired by the United Nations Development Programme (UNDP), and other consultants provided by the World Bank and by a regional bank. The mission had about twelve specialists who came to the country for a week. The Minister of Education asked us to prepare a paper diagnosing the main problems of the education system, identifying priorities and proposing a strategy for reform. The task was daunting even for such an experienced team – the average member of this team had about twenty years of education development experience. The task was helped because there were a number of good reports and assessments produced in-country upon which the team could draw, and statistical information was also readily available. Very competent staff of the ministries of education and planning were available to support the requests of the mission. Again in this case members of the team spent most of their time reading documents, writing their sections of the paper and consulting with each other. The team leader and the Minister of Education discussed a draft report. At the end of the mission, the final report proposing recommendations for educational change was delivered to the President of the Republic. There was little chance to implement the recommendations of this report; the Minister was replaced in six months because of communication problems with the teacher unions.

Perhaps it should not be surprising that these four cases, involving specialists from several continents and generations, and involving different international agencies and host countries, were so similar in the basic approach followed in providing technical assistance to identify needs and consider options: foreign experts came in, collected information, processed that information and discussed it with each other, and prepared a draft proposal or plan. This plan was discussed with the highest education authorities, frequently only the Minister of Education.

And the process finished. Final reports were produced; projects were bid; loans were processed.

It is obvious that this approach to exploring options to support education policy choices is not very participatory. Those who participate are experts; commonly foreign experts, sometimes national experts. It is clear that many people who will be influenced by the results of these choices have no voice in the process that has just been described. Many who hold a stake in the results of the proposed actions that will be based on the recommendations of the report do not have a chance to see the full range of options, nor do they have a chance to influence the process of selecting an option or a course of action. Much of the implementation research and literature highlights the problematic nature of this deficiency in policy design, and points out that implementation problems are just a way in which those who have not been consulted at the planning or decision-making stage make their voices heard (Grindle, 1980). Many will argue that implementation failure in education development reflects the problematic non-participatory nature of rational educational planning. Yet in spite of what the literature might suggest, planning in practice, as I have experienced it, is pretty well represented by the four cases presented here. These are not old cases; in fact they are quite recent. The actors involved, though some are very experienced, are not considered 'passé' or the 'old wave'. On the contrary, some of them are considered leaders in their own institutions and in the field.

These four cases illustrate precisely what educational planners are trained to do; the reason that there is so much convergence in the approaches followed is because the field of technical development assistance lacks successful alternative models that illustrate more participatory approaches of informing education choices. Most of the literature that criticizes educational planning does so from a theoretical or academic standpoint, and has failed to stimulate a paradigm shift in how technical assistance is provided. In effect, much of the critique of rational planning has lacked the power to inspire alternative approaches.

Education technical assistance in theory

Most of the literature on planning and policy analysis for educational development has not explored the role of participation in decision-making, or the extent to which participation and technical analysis can support each other. In a sense, much of the educational planning literature is written assuming that the planner is in the role of advising a single decision-maker who is highly placed in the organizational hierarchy and has authority to decide on directions for education policy reform. As the four cases illustrate, that is precisely what the foreign advisers did in each case.

An additional difficulty with much planning literature is that it assumes that educational problems have one solution and that the established techniques can identify it. For instance, a draft of an education policy paper currently in preparation at the World Bank states that rate-of-return methodologies can be used to decide how resources should be allocated to different levels of education (World Bank, 1995). Implicit in this is the view that the problems to be solved are 'convergent'; that is, they have one solution. As E. F. Schumacher has pointed out, many policy problems are 'divergent'; they do not have one 'correct' solution (Schumacher, 1977).

A state-of-the-art review of the technique of education sector assessment prepared in the 1970s, for instance, did not address the social and political context in which such assessments take place (Daniere, 1977). A more recent book presenting a methodology by which to carry out sector assessments again had no discussion about the organizational or political context in which such technical exercises would be carried out (Pigozzi and Cieutat, 1988). Ignoring the political dimension of planning and technical analysis, however, may ultimately lead to plans that have no impact on policy reform:

> A better understanding of the political dimension of planning, or of the management function of planners, would allow planners to play their role in a forthright fashion. They should not have to pursue their goals in devious ways or give the appearance of usurping the

authority of the Prince they serve ... Effective planning is a management function that involves planners in political transactions. (Benveniste, 1991, p. 33)

A review of experience in developing countries with planning concluded that the limitations on the information available to planners who rely only on analytical techniques yield less than optimal solutions. This review concluded that qualitative judgement is an essential ingredient in policy analysis, and that such judgement is best informed by consultation 'not only in different parts of the government, but also with businessmen and academics. Japan, Korea, and Brazil have, for some time, employed consultation to improve their economic management' (Agarwala, 1983, p. 16). This is consistent with the view that solving complex problems is a process of finding successive approximations; that any given answer to the problem can always be improved and that only open dialogue allows people to deal productively with such problems (Senge, 1990).

But the literature that links the political nature of educational planning to the means by which planning and policy analysis can improve with more participatory processes is scarce. A recent publication that analyses planning as a political process concludes that planners need to acquire power in support of their plans in order to help those plans be implemented, but does not see a useful role for participation as part of this process:

Planners avoid formal participatory schemes for several reasons:
Participatory schemes are time and resource consuming. The complex task of resolving the multiple interests of a large set of stakeholders cannot easily be accomplished in an open democratic forum.
Participatory schemes are too demanding on participants. Clients and beneficiaries are not necessarily sufficiently involved and capable of resolving issues.
Participatory schemes require complete openness and disclosure. As we shall see, this is not always desirable or possible ...
Planners are not trained in participatory management. They do not want to relinquish what little authority they happen to have and fear that their

professional autonomy will be challenged. (Benveniste, 1991, p. 47)

The lack of attention to participation in the process of education planning and technical analysis has long been recognized:

Planners and administrators are reasonable people in the main, working earnestly in the interests of the system as they see them. Why is it consultation and participation are not more characteristic of their work? A number of reasons can be suggested. Normally, because of the demands of the political system which they service, planners and administrators are working under extreme pressure. Time schedules have to be met and, at the same time, they have to be ready to answer questions which may arise at any time about any part of the system. Participation and consultation are time-consuming exercises. Most administrators would hold too, that in their experience, consulting with others has not been very productive. (Grassie, 1974, p. 23)

Research in fields other than education, however, would suggest that education policy reform is more likely to occur if analysis and planning can be linked productively with processes of consultation and participation. A recent work on the political economy of policy reform (Grindle and Thomas, 1991) proposes a framework for understanding policy choices that identifies a critical number of factors on which information could be sought, not exclusively from technical analysis but rather from consultation and other avenues of participation in decision-making.[1]

An analysis of a participatory consultation to develop an implementation strategy for disseminating a food policy paper in Kenya led to widely shared understanding and support for the recommendations of the paper and facilitated the achievement of the objectives of the ministries that participated. This study also concluded that participation facilitated responsiveness to political realities, constraints and opportunities (Cohen, 1984).

A study of the implementation of six development programmes concluded that participation facilitated implementation, particularly as the complexity of the programme and the environment increased (Paul, 1982, p. 205).

The importance of participation and ownership for the successful implementation of education policies is beginning to receive some attention. At a recent meeting of African ministers and permanent secretaries of education, participation was discussed in the context of 'ownership' of plans:

> A background paper prepared for the meeting listed the many factors hindering the successful implementation of activities to improve and expand education in sub-Saharan Africa. National conditions and how they influence effective implementation were analyzed and the *ownership* of the various programmes discussed.
>
> Mauritius provided an excellent example of how a national education plan could actually be formulated and implemented using local expertise ... with the help of many partners (professionals, political leaders, the private sector, etc.). It is a complex process involving a lot of learning-by-doing, negotiation, and the progressive development of national capacity. [This emphasizes] the need for programmes to be based on clear objectives defined by consulting all the partners involved. This helps to encourage participation and create a sense of *ownership* among all stakeholders.[2]

In sum, most of the literature on educational planning is silent on the political context in which planning operates. When politics is considered, it is generally treated as 'noise' or as an element that the planner has to control in order to increase the likelihood of success in plan implementation. Analysis on productive interactions between participation and technical analysis for education policy reform is lacking.

However, research in other development fields suggests that participation can be a very constructive force to improve both the quality of the policy, and policy implementation. To the extent that education policy analysis is an exercise in solving complex problems, only open dialogue that includes participation from multiple stakeholders and is informed by multiple disciplinary perspectives can facilitate organizational learning and a continuous approximation to better solutions.

The following section will present a case in which a participatory process was used to identify educational problems and priorities and to propose options for reform.

Breaking with tradition: orchestrating a participatory sector assessment in El Salvador

In the summer of 1993, the US AID mission to El Salvador issued a Request for Proposals (RFP) to conduct an assessment of the education sector. A parallel proposal called for an assessment of the health sector. As is common in the project cycle of US AID, these assessments were requested to help the US AID mission determine whether projects of technical assistance in these areas would be granted. Usually a sector assessment is followed by a team that designs a project to implement reforms in the sector. The project is then bid on competitively.

Under ordinary circumstances, there would have been little challenge in responding to this RFP. A US AID-funded project has sponsored the publication of a guide for how sector assessments should be conducted (Pigozzi and Cieutat, 1988) which provides detailed guidelines for planning the selection of foreign advisers and integrating them into a team that will carry out a sector assessment. The publication provides several examples of assessments conducted by the same project, which involved teams of foreign advisers who stayed in countries from eight weeks to over a year to complete their assignments.

I took the lead in preparing a response to the RFP for the education sector assessment at the Harvard Institute for International Development (HIID). Two events suggested that this project called for something other than 'business as usual'. The first was that the peace accords had only recently been signed in El Salvador after twelve years of civil war. When I approached the director of HIID to explore the idea of bidding for this RFP he asked, 'How would we be able to make a difference in this kind of context?' The reality that there were groups with conflicting points of view about the future of the country was all too obvious after twelve years of war. The second event was serendipitous: a colleague of mine was on mission abroad and had asked me to review the galley proofs of an article he had written on the politics of educational planning. I read these proofs at about the same time I was reading the RFP, which had come from the US AID mission in El Salvador.[3] Under the influence of these two events it did not seem that a standard team of experts would be acceptable or would have much impact among the factions that had been in conflict.

In preparing the response to the RFP we decided to establish a solid partnership with organizations in El Salvador that had high credibility among different political groups. We also decided that the assessment should be addressed to a wide spectrum of stakeholders who represented different groups in the society. We looked for organizations with the interest and capacity to participate in technical analysis of the necessary type and with strong credibility among the government, the ruling party, the business sector, and the groups that had been in opposition during the war. We invited two organizations to join in our proposal: the Business Foundation for Educational Development (FEPADE) and the Catholic University (UCA). Our discussions during the preparation of the proposal and the great mistrust of each of the organizations towards the other reaffirmed our perception of the highly fragmented and polarized society that the war had left and that the peace accords had not yet healed.

We proposed a simple model: the assessment would be conducted jointly by HIID, FEPADE and UCA, which would report to an advisory committee that would have broad representation from different groups in the society. There would be frequent dialogue with senior education officials, but this technical activity would be carried out not exclusively for the government but for the advisory committee. There were two reasons for this: first, there would be elections in 1994 and there was great uncertainty about their results, and second, the government in office, though supportive of the peace process, had been elected in the middle of the civil conflict in elections that did not have the support of all groups in the society. The proposal also emphasized that the process would have a healthy distance from the US AID mission, we would have limited meetings with US AID staff, the reports would be written in Spanish, and

US AID would not have veto power over the final products.

Those familiar with development assistance and with standard practices of US AID projects will recognize that ours was not a conventional proposal. It was too open-ended, offered US AID no guarantees about the final product, emphasized process over the technical quality of the product, and incorporated democratic politics as a central element of the work. In spite of, or because of this, HIID was awarded the contract to implement the project we had proposed. In September 1993 I arrived in San Salvador.

My first visit to the US AID mission suggested that the selection of our proposal had not had the support of all relevant people in the mission. We did have the clear support of four persons: the Director of the Office of Education, his deputy, a young, recently appointed professional and a local appointee in the education office. They were genuinely committed to supporting a democratic process of dialogue and were very helpful throughout the process of implementing the project. But they worked in an environment where less democratic practices were standard. An officer of the economics division in US AID greeted me by pointing out, 'I am Mr Value-Added Tax in this country; I am responsible for the adoption of the VAT here.' Whatever the merits of the idea of a value-added tax it struck me as odd that a foreign officer would take on attributions that are generally reserved to members of the Cabinet. I would later learn that complete sections of the national economic development plan had been written in the same office of economic analysis, and that it was standard practice for them to bring in consultants who would spend their entire sojourn in-country working out of offices in the US AID building (which incidentally is one of the most monumental structures of US AID in the world). Our proposal to spend most of our time in-country out of US AID offices was certainly contrary to practice in some of the units of the agency.

With the Director of Education and some of his staff, we began the work in earnest; our target was to complete a draft of the assessment before the end of the year. With input from the Minister of Education, our institutional collaborators and US

AID, an advisory committee was formed. The first meeting was to discuss with the committee the content that the assessment should address. The Minister decided that it would be better for her to distance herself publicly from the assessment, but agreed to meet one afternoon a week with the technical teams working on the project. She did send several representatives to the weekly meetings of the advisory committee.

The advisory committee included some fifty representatives of more than thirty organizations, including the Ministries of Education, Planning and Finance; Congress; a formerly armed group in opposition to the government (the principal opposition force); the Chamber of Commerce; the associations of exporters and industrialists; teacher unions; public and private universities; NGOs, and other relevant groups. Every week between September and December 1993 the committee held meetings with the professionals writing the chapters of the assessment.

At the first meeting we agreed that the assessment would have ten sections or chapters, covering each of the major subsectors of education (primary, secondary, higher) plus some special studies (technical–vocational, non-formal, financing and management). A technical team with consultants from HIID, UCA and FEPADE and with technical support from the Ministry of Education was organized in ten groups. These involved a total of thirty-five consultants, of whom twenty-two were Salvadoran nationals.

Each of the technical groups conducting the ten studies that were part of the sector assessment organized focus groups to explore issues and conclusions regarding each subject analysed in the assessment. For example, the group working on the non-formal education chapter organized a three-day seminar, to which more than thirty representatives of NGOs active in non-formal education were invited to discuss the principal questions of that study.

Although it was made clear to the committee that the final report would be the responsibility of the technical teams, in practice the weekly meetings served two purposes. On the one hand the meetings helped the technical teams writing the assessment understand better the perspectives of the advisory committee for policy-relevant analysis. This exchange helped the technical teams and the members of the committee better understand the complexity and multidimensional nature of the subjects being investigated. At the same time, the members of the committee were better able to ground their discussion on concrete issues and evidence as these were advanced by the technical teams. 'The final result was the outcome of a long process of exchange of ideas, or multiple rounds of feedback, of examining information from primary sources and experience, and of multiple drafts of each chapter' (president of FEPADE, in Barraza *et al.*, 1994).

The difficulties of bringing to the same table participants who had taken different sides during the conflict should not be underestimated. Even though peace agreements had been signed almost two years prior to beginning the assessment there had been no opportunities since the war (and for many years during it) for pluralistic committees to discuss national policy issues. Participation in the activity by different institutions such as the Ministry of Education, FEPADE, UCA, US AID and Harvard University made the activity sufficiently interesting for different groups to agree to participate also. Several of them indicated repeatedly that the reason they agreed to participate was that the mix of sponsoring institutions suggested that there was no ideological or party bias in the nature of the activity.

The organizers tried to maintain the content of the conversations at a level above local politics. For example, at the first meeting one of the participants, a former leader of the armed opposition, suggested that before we could agree on a path for education reform the committee should agree on a vision of the 'new man' for El Salvador. I replied that the objective was more modest, to find agreement on 'small problems' of the education system – 'nuts and bolts' kinds of issues.

At the time, some felt disappointed to hear that this committee would not tackle the 'big' questions such as the type of society that the education system would be building, but later on it became clear that some of the 'small problems' were not so small, and that it was possible to find agreement on them without addressing the reasons various groups perceived them as problems. For instance, all agreed that the fact that 15 per cent of children never entered first grade, and that one in four children among the poorest 20 per cent of the population never entered school at all, was a problem that needed urgent attention. In private conversations with members of the committee it was clear that this was seen as a problem for very different reasons by different political groups, but the committee concentrated on the problem and on possible solutions rather than on the reasons and the value systems by reference to which this was seen as a problem.

Towards the end of the year, members of the advisory committee received drafts of the various chapters of the assessment for review and comments. These drafts were also circulated among many staff in the ministry, in US AID offices, and among those who had participated in several of the focus groups. This served two purposes. First, it created an incentive for people actually to read the report – and from the extensive feedback we received we know they did read the drafts carefully. Second, the process helped the writers know their audience better, and to know which parts of the reports were not clear, which parts needed better argumentation, and which parts had to be reconsidered. This feedback process also provided opportunities to identify those who had been most alienated in the process and thus were potential enemies of the final report. We soon learned that an economics officer in US AID was most upset at the results of the study; he wrote a very strong memo to his chief proposing that US AID should suspend payment on the final product, which did not meet his standards of quality. At the heart of his opposition was a different ideological view from that of the specialists who had written the section on labour demand and costs and financing. Though we did not change the report, we spent a lot of time making sure his objections were well understood and properly addressed in the final report.

Procedures for dissemination

In January 1994, HIID and its institutional partners UCA and FEPADE conducted a series of work-shops, endorsed by the advisory committee, to present the results of the assessment and discuss them with key groups of stakeholders for education policy. A strategy was designed for dissemination of the findings of the assessment. Each chapter of the report was reproduced as a stand-alone document, with its own executive summary, to facilitate access to the information by specialized audiences. A special synthesis was prepared of the ten chapters, using many graphics and visual displays. A computerized graphics presentation was prepared to facilitate the exposition of the summary and of each of the chapters in different meetings. A press release was prepared for meetings with the media.

One of these meetings was with all presidential candidates, all of whom showed great interest in the subjects being discussed. The day after this meeting, the principal opposition candidate appeared in national news echoing some of the key themes and recommendations of the report. From that moment on education reform became a central issue in the electoral debate.

Another meeting was with senior officials in the Ministry of Education. As a result of this meeting the Minister decided to organize an eight-hour workshop to discuss the results of the assessment with key managers of the ministry. A meeting was held with 200 ministry staff, who came from the capital and from different regions of the country.

Meetings were held also with the press, with the Chamber of Commerce and the private sector, with the public and university communities, and with the Ministry of Planning. Some 500 copies of the final report were distributed upon request. As a result of this demand, the editorial centre of the UCA published 1,500 copies of the report, *La educación en El Salvador de cara al siglo XXI*, in 1994.[4]

Impact of the study

Less than a month after the presentation of the results of the assessment, the Minister of Education announced a modification of the curriculum of secondary education in line with the recommendations of the assessment. The ministry also began to implement a programme of administrative decentralization along the lines suggested in the corresponding chapter of the assessment. A group of private businesses actively lobbied Congress, using a chapter of the assessment as the principal source of their arguments, to prepare a decree to implement a law creating a national institute of technical training. Their lobby was based on the recommendation of the assessment which proposed a coordinating and regulatory role for the state, and responsibility for actual delivery of the training for the private sector.

After the new government took office in the summer of 1994, the Minister of Education was asked to stay in office, an unusual move of administrative continuity in Latin America. Most of the staff in the ministry remained. The former director of planning, who had actively participated in the advisory committee, became the Vice-Minister of Education.

Some of the areas of policy reform that can be linked to the assessment include:

1   The ministry has made it a policy priority to expand access in rural areas. New sections and new teacher appointments are being made, giving priority to the rural areas.
2   The ministry has begun to experiment with school autonomy; on a pilot basis schools will be given a modest fund, which teachers, principals and parents will direct to what they perceive as the greatest need to improve teaching effectiveness.
3   The ministry is making teacher training a priority area in the design of large education projects with funding from international development banks.
4   Administrative decentralization has continued, transferring responsibilities to the departments as suggested in the assessment. The Ministry of Planning finally approved this strategy in November 1994.
5   Parent and community participation has been fostered, not only by involving them in decision-making in the management of school funds, but also by establishing focus groups in communities to consult on educa-

tion issues. The Minister, in a series of public fora, is informing parents and the public at large about the conditions of schools and the main problems confronted by the education system. At the same time the Minister wants to rely on focus groups to receive feedback from teachers.
6   The Ministry is supporting innovations at the local level and is supporting a number of model schools with specially trained teachers to serve as trainers.

The content of the sector assessment has also been used in the negotiations between the government and the multilateral financial institutions as they design a programme of educational improvement that will cost about US$100 million.

Perhaps the most striking consequence of the assessment was that it unleashed a process of public discussion of education issues. Several organizations in the country produced their own reports on the problems of the education sector and on possible solutions to these problems (all these organizations had participated in the advisory committee of the assessment, and some had direct participation in the technical team writing the assessment). A think-tank on economic and social policy produced a policy brief on education and human resources, and sponsored several paid pages in the national press about the problems with and options for improving educational opportunities. The director of the social policy sector of this think-tank, who was a consultant working on the chapter of administrative reform in the sector assessment, became a vocal spokesperson for education issues in several national fora.

> Active participation by widely disparate groups in El Salvador has facilitated the analytical work and acceptance of its outcomes. A precedent-setting, much needed, national dialogue on education issues and policy is now underway in El Salvador. (Official from US AID, in Barraza *et al.*, 1994, p. 2)

Through the participatory methodology the sector assessment became a process of pluralistic reflection, and an opportunity to consider options for education reform. The final report has an excellent content, insufficient in itself to launch a rapid change in the education system, but of critical value to impress in the highest levels of decision making in the country that education in El Salvador should have the highest priority, and that a change is necessary not just in the funds assigned to the sector, but in the systems, procedures, decentralization and general improvement of teaching. (President of FEPADE, in Barraza *et al.*, 1994, p. 2)

The UCA produced, in addition to the publication of the sector assessment as a book, a special issue on education in a journal that regularly discusses social and economic topics. This issue drew directly from the chapters written by UCA staff in the assessment. A think-tank closely associated with the Christian Democratic Party produced two publications and sponsored a national forum of dialogue on education following the completion of the assessment. These publications drew on the assessment document. The senior person in charge of social policy in this centre – two had participated in the advisory committee – said that the meetings of the committee had worked as an advanced seminar generating much deeper understanding of education issues in the country. Similar comments were made by the person responsible for social policy in the think-tank:

The participatory methodology permitted a valuable transfer of technology; it provided the persons involved with an opportunity for professional enrichment. The conceptual and analytic skills of the national teams were expanded through collaboration with international consultants who found in each working team a counterpart with information, a national perspective and a space for transfer of technology. In this way the study achieved the best of international assistance and generated conditions favorable to implementation of the specific recommendations. (Staff member from think-tank in Barraza *et al.*, 1994, p. 4)

Most importantly, the advisory committee continued to work after the assessment was completed. In January 1995 they sponsored a national three-day forum on education reform. Over 200 people from 119 organizations participated, working in small groups of no more than ten people, divided by topic. The book published on the basis of the sector assessment was launched at this event and used as a major piece to support the small groups' discussions. The

Minister of Education legitimized the importance of the advisory committee by asking the members to meet periodically with her to review issues of education policy.

The Ministry of Education also had a series of one-day workshops with teachers in January 1995 to review the main problems of primary education and options for improvement. They prepared a video and handed out materials for discussion of educational problems. They used the synthesis of the HIID study as the base document for discussion, and a copy was handed out to all teachers in these workshops.

The education sector assessment in El Salvador served as an opportunity to establish new partnerships between university faculty and government officials, between the public and private sectors, between political parties, the business community, religious organizations and community groups. It stimulated a process of public dialogue about education and it opened new avenues to expand educational opportunities.

The selection of national institutions to work as technical counterparts was a great success. The partnerships HIID established with FEPADE, UCA and the various directorates of the Ministry of Education provided opportunities for participation from the outset. The configuration of an advisory committee with representatives of different sectors such as the teacher unions, the private sector, NGOs, also promoted levels of participation without precedent in the education sector in this country. (Minister of Education, in Barraza *et al.*, 1994)

Within a year of issuing the RFP for an education and health sector assessment, US AID had obtained completed products in both areas. The health sector assessment was conducted using more orthodox procedures, similar to the ones described in the first four cases presented in this chapter. The cost of the health assessment was more than twice the cost of the education assessment and the use of funds was also different. Most participants in the team were foreign consultants who had full responsibility for the different chapters of the assessment, and there were no Salvadorean counterparts among the authors of that study.

About 30 per cent of the HIID budget was sub-contracted to Salvadorean counterpart institutions and consultants. A large number of the consultants whom HIID brought to the project were colleagues from other Latin American countries who had expertise in specific areas.

In the summer of 1994, US AID bid a proposal to design and implement a social-sector reform project to cover education and health. HIID also submitted a proposal in this competition. Our plan was more complex than the one prepared for the education sector assessment in that it expanded the number of participating host-country counterpart organizations to six. We also expanded the spaces for consultation and dialogue to include the health sector and to include regional levels and town hall meetings. There was also an explicit attempt to set up a process that would allow the development of integrated approaches to address health and education projects simultaneously. HIID lost this competition to a reputable consortium of US-based consulting firms. Among the reasons offered by US AID were the insufficient technical quality of the HIID team (which included a number of Salvadorean professionals with limited international experience) and the complexity of the proposal.

The first task of this team was to design a project to respond to the needs and options identified in the assessment. This was accomplished by the end of February 1995. The feedback we received from several groups suggested that the use of a traditional approach to providing assistance was not satisfactory. The senior leadership of the Ministry of Education complained to US AID that four months into the project the team of technical advisers had not once discussed with ministry staff how they planned to approach the task. The ministry informed US AID that it was in a position to reject the eventual grant funds if it did not see that the project addressed its needs, and that it would rather rely on loans from the World Bank and the Inter-American Development Bank (which it was negotiating on the basis of the results of the sector assessment).

In February 1995 a high-level US AID officer wrote:

The Social Sector Reform Project has been troublesome for a variety of reasons. There was confusion about what an AID project could or should do with huge BID/World Bank loans coming down the pike. For me that never seemed much of an issue since the Banks said outright from the beginning that they will not work with civil society or the private sector – their loans are with the government, so they are not big on participation. This seems to me a crucial area that USAID could be involved in that doesn't require a ton of money, and we already have the seeds planted in Education with the Sector Assessment. The problem is that Health doesn't have those seeds planted, and it doesn't look like they are interested in planting them at the moment ... The Minister of Education has encouraged the Advisory Committee and FEPADE to get more pro-active in reform discussions. The doors are open on that side.

My opinion (shared by many others in this Mission) is that the design team of the Social Sector Reform Project was poorly organized and run. Even though there were some good people on the team, I would classify the overall effort as a complete failure.

First, they ran the effort in the traditional manner – a SWAT team of consultants from outside attending meetings but not *integrating* local actors from the start in the design effort. Second, they did not pick up on what people were saying (especially the Minister of Education) even when they were practically hit over the head with it – or if they did understand, they didn't listen. They insisted on proposing a 'COR' (communications operations research) methodology that they wanted to make the crux of the project.

Trying to sell a research-centered project to the Ministry of Education right now went over like a lead balloon. The Ministry of Education rejected the approach. The Ministry of Health ended up disliking it also.

About 2 weeks ago the mission leadership met with the Minister of Education and she said that in a meeting with the Ministries of Planning and Health they had all basically agreed that they would not accept the design of this project as they had seen it up until now. She whipped out the budget and pointed out the percentage breakdowns of TA, training, etc. and said it was unacceptable. This was not a surprise, in fact it was a relief both for us and for her to realize that we were on the same wavelength exactly. We told her that we would be checking with our Contracts Office to see what our options were at this point. (personal communication)

Eventually the government of El Salvador refused to accept the project which had been designed as a result of this activity, even though it was financed with grant funds. 'We'd rather borrow money to do something that makes sense to us than receive a gift for something that does not,' the Minister of Education said to the Director of US AID. In consultation with the Minister of Education US AID decided to use these funds to support a plan of activities to sustain institutional reform in education from FEPADE, the group which had worked as a partner in the preparation of the sector assessment. FEPADE invited HIID to design with them this plan of activities. Staff from UCA and other institutions which had participated in the earlier dialogue were involved in this activity. In May 1995 this group tried to pick up where they left off, and to recover the time spent between September 1994 and February 1995 when a technical assistance team tried to impose a traditional approach in a system that had learned to dialogue.

Lessons learned: conducting technical work to support policy dialogue

It is important to recognize that the activity discussed here took place in a context that is structurally not very participatory. US AID decided that it would pursue an education sector assessment independent of the views of the Minister of Education. Maybe it had already been decided that a project to support reform on education and health would take place prior to commissioning the assessment. So the opportunities for participation were to influence how the assessment would be conducted and the results it could provide, not to determine whether it would be conducted.

In spite of these structural constraints, the case documents that innovative approaches can be negotiated. This requires recognizing that the situation calls for something different from 'business as usual'. Because a participatory approach is so different from standard practice in this field it is to be expected that it will face resistance; the challenge is to recognize small openings, and to stay the course in a process that will sometimes be uphill. This case documents that even people who are initially opposed to a participatory methodology

can learn and change their minds about its merits. The attitude of the Minister of Education was initially lukewarm towards the assessment and the process we had proposed, and publicly she did not endorse it in any way – though she gave consent for it to be carried out and instructed her technical staff to cooperate. Her concerns were about conducting this activity just prior to the elections in a way that would not allow the ministry control over the findings. A year later, the same minister was launching a series of participatory activities, including appointing an advisory commission, which included a former leader of the armed rebellion and the rector of the national university (this commission was drawn from the advisory committee of the assessment). The ministry also conducted a series of workshops to discuss education problems with 2,000 teachers, at which the synthesis of the sector assessment was handed out as the base document for discussion. 'Although she qualifies it by saying, "Although we don't agree with *everything* in this study . . . ", the Minister cites the importance of that study over and over at every occasion' (US AID Education Officer).

The Minister also encouraged the advisory committee of the assessment to continue sponsoring fora for discussion such as the one which took place in January 1995.

The process of the assessment was also received initially with mixed feelings by the representatives of the former armed rebellion. After the study was completed, however, the presidential candidate for this group was the first to echo the findings and recommendations of the assessment in national news. This group organized an 'Educational Concertation' in late 1994, a meeting at which the importance of this study was highlighted, and the study was used as a basis for these deliberations.

Perhaps the most dramatic evidence of how people can change comes from an officer in the economic analysis unit at US AID. This person had proposed that HIID not be paid for this project for what he considered poor performance. In February 1995 he wrote me a letter, with no other purpose than to share his views about education and health:

It is my impression that if real reform comes about the results can be quite positive for El Salvador. This is a big if, however. It looks like we will be able to get some real reform in education, and I think much of that has to do with the very excellent work you did here. I am much less sanguine about health, which seems directionless. My sense is that health may need reform almost as much as education, so this is distressing to me. (US AID Economics Officer)

This case illustrates that it is possible to design processes of technical analysis to support the quality of education policy decisions and to integrate them into nascent democratic contexts. This requires a recognition of the political nature of planning, and the relevant groups with a stake in the outcome of planning (stakeholders) must be identified. Spaces must be created for collaboration between Ministries of Education and other organizations representing civil society, such as NGOs, universities or advisory committees. We have also learned that it is possible for ministries to have frank discussions with various stakeholders; these discussions are easier if they refer to the policy implications of technical analysis, but they can also include the conceptualization of problems that need attention.

One could argue over the merits of implementing a participatory process; even if this case shows that it is feasible, is there not a risk that broadening participation in the technical analysis of host country counterparts who have not had the same opportunities for advanced training in specialized analytical techniques would reduce the quality of the final product?

I contend that, on the contrary, the inclusion of multiple perspectives in the analysis enriches the quality of the final product. The techniques available for education policy analysis are not such that they can provide a single answer to the causes of and solutions to education problems. Findings about education problems are bound by the methodologies used to investigate them, by the way in which the phenomena of interest are defined and measured, by the events, moments, or people who are sampled, and by the hypotheses of those who investigate. This does not mean that one should dismiss the importance of rigorous enquiry into

educational problems, but it does mean that one should be humble about what such enquiry can yield. Maybe educational policy analysts and researchers can take inspiration from the impact of chaos theory in physics, which speaks of the infinite complexity of even simple systems and moves our understanding of science as 'truth' to understanding science as a process of discovery of patterns and probabilities.

Furthermore, educational problems as they are faced by policy-makers lack the precision to be found in a systematic study that can pre-specify all relevant variables. There are pedagogical, economic, legal, bureaucratic and other dimensions to the problems faced by decision-makers, and to the alternatives that can be considered. To bring up highly specialized expertise in rational analysis in order to examine problems and identify solutions is a useful exercise, but one that by definition simplifies the dimensions of the problem. Therefore, the consideration of alternatives should take place not within the simplified environment of the analyst – the hotel room, or the set of offices in which foreign consultants work – but in the real world, where concrete persons and groups express these multiple interests.

Some of the real problems faced by policy-makers have a complexity that defies easy answers. Policy analysis and strategic planning are therefore as much an exercise of discovery through rational enquiry as they are processes of managing negotiations of competing views on the problem.

Though the environment of the hotel room, the laptop and the reports, and the comfortable surroundings of the donor offices may offer security to the expert advisers, it is only by risking making oneself vulnerable to stakeholders, ministers and donor agencies by recognizing that we do not know all the answers, that there may be more than one answer, and that we need dialogue with others in order to understand the problem better, that it is possible to begin to appreciate the complexity of education issues as decision-makers face them; taking that risk is therefore the only course if one wants to provide advice which is relevant for real-life decision-making.

To conclude, the business of education reform exceeds the best intentions of decision-makers, no matter how highly placed they are. If an education system is to change its ways, what is needed is organizational learning, rather than learning by a single individual placed at the top. There are two reasons for this: one is that implementation of policy, and even policy definition, involves multiple participants; the second is that Ministers of Education and senior staff normally have a tenure too short relative to the time it takes educational innovations to influence learning conditions. The type of learning that has been presented here is not one where one person, the expert, teaches and others listen, but rather it is one of learning by discovery. Dialogue is an essential condition for that learning to take place. The expert must be willing to participate in this dialogue at a table with other stakeholders. The expert has a rightful place at that table, for the quality of the dialogue can be improved by this participation, but only with the recognition that the conversation has been going on before the expert's arrival and will continue when the expert departs.

Acknowledgements

I am grateful to all of those who have kept me informed of recent developments in El Salvador, especially Cecilia Gallardo de Cano, Minister of Education; Cynthia Rohl, US AID Education Specialist; José Luis Guzmán, from the Universidad Centro Americana; Héctor López, from FEPADE; and Sandra de Barraza from FUSADES.

Notes

1 Grindle and Thomas propose that the process of policy change is determined by three critical junctures which include perception of the policy and a number of characteristics of the policy such as the arenas of conflict and resources for implementation. These forces are likely to drive the politics of decision-making in ways which are ignored by most literature on educational planning. The notion that participation would be a mechanism by which to obtain information on these elements is my own inference, and not made explicitly in the book. In fact, the book does not contain the terms 'participation' or 'consultation' in its index, and one of the authors stated in a personal conversation that the literature on policy reform is very confined on this subject.

2 'Who owns the programmes? Issue raised during dialogue on African education'. Note on the Meeting of Donors to African Education Task Force in Angers, October 1993. In *IIEP Newsletter*, January–March, 1994.

3 The colleague was Noel McGinn, and the article was published as 'Politics of educational planning' (McGinn, 1994).

4 This book (Reimers, 1995) can be obtained from UCA Editores, Apartado Postal 01-575, San Salvador, El Salvador.

References

Agarwala, R. (1983) *Planning in Developing Countries: Lessons of Experience*. World Bank Staff Working Papers. Washington, DC: World Bank.

Barraza, S. *et al.* (1994) Participatory sector assessment in El Salvador, *Forum for Advancing Basic Education and Literacy* (September), pp. 4–6.

Benveniste, G. (1991) *Mastering the Politics of Planning*. San Francisco: Jossey-Bass.

Cohen, J. (1984) Participatory planning and Kenya's national food policy paper, *Stanford Food Research Institute Studies*, **19**(2), 187–213.

Daniere, A. (1977) The education sector assessment: evaluation of six Latin American countries, in R. Davis and N. McGinn (eds), *Analysis in Support of Educational Planning*. Mimeo, Harvard University.

Grassie, McC. (1974) *Participatory Planning in Education*. Paris: UNESCO, IIEP.

Grindle, M. (ed.) (1980) *Politics and Policy Implementation in the Third World*. Princeton, NJ: Princeton University Press.

Grindle, M. and Thomas, J. (1991) *Public Choices and Policy Change*. Baltimore: Johns Hopkins University Press.

McGinn, N. (1994) Politics of educational planning, in T. Husen and N. Postlethwaite (eds), *International Encyclopedia of Education*. Oxford: Pergamon, pp. 4595–602.

Paul, S. (1982) *Managing Development Programs: The Lessons of Success.* Boulder, CO: Westview Press.

Pigozzi, M. and Cieutat, V. (1988) *Education and Human Resources Sector Assessment Manual.* Tallahassee: Florida State University.

Reimers, F. (ed.) (1995) *La educación en El Salvador de cara al siglo XXI.* San Salvador: UCA Editores.

Schumacher, E. F. (1977) *A Guide for the Perplexed.* New York: Harper & Row.

Senge, P. (1990) *The Fifth Discipline: The Art and Practice of the Learning Organization.* New York: Currency Doubleday.

World Bank (1995) *Priorities and Strategies for Education.* Draft, 24 January.

7 Democratic Schooling, Transformation and Development

LYNN DAVIES

Introduction

This chapter focuses on the connections between the organization of schooling and the outcomes of equity, using gender as the key illustration. Much work on gender and development has centred on female access to education and on curriculum; there has also been some work on women teachers. Curiously, however, there has been little on the organization of the whole institution, and the effects of particular choices of management style and culture. This has a potential impact in two linked areas: we would need to know, first, how management policy impacts on (in)equity and gender relations within the school; and second, how management affects the social outcomes of the school, in terms both of any reproduction of 'masculine' ways of ordering the world and of future female participation in politics and decision-making.

Although a gender balance in formal education is an important aim, we should simultaneously ask exactly what the 'education' is that girls are being encouraged to attend. If going to school simply means exposure to gender-biased curricula and unchallenged masculinist modes of operation, then we might want to question its universal benefit. Is the schooling that we are asking parents and communities to support genuinely empowering and equitable? The relations of power and authority are key parts of the hidden curriculum of schooling, and yet there is an assumption in much of the effectiveness schooling research that 'culture' and management affect boys and girls equally. The lack of research on this is

understandable: a recent study on female motivation in Nepal (Joshi and Anderson, 1994) explained how the researchers wanted to engage in a larger study of school practices, but because of political unrest had to limit this part of the research, and focus more on the analysis of textbooks. It is always easier to get access to materials, and even to basic statistics on enrolment, than it is to embark on the in-depth ethnography which reveals the surrounding cultures of schools.

Because of a long-standing interest in this culture (see Davies, 1992, 1994), and in democracy as a vehicle for educational and national development, I want in this chapter to explore what is known about the effects of democratic or authoritarian modes of school operation, using gender divisions as the example. As will be seen, management cultures also have differential effects on other social divisions, such as social class, ethnicity, religion and 'ability'. It will be my argument that democratic schools are better placed to tackle all types of inequality and injustice, but in order to focus the discussion I will select gender as an international concern, and hope that this will generate discussion in other, equally important – and inextricably linked – areas. It is important that any mention of gender is not automatically relegated to a special section on 'women's education', but that it be seen as a highly significant signal of progress or stagnation within education and development as a whole. I first of all introduce the field by casting some doubts on the benefits of formal education in a range of countries; I then examine the evidence on the effects of bureaucracy, authoritarianism and patriarchy in schools;

I then bring together such themes by exploring what participation and transformation might mean, and raising some questions about the notion of 'empowerment'.

Is universal schooling a good thing?

The constant restructuring of education in most parts of the world means an equally constant need for vigilance about the effects of 'reform'. In the UK, for example, the introduction of a national curriculum was heralded as ensuring equal entitlement to knowledge; yet examining the content of such knowledge reveals a host of inequitable features. The privileging of maths, science and technology has by and large not questioned the masculine modes of thought and understanding which underpin such areas; geography and history, though not quite reverting to 'maps and chaps', have none the less attempted to go back to more nationalistic and heroic arenas; the reintroduction of competitive sport is a thinly disguised attempt to put Britain on the map again for male football and cricket; and most importantly, the demise of political education means the loss of a formal site for challenging government policy and social injustice. Together with a shift to market-based ideologies for school financing, the analyses are showing an increase in social polarization as a result of 'reforms' (Miles and Middleton, 1995).

Similarly, the effects on women of 'marketization' have been explored in countries such as China (Rai, 1994); and the gendered impact of structural adjustment policies has been revealed in African countries such as Zimbabwe (Gordon, 1994). So-called modernizing programmes, and certainly austerity programmes, have adverse effects on already disadvantaged groups. In many parts of the world we are seeing the gendered effects of an increase not only in fundamentalism, but also in other areas of religious expansionism. In Nicaragua, for example, Carr (1993) found that the demise of secularism and the attempt by the post-Sandinista government to combat the 'politicization' of education meant the Catholic Church

being given a major role in education. There was the creation of compulsory 'civic education' classes promulgating conservative Catholic doctrine; again, 'politics' was banned from the classroom, with no acknowledgement that all education about values has a political base. With increasingly 'fragile states' (Fuller, 1991) and severe economic cutbacks, the time and the sites for the crucial questioning of the social order may be disappearing in many schools all over the world. Precarious gains in arenas variously called 'social science', 'equal opportunities' or 'girl-friendly' policy are under threat.

The old saying, 'a little knowledge is a dangerous thing', has some interesting contemporary relevance in looking at the impact of female education. The fertility studies are intriguing here, for although it might be thought that there would be a straightforward connection between having more years of schooling and having lower numbers of children, the graph is actually bell-shaped. There are studies that show that girls with *some* education have more children on average than either girls with none or girls with, say, secondary education (Cochrane, 1982). It is interesting to speculate on the reasons for this, but one hypothesis would certainly have to relate to the content and style of the schooling experienced, and whether a little exposure to conventional norms and values simply reinforced traditional expectations for women, without the later benefits accruing to really functional literacy and the ability to articulate ideas. A study of 'rising education' for adolescents in rural India (Vlassoff, 1994) found that female youth was more traditional than twelve years previously, and although the girls' general knowledge had improved through going to school, they continued to see themselves in traditional domestic roles, whereas males saw education as opening up new opportunities. Low-fertility ideals were related to successful family planning propaganda, not formal education, which seemed to heighten conservatism. Similarly, education may provide avenues to employment, but working women may still be exploited by husbands and in-laws if they have learned no political or negotiating skills.

An article on Saudi Arabia revealed that female education had been greatly expanded, but that the education sector acted primarily as a means for the reproduction of gender divisions. The dual system, with gender-segregated schools and colleges, meant that although there were female role models as administrators of institutions, the overall management of education was male:

> These top-ranking male administrators make all the major decisions affecting female education from primary schools to universities. . . . Women have little decision-making power and complain that they merely implement decisions made by men far removed from the actual education process. Furthermore, Saudi women faculty are outside the 'old-boys' network, and do not have as much access to resources as their male colleagues. (El-Sanabary, 1994, p. 143)

The country has a gender-specific policy which restricts and limits the type of education women can receive, and what they can do with it after graduation. The explicit aim is to bring the woman up in a 'sound Islamic way' to become a good mother and homemaker, and to perform those jobs which 'suit her nature' such as teacher, nurse and doctor. El-Sanabary thus is able to make the claim, 'There is no hidden curriculum here.' Clearly differentiated curricula and female administrative and pedagogic isolation are intentionally instituted as a means of cultural conservation and social control.

This is not to say that segregated education cannot provide an arena for change. In spite of its limitations and restrictions, female education has opened up new options for Saudi women. On the private level, it has increased their negotiating power in the family. Several institutions provide low-cost on-site childcare facilities for the children of women students, teachers and staff, many of whom are young and experience many pregnancies and births during their education and employment. Hence it is important not to take an entirely deterministic view of schooling as a site for social reproduction, and to see where the spaces for contestation and struggle lie. The analysis of contradiction will become important: in the above example, the ideology of the family/motherly role for women led (as in the old USSR) to the provision of childcare facilities within the educational process, a management strategy exploitable for different sorts of female interests.

In examining cultures such as the 'gender regime' (Kessler *et al.*, 1985) within educational institutions, we need, then, to look at both their reproductive power and their possibilities for subversion.

Discourse and the gender regime

More recent analyses of education and social control have moved on from the notion of schooling as simply 'socializing into sex roles' to a more sophisticated exploration of 'discourse' within organizations. Discourse is a way of thinking and talking about the world; it involves the definition of people and events, the generation of categories and concepts. Discourse is language linked to the use of power, which creates and sets limits to the 'truths' by which we can understand our world. The binary opposition of 'man' and 'woman', and the understandings attached to these terms, is a key discourse. The use of language and discourse is central to 'hegemony', the dominance of one group or class over another: for hegemony refers to dominance by apparent consent rather than force, achieved by the shaping of reality through the successful diffusion of ideas, values and social 'rules'. Much more attention has been paid of late to masculinity (Connell, 1987; Mac an Ghaill, 1994) in educational settings, in particular hegemonic masculinity. The discourse around masculinity acts to shape concepts of what is 'normal' for boys, and – because femininity is constructed as a polar opposite in most cultures – what is 'normal' for girls. A discourse which posits the male as dominant and aggressive does not, however, necessarily always advantage men; the explorations show boys in schools as limited and constrained by such discourses, finding difficulty in expressing alternative versions of masculinity.

Yet because we all use language, and are active on a daily basis in the conscious or unconscious reproduction of or challenge to hegemony, such discourses are not uncontested. The exciting thing about contemporary analyses of discourse is the confirmation that social structures are only as permanent as the languages in daily use to describe them, and that therefore we all, as individuals, are implicated in their continuation – or dissolution. Whenever we rehearse the line, 'In our culture, women are expected to ... ', we reproduce, through the passive tense, the sense of an uncontestable determinism in social structure, one in which we (and individuals we know) have no part. Transformative teachers and schools, as we shall see later, use other discourses about gender. The other important feature is the acknowledgement that there are multiple discourses in daily use: discourses about religion, 'race' and class as well as sexuality. These are often in competition for hegemony, and again provide spaces for contestation.

In examining the cultures and discourses within educational organizations, it is important – if not always easy – to try to tease out which are products of a 'gender regime' and which are linked to other forms of knowledge and power. I look here first at hierarchical bureaucracy and then at authoritarianism and patriarchy both to assess their effects on gender equity, as mentioned in the introduction to this chapter and to trace the derivations and purposes of the discourses.

Hierarchical bureaucracy

Schools all over the world have been classified as typical bureaucracies, demonstrating both vertical and horizontal divisions (Harber, 1989). In a bureaucracy, activities and roles are separated according to job descriptions and specializations; decisions are made by virtue of one's position and level within the authority structure. Activities are circumscribed by rules and routines, with a divide between the personal and the public. In theory, bureaucracies should be exemplary sites for equity: the 'ideal-type' bureaucracy was in fact introduced in order to avoid the favouritism and personalization that would categorize, say, monarchies or oligarchies. The discourse around bureaucracy is that of rationality and efficiency; the networks are those of objective functions, not family or group connections. It could be argued that there is nothing implicitly gendered about bureaucracy.

However, in practice, it would seem that bureaucracies and the way they are interpreted remain good sites for the play of gender power. First, there is the question of whose 'rationality' is in play. The discourse of impartiality may operate to prevent the flexibility which subordinate groups may need. Acknowledgement of emotion and feeling, maternity and family leave, flexible working hours, autonomy to make decisions – all these may be downgraded in favour of a more tightly controllable and standardized culture. Yet it is these apparently highly personalized features which women in particular may require in order to function effectively in an organization, and to achieve progress.

The fact that bureaucracies appear to be objective in their operation acts of course to mask the possible imbalances in representation at the various levels. Our study of women and men in educational management in developing countries (Davies and Gunawardena, 1992) found men over-represented at upper levels of decision-making, whether in ministries of education or senior management of educational institutions. Men felt a greater sense of ownership of the management process, and felt more confident about their competence in a range of administrative tasks – even if they had never done them. Women, in contrast, were more realistic about their capabilities, and sometimes needed persuasion to take on managerial posts that would elevate them above colleagues. We argued in this study that flatter, more collegial and more rotational structures and styles would enable women – and some of the less competitive men – to experience management without having to leave classrooms permanently or to fragment previous relationships.

Even apparently democratic structures within bureaucracies such as committees may mask the fact that the academic gatekeepers are predominantly male. Mannathoko (1994), in her study of teacher education in Botswana, found differences between the flatter 'professional' bureaucracy of the university and the more mechanistic one of the colleges. The decentralized system of authority of a professional bureaucracy replaces extended hierarchies and line management through a series of committees, with issues being discussed at various levels, and with apparently full participation. However, the reality was that policies, plans and regulations had to go through the various committees, and as they moved up the ladder and got cleared, they did not necessarily go back down again. The top management could quite easily use the committees to delay or block implementation of policies and programmes they did not favour. This was done by arguing that new proposals were not up to standard, proper procedures had not been followed, or consultation had not been carried out. She found that some lecturers did not participate in the discussions, and that because of the pyramidal hierarchy of the committees themselves, with females concentrated at the bottom levels, decision-making was still predominantly in the hands of men. (There were significant age dimensions here too, with younger members of staff feeling disenfranchised.) The exclusion of women was not as stark as in the Saudi Arabian example mentioned earlier, but in some ways, because it falls into the hidden curriculum of the organization and is less transparent, the discourse is not so easy to challenge.

Fuller's study of Malawi has an excellent disclosure of the ability of bureaucracy to disempower teachers. Here he is talking of the penetration of state bureaucracy and the discourse of 'modernity' into the lives and work of classroom teachers:

> The fragile state, attempting to implement a modern bureaucratic form of organization, speaks to school headmasters. Despite infrequent direct regulation by state inspectors or district officers ... most headmasters proceed with at least the symbols of rational administration: routinising the teachers' actions through lesson plans, arranging simple bits of knowledge into thirty-five minute segments, and admonishing teachers to transmit Western signals of virtue and character (Western-style uniforms, promptness and cleanliness) ... No one asks whether such practices boost pupil achievement; they are simply seen as basic forms of organization, necessary for boosting the school's legitimacy and the teacher's authority... Teachers may come to feel little professional autonomy or control over their work ... Thus classic bureaucratic controls which link the strong central

state and local headmasters are simply passed on: headmasters, mimicking the form of control to which they are subjected, attempt to rationally control and homogenise the behaviour of their teachers. (Fuller, 1991, pp. 114–15)

Fuller does not go into the effects on gender, being more concerned about social class formation; however, clues start to emerge, if only from the unquestioned nomenclature of 'headmaster'. The point is that when there is acceptance of a discourse, particularly one so heavily oriented towards control, there is smaller space for challenge – either by teachers or students – to the accepted order. In the case of Malawian society, this is indeed a gendered order. The prime aim of mass schooling, to socialize children into the existing culture, does not provide an official arena to question that tradition. The irony is that a 'modernizing' discourse so firmly acts to retain existing historical traditions and divisions.

The centrality of bureaucracy to the perpetuation of state and institutional order is confirmed by Dovey in talking of South Africa. He claims that

> it seems unlikely that the state will change the form of organization of formal educational provision in South Africa from that of bureaucracy. Bureaucratic, or role, cultures, provide ruling groups with an effective means of control over such provision, and the power struggles of the past within the arena of education are likely to continue into the future, irrespective of who governs South Africa. (Dovey, 1993, p. 7)

Dovey looks therefore to the non-formal education (NFE) sector as being the site which would promote the interests of the disadvantaged. This is as long as NFE itself is not hierarchical, as the NFE literature has countless examples of 'top-down' organized literacy programmes failing because of low motivation to attend by targeted populations.

A significant and fascinating study in Zambia by Mwansa (1994) confirms this, and tackles the gender issue head-on. He studied four literacy classes in rural and urban areas, and discovered two kinds of leadership structure which generated different types of relationship. One was hierarchical (with an appointed class committee) and the other non-hierarchical (with rotational leadership). In the only class with a large number of male participants, the Social Development Assistant had intentionally given positions of leadership to men so that they could be attracted to stay:

> It is not many men who are interested in literacy. Those who are interested I give them posts. For example when they get together I ask men to pray for the group. I give them anything that makes them take over some responsibility from me so that they can stay. (p. 166)

My inference from such a discursive statement is that there is a belief that men cannot learn unless they are somehow in charge of others. In fact, problems and conflicts emerged within this committee and the class, with accusations of stealing, of undemocratic behaviour and of favouritism. The men saw the occupation of positions of leadership as a way of gaining control over others. In the female classes, in contrast, leadership was non-hierarchical. In the rural site there were no permanent class monitors and no chairperson. The position of a monitor was rotational from time to time, with the women deciding who would be the next:

> Even where the teachers tried to appoint leaders women chose to share the responsibilities. In the urban site ... the only male participant wanted to play the leadership role alone but was restrained because the women looked to his wife for leadership. (Mwansa, 1994, p. 166)

Mwansa comments: 'Unless leadership roles are properly explained and those who occupy them prepared for them, the tendency to dominate, to command and not to consult is likely to grow and contribute to misunderstandings among participants' (ibid.); he also asks for officials to 'recognize leadership potential among women' (ibid.).

I would take perhaps a slightly different interpretation of the findings, and not ask for more management training for men, or for more women in 'leadership', but would underline the benefits of the continuous sharing of responsibilities which was preferred by the women's groups. I think it no accident that there were gendered differences in preferred organization styles; the study points up the dangers and inexorable tendencies towards (masculinized) control ideologies and practices, once designated 'leaders' are put in place. As I narrated in *Women and Men in Educational Man-agement* (Davies and Gunawardena, 1992), I had started out with the idea of getting more women into management, but ended with questioning what this management was that excluded so many women, and whether 'entryism' was the right discourse. Schulz, too, in her (1994) study of Nepalese and Canadian female teachers, warns of seeing (fewer) women teachers just as 'negative numbers', of focusing on 'future absence, not present presence'. To understand the cultures of organization, we should explore what women and men actually do and contribute, rather than simply cast the 'problem' as one of imbalance within whatever hierarchy is there.

Authoritarianism and patriarchy

We have seen from the above discussion that bureaucracy, although not explicitly gendered, none the less may lend itself to hidden inequalities because of both the masking of male gatekeeping at important levels within the hierarchy and the acceptance of discourses of control centred round 'leadership'. Linked features are those of authoritarianism and patriarchy. Authoritarianism is conventionally defined as the antithesis to democracy – that is, management by decree rather than participation; patriarchy as the exercise of power through the 'father' head, and the acceptance of the control of men over women. In the feminist literature, the two are often conflated. Kenway (1995), for example, defines patriarchy as 'the institutional arrangement by which men as a sex-class exert power over women'. She explains:

> The particular focus of radical feminism's critique of the state has been on its complicity in sustaining the patriarchal family; its judicial and other arrangements concerning matters of rape, domestic violence, prostitution, abortion, pornography and reproductive technology; and its involvement in militarism. (p. 123)

The question, then, is how far schools are patriarchal. Certainly they can be violent places; certainly male power can be used in harassment and in initiating sexual relationships with female pupils; certainly the discourse in many is militaristic. A few examples will suffice.

Corporal punishment, although now illegal in most Western countries, is common in many parts of Africa and South-East Asia. Children are regularly beaten, not just for behavioural offences, but for making mistakes in answering questions. A colleague in Botswana recounted to me how, when visiting a rural secondary school to encourage students to come to the university, a girl asked him whether students got beaten for not knowing the answer. 'And if they think they know they answer, and put up their hand, and get it wrong, do they not get beaten twice as hard as if they just didn't know?' Similarly, 'excessive corporal punishment' was found to be a feature of primary schools in Thailand (Chantavanich *et al.*, 1990). In South Korea, not just individual beatings but class beatings are common, with the whole class being punished for one child's offence (Kang, 1995). Such routinized violence is no respecter of gender, and can be common in all-girls' schools as well. I recall, before corporal punishment was outlawed in the UK, a school I was researching reintroducing the cane for girls, in line with what it saw as its equal opportunities policy (Davies, 1984). We could spend interesting time arguing whether if both boys and girls are beaten equally, this is then a gender issue; that is, whether it is a demonstration of patriarchy or just oppressive authoritarianism. Indeed, mothers and female teachers also beat children (as I shall discuss below). I would hold none the less that it is probably more a reflection of patriarchal control than matriarchal, linked as it is to ways in which men control wives and display dominance within the family. Domestic violence is far more common with women as victims. The prime concern, however, is that institutionalized violence is an abuse of human rights, and acts to brutalize both the institution and the victim. Within existing discourses and expectations for boys and girls, it probably has different effects, acting to confirm violence and aggression as acceptable means of control and display for males, but for females as something that they have to endure.

Institutional violence is also inextricably linked to other forms of the use of power. Harassment of females is not uncommon in educational institutions, nor is the pressure to have a sexual relationship in exchange for good grades (Mannathoko, 1995). The various combinations of male–female, teacher–pupil lead to different kinds of the use of sexuality for power, but the most common appears to be male teachers using a power position with regard to female pupils. I documented some of this previously in a discussion of teacher deviance (Davies, 1993), noting how there can be acceptance of male teachers having uncontrollable urges which are only fuelled by apparently promiscuous girls; or there can be girls expelled for pregnancy but not the father (whether pupil or teacher). In examining the gendered culture of a school or college, it is important therefore to identify the discourses attached to 'normal masculinity', and the justifications for particular types of relationships or interactions. These can be revealed in the sanctions – or lack of them – for particular types of sexual behaviour or harassment. Joshi and Anderson noted in their study of Nepalese classrooms that there was strict sex segregation, with girls usually sitting at the back of the classroom:

> The argument presented by teachers for such practices was that the children preferred such arrangements and that as boys at this age were physically less well developed than girls it was appropriate that boys were not overshadowed by girls. *Girls also felt safe at the rear of the classrooms as they were less likely then to be harassed or teased by boys.* [italics added] (Joshi and Anderson, 1994, p. 177)

The relevant point here is that there appears to be no school policy nor attempt by teachers to outlaw such harassment. Instead there was the institutionalization of patriarchy through particular militaristic practices:

> The practice of lining up outside prior to school, for assembly and the national anthem also reinforced the secondary position of girls. Boys were always at the front and preceded the girls as they marched to class, a replication of the 'follow me' approach of a male dominated society. (ibid.)

Authoritarianism therefore is also supported through a whole range of military devices and discourses in schools, with playgrounds like parade grounds, rigid uniform rules, codified deference patterns and differentiated rules and privileges for different ranks. The need for discipline and control means that it is no accident that schools resemble army corps, wanting blind obedience from the troops. Again, such regimes rarely provide space for that questioning of the moral order which is so fundamental to social change and greater equity.

Yet we have to be careful in simply placing schools on a continuum from democratic to authoritarian. It is easy to pick out the shock-horror instances of repression, and infer – or imply – that this is a totalizing and brutalizing regime; or conversely to find a happy school with child-centred classrooms and assume that the management is democratic and convivial. We need full ethnographies of schools to uncover the complexities and the effects. A fascinating study by Moll (unpublished) of a rural South African school found marked discontinuities between the formal and the informal management. Formally, the school was 'authoritarian' in the sense of relying on non-participatory teaching methods, drilling and frequent corporal punishment. The principal was the only one who appeared to make any decisions with regard to the school, and she set the timetable and spent most of the day issuing curt instructions to staff and students. Yet Moll realized after a few days in the school that he was missing something. Paradoxes had to be solved. There seemed to be no friction with regard to management, and none of the teachers resented the reprimands from the head, nor showed any inclination to engage in any part of school administration themselves. What Moll uncovered was a hidden, and different, style of social organization. The teaching and the administration were secondary in the teachers' eyes to survival in difficult economic circumstances:

> The sense of a merely ceremonial, institutionalized pecking order, with prescribed rights and duties beyond the realm of the educational, is inescapable. The longer I spent in the school, the more I realized that, as a social organization, it had very little to do with instruction and learning; rather it was a support network for a group of people battling to cope with overwhelming odds. (Moll, in press)

The real 'management' activities in this institution took place among the teachers outside school time. All the women on the staff (and excluding the two male teachers) met together at length before and after school, where they shared food, administered a savings club, and swapped clothing and other resources. They discussed school matters, but largely at the level of anecdote, and did not discuss educational practices or policies.

> In this way they sustained a close social support and friendship network as a basis for running the school. Here, all were equals, the principal amongst them. And here, it became clear to me, the real (albeit informal) management of the school took place. (ibid.)

Sebakwane (1994) had discovered a similar support network among women teachers in another of the South African homelands, with cooking clubs, condolence clubs and birthday clubs as well as saving schemes. The question arises, then, as to whether such 'collectivity' is gender-specific, or 'African', or the response of any marginalized group. Although it may be some combination of these, I would suggest there were certainly gendered elements to it. Chantavanich *et al.* (1990) also noted good relationships among teachers of the same age group in Thailand, and among teams of young female teachers. The teams 'worked in unison at the schools, e.g. staying late to coach students in sports, decorating the schools, and helping each other with their routine jobs when something unexpected occurred' (p. 136). Again the schools themselves were hardly democratic in formal organization, and had poor relationships with the parents and community (parents had to sit on the floor to see the teacher, while the teacher sat on a chair); yet the seeds for a supportive collegial management were there in some schools.

The perhaps sad thing is that none of this support and collegiality seemed to percolate through to the pupils. In Moll's study the female teachers' preferred style of discipline was lashing out with a switch; only one of the teachers attempted to provide interesting visual material for her class. There is no necessary connection between the learning culture of the school and either the gender of the teachers or their informal ways of forming relationships with each other. Female teachers can reproduce just as authoritarian, and indeed patriarchal, regimes as their male counterparts, particularly in conditions of stringency.

Nor, it must be said, does patriarchy disadvantage only females. Mwansa's study of literacy programmes in Zambia found men dropping out more frequently than women. The men had been socialized through arenas such as their initiation camps to relate only with men. The camps were 'exclusive, militaristic and highly regimented'. The men had difficulty with the mixed-sex classes, and held patriarchal attitudes that a woman should not look more clever than a man. They therefore, as we saw earlier, attempted to dominate the classes, but felt extreme embarrassment and fear about exposing personal ignorance. They felt 'too big for literacy', and did not want to be among people considered to be illiterate. Whereas women readily admitted being unable to read and write, men were secretive and individualistic.

> When the teacher asks questions normally there would follow a short spell of whispers among women and one of them would provide the correct answer. Men would sometimes try out answers on their own and if they made mistakes they would stay quiet for a while without trying again. (Mwansa, 1994, p. 160)

It was clear from the study that women were better able to benefit from the classes, being less bound up with pride and status.

Such conditioning is not of course peculiar to developing countries; recent work on masculinity in the UK (for example Mac an Ghaill, 1994) shows the limitations for boys of the confinement to a single aggressive 'macho' style of masculinity within schools, and the contradictions this causes, particularly in relationships with peers of either sex. The link with ethnicity is significant, in that ethnic minority males may use patriarchy as a means of demonstrating superiority in the face of discrimination and subjugation on other fronts.

The reason why it is so hard to disentangle authoritarianism, bureaucracy and patriarchy is that they substitute for each other in the reaction to powerlessness and in the attempt to gain power. Our concern should perhaps be not so much in the causes as in the effects, and in attempting to assess the benefits of styles of school organization which are not centred around control.

Democracy, empowerment and transformation

What is common to authoritarianism, bureaucracy and patriarchy is hierarchy, the attempt to maintain dominance by subordinating another. It is based on a vertical conception of power and status, that you cannot be respected unless you are superior. Democracy, on the other hand, is based on the notion of equal respect, the premise that it is possible to improve everyone's life situation cooperatively rather than competitively. Democracy thus sits uneasily with most schooling, based as this is on competitive individualism and examination success. None the less, we have sufficient examples from a range of countries to show that schools applying democratic practice are not only feasible but actually as effective as, or more effective than, conventional authoritarian schools. Democratic schools have a number of key features: power-sharing in school management; flexibility and autonomy in learning; a formal focus on political education for participation; and a concern for equal rights among staff and students. One of the underpinning features is the focus on raising everyone's self-esteem (rather than the attempt to humiliate which is the cornerstone of repressive schooling), and it is here that we can trace the gender effects.

The 'New School Program' in Colombia (reported by Colbert *et al.*, 1993) was a radical new initiative for primary education which promoted active and reflective learning, a flexible promotion system, and the attempt to develop children's cooperation, comradeship, solidarity and civic, participatory and democratic attitudes. It was based on self-instructional study guides and the use of learning centres and school libraries; children could come in and out of school according to family and work needs. Pupils were organized in committees and learned group decision-making, and teachers too were trained at college, through democratic and active learning ways, to teach multi-grade and flexible classes. One of the key aspects of the very positive evaluation was that

> Children in the New School Program were found to have a much higher level of self-esteem than those

enrolled in rural schools where there is a teacher for each grade. The fact that self-esteem of girls equalled that of boys is particularly important; more participatory classrooms appear to help girls' self-esteem ... in tests on socio-civic behaviour, self-esteem and selected subjects ... New School children scored considerably higher than those in traditional rural schools. (Colbert *et al.*, 1993, pp. 63–4)

Similarly, Leonardos reports on the CIEP schools in Brazil, which were public democratic schools designed for disadvantaged students:

> the classroom pedagogy was marked by dialogues and debates in which the teacher shared the stage with the students. The teacher's feedback to students was predominantly constructive; there was a constant concern with building students' self-esteem ... At the CIEP, students were encouraged to take a critical perspective – to question the reason and the meaning of what they were learning. (Leonardos, 1993, pp. 80–1)

The point about both these initiatives is that they were system-level ones, with democratic organization and a questioning pedagogy sanctioned by the state. Elsewhere, it is more difficult for individual teachers to raise self-esteem and political awareness unless they are able to do so as part of a whole-school approach and, ideally, in a national framework. If the whole regime is designed to subjugate, and teachers trained simply to transmit the syllabus, then transformative individuals have a more onerous task. For them to impact on gender equity, there has to be a formal commitment by the school to pupil participation, to cooperative working and to maximizing self-esteem for all. Studies of women's literacy projects have found that 'A superior and patronizing teaching attitude discourages interest, while a democratic, open and involved attitude, treating the learners as equal adults, and creating an atmosphere of confidence, is found to have a positive influence on attendance and results' (Lind, 1992). Lind goes on to assert that women's participation in literacy is directly empowering, in that the woman integrates into a new reference and support group, learns new skills and has a potential new role in the family as well as paid employment: while she is away at classes, family responsibilities sometimes fall upon the male! The claim is that the ability to participate in political discussions and pro-

grammes means that 'a general democratization of society may follow'. I will discuss that claim later in the chapter.

Adult literacy programmes have the major benefit, of course, of not being about selection and competitive examinations. It would seem easier to have equitable pedagogic methods when mass discipline is not an issue. In formal education, we have to look at the whole ethos of the school within which a critical pedagogy might take root and attitude change occur. A study by John and Osborn (1992), for example, compared two secondary schools in the UK, one traditional and authoritarian and one democratic, in terms of pupils' civic attitudes. The traditional school laid stress on formal rules and didactic teaching, with just a four-week block on civic education. The democratic school was a community one with integrated and negotiated curriculum, a fully integrated political education programme, an equal opportunities policy and elected positions for all decision-making. There were not huge differences in attitudes among the pupils, but the democratic school pupils were more ardent supporters of race and gender equality and displayed a greater scepticism about the royal family and about whether the government operated democratically. The article concludes that the findings are suggestive rather than conclusive, and that further research is necessary. Even in the democratic schools in Brazil and Colombia cited above, we have as yet little long-term evidence of the empowerment of either females or males. For this, as I have argued elsewhere (Davies, 1995), we will need performance indicators of democracy which will track outcomes of empowered behaviour such as political participation, new economic roles or different family relationships.

At present we have only educated guesswork. We have seen that conventional authoritarian schools do not empower either males or females. Acting as they do mainly to reproduce rather than challenge existing patterns of inequality and dominance, they limit both men and women, but particularly women. My assumption is that democratic schools which, crucially, treat pupils as adults and insist that they participate and question will, through both political skills and self-esteem, act in the same way as some adult literacy classes: they can begin to empower participants. Whether such empowerment, however, will do anything to bridge the 'gender gap' in employment and in higher education is another unknown, in that men are equally capable of benefiting from the empowerment. It would only work if mutual respect and tolerance for a variety of masculinities, femininities, sexualities and competences were truly absorbed.

Mixed or single-sex democracy?

This leads to the thorny question of mixed or single-sex democratic environments. There are arguments from different parts of Africa that women, because of previous subjugation, need an 'enabling environment' in order to take risks and gain confidence, hence a women-only setting (Mwansa, 1994; Erinosho, 1994). In Peru, the converse was reported, that coeducational classes liberate to a small degree the aggressive impulse in girls while encouraging a restraining impulse in boys (Sara-Lafosse, 1992). Girls' achievements are usually higher in single-sex institutions, but this may be compounded by social class and religious factors, and is not a straight gender issue. Single-sex institutions are not by nature any more or less democratic; women can oppress other women and, as we have seen, act in equally authoritarian ways. It is a question of whether the academic confidence gained by girls from not having to compete with boys and not having to display daily femininity counteracts the lack of opportunity to experience the debate and mutual respect or critique which would come from a mixed democratic environment. It also depends on whether unreconstructed boys are still able to maintain dominance as adult males. The importance of challenging gender relations means both sides having to learn values of equity and democracy.

The Center for Living Democracy in Brattleboro, Vermont, for example, stresses that democratic citizens are not born. They learn the arts of democracy just as they learn sports, history or reading:

by experience and training. Some of these 'arts' of democracy are listed as dialogue, negotiation, evaluation and reflection, public judgement and political imagination – letting go of today's 'givens' in order to re-image the future (quoted by Harber, 1995).

Participation?

Harber makes the point that the arts of democracy are not just about 'participation' (for participation rates were fairly high in Nazi Germany), but about *how* we participate, and with what underlying values. Tolerance of diversity and respect for evidence, plus regarding all people as having equal social and political rights, would be key values. The now defunct Schools Council in the UK promoted the role of the school in this:

> Some values, like those of democracy, tolerance and responsibility, grow only with experience of them. Social education arises from a school's ethos, its organization and its relation with the community. The way a school organizes its staff and pupils and its formal rules, says a great deal about its real values and attitudes. Schools need to practise what they seek to promote. (Schools Council, 1981)

Non-formal education, too, may have to examine its claims to 'participation'. In an impressive critique of the Mahila Samakhya (education for women's equality) project in India, Dighe points out that the project will not be able to achieve its stated objectives, as it is based on wrong premises. One relates to the 'participatory' nature of the project:

> The assumption is that despite the hierarchical, bureaucratic ethos that presently prevails, it would be possible to bring about a change to participatory management styles by fostering a partnership relationship between the bureaucracy and the voluntary agencies. However, advocates of participatory approach well know that there can be comparatively weak forms of client participation in which there is a top-down initiation with some cursory consultation with low-power groups about their needs and

interests. In such a situation, participation becomes ritualistic rather than substantive since decision-making and power relations are not altered (nor are they intended to be) ... If the existing national leadership is not committed to the ideology and policy of power realignment in favour of the poor, it is possible that strong client participation would only be regarded as subversive. (Dighe, 1992, pp. 175–6)

The second false premise was that in building a positive self-image women could become active participants in the process of development. The assumption was that, as individuals, women would become more efficient and productive and there would be an overall improvement in their social and economic well-being. Yet Mahila Samakhya was 'particularly quiet' about the manner in which economic well-being would be brought about; there was a 'naive assumption' that the programme would provide an alternative challenge to upward mobility so that inequalities would be reduced. Yet the 'individual deficit' viewpoint to which the programme subscribed did not get to the root of the maldistribution of power and resources. It was 'person-centred' not 'system-centred', not explicating how changing individual attitudes would somehow restructure society. The 'parameters of empowerment' elaborated by the project included developing the ability to think critically and encouraging group action to bring about change in society; yet, as Dighe points out, 'An unresolved dilemma for "Mahila Samakhya" is why the government should cooperate in the nurturance of a process that has as one of its major goals redistribution of power away from the centre towards the formerly low-power periphery' (Dighe, 1992, p. 180). Changes in individuals' social meanings and awareness *can* aggregate to produce a certain 'critical density', when there comes into existence potential for assertive, even organized, political action. The participatory approach to adult learning has tremendous pedagogical advantages. 'But in the absence of linkages with wide ongoing class struggles and socio-political movements, the highly cherished goal of empowerment of women would not be realized' (ibid., p. 181).

It is my contention, then, that 'empowerment' will not come simply from sending girls and boys

to school or literacy classes. Nor will it come from formal 'civic education' or girls-only maths classes. Nor will it come from participatory approaches which are not openly linked into wider movements for social change. The really successful projects which have created the potential for transformation have been those initiated and backed by governments – and which target both sexes.

Empowerment?

I would want therefore to treat with care this notion of 'empowerment' which is so much part of current discourse about equity. There are dangers that this, like 'participation', will become just another fuzzy buzzword, or 'symbolic political language', as Troyna (1994) reminds us. Gore deconstructs the notion by breaking down its parts, arguing that empowerment

> carries with it an agent of empowerment (someone, or something, doing the empowering), a notion of power as property (to *em*-power implies to give or confer power) and a vision or desired end state (some vision of what it is to be empowered and the possibility of a state of empowerment). (Gore, 1993, pp. 73–4)

The problem, then, is that 'empowerment' in some ways still presents an image of the passive recipient of power, a person for whom power is encouraged or bestowed. The implication is that individuals or groups do not have any power and must be given it: in some ways this does not move much beyond the deficit approach to women as a 'disadvantaged group'. The other problem is that in our somewhat competitive notions of power, we tend to assume that power means power *over* others, or that women will gain power at the expense of men. Authoritarian schooling *may* empower women through providing academic knowledge and credentials which enable them to compete; but this is not actually the aim of democratic schooling. Nor will the presence of even significant numbers of empowered women necessarily do much for gender equity unless those women – and their male colleagues – are committed to social transformation and the progress of other, less advantaged groups.

There has therefore been quite a strong critique mounted on the so-called 'empowering' properties of critical pedagogy and ethnographic research. Simply giving students 'a voice' through dialogue in the classroom or through revealing their perceptions and experiences in 'authentic' qualitative research does not of itself provide them with long-term competences and orientations for change (Troyna, 1994). As Ellsworth comments, 'Strategies such as student empowerment and dialogue give the illusion of equality while in fact leaving the authoritarian nature of the teacher/student relationship intact' (1989, p. 306). I would prefer, then, the notion of 'transformative' education rather than 'empowering', in that first, it carries with it a social rather than individual connotation; and second, that it implies an active engagement with change rather than being awarded rations of power. It is true that 'transformation', like 'empowerment', does not give a picture of what precise end is envisaged; but it would be inappropriate in a truly democratic political environment to prescribe and circumscribe such ends. The whole point about democratic education and a democratic constitution is that it seeks constantly to review and challenge existing practices – albeit within values of equity and social justice.

Conclusion: the democratic apprenticeship

Democratic schooling works from the premise that we all have 'power' within us, but that in fact this needs *practice* in recognizing, in exercising responsibly as well as in articulating. Models we have of democratic schools are ones where pupils exercise choices about roles, rules, relationships and learning. They are flexible. Some of this flexibility has come from a recognition of gendered needs, for example with shift schools in Ghana ensuring that girls who are contracted as housemaids can fulfil both educational and economic needs (Griffiths and Parker-Jenkins, 1994). Yet such flexibility should be merely part of a wider recognition of education adapting to children's needs rather than the other way round. Williams (1994), writing in an edition of *Forum* on 'Approaching democracy and education', lists solutions to problems of school attendance, such as permitting siblings to attend class or providing day-care centres for siblings, shift and seasonal schooling, non-graded unit-based curricula, allowing children to progress at their own pace, second-chance programmes, and the elimination of examinations in the early grades. These are in fact important features of the democratic schools in Colombia and Brazil cited earlier. Yet they are not there simply to prevent drop-out. They are there as part of an ethos which enables children to make responsible choices about their learning and to exercise political skills.

I have argued that the skills and orientations which are particularly important for equity are those of challenging existing unjust social, political and economic structures. The apprenticeship in this comes from observing teachers challenging discrimination, abuse and injustice in classrooms and wider settings, and from practising using power responsibly in school settings. This requires an openly sanctioned democratic management of the school, with features such as student councils, student representation and rotational leadership. This is not instant empowerment, but an apprenticeship in democracy – and one which females and males must undergo simultaneously.

We should beware the 'totalizing fallacy' that all women are dispossessed. Identities are contingent, so that in some contexts we are powerful, in others less so; sometimes gender is significant, sometimes not as significant as, say, age or 'race'. Gender equity paradoxically therefore will not come from a focus on 'women and girls', but from the struggle towards a society which has a respect for all equal rights and appreciation of all diversity. It has been the contention of this chapter that democratic schooling and democratic apprenticeship are first steps towards such a transformation.

References

Carr, M. (1993) Educational politics pushes children on to the streets, *Times Educational Supplement*, 24 December 1993, p. 10.

Chantavanich, A., Chantavanich, S. and Fry, G. (1990) *Evaluating Primary Education: Qualitative and Quantitative Studies in Thailand*. Ottawa: International Development Research Centre.

Cochrane, S. (1982) Education and fertility: an expanded examination of the evidence, in G. Kelly and C. Elliott (eds), *Women's Education in the Third World: Comparative Perspectives*. Albany: State University of New York Press.

Colbert, V., Chiappe, C. and Arboleda, J. (1993) The New School Program: more and better primary education for children in rural areas in Colombia, in H. Levin and M. Lockheed (eds), *Effective Schools in Developing Countries*. London: Falmer Press.

Connell, R. (1987) *Gender and Power*. Cambridge: Polity Press.

Davies, L. (1984) *Pupil Power: Deviance and Gender in School*. Lewes: Falmer Press.

Davies, L. (1992) School power cultures under economic constraint, *Educational Review*, **43**(2), 127–36.

Davies, L. (1993) Teachers as implementers or resisters, *International Journal of Educational Development*, **12**(4), 161–70.

Davies, L. (1994) *Beyond Authoritarian School Management: The Challenge for Transparency*. Ticknall: Education Now.

Davies, L. (1995) International indicators of democratic schools, in C. Harber (ed.), *Developing Democratic Education*. Ticknall: Education Now.

Davies, L. and Gunawardena, C. (1992) *Women and Men in Educational Management: An International Inquiry*. Paris: International Institute for Educational Planning.

Dighe, A. (1992) Education for women's equality: a pipe dream? A case from India, in *Women and Literacy: Yesterday, Today and Tomorrow*. Nordic Association for the Study of Education in Developing Countries Symposium Report, UNESCO.

Dovey, K. (1993) The role of non-formal education in South Africa, paper presented at the Oxford Conference on the Changing Role of the State in Educational Development, Oxford, September.

Ellsworth, E. (1989) Why doesn't this feel empowering? Working through the repressive myths of critical pedagogy, *Harvard Educational Review*, **59**, 297–324.

El-Sanabary, N. (1994) Female education in Saudi Arabia and the reproduction of gender divisions, *Gender and Education*, **6**(2), 141–50.

Erinosho, S. (1994) Nigerian women in science and technology, *Gender and Education*, **6**(2), 201–13.

Fuller, B. (1991) *Growing Up Modern: The Western State Builds Third World Schools*. London: Routledge.

Gordon, R. (1994) Education policy and gender in Zimbabwe, *Gender and Education*, **6**(2), 131–41.

Gore, J. (1993) *The Struggle for Pedagogies*. London: Routledge.

Griffiths, M. and Parker-Jenkins, M. (1994) Methodological and ethical dilemmas in international research: school attendance and gender in Ghana, *Oxford Review of Education*, **20**(4), 441–59.

Harber, C. (1989) *Politics in African Education*. London: Macmillan.

Harber, C. (1995) Democratic education and the international agenda, in C. Harber (ed.), *Developing Democratic Education*. Ticknall: Education Now.

John, P. and Osborn, A. (1992) The influence of school ethos on pupil citizenship attitudes, *Educational Review*, **44**(2), 153–65.

Joshi, G. and Anderson, J. (1994) Female motivation in the patriarchal school: an analysis of primary textbooks and school organization in Nepal, *Gender and Education*, **6**(2), 169–82.

Kang, S. W. (1995) Education, democracy and human rights in South Korea. Unpublished paper, University of Birmingham.

Kenway, J. (1995) Feminist theories of the state: to be or not to be? in M. Blair, J. Holland and S. Sheldon (eds), *Identity and Diversity: Gender and the Experience of Education*. Clevedon, Avon: Multilingual Matters/ Open University Press.

Kessler, S., Ashenden, D., Connell, R. and Dowsett, G. (1985) Gender relations in secondary schooling, *British Journal of Sociology of Education*, **6**(2), 133–54.

Leonardos, A. (1993) CIEP: a democratic school model for educating economically disadvantaged students in Brazil, in H. Levin and M. Lockheed (eds), *Effective Schools in Developing Countries*. London: Falmer Press.

Lind, A. (1992) Literacy: a tool for the empowerment of women? Women's participation in literacy programmes of the Third World, in *Women and Literacy, Yesterday, Today and Tomorrow*. Nordic Association for the Study of Education in Developing Countries Symposium Report, UNESCO.

Mac an Ghaill, M. (1994) *The Making of Men: Masculinities, Sexualities and Schooling*. Milton Keynes: Open University Press.

Mannathoko, C. (1994) Democracy in the management of teacher education in Botswana, *British Journal of Sociology of Education*, **15** (4), 481–96.

Mannathoko, C. (1995) Gender, ideology and the state in Botswana teacher education. Unpublished Ph.D. thesis, University of Birmingham.

Miles, S. and Middleton, S. (1995) Girls' education in the balance: the ERA and inequality, in L. Dawtrey, J. Holland, M. Hammer and S. Sheldon (eds), *Equality and Inequality in Education Policy*. Clevedon, Avon: Multilingual Matters/Open University Press.

Moll, I. For the sake of form: managing a rural South African school, *International Journal of Educational Development*, in press.

Mwansa, D. (1994) Community perspectives on gender, participation and culture in Zambian literacy programmes, *Gender and Education*, **6** (2), 151–68.

Rai, S. (1994) Modernization and gender: education and employment in post-Mao China, *Gender and Education*, **6**(2), 119–30.

Sara-Lafosse, V. (1992) Coeducational settings and educational and social outcomes in Peru, in N. Strom-quist (ed.), *Women and Education in Latin America: Knowledge. Power and Change*. Boulder, CO, and London: Lynne Rienner Publishers.

Schools Council (1981) *The Practical Curriculum* (quoted in Harber, 1995).

Schultz, L. (1994) Your daughters are not daughters but sons: field notes on being and becoming a woman teacher in Nepal and in Canada, *Gender and Education*, **6**(2), 183–200.

Sebakwane, S. (1994) Gender relations in Lebowe secondary schools, *Perspectives in Education*, **15**(1), 83–99.

Troyna, B. (1994) Blind faith? Empowerment and educational research, *International Studies in the Sociology of Education*, **4**(1), 3–24.

Vlassoff, C. (1994) Hope or despair? Rising education and the status of adolescent females in rural India, *International Journal of Educational Development*, **14**(1), 3–12.

Williams, J. (1994) The role of the community in education, *Forum for Advancing Basic Education and Literacy*, **3** (4), 20–1.

8 The Dissemination of Educational Research

KENNETH KING

The aim of this chapter is to highlight the important role played by educational research in a global context, and to try to draw a balance of advantage and disadvantage for developing countries from the modes and content of that distribution. The chapter is concerned exclusively with educational research, although some of the implications may also apply to other spheres of human knowledge. In this context, the chapter has three major foci: first, it considers the international environment within which the findings of educational research are made available. It argues that the advances in the field of educational technology and their impact on educational research appear to be widening the gap between developing and industrialized societies, while at the same time stimulating ever more intensive interaction and exchange among researchers within and across countries of the Organization for Economic Co-operation and Development (OECD). There are, however, a number of important exceptions to this general pattern, and these are discussed in the text. Second, the chapter discusses and reviews the principal vehicles for the dissemination of educational research with particular attention to those which may have potential for bridging the above-mentioned gap between developing and industrialized countries. Third, the chapter considers the somewhat vexed question of the relationship between research and its dissemination and impact on policy.

Research dissemination in a global context

The past decade has witnessed a substantial change in the world environment for research dissemination. A large number of the poorer countries in the developing world are, through economic crisis, debt, internal strife and imposed structural adjustment, less able than previously to sustain the infrastructure of higher education on which research has to depend. This has occurred at the same time as there has been an explosion in demand for higher education and, in some cases, an explosion in numbers.

Quality has been threatened, as is evidenced by the increasing difficulty faced by university and other libraries in maintaining and updating their collections, most particularly of those books and journals that require to be paid for in hard currencies at an exchange rate that reflects the massive and continuing devaluations of local currencies. Few universities have been able to institute programmes for the computerizing of their stock; librarians are often untrained; and on- and off-line computer searches, so much used in industrialized countries, are usually out of the question. Moreover, those essential elements of professional development such as in-house journals, study visits, exchanges and attendance at international and regional conferences, as well as visits by distinguished scholars, have also fallen victim to the need just to pay staff salaries.

Research production is also weakened in developing countries by the problems universities face in recruiting, retaining and adequately rewarding staff sufficiently for them to pursue full-time teaching and research careers. Inadequate remuneration has inevitably led to staff effectively working part time, whatever their nominal status. Additional income has had to be sought in ways that may be far removed from conventional research and teaching careers, with the certain result that research output in many countries has been reduced in both quantity and quality. In other words, there is less high-quality research to be disseminated from some countries in the world.

Since the end of the 1980s and the demise of the Cold War, the number of countries seen to be sharing similar infrastructural weaknesses, previously associated with the developing world, is increasing. However difficult the contacts between East and West and East and South were during the Cold War, many exchanges did take place, and the Soviet Union's and Eastern bloc's currencies were sufficiently strong for their own scholars to sustain a reasonable status in society and to allow for the purchase of essential bibliographical materials. Now many of the successor states of the Soviet Union are no longer able to profit from the research and other linkages which once existed within and across the Soviet Union and Eastern bloc. Moreover, they still have few existing contacts with Western educational research and very limited resources with which to initiate and sustain such contacts.

In the majority of OECD countries and in a number of the newly industrializing countries (NICs), cheaper and more powerful communications technology has encouraged much more rapid exchange of information in general and of educational research findings in particular, as a by-product of this technology revolution. The now massive storage, search and retrieval capacities associated with the specialized databases contained on compact discs (CD-ROM) provide to ordinary university students possibilities for literature review that would earlier have required considerable expertise and a great deal of time. Similarly, for academics concerned with the dissemination of their academic research, the process of publishing in recognized and refereed outlets leads automatically to the abstracts of their articles or books becoming part of these integrated and specialized databases.

Academics in the developing countries who publish in recognized journals have, of course, the same facility in theory, but the weaknesses in research infrastructure in these countries, including a lack of local funds for research, have made it increasingly difficult for them to publish in those journals which are scanned for entry to computerized databases.

The incorporation of research findings into the relevant specialized databases is a process that has also dramatically facilitated research dissemination. This incorporation is, however, an activity that has proceeded according to a set of organizational assumptions that have tended further to divide the research production of the poorer from the richer countries. For one thing, these international databases appear to have had criteria for inclusion of research material which inevitably lead to the exclusion of much of the research production that depends on the sometimes irregularly produced, locally circulated journals of many developing countries. The same is likely to be true of locally published books. By not being connected to the increasingly global publishing networks, such local research products may well not reach the compilers of specialized databases. Even within the industrialized world, research dissemination into these influential databases will be much more likely if the work is written in English or, to a lesser extent, French or Spanish than if it is in other European languages.

The incorporation of a great deal of easily accessible research into CD-ROM databases has been acknowledged as a dramatic improvement in data storage and dissemination, since the keywords and abstract from any single source can be readily identified and listed along with all other items that have the particular keywords being used in the search. The fact that a single CD-ROM computer disc can contain tens of thousands of abstracts and cover a whole field of enquiry such as social sciences or education abstracts for over a ten-year period has suggested to some analysts the possibility that this CD-ROM format could help to narrow the infrastructure gap between the libraries of the developing and industrialized world. It is certainly the case that for the cost of the CD-ROM reader and several database discs, an external agency could provide a wealth of abstracted information not currently available to poorer countries. Access to the abstracts alone, however, and not to the full texts of the original documents, articles and books, may by itself not compensate for the lack of up-to-date materials in the libraries of developing countries. Although developments with the worldwide web seem likely to make available access both to the abstracts and the full texts, this will still depend on a minimum level of computer infrastructure.

By contrast, in an industrialized country the search process may reveal a number of important articles, which can either be consulted in full in the library, or be accessed through other networked libraries or databases. This progressive interlinking of major data sources in the OECD countries is rapidly increasing the research dissemination potential in these environments. In addition, the spread of high-powered personal computing and the networking of whole universities and groups of users are making it possible for researchers to transfer directly to their own computers the outcomes of complex searches through these large databases. Within the OECD countries, therefore, the process of research dissemination has been dramatically changed by the ownership of personal computers which can be linked into larger and more powerful networks. The cost of a personal computer in the OECD countries is less than a tenth or fifteenth of an average university salary, whereas for many developing countries a microcomputer is much more than an entire annual salary, and would usually have to be purchased in a difficult-to-obtain hard currency.

The same is true of many of the accompaniments of the information revolution. Researchers in industrialized countries, including the NICs, will routinely have fax numbers along with telephone numbers on their business cards. Many will also include a personal electronic mail (e-mail) number. These facilities have many implications for rapid research dissemination among those who possess them. A researcher in the middle of composition can check on or ask for a piece of research data from a colleague, whether that colleague is located in Japan, the USA or elsewhere, and may well have the information back within an hour, subject only to the availability of the overseas colleague and the time zone being favourable. Similarly, within a few minutes, researchers can hear of a particular conference, can check on the possibility of being included in a particular session with the conference organizers, and can transmit the abstract of their proposed paper. They can also scan the conference programme through the Internet.

There is, thus, the possibility now for researchers linked by e-mail and fax to carry out a great deal of research dissemination at very little cost but at enormous speed. For researchers whose institutions are linked into the various text-packaging systems, it is entirely possible for two or three authors to work on parts of the same text and for the whole manuscript of several hundred pages to be moved around the world very easily.

Another dimension of research dissemination in the OECD countries that has been substantially transformed in the 1980s and 1990s has been the ability of researchers to produce, through laser printing and desktop publishing, a quality of printed output which is much closer to commercial publishing. The older distinctions in universities between Roneo- or Gestetner-produced papers (typed on to stencils and run off on manual or electric inking machines) and published papers have been significantly reduced. As a consequence, research results in research papers can be disseminated to wider audiences much more rapidly than before, and there is much greater scope for individual researchers, independently of the formal databases or commercial publishers, to disseminate their findings.

This potential for research dissemination and retrieval, which appears to be growing incrementally in the NICs and OECD countries, has not been paralleled in the developing world. There is, however, at least one exception to this growing information gap between North and South, and that is the regional education research and documentation network in Latin America, called REDUC (Red Latinoamericana de Información y Documentación). This structure has built up across the continent a network of national documentation centres that link into a cooperative organization for collecting and abstracting education research on Latin America, and making it available through conventional published collections (*resúmenes analíticos*), microfiche, hypertext and CD-ROM technology. This outstanding project has captured a significant proportion of the Latin American research output on education and vocational training over the past twenty years. The number of abstracts in 1992 reached 20,000 and the number of participating countries seventeen. The importance of this unique database on education research within an entire continent has underlined the advantage of operating in a single common language (in this case Spanish) and of securing over an extended period the substantial external funding needed to sustain it.

Mechanisms for the dissemination of educational research

In discussing the global information environment, several of the key modalities for research dissemination have already been mentioned, and in particular the routine collection and abstracting of research findings into specialized computer databases which are accessible to researchers and students, as well as potentially to policy-makers, in institutions that have access to this particular information technology. There are a number of other means for research dissemination that must be acknowledged, but where none the less those in developing countries are at an increasing disadvantage. For illustrative purposes the role of conferences, research networks and international organizations in the transfer of research findings will be briefly explored.

Conferences

Despite the massive rise of telecommunication technology and access to research results via the new information systems described earlier, several of the older forms of research dissemination appear not to have lost their attraction. The academic conference has not been undermined, for example, by the many alternative means of acquir-

ing research results. This can partly be explained by the importance of the human or personal dimension of research dissemination. Face-to-face interactive communication, dispute and debate can all to some extent be captured in teleconferencing, but there are still many dimensions of the successful research conference that cannot yet be acquired through other modalities.

Conferences have a very important function of facilitating the interaction of apprentice and established researchers, and they provide the mechanisms for the development and maintenance of less formal mechanisms for research dissemination. One of these would certainly be the 'informal college', a grouping of researchers working in different locations but on a similar theme or disciplinary region. The informal college encourages discussion, dissemination and future planning of research that may be nowhere captured in the formal conference record or in any of the available papers. It also underlines the importance in educational research and its dissemination of the personal and affective factors and dimensions.

Conferences are likely to remain popular, since they combine the formal, scientific model of research dissemination with the less formal mechanisms. Conferences, for example, provide many opportunities for the linkages between researchers and academic job markets to be explored. And here too it is well known that the personal, non-cognitive dimensions of researchers may prove also to be important for recruitment decisions. The relationships among good research, its dissemination and the recruitment of researchers are complicated by the interplay of cognitive and non-cognitive aspects of the research process.

Research networking

Another important vehicle for research dissemination is the network. One network, REDUC, has already been mentioned, and is responsible for carrying a great deal of research traffic within Latin America. Networks cover a considerable diversity of styles, membership and assumptions. They straddle the professional associations concerned with educational research, or, more accurately, with many different subfields of educational research, on the one hand, and the minimally institutionalized collections of like-minded researchers on the other. One of their assumptions seems to be linked with the importance of transferring information quickly round the nodes of the network. This characteristic emphasizes the speed with which the research networks can share information through many different modalities, such as newsletters, electronic bulletin boards, e-mail and fax. Such modalities tend to underline the democratizing aspects of networking. The other side of networking is equally evident, underlining the fact that networks are to some extent like clubs with limited membership. The transfer of information, therefore, will be limited to those who are members.

International organizations

No account of research dissemination in the field of education would be complete without mention of the role and power of the international organizations. Their powerful role arises not only through the research which they do and the immediacy of its dissemination, but also from the way in which that research, both in style and content, can be rapidly embodied in educational projects, and not least in the technical assistance dimensions.

These organizations also have the financial resources and the influence over the financially weakest and most dependent nations to make sure that their findings of educational research are taken very seriously. Only more recently have such organizations begun to turn to a much more participatory concept of project design and implementation, which can respect local knowledge and its value. But in the competition between local and international knowledge, there is little doubt which will prevail, given the paradigms and power of many international organizations.

The contrasts among these three faces of research dissemination are important for emphasizing that research dissemination is not an unproblematic objective, but one suffused with underlying assumptions and values, not least about which knowledge (and methodology) is most worthwhile. Research results or research information may be perceived as a kind of capital within the larger research community. The careful manipulation and utilization of one set of research results may lead to further funding and in turn further research grants. The process is often cumulative. A very open approach to research and its dissemination may reduce the comparative advantage of one researcher or research team as against another. A more closed approach towards the distribution of highly valued information – for example, about key meetings or the availability of research grants – may increase that advantage.

The different aspects of research networking may be used to consider the impact of networks on the information gap between North and South. There are certainly a number of networks, associated in many cases with the multilateral and bilateral agencies, the specialized agencies of the United Nations, and the international non-governmental organizations (NGOs) which are dedicated to providing information, at little or no cost, to the South. Diligent researchers in the South may be able to access a great deal of research information by becoming a member of one of these networks, and from them further connections may flow in the form of bulletins, newsletters and information about meetings and conferences.

But precisely because the research environment in the South is so weak, for reasons referred to earlier among others, as well as because of the different cultural traditions in many societies about the ownership of knowledge, it is sometimes the case that even when scarce research information is made available to a single point in such institutions, it then remains undisseminated for cultural reasons or through lack of communication capacity. The sheer scarcity in the South of research information and of opportunities to attend international research meetings may paradoxically make research dissemination more problematic than in the research-rich North.

Research dissemination and policy impact

Finally in this consideration of research and its dissemination, it is important to consider the frequently voiced aspiration on the part of some educational researchers that research should influence policy. The notion that research should somehow translate into policy derives from a view of research and policy which almost certainly pays insufficient attention to the differences in the culture of research and the culture of policy. Indeed, it may be more accurate to speak of research cultures and policy cultures, since there is certainly not a single variety of each. Be that as it may, it would appear that the primary targets of most research dissemination strategies are other researchers, through academic conferences, academic journals and the communications of learned societies. This is understandable, since the rewards and promotion tracks for academic research are intimately connected with publication in these very outlets.

The culture of policy-making, on the other hand, would appear to be far removed from the circles of academic papers, journals and specialized databases. Yet it is clear, at least in the North, that educational policy institutions, whether ministries of education, education project implementation units or education divisions of aid agencies, do all disseminate policy and policy papers which are informed, sometimes selectively, by commissioned educational research. Certainly the type of policy research associated with such institutions has its own character, which is in many ways different from the norms of academic research. Even when it is actually carried out by academics, in the form of contract or commissioned research, it may not be treated in the same way, or presented in the same register, as conventional research. For one thing, commissioned research may not be in the public domain, but may be owned by the contracting agency, which may maintain restrictions on its publication and further dissemination. The products may, in any case, not appear in any of the regular vehicles of dissemination. In other

words, such contract research may exhibit a different set of values and assumptions about openness of content and results as compared with ordinary academic research. And yet, once the findings of commissioned research have been incorporated into a major policy paper or a national report on education, these final products are often very widely disseminated indeed.

Again, there would appear to be major differences between research and policy-making in the North and the South. One additional complication arises for educational research dissemination in the South by dint of the fact that in many countries Northern aid agencies are seeking to reform the educational policy-making of national governments and are thus bringing to bear on Southern governments and their policies the conclusions of major reports and policy papers produced in the North. In this way, research commissioned in one context, sometimes with limited applicability outside that context, may be disseminated by aid agencies in another and used to legitimate educational policy decisions. This dubious use of educational research findings represents an increasing hazard for researchers and policy-makers in the South.

Conclusion

The scope for the dissemination of educational research, as well as its volume, has grown dramatically in the 1980s and early 1990s. New forms of educational research are being facilitated by the technological breakthroughs of the past decade, not least in the field of meta-studies and analytical compilations of research studies into composite reviews. Owing to the increasing pressure on academics in the North to publish or see their institution downgraded, the dilemma may well be how best to absorb the consequences of the global information revolution, and strike a balance between the pursuit of their own research priorities and the need to accommodate the most relevant findings from the mass of those to which they now have very easy access. In many of the weaker countries of the South, by contrast, both the pursuit of independent research and the regular receipt of the world's research output in any particular field is in increasing crisis, and likely to be more so for the foreseeable future. To avoid this further widening of the gap between North and South, new strategies will be needed from the North and the South and from the aid agencies which support education projects in the South. Not only will greater attention have to be paid to the consequences for the South of a global information revolution, from which only the North will be able to draw full advantage, but renewed attention will have to be given to newer modalities which might still enable the South to leapfrog some of the stages of educational research and its dissemination through which the North has had to pass.

Note

An earlier version of this chapter was published as 'The dissemination of educational research' in the *International Encyclopedia of Education*. Oxford: Pergamon, 1994.

Further reading

Gmelin, W. and King, K. (eds) (1992) *Strengthening Analytical and Research Capacities in Developing Countries*. Bonn: German Foundation for International Development.

Hudson, B. *et al.* (1980) *Knowledge Networks for Educational Planning: Issues and Strategies*. Research Report 36. Paris: International Institute for Educational Planning, UNESCO.

International Institute for Educational Planning (1991) *Strengthening Educational Research in Developing Countries*. Paris: IIEP, UNESCO.

King, K. (1991) *Aid and Education in the Developing World*. Harlow: Longman.

McGinn, N. F. and Borden, A. M. (1995) *Framing Questions, Constructing Answers: Linking Research with Education Policy for Developing Countries*. Harvard Studies in International Development. Cambridge, MA: Harvard Institute for International Development.

NORRAG News (1992) Special issue on Networking in Education and Training, no. 13, December. Edinburgh: Centre of African Studies, University of Edinburgh.

REDUC, *Resúmenes analíticos en educación*, serial publication of abstracts of REDUC (Red Latinoamericana de Información y Documentación). Santiago, Chile: CIDE.

Shaeffer, S. and Nkinyangi, J. (eds) (1983) *Educational Research Environments in the Developing World*. Ottawa: International Development Research Centre.

9 The Role of Aid Agencies and Academic Institutions in Reducing Educational Dependence

CAROL A. KOCHHAR

Introduction

Global transformations occurring in economic, social and political arenas are affecting the economic and human resource potential of developing nations. Economic transformations and new technology are also altering the nature of work and the workplace in both developed and developing nations. In many developing nations new international economic policies are emerging which reflect countries' efforts to enter the industrial world, rather than just narrowly sustaining themselves. These transformations require country responses to educate and prepare all children and youth to participate in local and country-level economic and social changes. Such participation requires first and foremost the establishment of a coherent system of universal primary education which can ensure both the *right to access* to and the *means for acquiring* an education. Legal rights and assurances are empty unless there is a clear commitment of resources to provide the *means* for obtaining knowledge and skills relevant for community and national participation. The goal of universal primary education for all is central to the goals of broader economic growth within developing countries. Developing countries and countries in social and economic decline have depended on substantial assistance in order to accomplish these goals. Reducing the dependence of chronically underdeveloped nations requires not only economic development assistance but investment in human resources. Such a strategy is grounded in the assumption that greater educational and economic opportunity will bring social stability and self-determination. The use of aid for economic development and institution-building for self-reliant development must necessarily involve cooperation among various academic, governmental, business and non-governmental institutions in both developed and developing nations.

There is widespread evidence that foreign aid has not helped produce the broad-based economic and social development results expected by aid agencies. In many cases humanitarian aid has created long-term dependence and has done little to spur economic development. There is also considerable evidence being accumulated that shows that even specific economic aid seems to hinder development more than promote it (Bandow, 1985; Packenham, 1992).

Aid agencies, or 'helping' organizations, have often contributed to dependence in many ways. Major aid agencies have not promoted the full participation in the practical and policy decisions about development by the people who are affected by them. The conditions that have led to such dependence are examined in order better to understand the connection between economic dependence, educational dependence and the right to universal basic education for all citizens. This examination is then followed by the raising of a new set of assumptions about educational empowerment and interdependence, promotion of inclusive education, and the strategies needed to promote it from an intersectoral approach (shared responsibility). An intersectoral approach means that the goals of education are integrally linked to goals of improved nutrition and health conditions as preconditions for learning and sustained participation in primary education.

A major theme in this chapter is that aid agencies can be most successful in playing a significant role in fostering self-sustaining education development in countries where there is genuine desire on the part of the people to accept change, and the political process is conducive to broad-based social and political change. The involvement of aid agencies and developed nations in the affairs of the world places new demands on education and human resource development. Yet, according to some development experts, few educational development efforts have been thought through in terms of ends and means (Ingham, 1993; Brademus, 1987; Lema, n.d.). If aid agencies are not to waste human and financial resources, their leaders must begin to think through what is being accomplished under the rubric of 'educational assistance'. Dependency theory and its application in educational development are important because of the sheer magnitude of the impact of these ideas upon developing countries and because they provide a window through which to view broader development issues. Important philosophical questions related to educational development initiatives are: education for whom, when, how, according to what priorities, in what areas, and for what ultimate aims?

Failure of aid agencies and academic institutions to achieve their goals

Unhelpful economic assistance

Zimmerman (1993) concludes that over the past half century, the United States and other developed nations have spent billions of dollars on foreign economic assistance which has largely failed to achieve its economic and social development goals. Instead, it has been used as a tool to promote the political and security objectives of the assisting nations. Such assistance has failed primarily because it has been politically driven, and 'promotes the trappings of modernization, but not necessarily development' (p. 234). Zimmerman argues that lack of attention to such objectives of empowerment of people – particularly in education – ultimately undermines short-term political and security successes. Recently, development economists have been criticized for applying a 'goods-centered' view of development rather than a 'people-centered' development ethic (Ingham, 1993). Efforts by aid agencies which create ineffective assistance and which fail to 'teach people how to fish' help ensure that aid agencies continue indefinitely providing welfare-type assistance. They fail to create conditions for self-sufficiency and self-determination with the broadest possible participation by host country leaders and citizens.

Economic dependence and universal access to education

The development process in many recipient nations has not significantly affected the majority of their people. Also, conditions that have led to unhelpful economic assistance for social-sector development have often created unhelpful educational assistance and educational dependence.- International development experts have observed that external aid counts for about 9 to 10 per cent of all expenditures on education and that this money tends to be invested in the most urgently needed and useful activities and resources (Ingham, 1993; Hurst, 1981). For example, the bilateral donors of the Organization for Economic Cooperation and Development (OECD) allocate about 12 per cent of their total aid to education on average. Japan and the USA spend less that 3 per cent, whereas Norway and France spend 28 and 34 per cent respectively (Hurst, 1981). The World Bank, by contrast, lends about 6 to 7 per cent of its funds in education. Although aid to education represents a small percentage of technical assistance loans, its impact on policy-making in developing regions is often significant (Bujazan *et al.*, 1987). The demand for technical assistance continues indefinitely when the skills and expertise required cannot be supplied locally. Aid may have helped expand education by providing buildings and teachers, but it has not contributed significantly to the development of coherent educational *systems*. The reorientation of aid agencies towards the development of strategies for empowerment within the recipient country will help to overcome barriers to the goal of universal primary education and the inclusion of all children, youth and adults in education.

The goal of providing universal primary education for all is central to the goals of broader economic growth within recipient countries. Education has been referred to by many international experts as the key to country development. The task of educational assistance efforts is to focus on the function of education in the total effort to improve the conditions of life in rapidly developing societies and to impact the total process by which people are *motivated to help themselves* through communication and national and international action. 'Education' includes informal, community and adult education as well as that which goes on inside schools and universities. Issues of dependence affect the major goals of education: individual and personal development (longevity and knowledge), wealth creation consistent with environmental sustainability, and democratic nation-building. Fostering dependence is in direct opposition to the assumption that ownership and self-determination and the involvement of local communities in control of their own destiny are critical factors in each of these areas of educational development. Traditionally, aid agencies have focused their efforts on supporting infrastructure development for education (school buildings, materials, etc.) but not on changing social, economic or political structures to create new values and attitudes which can affect education (Zimmerman, 1993; Ingham, 1993; Sayigh, 1991, 1982).

Conditions of children and the need for educational development

The current conditions for children in most developing nations necessitate a continued commitment from developed nations to assist with educational development. Many developing countries, such as those in Asia and Latin America, have made significant gains in human resources in the past fifty years. The overall death rate in developing regions has improved from 25–30 per thousand in the 1950s to 10–15 per thousand in the 1980s. Life expectancy has risen from 40 years in 1945 to 62 years in the 1990s. Literacy rates have increased greatly since 1945, with enrolments in higher education increasing by a factor of 20; in secondary education by a factor of 15; and in primary education by a factor of 5 (Ingham, 1993; United Nations, 1992). It is important to recognize these achievements, but also to realize the growing difficulties developing countries are having in continuity such progress in the face of severely limited or diminishing resources.

During the past few decades there has been an expansion of school enrolments throughout the developing regions, but the rapid population increases threaten to erase the impacts of these achievements. It is estimated that between 1980 and 2000 the world's population will increase from 4.5 to 6 billion persons (Hurst, 1981). Of the total population of school age children, there is a large portion who are not gaining access to primary education. These include the following:

1   Approximately one-third of the children of primary school age in the developing countries do not attend school at all (Lynch, 1994; Hurst, 1981).

2   About a third of the adult population is illiterate.

3   It is estimated that there are some 130 million children between the ages of 6 and 11, many with impairments and learning disabilities, who are not receiving any kind of basic or primary education, 60 per cent of them girls (UNICEF, 1991).

4   More than one-third of children entering the first grade in many countries in Asia fail to

reach the end of the primary cycle (Mingat and Tan, 1992).

5   The World Health Organization (1992) estimates that of children who have severe and multiple impairments, only about 1 to 2 per cent receive institutional services and the majority are excluded totally from school.

With the significant expansion of primary education in the past decade, many children with special learning needs have been enrolling in primary schools. These children are at risk of repeating or dropping out because of poverty, hunger, malnutrition, environmental or cultural reasons, or have minor impairments that impede their performance (Lynch, 1995). Many educators also believe that high drop-out and repetition rates reflect learning problems and that poor educational provision is the root cause. The size of the population of children with special educational needs in many developing countries is difficult to quantify owing to the lack of standardized screening instruments to diagnose impairments, the absence of clear standards for what constitutes disability, the lack of properly conducted population studies, lack of knowledge on the part of governments that are reporting data, and the fact that some impairments are reversible and disabilities can be overcome (Lynch, 1994; Jonsson, 1993).

The world prevalence rate for impairments was estimated by the World Health Organization and the United Nations Children's Fund (1978) to be about 19 per cent. This figure has been generally accepted and adopted by other United Nations agencies (the ILO, UNESCO, UNICEF) and international non-governmental organizations (NGOs) concerned with disability issues. On the basis of a 10 per cent figure, the total number of persons with impairments in the world was approximately 450 million in 1980, 500 million in 1990, and is expected to rise to well over 600 million by the end of this century (approximately 40 per cent of this population is expected to comprise school age children). UNICEF estimates that 140 million children with learning difficulties and significant impairments are living in developing countries, 88 million of them in Asia, 18 million in Africa, 13 million in Latin America. Only 11 million live in

Europe and 6 million in North America. One family in four is estimated to be affected by impairment in one way or another over the life of the school age children (UNICEF, 1991; UNESCO, 1990; WHO, 1978). The magnitude of the population of children in need of specialized educational services requires that educational development efforts promote inclusion of all children in the educational system. The goal of universal primary education for all is central to the goals of economic and political empowerment in developing countries.

Educational dependence and its promotion by aid agencies and academic institutions
Conventional development theory which has been driving aid agency policies over the past few decades is being re-evaluated in light of newly accumulated research on the questionable impact of development aid. An Agency for International Development (AID, 1989) review of the impact of foreign assistance by the USA concluded that 'all too often, dependency seems to have won out over development ... only a handful of countries that started receiving US assistance in the 1950s and 1960s have ever graduated from dependent status' (p. 111–12). In the 1960s and earlier it was noted by several diplomacy experts that these efforts had not contributed to long-term development goals shared by aid agencies and host countries (McGhee, 1967; Kennedy, 1961; Osgood, 1953). Ironically, with the Foreign Assistance Act of 1961, Congress established the AID to administer economic aid and advance US policy objectives. The goals of military aid and development assistance were integrated.

Development assistance is provided to host countries by a variety of institutions including governmental organizations, private voluntary organizations, non-governmental organizations, academic institutions and business organizations. Many developing countries rely upon external agencies in the development of education from policy and planning to major reform efforts at all educational levels, both formal and informal. The lure of assistance is considerable and if an agency is willing to finance certain kinds of projects, then the host government is likely to arrange its educational plan to accommodate the projects it deems fundable (Spaulding, 1981). For example, for decades before the Marxist government took over in 1978, Afghanistan pursued a policy of educational 'non-alignment', which meant that it initiated a variety of projects in many educational fields that foreign donors were willing to support. A patchwork of programmes were funded by the Germans, French, Americans, the then Soviet Union, UNESCO and the World Bank, and others, each with little relationship to one another (McGinn *et al.*, 1985; Spaulding, 1981). The non-alignment policy of the government allowed various external agencies to do what they liked as long as they financed it. The Afghan government, like many other developing countries at that time, lacked planning capacity to develop an integrated education system.

There are many factors related to these organizations and aid agencies which create ineffective assistance, continue indefinitely providing welfare-type assistance, and fail to develop coherent educational planning. Welfare-oriented assistance does not promote sustainable development, which has been defined as empowering people, creating self-sufficiency and self-determination with the broadest possible participation by host country leaders and the people who will be affected (Hasanain, 1995; Zimmerman, 1993; Packenham, 1992; AID, 1992; Sayigh, 1991; Bujazan *et al.*, 1987; Lema, n.d.).

What is educational dependence, who contributes to it and what are the impacts of such dependence on education development? What is the role of governmental, non-governmental and academic institutions on continuation of educational development in developing nations? Sumner and Erickson (1985) defined development as a growth in the number of feasible choices available to the host country which contributes to long-term growth but which may even hamper the country's progress if relief becomes permanent. International assistance is aimed at helping to promote a sustained expansion of another nation's overall economic well-being.

Chambers (1983) referred to dependence as the 'deprivation trap', a mutually reinforcing situation

of powerlessness, vulnerability, physical weakness, poverty and isolation into which the majority of poor people are locked. Such disenfranchisement is associated with strong centralization and professionalization of development efforts, including reliance on external expertise. For example, educational research efforts are important to developing countries because they stimulate the development, reform and organization of educational practices and help train internal experts. Foreign funds for research are often necessary because of the absence of local research money. In the southern core of Latin America, social science research institutes, including those concerned with education, have reconstituted themselves as private centres outside the universities and are entirely dependent on foreign funds. Short-term externally funded research efforts tend to be insecure, pay little attention to the research environment, local norms and structures, tend to exclude participation by local students and scholars, and tend not to reflect local conditions and priorities (King, 1981). Under these conditions, the likelihood is that the research information generated will not be relevant for long-term, sustainable development. It is also unlikely that there will be recipient government interest in the findings since these centres are outside the regular university system and therefore have little formal responsibility for training a new generation of students for research.

Certain forces in society tend to centralize, rather than decentralize, development activities and to contribute to dependency. Sayigh (1982, 1991) suggests four characteristics central to the 'dependency school' of development:

1   a small group of advanced Western countries dominate a group of less developed countries;
2   these dominant countries transfer power to transnational corporations in the form of 'foreign aid' and skim the economic surplus generated in the recipient country;
3   these dominant countries inhibit self-determination and development in the host countries, thereby perpetuating dependence and underdevelopment; and

4 internal country factors such as class structure, interest groups, and institutions designed to serve the powerful also perpetuate a dependency relationship with external agencies.

In summary, the countries receiving outside aid remained incapable on developing from within in a sustainable manner.

In terms of social and educational progress in developing countries, conditions such as those described earlier perpetuate gross and widening maldistribution of wealth and income, poorly spread health services and persistence of disease, insufficient manpower development and technical training, high rates of unemployment, limited access to education, particularly by women, insufficient and faulty formal education systems and philosophies, a narrow base of political participation and lack of respect for basic rights and individual freedom. For educational development assistance to be effective, it must increase the net investment in the *means* of education in poor countries, encourage nations to adopt educational policy reforms, encourage nations to adopt policies of universal rights to education at all levels, improve the access of women to education at all levels, and involve both private and public institutions (Ingham, 1993; Clark, 1992; Sumner and Erickson, 1985). The participation of women is another factor with an important relationship to continued educational dependency. Women may be denied access to education at all levels because of structural barriers created by aid agencies and academic institutions.

Table 9.1 summarizes the work of numerous writers in dependence and development theory and presents features of host country dependence on aid agencies with implications for educational development.

The definition of development proposed by Norman Jacobs (1971) reflects the recognition that development means commitment to change and empowerment, and is an open-ended commitment to objectivity. According to Jacob's definition, innovation is accepted or rejected according to whether or not it contributes to maximizing the society's potential. The principles of dependence apply not only to developing nations, but also to more advanced nations such as those in the Middle East, which are currently facing conditions in which there is a dismantling of social, economic, cultural, educational and psychological fabrics that have been crucial to their survival for centuries. These influences are due both to factors that are external to the country – the influence of multinational corporations or governments – and to internal factors such as conflicts among subpopulation groups (Fasheh, 1995). The requirement in time and energy needed to deal with the underlying problems of cultural dependence and societal restructuring presents an overwhelming challenge to the country's capacity to address the demands of educating and preparing children, youth and adults for the work of the nation. It is helpful to examine the purposes of different aid agencies involved in educational development and review examples of how each contributes to dependence as defined in Table 9.1.

How aid agencies contribute to dependence

Governmental institutions such as AID and the Peace Corps provide economic support funds, development assistance to support social and economic programmes, and food aid. The US Peace Corps sends qualified men and women to help meet the needs of developing countries, as specified by the Peace Corps Act 1961. Governmental organizations also work closely with *academic institutions* in implementing aid projects. Often external governmental personnel are viewed by recipient country leaders as pursuing their own political or social agendas and lacking genuine concern for the country's people. Government agency personnel may also be reluctant to gather the cultural and political information that could be relevant for educational development efforts because they do not want to be misinterpreted as having a political agenda (North, 1989). *Multinational institutions* include organizations such as the International Monetary Fund (IMF), the

Table 9.1 Characteristics of dependence and implications for educational development

Broad characteristics	Implications for educational development
External aid is viewed as an entitlement and the host country views the aid agency as a 'saviour'.	Educational aid is viewed as an entitlement and the host country may operate under the belief that it lacks the resources for anything other than the basic survival needs of its people.
Aid funds are used to support the country's own existing governmental organizations.	The country's existing governmental organizations fail to support equitable educational development, are inefficient or inequitable in providing education, and are unable to support broad and intersectoral educational development. Assistance levels are not based on the recipient government's capacity to use the assistance effectively for economic and social purposes.
The country cannot sustain development initiatives.	Aid-initiated educational development projects are terminated when the aid declines; minimal or no local and national-level resources are invested in the projects. There is a tendency to spend the money too fast (more money is available than there are projects).
The host country fails to use aid to develop and expand its own human, natural and financial resources.	Generally, aid is focused not on basic educational needs, but rather on continuing and advanced education of the country's privileged and élite. The educational aid is devoted to activities, particularly in higher education, which benefit only rich and élite segments of the population instead of achieving a broader distribution of resources to permit broader participation by the population.
The host country capitulates to the agendas of external agencies.	The host country leaders adopt the educational agendas of external agencies and fail to insist on their own internal goals for education and define their own educational performance measures or outcomes.
The host country fails to achieve meaningful political freedom.	Country leaders lack understanding of the relationship between political freedom and education development and the goal of universal access; they do not view schools as a major instrument or socializing agency where learning about democracy and free enterprise takes place.
Legal instruments are not set up so as to support broad development.	There is a failure to achieve broad social reform and limited impact on legal reform. Legal instruments are not developed to support the goals of universal primary education, equal access to education for all and, most importantly, the *means* for acquiring education. Aid projects that concentrate solely on developing legal rights instruments without developing the means for acquiring quality basic education are not likely to result in sustainable educational progress.
Strong central government control over the development processes (Zimmerman, 1993).	There is a failure to establish educational programmes which directly support the democratization process. International development efforts unwittingly perpetuate social and economic inequities in recipient countries. People of underdeveloped countries are represented at aid conferences by élites who lack the will to solve the problems of the vast majority.
Participation of local people in planning, allocation of aid and in decisions that affect their destinies does not occur.	Local participation in planning educational projects, setting educational priorities, and allocating aid for education is weak.
Representation of women in development projects is limited.	Participation in educational planning and access to basic and higher education are limited for the general population, particularly for women.
Sound development criteria are not adhered to.	Educational projects may develop through the initiation of a variety of internal organizations and may not complement each other or have connections with each other. A coherent system of educational development fails to emerge.
Since there is limited involvement of local communities in the project planning, local ownership over the project and commitment to change by host country leaders fail to occur.	Educational development projects are viewed by host country leaders as 'belonging' to the external agency or foreign aid entity and therefore there is a 'hands-off' policy and lack of commitment to internal change or reform.
There is limited change in broader social, economic or political structures to create new values and attitudes.	When there is little change in broader social, economic or political structures, new values crucial to educational development – equity, local participation, inclusion, universal primary education, holistic and developmental frameworks for education, child-centred strategies – are not developed.
Aid recipients do not feel more empowered or in control of their destinies as a result of the aid or assistance.	Educational leaders do not feel empowered or in control of the distribution of educational aid and the substance and structure of educational programmes. Lack of self-determination makes universal primary education less accessible for children, youth, families and adult citizens.

Broad characteristics	Implications for educational development.
Host country leaders may manipulate aid agents to reverse negotiated policies.	Host country leaders may manipulate aid agents to renegotiate policies crucial for educational development or may seek reversals or waivers of initial conditions for educational reform, thereby preventing or slowing authentic and meaningful change.
The host country continues to rely upon external expertise; internal dialogue and consensus-building on policies fail to occur.	The host country continues to rely upon external personnel and experts for support rather than build internal capacity and expertise through technical training and higher education. Host country leadership is unable to create internal dialogue and consensus-building on educational policy issues crucial to implementation of universal basic education for all, and to facilitate new internal coalitions to support education reforms.
Host country is unable to project or assess its own needs.	Educational needs of the general population may not be assessed, or there may be minimal or no participation of local leaders in the establishment of educational priorities; the needs of the few are represented in country-level educational development and policy discussions.
Aid agencies and host countries pay little attention to monitoring and have weak communication systems by which to manage projects.	There is a lack of continuous, informal communication at the working level on educational development issues. Excessive bureaucracy of the educational aid agencies weakens leadership and vision and there is high ambiguity regarding the purposes and implementation approaches to the aid. Educational planning processes avoid clear delineation of responsibilities.
Traditional beliefs about democracy and economic development need to be reassessed.	Western traditional belief is that democracy depends first on achieving strong economic development; the reverse may be true because democracy improves the chance for sustainable economic growth by ensuring the broadest possible participation by empowered people. Aid agencies and host countries fail to foster self-sustaining political, social and economic institutions, and promote active participation from and with the increasingly empowered and knowledgeable people (Sayigh, 1991; Zimmerman, 1993).
There is mistrust between host countries and donor nations and cultures.	Host country leaders view donor agencies and nations with scepticism and believe that aid agencies seek control over information for purposes of bringing about changes in values, orientations and cultures and of the imposition of the Western capitalist consumer culture (Sayigh, 1991; Galtung *et al.*, 1980).
Aid is used solely for infrastructure development without addressing human resource needs.	Aid is devoted to the building of school buildings and little is used to invest in training and retaining teachers who can provide appropriate and relevant education. There is little focus on facilitating or identifying development-oriented leadership within the educational system and other sectors such as business, the media and labour.
Host countries do not use aid to coordinate resources and help use them efficiently.	Education development is not linked with health-related and nutritional improvements (health as the pre-condition for schooling). There may be a tendency toward over-specialization of experts and academic personnel and a general failure to understand problems from an intersectoral or multi-disciplinary perspective.
There are conflicts between the longer-term goals of development and short-term goals of political considerations.	Educational projects tend to be implemented as short-term projects that may catch the attention of those in political power, but there is little coherence and connection among such projects.
Long-term plans are poorly articulated and communicated.	There is a lack of adequate long-term educational development plans and lack of an active voice of implementers in such planning. Documents are written in the passive voice, which obscures responsibility among agencies and leads to a general atrophy of communication.
Aid agencies develop plans in isolation from the recipient countries.	Educational aid agendas are developed without adequate participation of recipient countries, recognition of the political and bureaucratic contexts of each project, or serious dialogue on educational development issues and priorities between aid agencies and recipient countries. There may also be a lack of political analysis skills to take into account the political factors that create barriers to sustainable educational development, and ignorance of local languages and social and political cultures.

World Bank and the United Nations Development Programme (UNDP), the Asian Development Fund and the African Development Fund. These institutions provide economic aid and enforce tough development-oriented conditions (Zimmerman, 1993). *Private voluntary organizations* (PVOs) channel donor government and aid agency funds through private voluntary organizations and other *non-governmental organizations* (NGOs).

Barriers can be created when the objectives of multinational or non-governmental organizations conflict with or are unwelcome in the country-specific context. For example, vigorous promotion of women's participation in development projects can create resistance in Muslim countries (Zimmerman, 1993). Similarly, promoting inclusion of all individuals, including girls, and individuals with impairments, in educational activities and planning may create resistance, particularly when local people and leaders have superstitious beliefs about women or individuals with disabilities. Aid agreements are more effective when they address these barriers and include provisions or conditions in project agreements that promote inclusive educational policies and practices. In addition, aid organizations often have special interests and conduct projects on their own with considerable independence and detachment from local decision-making. They often contribute to a patchwork of programmes with their own teams of experts, which fragments efforts at building coherent educational systems within developing countries (Mason, 1990; Spaulding, 1981). Training programmes of various technical assistance efforts are also often managed in a similar way, supplying cadres of trained personnel who are extensions of the institutions in which they are trained, but who do not share common educational development goals and ideologies.

Academic institutions include colleges and universities within countries as well as international units which serve more than one country. Technical assistance of academic institutions is a major channel for technology transfer from high-income to low-income countries. This assistance may involve sending experts to work in developing countries to help them make better use of their existing resources, and providing education and training at home or abroad for citizens of those countries to help them add to the country's human resources. Deficiencies of these forms of technical assistance have been discussed by many international development experts (Packenham, 1992; Wilhelm and Feinstein, 1984). A common form of technical assistance in educational development has been that in which an expatriate resident adviser or expert works with a local 'counterpart', or someone to be trained on the job and, theoretically, take over when the expert leaves. These forms of technical assistance have been found problematic because recruitment of the right people where they are most needed is difficult. Also, the 'experts' are usually better paid, and are viewed by their local counterparts as having questionable commitment to the country in which they are working. The training of the successor, if it occurs at all, is often ineffective, and the transfer of responsibility for educational development and expertise fails to take place (Berg, 1984). Commitments to educational development were made from the 1950s to the 1970s by many multinational organizations such as the World Bank, UNESCO, the Organisation for Economic Co-operation and Development (OECD) and the North Atlantic Treaty Organization (NATO). Many developing countries became increasingly dependent on these multinational organizations, particularly for higher education development (Clark, 1992; Clark *et al.*, 1991).

Academic institutions can also contribute to country dependence by becoming as dependent upon the aid project as are the recipients. In addition, academic institutions promote dependence by not adhering to sound development criteria. For example, in one case, three project evaluations between 1979 and 1984 found that the Massachusetts Institute of Technology in the USA had failed to correct deficiencies that were impeding attainment of its project objective: self-sustaining research capacity within the Egyptian university community (Zimmerman, 1993). Universities often have special interests that impede sustainable development in host countries. Universities create training programmes for host countries and bring country leaders and personnel to the USA for short-term training or long-term advanced education. Yet universities are prone to use their connections with central governments to maintain access to aid funds and obtain earmarks, even when their performance may have limited benefit for the host country. Universities can be very effective development agents, but they can also create resentment when the recipient country cannot easily terminate a contract for non-performance. In these cases, the aid contracts serve to help the universities gain access to host country information rather then achieving transfer of knowledge and technology to that recipient (Pianin, 1992). The aid is viewed by the recipient country as providing returns primarily to the aid agency or donor nation and not to the recipient country for purposes of promoting self-sustaining educational development.

Business and labour groups provide assistance in economic reforms and development of enterprises. Often these agencies, too, become as dependent upon the aid as are the recipients. Some large businesses use their connections with the US Congress and with other central governments to create laws and regulations that benefit them and may continue the dependence of the host country on goods, cash aid or political influence. Such special interests impede policy dialogues and reduce the likelihood that sustained and self-sustaining capacity will be developed. Business interests often favour private organizations over public ones, making it less likely that public organizations will get the help they need to improve their efficiency and make needed reforms.

Continued educational dependence is created and perpetuated by a variety of aid agencies and academic institutions. Many international observers are reassessing the reforms and development efforts sponsored by aid agencies, many of which have been criticized as paternalistic interventions in the name of equality. As Lionel Trilling wrote in 1947, 'moral passions are even more willful and imperious and impatient than the self-seeking passions ... Some paradox in our nature leads us, once we have made our fellow men the objects of our enlightened self-interest, to go and to make them the objects of our pity, then our wisdom, ultimately of our coercion' (p. 72). Though civil rights interests have awakened special-interest

groups to the need for grassroots organization, such change is often accompanied by a healthy local scepticism towards new laws, regulations and policies, and a natural vigilance on the part of local people in seeking to protect themselves and their communities from 'coercion' and the invasive power of government and external agencies.

Need for a paradigm shift

Economists and social scientists alike have called for a change in the philosophy of development policy to reflect the primacy of the human dimension and the promise of self-reliant development. What is self-reliant or self-sustaining development and what are its implications for educational development? Over the past two decades, several development experts have defined development in a manner that incorporates concepts of country, community and individual self-reliance. Jacobs (1971) used the term 'development' to include empowerment as part of the change process. The word 'development' should be understood to include the concept of empowerment of people as individuals and groups seeking to control their own destinies. Rather than a method of transferring know-how, 'empowered development' means a process of *developing* know-how – a process, for example, of finding out what will work in Bangladesh, rather than simply transferring what has been found to work in New York or London.

Galtung *et al.* (1980) identified thirteen points which define 'self-reliant development', among which is included a change in the country's priorities towards production for the basic needs of those most in need, compatibility with local conditions and, greater participation of the general population. Zimmerman (1993) refers to 'genuine' development, which, like Slater's (1989) 'authentic development', is viewed as inseparable from the sustainable growth of democracy and peace. According to Sayigh (1991, p. 95), self-reliant development is characterized by the following aspects:

1   The country expresses determination to seek regeneration and to depend on itself to the maximum extent possible.

2   The practice of self-reliance applies to the individual village or community and the whole-country level.

3   Self-reliance means cooperation within villages and communities for self-help, cooperation and exchange with other communities, establishment of strategies and structures for action, awareness of the power of self-reliance and cooperation, and promotion of philosophies, attitudes, values and patterns of behaviour and policies which all serve the pursuit of self-reliance at the local and national level and beyond at the regional level.

Jameson *et al.* (1991) outlined five human development aspects that economists need to take into account in order to pursue people-oriented development policies, namely attention to expanding capabilities, focusing on beneficiaries, the role of women, culture sensitivity, and assessing social costs. These themes are also reflected in the work of many contemporary development writers.

1   *Focus on expanding capabilities.* Distributional objectives should be placed ahead of the goal of economic growth. Economic development means expanding capabilities. Development questions, therefore, are framed in terms of human outcomes: what are people capable of doing? A people-oriented approach addresses the question, 'Can people read and write?', not 'How much is being spent on primary education?' It asks, 'Are people living longer?', not 'What is the expenditure on health?' It is obvious that an individual who is illiterate and in poor health does not have the same capabilities, even if he or she has the same level of income, as someone who is literate and healthy.

2   *Place beneficiaries at the centre.* People-oriented development policies refer to people as beneficiaries, to be benefited, rather than as 'problems', or 'target groups', to be 'impacted' by policy. If the technicians, bureaucrats and planners are viewed as the 'solutions', then the potential contributions that can be made by the beneficiaries are often discounted. In implementing people-oriented policies, attention to the needs of the poor in developing countries becomes central in aid policies and bilateral and multinational aid for education is provided first and foremost to support host government undertakings (Wilhelm and Feinstein, 1984).

3   *Meaningful participation of women.* People-oriented development acknowledges the role of women because they bear a disproportionate share of poverty and because they play an essential role in family development and productive community activities. This involves changing traditional perceptions of women and rejecting arguments for the subordination of women. External investments in education have been found to be responsible for supporting practices that deny women equal access to higher education and lower women's relative access to educational, economic and political resources (Meillassoux, 1981; United Nations, 1988).

Sustainable educational development requires the representation of all segments of the population in the development effort, particularly women. Women are particularly important in educational development because they are the primary nurturers and trainers of the next generation, particularly at the elementary and secondary levels. In the USA the strength of the Catholic elementary schools has been attributed to the efforts of women educators. Women are central for early childhood development, and in countries which emphasize the role of women in raising children, such as Islamic nations, formalization of women's role in childhood education through higher education and preparation for teaching would advance educational development (Hasanain, 1995).

Several barriers to women's success have been pointed out by Clark (1992) in a study of sixty-six non-core countries, and include the adoption of Western definitions of women's 'proper place', the rise of patriarchal control in manufacturing and other institutions, and limited governmental regulations against gender discrimination. These forces also provide disincentives for women to pursue higher education, whereas they provide relative incentives for men to do so, and provide no incentives for university officials to locate qualified women. For example, in the Middle East, which has developed substantial natural resources and national income, observable attention is given to the education and training of men but there is no comparable effort for women (Hasanain, 1995). At the national level, various countries are experiencing increased pressure to place more emphasis on the development of women.

4   *Promote culture sensitivity.* People-oriented policies are culture sensitive, and appreciate the relationship between development and the dominant mores of a society. Development efforts are more likely to reduce resistance to change when they incorporate an appreciation for the cultural history and values of the people (Ingham, 1993; Jameson, *et al.* 1991).

5   *Assessing social costs.* Economists often argue that development means sacrifices now for future generations. But it is important for development implementers to consider the limits that should be placed on the high social costs demanded of the present generation (Jameson, *et al.* 1991).

The definition of development as human development requires that we look beyond economic measures of progress to consider a wide range of social measures.

Development and empowerment

The traditional view of development has been economic, or a goods-oriented view. When development is defined more broadly, as human development, what is proposed is a people-oriented view of development that can achieve longer-term results. Today's emphasis on grassroots participation in educational development was foreshadowed in the 1950s and 1960s by development strategies which viewed rural projects as a way to reduce large-scale poverty. By increasing local participation, development efforts would better reflect the realities of local development, enfranchise the economically weak, and harness the talents of women (Ingham, 1993). The definition of dependency reduction and country development as human development requires that a range of social indicators be considered in developing self-sustaining strategies.

Development is also about justice and human rights as well as economic growth (Mason, 1990). The United Nations community generally recognizes three categories of human rights: economic, social and political. Economic rights include the right to work, to change jobs, to relocate and to advocate safe working conditions and fair wages. Social rights include the rights to education, basic health care, and adequate food and nutrition. Political rights include the right to free speech, to be allowed to organize political groups, free and fair elections, and access to information. Educational development relates to each of these categories of rights. For example, aid agencies have helped build schools and health clinics, train teachers and health workers, and improve access to food and nutrition. Aid programmes have also helped create new employment opportunities through the creation of large infrastructure projects, cooperative organizations and vocational training programmes. The political process is essential to creating a human rights environment that is conducive to the development of people (Mason, 1990).

McGinn *et al.* (1985) suggested that successful, sustainable educational reforms are most effectively explained by a *political paradigm.* This framework highlights the political quality of decisions made by competing interest groups including aid agency operatives, project directors, ministers of education and political educational leaders. Each attempts to control scarce resources, in terms of both funds and legitimacy. Political processes account for much of the decision-making about setting priorities. Both practical knowledge (commonplace know-how) and theoretical knowledge (scientific, predictive and quantifiable) are needed to make educational policy choices, requiring a blend of technical and political forces (Bujazan *et al.*, 1987).

Traditional economists involved in development efforts have not been concerned with the question of whether development was 'sustainable' or could go on indefinitely (Ingham, 1993; Tisdell, 1988). Self-sustainable educational development recognizes that the wealth of a nation resides more in its people than in any other resources and creates new power in both individuals and organizations. Morris's physical quality of life index aggregated three social measures, including life expectancy at age 1, infant mortality and the literacy rate, in order to provide international comparisons (Morris and Adelman, 1989). The UNDP (United Nations, 1992) produce a *Human Development Report* which ranks countries by their success in meeting human needs. Countries that rank low in national income per capita may rank high on a human development index if people live relatively long lives, are mostly literate, and have enough purchasing power to rise above poverty (Ingham, 1993). Dasgupta and Wheale (1992) refined these measures of development to include political and civil rights indicators and examined fifty countries. Rights to political liberty meant citizens' rights to play a part in determining who governs their country and what its laws are, and civil liberty means the rights of the individual *vis-à-vis* the state. Dasgupta and Wheale found that a majority of poor in developing countries have severe deprivation of political and civil liberties; the poor but exceptionally liberal countries were few in number, notably Botswana, the Gambia, India, Mauritius and Sri Lanka. Countries whose citizens enjoyed greater political and civil liberties also performed better on people-centred measures for development.

Goulet (1992) uses the term 'authentic development' and defines participation of people as deprofessionalization in all aspects of life, including schooling, health and planning, in order to make people more responsible for their well-being. Participation enables people to become subjects rather than objects of their own destinies. The United Nations Economic and Social Council (1993) refers to self-sustaining development as an organized effort to increase control over resources and institutions for groups excluded from such control. Participation can empower the poor and permit them a greater choice and control over their rights and their futures. Participation is often a feature of 'bottom-up' development. 'Development from below', as defined by Stöhr and Taylor (1981), requires a redirection of decision-making and a decentralization and dispersal of resource allocations and administrative power to regional and local community levels.

Fasheh (1995, p. 71) discusses the role of 'community building' in reducing educational dependency and defines it as involving five sublevels:

1 developing the ability to express personal experiences and observed phenomena;
2 developing the ability to redefine terms and concepts, to explain experiences and phenomena, and to see 'wholes', or construct one's own knowledge;
3 developing the ability to generate, acquire and manage information;
4 building social formations such as small groups or teams and forms of communication that are effective in solving problems and addressing needs; and
5 building at the spiritual and value development level as part of achieving a common vision.

According to Fasheh, educational institution-building at the community level encompasses all five levels and refers to developing an environment within an institution that is conducive to learning, commitment, and taking initiative. Most importantly, at the community level it involves learning, or acquiring the means to learn, to communicate, build and produce. Acquiring the *means* to learn is a much more basic need than acquiring ready-made knowledge or technical know-how and is even more fundamental than acquiring the right to an education.

Bujazan *et al.* (1987, p. 169) suggest a three-dimensional conceptual model to help understand aid agency activity in developing regions and their role in facilitating educational interdependence and local empowerment. This three-dimensional model maps decision-making (*x*-axis) over phase time (*y*-axis) with a third axis (z-axis) of political–technical index. The level and phase time dimensions map a direct relationship in which higher levels of decision-making (policy mandates by aid agency directors, for example) are associated with the initial phases of agency aid to education. As policies become translated into practice, the responsibility for educational development shifts to lower levels of the system: to regional missions, project directors and local educators. The third dimension, the technical–political index, relates to the 'slippage' or breakdown in project implementation. Such slippage results from political factors such as resistance of recipients to legitimizing the values of academic institutions and donor agencies, hostility toward 'received' educational concepts, and technical factors such as misfit of people to responsibilities, and poor articulation among project components. This model describes a 'transfer of responsibility' curve in which an educational aid effort has as a central goal the transfer of decision-making and resource allocation to local areas and indigenous populations.

Reducing educational dependence: a shift toward basic and primary education

Over the past few decades, aid agencies have incorporated education goals into broader economic development and poverty reduction projects. Since the 1960s, educational development strategies by aid agencies have also shifted from higher education development in recipient countries to basic education and greater participation of the general population in education. Over the past three decades, large aid agencies such as the World Bank have also altered their original policies related to educational development (Bujazan *et al.*, 1987). The World Bank initiated its first educational loan in 1963 and the Bank's role was very restricted in terms of 'priority' education projects, focusing mainly on technical vocational training and general secondary education. A narrow interpretation of the human capital contribu-

tion guided the agency strategies (World Bank, 1974, 1980). The Bank later altered its policy to promote a broader conceptualization of the education–development relationship and highlighted relevance, efficiency and economy as key educational issues. The new policy was aimed at projects like vocational training, which would produce trained manpower, and placed more emphasis on technical assistance (World Bank, 1971). Additionally, a heightened emphasis was placed on primary and basic education for young people and adults, and also on participation of minorities, rural development and equity. The rationale for promoting basic education was based upon a shift from a solely humanitarian view of education as a function of human rights to an incorporation of the economists' arguments of its investment value. In the late 1970s, as research evidence mounted about the ineffectiveness of aid projects and as population increases and the social rates of return with each level and type of assistance were considered, basic education became viewed as the cornerstone of development (Psacharapoulos, 1983).

Other multinational agencies have also shifted educational aid policies to promote basic education and greater participation of the general population in education. The Inter-American Development Bank has advocated the principle that expenditure on education be regarded as investment in human capital, rather than as consumption (Bujazan *et al.*, 1987). For example, US AID education sector and Caribbean Basic Initiative funds also shifted aid policies significantly during the 1970s. New categories of aid were created for non-formal education, basic skills and primary education, participation of women and the urban and rural poor (Method and Shaw, 1981). In addition, the aid policies of each of these institutions called for stronger coordination between donor agencies and host countries, manpower planning within the wider economic context, and collaborative planning with recipient countries (Zimmerman, 1993; Warren, 1984). In the 1980s in Latin American and Caribbean countries, the quality and total coverage of education for meeting the demand for labour in productive sectors and training additional personnel in science and technology became the primary strategies for aid agencies.

Although decentralization of educational aid projects and broader participation may be difficult goals to achieve, they can be facilitated by outside agencies in several sectors. In this context, at least four sectors are necessary for sustainable economic development: the education process, business enterprise, the legal system and individuals (Zimmerman, 1993).

The role of academic institutions and the education process in reducing educational dependence

Educational opportunity is expanding dramatically in almost all developing countries. Self-reliant development involves a commitment to build the educational systems of developing nations at all levels, from basic education to higher education. Assistance organizations have been and are influencing the direction of this expansion in terms of the kinds of educational programmes that receive priority and in how these programmes are implemented once they are adopted (Zimmerman, 1993; Spaulding, 1981). The involvement of aid agencies and nations in the affairs of the world places new demands on education and human resource development. The goal of educational efforts in aid projects is to prepare country leaders for wise public leadership in governance in a critically interdependent and rapidly changing and evolving world (Brademus, 1987). An education process that provides good basic knowledge and stimulates free enquiry and research begins in elementary school and culminates in universities that are unfettered by policy, or by military or religious intervention. Reducing the dependence of chronically underdeveloped nations requires educational development strategies that are based on the theory that greater educational opportunity will bring about social stability through the creation of a middle class and help build a trained labour force. The use of aid for economic development and institution-building for self-reliant de-

velopment must necessarily involve the academic institutions of advanced nations. Academic institutions and aid agencies have assumed the obligation of providing help to support the development of higher education and to exchange knowledge about educational development among developed and developing nations.

In 1961, the Ford Foundation's Committee on the University and World Affairs summarized the role of the university in a free society:

> The American university has a public purpose, whether in domestic or world affairs, founded upon the traditions of American society and the heritage of other great universities in history. The purpose is the advancement of human welfare through the enlargement and communication of knowledge in a spirit of free inquiry. At its best, the university frees individual minds as it develops competence for the higher pursuits of life. It widens the horizons of the nation's judgement while supplying skills essential to the nation's tasks. As part of a larger community of scholarship, it also cooperates in an effort to enlarge man's understanding of the world and thereby to promote the welfare of mankind. The American university adds a third form of service to the society that nurtures it – activities such as professional training, consultations, extension work, and continuing education, serving directly the broader society beyond the campus. (Ford Foundation Committee, 1961, p. 9)

After the experiences of two world wars, society began to view US institutions, including the university, as embracing the concept of a truly worldwide spectrum of social needs. The USA and other Western nations, exhibiting a new involvement in world affairs, have taken on many new activities in Asia, Africa, Latin America, Russia and the Baltic States. These include research on economic, political and social development of newly independent nations; educating foreign students in large numbers; and projects in developing countries to help build and strengthen educational institutions.

Many developing nations have only relatively recently become independent and many have small educational structures and very little higher education. More expanded systems of higher education were required to supply the manpower needed to lead them in social and economic development. For example, during the neocolonial period in India, Africa and Latin America, Western education institutions and aid agencies helped to stimulate the development of nationalism, and production plants and local markets developed. Multinational aid agencies and corporations discovered the advantages of training and employing indigenous managers who could buffer local resistance and hostilities. The goal of such colonial development efforts, as articulated in the British Colonial Development and Welfare Acts after World War II, was to 'facilitate the eventual assumption of full control and financing by the dependent territory concerned' (Sharp, 1952, p. 14). Over half of the total outlay of funds under the Acts was earmarked for education at all levels, training for colonial service, and scientific research in the Caribbean Region, South-East Asian territories and British dependencies in the Mediterranean, Middle East, Western Pacific and Africa. In Africa, Westernized manpower became abundant because of the success of African universities in socializing local personnel to Western ways, thus reducing dependence upon external consultants (Clark, 1992; Mazrui, 1978).

A variety of public and private foundations and organizations provided many forms of educational assistance including helping teachers develop instructional skills, providing independent consultation by university faculty to country institutions, providing direct funding for educational institutions or educational projects, staffing academic institutions in developing countries with teaching scholars, opening higher education in developed nations to students from other countries to study abroad, and working with governments in planning and analysis to address national-level educational issues (US General Accounting Office, 1990; Ticknor, 1988; Brademus, 1966).

The 1960s was a period of experimentation and innovation in economic and educational development, and universities were involved in many important developments in the twenty-year period after World War II. Programmes were launched in several key Western universities for the development of materials and training of teachers and other professionals, and the exchange of scholars. The Fulbright Program, which was established in 1946, initiated the exchange of scholars in sixty countries (Woods, 1995). University contracts for institution-building abroad became integral to foreign aid activities. During the 1960s, universities began to focus less on direct aid and more on interinstitutional cooperation in order to foster greater participation by developing country leaders and therefore maximize potential benefits (Marvel, 1966). Thus, during the 1960s and 1970s the stated aim of development shifted from promoting modern sector development to redistributing the benefits of development to favour poor and more disadvantaged populations and to secure their participation in the creation of these benefits (Zimmerman, 1993; Hurst, 1981). In education this has primarily meant promoting 'democratization' of enrolment patterns, or equity in educational policies at all levels.

Several trends in academic institutions towards fostering interdependence and international collaboration were summarized by the Institute of Advanced Projects (1966, pp. 81–2). They are still applicable today and include the following:

1 rapid growth of international programmes within academic institutions in Western nations;
2 increased cooperation with institutions and agencies other than colleges and universities in host countries;
3 significant involvement of universities in assistance to developing countries through short- and long-term assignments connected to development aid;
4 a growing awareness of the need to assist with the development of the educational infrastructure in developing nations, including primary and secondary education; and
5 facilitation of recipient responsibilities and a focus on fostering administrative and managerial competence within educational agencies themselves.

Aid agencies contribute to sustainability of change in host countries by building linkages with recipient country institutions, particularly universities and research institutions which are viewed as the best prospects for long-term development impact (AID, 1987). Often these linkages are made between universities and private aid agencies. For example, in Malaysia a programme for training headmasters from schools in the Maldives was developed by the Asia Foundation in coordination with US aid agencies and regional universities. Similar institutional development projects in Korea, Bangladesh and Indonesia during the 1960s and 1970s are now self-sustaining (Zimmerman, 1993). Between 1967 and 1980, the Southeast Asia Ministers of Education Organization, with support from US aid agencies, established five regional academic institutions aimed at educational and public health development: the Regional Center for Educational Innovation and Technology, the Regional Center for Education in Science and Mathematics, the Regional English Language Center, the Regional Center for Graduate Study and Research in Agriculture, and the Regional Center for Tropical Biology.

Aid-agency-supported training programmes, often called 'participant training', which develop internal expertise may be the aid tool best suited for advancing both development and political objectives (Zimmerman, 1993). Participant training has long-term impact because it creates a cadre of professionals who can advance the goals of universal primary education and coherent educational planning. Also, those involved in participant training often have a chance to witness the democratic political process and to address human rights issues. Contacts, however, need to be maintained over time to strengthen relationships with the returned participants. Two important lessons learned from the Central American Peace Scholarship programme (CAPS) are that participant training needs to be adapted to local realities, and that the capacity of the local organizations to hire the trainees and use their expertise after the training must be strengthened. Development impact comes from the trainees' empowerment as they apply their new skills within their communities (Chesterfield *et al.*, 1989).

Universities can be particularly helpful in providing assistance to foster sustainable development. University personnel in university-linked projects have unique opportunities to develop understanding that is sometimes deeper than is possible for other governmental or diplomatic officers. Often they have unique insight and information about a given country's social and political events (North, 1989). Universities can be helpful when they form consortia of academic institutions which are incorporated into aid projects. For example, under the Foreign Assistance Act, in recognition that development required changes in institutions, university research and training projects were incorporated into AID projects. Universities involved included Stanford University, which conducted research on effective participatory methods, Northwestern University, which looked at modernization and sociopolitical participation, Fletcher School at Tufts University, which trained in social and political aspects of development, and Yale University, which examined the role of law and legal institutions (Mason, 1990).

Such efforts to foster interdependence in educational development have been difficult to achieve. The ties of newly independent countries have proved strong and have led to resistance to change and the continued use of foreign aid to support traditional practices (Ingham, 1993; Brademus, 1987). Also, aid agencies were finding that many of the problems in the development of higher education could be traced to problems in primary and secondary education, which meant that a refocusing from higher education to basic education was indicated. There was a growing realization among academic institutions that the provision of universal primary education was central to the goals of broader economic growth and interdependence among developed nations.

The shift from higher education to basic education raises questions about how to achieve these goals that must be clarified by aid agencies and academic institutions. Should the American or European systems of education be introduced or are there other ways of achieving these goals? Should the existing system in the recipient country be strengthened without substantial reforms and what should be done if the system resists change? Questions such as these must be answered if policies are to be developed which can govern the aid efforts, use resources efficiently and promote self-reliant educational development. If primary education and the full participation of all citizens are vital for economic development, then the educational process at all levels must be inclusive of children of all ethnic origins, languages and dialects, and should include both girls and boys, and children with impairments. The human service delivery paradigm for primary education has to change in order to create inclusive educational programmes.

There are many strategies for improving foreign assistance through academic institutions which can foster inclusive and self-sustainable educational development.

Degree of control of policy-making. Developed nations help foster self-reliance when they resist becoming involved in detailed educational policy-making in recipient nations. Residents of a developing country better understand how things work there. Therefore, when a donor and a recipient nation have agreed on the appropriate role for collective action and on how best to use assistance funds to encourage educational development, the donor should not attempt to control the recipient from the outside. People in poor nations need to exercise judgement about how development should proceed, and attempts to impose development plans may be futile (Sumner and Erickson, 1985).

Broader participation. Exchange programmes should make a concerted effort to seek out and select more 'have-nots' with promise and talent and the desire to promote desirable social and economic change. This is important to prevent the exchange experience from becoming a privilege restricted solely to the élite. Such a policy will avoid accentuating a bias toward upper-income groups (Zimmerman, 1993; Ingham, 1993; Hurst, 1981).

Coordination. Better coordination is needed among various governmental agencies, academic agencies and sectors involved in educational development.

Internal capacity building. The character of the educational development initiative in any given country must be determined by the needs and character of that country, and country-by-country

planning is essential. The educational development effort must be centred on strengthening of the educational and social institutions of the country through facilitation of leadership, building up local universities and educational agencies, and providing training and exchange specifically focused on internal capacity-building. Host country students studying in Western universities should be encouraged to engage in community action or practise teaching in that nation.

Broad educational strategy. Universities can help developing countries shape an educational strategy to govern its investment in education. No single discipline within the university can have a monopoly. Universities can be enlisted in the tasks of modernizing existing universities in developing nations slowly and patiently.

Adequate time for development. Adequate time should be planned for training institutions to assemble faculty, prepare an integrated curriculum and engage country leaders. Five- to ten-year plans are more appropriate for achieving sustainable development than are short-term projects.

Research and evaluation. Research is needed to analyse and appraise recent Western aid programmes aimed at improving educational systems and processes. This research should be designed to describe and assess the educational practices, theories and assumptions upon which the aid initiative has been based, to evaluate what has happened under varying conditions in different countries as a result of these policies, and to formulate principles that may guide the improvement of educational assistance in the future. Much more needs to be learned about the advantages and disadvantages of the training programmes for students and educators from other countries who come to Western nations to study in the field of education, and what happens to them when they return home. Some preliminary directions for research on development summarized by King (1991) include the following:

1   Attention should be given by international agencies to unfunded research on educational development being carried out in developing

countries; much non-funded research may be very promising and may be addressing local conditions and priorities.

2   Funded research has led to greater overseas support of quantitative survey research rather than research less concerned with the collection and analysis of large data sets.

3   Relations between recipients and donor agencies are much more personalized than those between research councils and academics; informal networks may promote the development of small international groups of 'élite research brokers' between outside funds and local institutions. The motives and goals of such brokers may not be beneficial to meeting the educational priorities and needs of the country or region.

4   Educational research priorities should be set inside the countries where the research will take place so that it can be responsive to local conditions and needs.

5   In the successful pursuit of interdisciplinary research in education, much longer periods of support at perhaps lower levels of funding may be more beneficial than short-term funding at high levels.

Although there may be limited funding for educational research in developing countries, its impact on policy-making in a region is significant. Aid efforts must help maximize the building of local sources for the funding of research and help establish an internal research infrastructure through country universities.

The role of private and non-governmental agencies in reducing educational dependence

The private and non-profit sectors promote a wide range of educational development activities through private aid agencies and non-governmental organizations (PVOs and NGOs) and foundations. These organizations, such as the International Council for Educational Development and Academy for Educational Development,

may be attached to larger multinational aid agencies and provide inputs into governments and policy for educational development. They seek contracts through aid agencies and often undertake studies on their own initiative which seek to influence aid policies. Private aid organizations include the Catholic relief services and CARE, the Church World Service, the International Human Assistance Program, World Vision International, Africare and the American Jewish Joint Distribution Committee. These specialized organizations operate projects involving medicine, education, nutrition and agriculture, child sponsorship and organizational development. PVOs, NGOS and foundations can provide quick, flexible responses for individuals and organizations that they help, can focus programmes more narrowly, and have less cumbersome reporting requirements and bureaucracies. Foundations have played a decisive role in support of education in developing nations by providing venture capital for projects. For example, in the USA the Rockefeller Foundation, Carnegie and Ford Foundations provide resources to support personnel for overseas projects, research by individuals and groups, graduate training and research centres in developing nations, and interinstitutional cooperation to share scarce resources.

Private and non-governmental agencies have been instrumental in promoting human rights goals of aid agencies (Zimmerman, 1993; Sayigh, 1991; Mason, 1990). US AID distributes funds for human rights activities and the development of human rights organizations through various foundations and organizations. Such support strengthens the legal systems to increase access to judicial processes. When educational discrimination and exclusion occur, due process is essential to support educational goals of equal access to primary education for all. Human rights organizations have sponsored human rights training and have promoted activities such as conferences, training programmes, local research and scholarship programmes in Latin America, the Caribbean, Africa and the Middle East.

PVOs and NGOs often work very closely with local governments in aid projects. They can be particularly effective because they can strengthen local government administrations, facilitate local participation in the planning and implementation of education development projects, and help local governments eventually raise their own revenues for programmes and services. Non-governmental organizations can help communicate the idea that local people should have a say in how funds for education development in their villages or communities should be spent.

The role of governments and policy-making institutions in reducing educational dependence

International efforts for developing self-reliant educational development involve long-term commitments from the governments of developed nations. Government agencies also view universities as a major national resource for personnel, research and training, and seek the services of universities for technical assistance in educational development. Brademus, crafting the preamble to the text of the US Congressional Task Force on International Education in 1966, was particularly eloquent in its articulation of the aims of US commitment to educational development as a central component of international development:

> Schooled in the grief of war, we know certain truths are self-evident in every nation on this earth:
>
> • Ideas, not armaments, will shape our lasting prospects for peace.
> • The conduct of our foreign policy will advance not faster than the curriculum of our classrooms.
> • The knowledge of citizens is one treasure which grows only when it is shared.

International education cannot be the work of one country. It is the responsibility and promise of all nations. It calls for free exchange and full collaboration. To this end, I propose to strengthen our capacity for international educational cooperation, stimulate exchange with students and teachers of other lands, assist the progress of education in developing nations, and build new bridges of international understanding. (US Congress, 1966, p. 17)

The Task Force on International Education outlined the goals of the programme of international education that has formed the basis for US commitment for almost thirty years, and comprises the following organizations:

1   a Council on International Education
2   a Corps of Education Officers to serve in the US Foreign Service
3   new programmes in international studies for elementary and secondary school
4   centres of international research and training
5   exchange with the students and teachers of other lands
6   school-to-school partnerships
7   an exchange Peace Corps
8   an education placement service
9   expanded AID programmes of education assistance
10 new techniques for teaching basic education and fighting illiteracy
11 programmes for summer teaching and teaching of English abroad
12 binational education foundations
13 conferences of leaders and experts
14 programmes to increase the flow of books and educational materials
15 responses to improve the quality of US schools and colleges abroad
16 special programmes for future leaders studying in the USA

The role of multinational business enterprise in reducing education dependence

Business and industry enterprises (capital and labour) encourage change in policies through the political process when such change is necessary to create continued productive and innovative investment and growth by individuals and business organizations. Business enterprises are vital in the planning of primary and secondary education curriculums as well as work preparation. Relevant vocational experiences can be taught concurrently with primary education to prepare children and youth for work in the communities.

Business–education partnerships can take many forms, though such relationships in the USA and European nations typically involve providing educators with advice, donations of equipment, space, and direct financial assistance to schools or educational development initiatives. Businesses and industries can help schools combine basic academic skills with needed workplace knowledge and job skills, and help to ensure that schools relate what is taught in school to what is required for participation in the work of the local community. There are some grand programmes that supply computers and other classroom items to participating schools. Businesses have also adopted schools, offering technical help, management skills, apprenticeship and work experience programmes, and have funded higher education initiatives (Kochhar and Erickson, 1993).

Business and industry enterprises need literate and educated workers, and their investments can produce long-term results. Businesses can also be a powerful political force for promoting educational change and empowerment of the workforce. Schools in most developing nations cannot rely entirely on external or internal funds to reform and expand services for a diverse population of learners. Educational expenses take huge shares of revenues and any hopes of significant assistance must depend on outside help (National Symposium on Partners in Education, 1990).

The role of the legal system in reducing education dependence

The legal system creates and enforce rules fair to all individuals and enterprises. The laws and courts define and enforce respect for rights, fair production of wealth, and possession of property independent from government control. The legal system plays a vital role in protecting the rights of individuals to equal access to educational opportunities and full participation by all families and

children in available programmes. The legal system is also essential for combating discrimination and exclusion of those children who are more difficult to serve. Such exclusion eliminates their chance for future economic participation and independence, and continues their dependence on their families and communities.

But how do aid agency administrators know whether their efforts to advance human rights in a host country have resulted in measurable achievements? In 1990 the US AID organization developed an evaluation to assess projects which focuses on legal institution-building. The evaluation uses four effectiveness criteria (Mason, 1990):

1. management organization, including monitoring and evaluation;
2. institution-building effectiveness and impacts on legal reform;
3. improvements in human rights; and
4. sustainability.

These criteria are also relevant and useful for evaluating educational development in developing countries since they focus on whether educational development efforts, including equity policies, are likely to be sustained when the aid is discontinued. Four important lessons were learned by AID as a result of evaluation of numerous aid projects:

1. The transfer of the substance and processes of democratic and participatory development was a critical factor in educational sustainability.
2. The host country or some group within the society should initiate democratic and human rights efforts; using aid for human rights activities requires host country cooperation.
3. Intermediary and non-governmental organizations are the ideal entities to develop human rights activities.
4. Human rights activities require a low profile because they have the potential to become politicized and emotionalized.

As Mason puts it, 'the success of legal institution building efforts results not from the degree of publicity but the number of people whose rights are positively affected and the extent to which these efforts penetrate the institutions they are intended to serve' (1990, pp. 22–3).

The role of empowered individuals in reducing educational dependence

Zimmerman (1993) claims that the democratic political process achieves its highest efficiency in direct proportion to the degree that individuals and families accept responsibility for defining and pursuing their own utopias. Zimmerman draws a distinction between *modernizing* and *developing* people. People can be *modernized* through skill enhancement to perform new jobs with new technology, or to produce high-technology products. People who are *developed*, however, have or can acquire the capacity to empower themselves – socially, politically and economically. Individuals can make their own choices and be responsible for them. Furthermore, a successful free market depends upon the productivity, risk-taking and imagination of individuals. The educational system must be a free, broad-based and inclusive educational process and teach respect for the freedom and personal responsibility of the individual. Individuals can contribute to local and national development by identifying and communicating their personal needs and objectives and improving and expanding their knowledge and skills. Governments can create opportunities for innovative individuals to profit from their efforts for productive self-growth. Individuals can provide input into the evaluation of the aid efforts to determine whether they are actually providing benefits at the local and individual level.

Aid agencies and their development efforts in the education sector must be prepared to collaborate with recipient country governmental, academic, business and other leaders and to foster commitment within the host country in the way political, social and economic power is created and shared.

Linking universities, governments, and non-governmental organizations in an international project to promote inclusive educational policies

The goals of one recent educational development project, the US–Baltic Consortium, may provide more specific examination of the goals of collaborative educational development between the USA and the deteriorating countries of Russia and the Baltic States. The US–Baltic Consortium was recently established by the efforts of Dr Judy Smith-Davis, an educational consultant for the US Department of Education and other private non-profit educational organizations. The collaboration emerged out of a series of visits to Russia in the early 1990s which resulted in an invitation by the Ministry of Education in Russia to arrange a visit by US educators to meet Russian educators in a series of seminars and informal exchanges. This invitation spurred the formation of a private non-profit organization, directed by Dr Smith-Davis. Dr Smith-Davis's vision is to help empower educators in Russia and the Baltic States to explore, define and pursue education reforms and development through professional and personal exchanges among experts. The US–Baltic organization is a loose collaboration of universities throughout the USA, Russia and the Baltic States, the US Office of Special Education and the Russian Ministry of Education, and several private non-profit professional associations in both countries. Since 1993 there have been numerous visits by groups of American educators to Moscow, St Petersburg and surrounding cities, and also to the Baltic States. American educators, legal consultants, state educational directors and special-education experts have participated in seminars to share practical and operational strategies for developing inclusive educational programmes. Policy seminars between US and Russian educators have helped to formulate legal statutes to promote the right to education for all children and to promote inclusive practices that could help reverse the current system of segregation and institutionalization of children with impairments away from their families, peers and communities. The Russian Ministry of Education has drafted a preliminary document which mirrors the Individuals With Disabilities Education Act, which provides the legal authority and regulatory structure for special-educational services in the USA.

Future missions of Russian educators to the USA are planned, as well as special conferences between the US Department of Education, Russian educational officials and universities. Several universities, including the George Washington University's Department of Teacher Preparation and Special Education, have developed the framework for an international component to be integrated into the current doctoral training programme. This component is designed to provide those in educational leadership training with a broader international perspective on inclusive educational policies and practices. The content of this international component is centred on issues related to five major groups of individuals who are largely excluded from the mainstream education and employment training systems in both developed and developing countries:

1   needs (educational, health and human service) of children and youth who are currently enrolled in primary, middle or secondary schools;
2   needs of children and youth who are currently enrolled in schools, but are not progressing;
3   needs of children and youth who have severe impairments and complex educational needs that are not being addressed;
4   needs of children and youth who have dropped out of schools and are receiving no services; and
5   needs of adults who are illiterate and not receiving services.

The curriculum component addresses the following themes related to inclusive educational development and reduction of country, community and individual dependence.

Broader strategic policy themes

1   Issues related to international and national policies for promoting coherent sustainable educational development and reducing educational dependence;

2   the link between education and poverty alleviation (coordinating service and human resource systems; coordinating governmental and non-governmental organizations);
3   improving the quality of primary education (paradigm shifts needed);
4   developing international and country-level legal instruments to promote educational rights, inclusive educational practices and human services needs of children and adults;
5   developing a system of education and human services personnel development for children, youth and adults;
6   capacity-building in educational and human services training institutions; transfer of knowledge from effective efforts of other developing nations; and
7   a framework for making strategic national choices and for making operational choices at institutional and instructional levels.

Practical and operational issues

1   Understanding the link between educational progress of children and the economic context in villages; relationship between poverty, work and early school drop-out;
2   developing health and nutritional supports, linking public health services and school programmes, and exploring the relationship between nutritional/health status and enrolment and progress in education;
3   status of current school enrolment; assisting children to enrol and attend school;
4   strategies for addressing drop-out, low attendance and grade repetition, and strategies for outreach to children and youth who are not enrolled or who have dropped out;
5   developing special instructional strategies, supports and accommodations in the general educational setting for learners with cognitive, physical or health impairments;
6   developing vocational skill and work preparation training programmes that support local economic development needs, including strategies for integrating basic academic curriculum, vocational skill training and community-based work experiences;

7 developing literacy classes for adults, and the families of schoolchildren;

8 linking social services and developing family supports;

9 special issues related to the development of girls and women, including equity in access to basic and advanced education, teenage pregnancy and pre-natal health care, cultural attitudes toward women and education;

10 developing basic services in remote areas;

11 developing special strategies and supports for workers with cognitive, physical or health impairments; and

12 developing skilled teachers and addressing issues related to personnel supply and demand.

This curriculum component will also require leaders in training to participate in international development and research activities and to communicate their experiences through international journals and conferences.

Conclusion: new assumptions for sustainable educational development

Reducing dependency relationship means shifting the power from central governments or aid agencies and promoting the empowerment of individuals and educational organizations within communities to determine their own destinies. It means participatory change processes and building decision-making at the local level. Simply put, change must be mutually constructed among aid agencies, academic institutions and the beneficiaries of assistance.

In order to achieve these new relationships, a fundamental paradigm shift in values and actions for aid agencies is required. A key assumption for facilitating sustainable educational development is that it must transfer the substance and processes of democracy. The four conditions that are necessary for sustainable economic development outlined above – the *education process, business enterprise*, the *legal system* and *individuals* – are

applicable to educational development efforts which can reduce country dependence. An infrastructure for schools, school administration and resource development, teachers and instructional materials is essential. Business enterprises are vital in the planning of primary education curricula and vocational training to prepare children for work. Curricula must be realistic and relevant to community cultural conditions and available economic opportunities. The legal system must understand and support efforts to advance the idea that broad human rights efforts must incorporate the basic right to universal primary education. Academic institutions must maintain as their chief mission – whether through training, technical assistance or research – the development and sustainability of coherent systems of basic education which are accessible by all citizens. At the core of these efforts must be the following ideas:

1 The needs of the child or individual are at the centre of educational development efforts.

2 School systems must be responsive to the individual needs of a diverse population of children.

3 The needs of the individual child determine the kinds of educational programme that are to be developed and the educational policy choices that are chosen at the country and local levels.

This philosophy of individual-centredness departs from the traditional philosophy in which a generic national curriculum or set of standardized teaching practices determines the content and processes of educational programs. The child-centred philosophy must also address a holistic approach to educating children within the social and economic context of individual communities. The effects of poor nutrition and health on children's learning ability are a major cause of inefficiency and lack of sustainability of primary education. The focus is beginning to shift to an appreciation of learner-related factors, or the linkage between the education/learning process and the readiness for learning with which children arrive at school. Sustainable educational development must be participatory and inclusive. Educational development, therefore, must address the needs of all populations of children and their families in order to achieve a sustainable link between human resources and economic development, between dependence and interdependence.

References

AID (1987) *Costs of Initiation Mechanism for New Relationships with Advanced Developing Countries* (a report prepared for AID's Asia-Near East Bureau by Robert Zimmerman, 23 December. Washington, DC: Agency for International Development.

AID (1989) *Development and the National Interest.* Washington, DC: Agency for International Development.

AID (1992) FY 1992 CP, Annex I, Africa, p. 422.

Bandow, D. (1985) *US Aid to the Developing World: A Free Market Agenda.* Washington, DC: Heritage Foundation.

Berg, E. (1984) The effectiveness of economic assistance, in J. Wilhelm and G. Feinstein (eds), *US Foreign Assistance: Investment or Folly?* New York: Praeger.

Brademus, J. (1966) International education in the 1970's: its needs and costs. *NVEA Spectator*, **35**(4), 4–7

Brademus, J. (1987) *The Politics of Education: Conflicts and Consensus on Capitol Hill.* Norman, OK: University of Oklahoma Press.

Bujazan, M., Hare, S., Belle, T. and Stafford, L. (1987) International agency assistance to education in Latin America and the Caribbean, 1970–1984: technical and political decision-making, *Comparative Education*, **23**(2), 161–71.

Chambers, R. (1983) *Rural Development: Putting the Last First.* New York: Longman.

Chesterfield, R. (1989) *CAPS Case Studies, Phase II: Clasp II Design-related Data Collection, Final Report.* (Prepared by the Academy for Educational Development and Juarez and Associates, 1 August).

Clark, R. (1992) Multinational corporate investment and women's participation in higher education in non-core nations, *Sociology of Education*, **65** (January), 37–47.

Clark, R., Ramsbey, T. and Adler, E. (1991) Culture, gender and labor force participation: a cross-national study, *Gender and Society*, **5**, 47–66.

Dasgupta, P. and Wheale, M. (1992) On measuring the quality of life, *World Development*, **20**(1), 119–32.

Fasheh, M. (1995) The reading campaign experience within Palestinian society: innovative strategies for learning and building community, *Harvard Educational Review*, **65**(1), 66–92.

Ford Foundation Committee on the University and World Affairs (1961).

Galtung, J., O'Brien, P. and Preisewerk, R. (eds) (1980) *Self-Reliance: A Strategy for Development.* London: Bogle-L'Ouverture Publications.

Goulet, D. (1992) Development: creator and destroyer of values. *World Development*, **20**(3), 467–75.

Hasanain, M. (1995) Education of women and supportive services: a proposal for Saudi society. Unpublished paper, The George Washington University, Washington, DC.

Hurst, P. (1981) Aid educational development: rhetoric and reality, *Comparative Education*, **17**(2), 117–25.

Ingham, B. (1993) The meaning of development: interactions between 'new' and 'old' ideas, *World Development*, **21**(11), 1803–21.

Institute of Advanced Projects, East–West Center (1966) *The International Programs of American Universities.* East Lansing: Michigan State University.

Jacobs, N. (1971) *Modernization without Development: Thailand as an Asian Case Study.* New York: Praeger.

Jameson, K. P., Vogel, T. and Grayson, G. (1991) Latin America: three reports. *Commonweal*, **118**(18), 609–11

Jonsson, T. (1993) *Special Needs Education: Policy and Planning.* Paris: UNESCO.

Kennedy, J. F. (1961) The Peace Corps. Message to Congress. In *Vital Speeches*, 27, no. 11 (15 March), pp. 325–6. Washington, DC: The Peace Corps.

King, K. (1981) Dilemmas of research aid to education in developing countries, *Comparative Education*, **17**(2), 247–54.

Kochhar, C . and Erickson, M. (1993). *Partnerships for the 21st Century: Developing Business–Education Partnerships for School Improvement.* Rockville, MD: Aspen Publishers.

Lema, A. A. (n.d.) *Education and Self-Reliance: A Brief Survey of Self-reliant Activities in Some Tanzanian Schools and Colleges.* Dar es Salaam: Institute of Education, University of Dar es Salaam.

Lynch, J. (1995) *Primary Education for All, Including Children with Special Needs.* World Bank Technical Paper 261. Washington, DC: Asia Technical Department, Population and Human Resources Division.

McGhee, G. C. (1967) The American ambassador today. Address delivered at the Fourth Graduation Exercises of the Senior Seminar in Foreign Policy, Foreign Services Institute, Washington, DC, 8 June.

McGinn, N., Barra, N. and Harris, C. (1985) Making education relevant: recent efforts in Latin America to fit education to economic policy. Paper presented at the Comparative and International Education Society Annual Meeting, Stanford University, California.

Marvel, W. W. (1966) *The University Looks Abroad: Approaches to World Affairs at Six American Universities*. New York: Education and World Affairs.

Mason, J. P. (1990) *AID's Experience with Democratic Initiatives: A Review of Regional Programs in Legal Institution Building*. AID Program Evaluation Discussion Paper 29: Washington, DC: AID.

Mazrui, A. (1978) The African university as a multinational corporation: problems of penetration and dependence, in P. G. Altbach and G. P. Kelly (eds), *Education and Colonialism*. New York: Longman, pp. 331–52.

Meillassoux, C. (1981) *Maidens, Meals and Money*. Cambridge: Cambridge University Press.

Method, F. and Shaw, S. (1981) *AID Assistance to Education: A Retrospective Study*. Washington, DC: Creative Associates.

Mingat, A. and Tan, J. (1992) *Education in Asia: A Comparative Study of Cost and Financing*. Washington, DC: World Bank.

Morris, C. and Adelman, I. (1989) Nineteenth century development experience and lessons for today, *World Development*, **17**(9), 1417–32.

North, W. H. (1989) Development specialists, managers and diplomats, *Foreign Service Journal*, May, p. 39.

Osgood, R. E. (1953) *Ideals and Self-Interest in America's Foreign Relations*. Chicago: Phoenix Books, imprint of the University of Chicago Press.

Packenham, R. (1992) *The Dependency Movement*. Cambridge, MA: Harvard University Press.

Pianin, E. (1992) Academic pork fills favored school larders, *Washington Post*, September 5.

Psacharapoulos, G. (1983) Education as an investment, *Development Digest*, **21**, 59–66.

Sayigh, Y. A. (1991) *Elusive Development: From Dependence to Self-Reliance in the Arab Regions*. London: Routledge.

Sharp, W. (1952) *International Technical Assistance: Programs and Organization*. Chicago: Public Administration Services.

Slater, D. (1989) Territorial power and the peripheral state: the issue of decentralization, *Development and Change*, **20**, 501–31.

Spaulding, S. (1981) Needed research on the impact of international assistance organizations on the development of education, *Comparative Education*, **17**(2), 207–13.

Stöhr, W. and Taylor, D. (eds) (1981) *Development from Above or Below?* London: Wiley.

Sumner, D. A. and Erickson, E. W. (1985) The theory and practice of development aid, in D. Bandow (ed.), *US Aid to the Developing World: A Free Market Agenda*. Washington, DC: Heritage Foundation.

Ticknor, S. (1988) The aid charade and recipient politics. Paper delivered at the American Political Science Association Annual Conference, Washington, DC, August.

Tisdell, C. (1988) Sustainable development: differing perspectives of ecologists and economists, and relevance to LDCs, *World Development*, **16**(3), 373–84.

Trilling, L. (1947) The uncertain future of the humanistic educational model, *American Scholar*, **44**(1), 52–67.

UNICEF (1991) *The State of the World's Children 1991*. New York: Oxford University Press.

United Nations (1992) *Human Development Report*. New York: Oxford University Press, published for the United Nations Development Programme.

United Nations Center for Human Rights (1980) The International Bill of Human Rights, in *Human Rights* (Fact sheet no.2.). Geneva: United Nations.

United Nations Economic and Social Council (1993) *Selected Issues in Fields of Activity of the Commission and Reports on Its Regional Institutions: Agenda for Action for the Asian and Pacific Decade of Disabled Persons, 1993–2000* (E/ESCAP/902, 21 January 1993). Bangkok: ESCAP.

US Congress (1966) *International Education: Past, Present, Problems and Prospects*. Committee on Education and Labor, US House of Representatives, October.

Warren, M. (1984) *AID and Education: A Sector Report on Lessons Learned*. AID Program Evaluation Reports 12. Washington, DC: US AID.

Wilhelm, J. and Feinstein, G. (eds) (1984) *US Foreign Assistance: Investment or Folly?*. New York: Praeger.

Woods, R. B. (1995) J. William Fulbright, *Academe*, May–June, 20–2.

World Bank (1971) *World Bank/International Development Association Annual Report 1971*. Washington, DC: World Bank.

World Bank (1974) *Education Sector Policy Paper*. Washington, DC: World Bank.

World Bank (1980b) *Education Sector Policy Paper*. Washington, DC: World Bank.

World Health Organization and United Nations Children's Fund (1978) *Primary Health Care: A Report on the International Conference on Primary Health Care, Alma-Ata, USSR, September 6-12, 1978*. Geneva and New York: WHO and UNICEF.

World Health Organization (1980) *International Classification of Impairments, Disabilities, and Handicaps: A Manual of Classification Relating to the Consequence of Disease*. Geneva: WHO.

World Health Organization (1992) *National Strategies for Overcoming Micronutrient Malnutrition* (45th World Health Assembly, Doc. A45/17). Geneva: WHO.

Zimmerman, R. F. (1993) *Dollars, Diplomacy and Dependency: Dilemmas of US Economic Aid.* Boulder, CO: Lynne Rienner.

Further reading

American Vocational Association (1994). Clinton signs voc ed appropriations. *Vocational Education Weekly,* **7**(24), 4.

Barnett, W. (1991) Benefits of compensatory preschool education. *Journal of Human Resources,* **37**(2), 279–311.

Blomstrom, M. and Hettne, B. (1984) *Development Theory in Transition – the Dependency Debate and beyond: Third World Responses.* London: Zed Books.

Brouillette, R. (1995). The future of special education: who will pay the bill? in R. Brouillette and P. Mittler (eds), *The Future of Special Education.* London: Kogan Page.

Business Roundtable (1990) *Essential Components of a Successful Education System: The Business Roundtable Education Public Policy Agenda.* New York: Business Roundtable, p. 2.

Carnoy (1980) International institutions and educational policy: a review of education-sector policy. *Prospects,* **10**, 265–83.

Chilcote, R. H. (1977) Dependency: a critical synthesis of the literature, in Janet Abu-Lughod and Richard Hay, Jr. (eds), *Third World Urbanization.* New York, London and Toronto: Methuen.

Clark, G. and Kolstoe, O. (1995) *Career Development and Transition Education for Adolescents with Disabilities,* 2nd edn. Boston: Allyn & Bacon.

Committee on the University and World Affairs (1961) *The University and World Affairs.* New York: Ford Foundation, p. 9.

Council for Exceptional Children (1995) CEC launches drive to protect IDEA, special education funding. *CEC Today,* **1**(10), February. Reston, Virginia.

Davidson, P. W., Goode, D. A. and Kendig, J. W. Developmental disabilities related education, technical assistance, and research activities in developing nations, *Mental Retardation,* **30**(5), 269–75.

Educational Excellence Act of 1989: Fact Sheet. (1989, April 5). Press Release. Washington, DC.

Education Goals Panel (1993) *Summary of the National Education Summit.* Washington, DC.

Education USA, March 1, 1993, 1–2.

Everson, J. M., Barcus, M., Moon, M. S. and Morton, (1987) *Achieving Outcome: A Guide to Interagency Training in Transition and Supported Employment.* Richmond: Virginia Commonwealth University, Project Transition into Employment.

Galbraith, J. K. (1983) *The Voice of the Poor: Essays in Economic and Political Pressures.* London: Harvard University Press.

Gordon, E. (1973) Broadening the concept of career education, in McClure and Buan (eds), *Essays on Career Education.* Portland, OR: Northwest Regional Educational Laboratory.

Goulet, D. (1989) Participation in development: New avenues. *World Development,* **17**(2), 165–78.

Halloran, W. Personal communication with Dr Halloran, a Fulbright Scholar in India and assisting with the development of special education and school-to-work transition services. October 15, 1994.

Harris, L. and Associates, Inc. (1989) *The ICD Survey of Disabled Americans: Bringing Disabled Americans into the Mainstream: A Nationwide Survey of 10,000 Disabled People.* New York.

Hehir, J. B. (1990) The United States and human rights: policy for the 1990s in light of the past, In Kenneth A. Oye, Robert J. Lieber, and Donald Rothchild (eds.), *Eagle in a New World: American Grand Strategy in the Post-Cold War Era.* New York: HarperCollins, pp. 9–10.

Johnston, R. (1995) Lobbyists split over unfunded bill. *Education Week,* 18 January.

Kearns, D. T. (1988) An education recovery plan for America, *Phi Delta Kappan,* (4), 565–70.

Kiernan, W. and Schalock, R. (1989) *Economics, Industry and Disability.* Baltimore: Paul H. Brookes Publishing Co.

Kochhar, C. (1994) Capital Capsule: National policy agenda for school-to-work transition. *Journal of Vocational Special Needs Education,* Spring, 35–6.

Kochhar, C. and Barnes, A. (1992) Crossroads of opportunity: integrating the IDEA, Perkins and ADA to support transition for youth with disabilities. *Journal of Vocational Special Needs Education,* (2), 15–21.

Kochhar, C. and Deschamps, A. (1991) Policy crossroads in preserving the right of passage to independence for special learners: implications of recent changes in national vocational and special education policies. *Journal of Vocational Special Needs Education (3),* 25–30.

McGinn, N. and Street, S. (1985) Educational decentralization in Latin America: National policy or factional struggle. Paper presented at the Comparative and International Education Society Annual Meeting, Stanford University, California.

Mangum, G. (1973) Manpower programs as career education. In Doug McClure and Buan, (eds), *Essays on Career Education.* Portland, OR: Northwest Regional Educational Laboratory.

Maresca, J. J. (1986) Leaders and experts, *Foreign Service Journal,* March, 32.

Mittler, P. (1992) International visions of excellence for children with disabilities. Speech presented at the

International Convention of the Council for Exceptional Children, Baltimore, Maryland, April 2–3.

National Commission on Employment Policy (1981) *Youth Transition*. Washington, DC.

National Commission on Excellence in Education. (1983) *A Nation at Risk: The Imperative for Education Reform*. Washington, DC: US Government Printing Office.

National Education Goals Panel (1993) *Handbook for Local Goals Reports: Building a Community of Learners*. Washington, DC.

National Symposium on Partners in Education, Corporate Foundations Seminar, Washington, DC, November, 1990.

Paulston, R. (1977) Social and educational change: conceptual frameworks. *Comparative Education Review*, **21**, 370–95.

President's Education Summit with Governors (1989) Joint statement, September 27–8, University of Virginia.

Preston, P. W. (1985) *New Trends in Development Theory, Essays in Development and Social Theory*. London: Routledge & Kegan Paul.

Psacharapoulos, G. (1981) The World Bank in the world of education: some policy changes and some remnants. *Comparative Education*, **17**, 141–46.

Reich, R. (1991) *The Work of Nations: Preparing Ourselves for 21st Century Capitalism*. New York: Alfred A. Knopf.

Rigden, D. (1992) *Business and the Schools: Guide to Effective Programs*. New York: Council for Aid to Education.

Rist, R. (1990) Usefulness of research in the policy process, in C. Kochhar (ed.), *Excellence in Doctoral Leadership Training in Special Education, 1990*. Joint publication of the US Office of Special Education Programs and the George Washington University, Washington, DC.

Roger, C. R. (1987) *Foreign Aid Reconsidered*. Baltimore: Johns Hopkins University Press.

Rusch, F., Destafano, L., Chadsey-Rusch, J., Phelps, L., Szymanski, E. (1992) *Transition from School to Adult Life: Models, Linkages and Policy*. Sycamore, IL: Sycamore Publishing Company.

Schalock, R. L., Wolzen, B., Feis, P., Ross, I., Werbel, G. and Peterson, K. (1985) *Post-secondary Community Placement of Mentally Retarded Individuals: A Five Year Follow-up Analysis*. Unpublished manuscript.

Semyonov, M. and Shenhav, Y. (1988) Investment dependence, economic development, and female employment opportunities in less developed countries. *Social Science Quarterly*, **69**, 961–78.

Shapiro, H. (1990) Society, ideology and the reform of special education: a study of the limits of educational change, *Educational Theory*, **30**(3), 237–50.

Sitlington, P. (1992) *Iowa Follow-up Study for Youth with Disabilities*. Des Moines: Iowa Department of Education.

Thagard, P. (1992) *Conceptual Revolutions*. Princeton, NJ: Princeton University Press.

UNDP, UNESCO, UNICEF, World Bank (1990a) *Final Report: World Conference on Education for All: Meeting Basic Learning Needs*. New York: The Inter-Agency Commission.

UNDP, UNESCO, UNICEF, World Bank (1990b) *World Declaration on Education for All and Framework for Action to Meet Basic Learning Needs*. New York: Thew Inter-Agency Commission.

UNESCO (1991) *World Educational Report*. Paris: UNESCO, p. 51.

UNESCO and Ministry of Education and Science, Spain (1994) *The Salamanca Statement and Framework for Action on Special Needs Education*. Paris: UNESCO.

UNICEF (1979) *Childhood Disability: Its Prevention and Rehabilitation*. New York: UNICEF, Document E/ICEF/L. 1410, p. 10.

Usdan, M. (1992) Down to business, in *America's Agenda*, Autumn New York: Scholastic, Inc.

US Department of Education (1988) *Education Partnerships: State Legislation and Initiatives*. Washington, DC: Office of Private Sector Initiatives.

US Department of Education (1991) *America 2000: An Education Strategy*. Washington, DC.

US Department of Education (1994) Improving America's Schools Act Passes, *Goals 2000 Community Update*, **18**, November, 1994.

US Department of Education. The Secretary's Commission on Achieving Necessary Skills (1992a). *What Work Requires of Schools: A SCANS Report for AMERICA 2000*. Washington, DC: US Government Printing Office. Order number 029-000-00433-1.

US Department of Education. The Secretary's Commission on Achieving Necessary Skills (1992b) *Learning a Living – Part One*. Washington, DC: US Government Printing Office. Order number 029-000-00439-1.

US Department of Education (1993) *Goals 2000: Getting Communities Started*. Office of the Secretary of Education. Washington, DC: US Government Printing Office.

US Department of Education, Office of Special Education Programs. *1992 Report to Congress on the Implementation of the Individuals with Disabilities Education Act*. Washington, DC.

US Department of Education, Office of Special Education Programs. *Eleventh Annual Report to Congress on the Implementation of the Individuals with Disabilities Education Act*. Washington, DC.

US Department of Education, Office of Vocational and Adult Education. *National Assessment of Vocational*

Education Interim Report to Congress. Washington, DC, January 1994.

US Department of Education, Office of Special Education Programs. *New Directions for Implementation of IDEA*. Washington, DC, December 1994.

US Department of Education, Office of Vocational and Adult Education. *National Assessment of Vocational Education Final Report to Congress*. Washington, DC, June 1994.

US Department of Labor (1981) *Report of the National Commission on Employment Policy*. Washington, DC.

US Department of Labor (1991) *What Work Requires of Schools*. Washington, DC.

US Department of Labor (1992) *Learning a Living: A Blueprint for High Performance*. Washington, DC.

US General Accounting Office (1994) *Multiple Employment Training Programs*. (GAO/HEHS-94–193). Washington, DC.

US General Accounting Office (1989) *Vocational Education: Opportunity to Prepare for the Future*. (GAO/HRD-89-55). Washington, DC: US Government Printing Office.

US General Accounting Office, Human Resource Division (1990) *Peace Corps: Meeting the Challenges of the 1990s*, May, 9–12.

US General Accounting Office (1992) *Apprenticeship Training: Administration, Use and Equal Opportunity*. (GAO/HRD-92-43). Washington, DC: US Government Printing Office.

US General Accounting Office, Human Resource Division (1992) *Integrating Human Services: Linking At-Risk Families with Services More Successful Than System Reform Efforts*. Report to the Chairman, Subcommittee on Children, Family, Drugs and Alcoholism, Committee on Labor and Human Resources, US Senate.

US General Accounting Office (1993) *The Job Training Partnership Act: Potential for Program Improvements But National Job Training Strategy Needed*. (GAO/T-HRD-93-18). Washington, DC.

US General Accounting Office (1993) *System-wide Education Reform: Federal Leadership Could Facilitate District Level Efforts*. (GAO/HRD-93-97). Washington, DC: US Government Printing Office.

US General Accounting Office (1994) *Transition from School: Linking Education and Worksite Training*. (GAO/HRD-91-105). Washington, DC: US Government Printing Office.

US General Accounting Office (1994) *Occupational Skills Standards: Experience Shows Industry Involvement to Be Key*. (GAO/HEHS-94-193). Washington, DC.

US News and World Report (1993) *Separate and Unequal: How Special Education Programs Are Cheating Our Children and Costing Taxpayers Billions Each Year*. December 13, pp. 26–38.

US Office of Special Education (1990) *Twelfth Annual Report to Congress on Implementation of the Education of the Handicapped Act*. Washington, DC.

US Office of Special Education (1993) *Fifteenth Annual Report to Congress on Implementation of the Education of the Handicapped Act*. Washington, DC.

Wagner, M. (1989) *National Longitudinal Transition Study*. Palo Alto: SRI International.

Wagner, M. *et al.* (1990) *Report from the National Longitudinal Transition Study*. San Francisco: SRI International.

Wagner, M. *et al.* (1993) *Summary Findings of the National Longitudinal Transition Study*. San Francisco: SRI International.

World Bank (1980a) *World Bank Annual Report 1980*. Washington, DC: World Bank.

World Bank (1984) *World Bank Annual Report 1984*. Washington, DC: World Bank.

World Bank (1992) *Primary Education for All Including Children with Special Needs*. World Bank Regional Study. Asia Technical Division. Washington DC.

Part Three

Human Rights and Educational Entitlements

10 Education for Human Rights and Development in Ethiopia

AUDREY OSLER

Introduction

This chapter considers the opportunities for introducing education for human rights and development in a context where there have been recent and extreme abuses of human rights, and where there remain political uncertainty and economic crisis. It reviews attitudes to human rights education among educators in Ethiopia, many of whom have direct experience of human rights abuses under the Mengistu regime. It assesses the potential of education for human rights and development to contribute to the rebuilding of the country, in particular the contribution that it might make to the development of political freedom and democracy.

Discussion of educational innovation in Ethiopia needs to be set within the context of the country's recent political history. It is also important to remember that Ethiopia's history is complex and somewhat confusing to outsiders, and that explanations of recent events continue to be contested by various political factions within Ethiopia. It is perhaps inevitable in such a context that predictions of future developments are difficult to make, yet the process of educational planning requires such forward thinking. The current government is attempting a transformation of the political structure, and education clearly has a part to play in this process. The government's proposals for human rights education within the new programme of civics education are examined, and consideration given to those factors which support and hinder its implementation, setting this discussion within the broader political framework.

I examine initiatives to promote education for human rights and development, drawing on the experience of two study visits to Ethiopia. The first visit, in November 1992, included the presentation of two workshops in Addis Ababa. The first of these, organized in partnership with the Ethiopian Ministry of Education, was on human rights education; participants included officials in the Ministries of Education and Justice, curriculum developers, teacher educators, school inspectors and teachers. The second workshop focused on basic training in human rights principles and practice for senior police officers. A number of visits were also made to local schools. The second visit took place in January 1994 and focused on the role of the mass media in promoting education for human rights, both through the schools' broadcasting services and directly to the general public.[1] This second visit included meetings with recently formed Ethiopian human rights organizations in Addis Ababa, discussions with the Educational Mass Media Agency, and visits to schools and meetings with teachers, pupils, local education officers and teacher educators in the Bahir Dar and Gonder regions. Both visits were made under the auspices of the Carter Center of Emory University, Atlanta, which has initiated a wide-ranging programme of activities in Ethiopia aimed to promote human rights.[2] Before these experiences are discussed a brief overview of the economic and political context in Ethiopia is offered.

The economic and political context

In the mid-1980s Ethiopia's plight temporarily became the concern of millions of ordinary people in Europe and elsewhere, following Michael Buerk's graphic report for BBC television news, when images of famine and starvation were beamed across the world. Yet the famine was not the 'natural disaster' that many may have taken it to be: the previous ten years had been marked by civil wars and political violence which had devastated much of the country. The seventeen years of the Mengistu regime saw appalling abuses of human rights in which over a million people are estimated to have died from famine and in which 100,000 people were imprisoned or tortured for political reasons and tens of thousands more 'disappeared' or were extrajudicially executed (Amnesty International, 1991a). The period also saw the flight of over 1 million refugees, who left their homes to avoid not only famine but also political persecution, military conscription and forced resettlement.

In 1991, while US-sponsored peace talks were taking place in London, the combined forces of the Ethiopian People's Revolutionary Democratic Front (EPRDF) and the Eritrean People's Liberation Front (EPLF) finally achieved a military victory over the Mengistu regime after a prolonged and extremely violent struggle. In May 1991 the EPRDF gained control of Addis Ababa, and Mengistu fled to Zimbabwe. In July a national political conference was convened in Addis Ababa and a Transitional Charter was established for the country, which was designed to remain operational until the establishment of a permanent constitution. The Universal Declaration of Human Rights was accepted by the conference as a basis for future development and was incorporated into the Transitional Charter. Promises were also made of democracy and self-determination for the Ethiopian peoples. The conference was significant in that it included a broad range of Ethiopian peoples and interests, including not only the EPRDF and the Oromo People's Liberation Front (OLF) but also many other liberation organizations and representatives of various ethnic groups. The conference agreed to establish a constitution, to hold regional elections at an early date and to hold national elections by the end of 1993. Meles Zenawi, the leader of the EPRDF, became president of the Transitional Government and an eighty-seven-member Council of Representatives was estab-

lished, including thirty-two EPRDF representatives, twelve from the OLF and a range of others chosen from other interests and ethnic groups (de Waal, 1994). The EPLF did not take part in the conference but instead established a Provisional Government in Eritrea and set about working for a referendum on Eritrean independence. The referendum took place in April 1993 and Eritrea is now independent.

Since 1991 a number of international organizations have begun working with the Transitional Government of the Ethiopian People's Revolutionary Democratic Front (EPRDF) to rebuild the economy, resolve the immediate problem of continuing food shortages, develop environmental and conservation programmes to avoid further damage to the land, and help develop a new constitution based on democracy and respect for fundamental human rights. Public awareness and understanding of human rights is clearly an important part of the process of building a new Ethiopia, and one goal is to incorporate teaching and learning about human rights and development within the formal education system. Nevertheless, in a large country with over forty ethnic groups, many of which suffered or were neglected under the previous regime, the task of promoting a new participative political climate is fraught with difficulties.

Ethiopia's GNP per capita in 1991 was US$120, the third lowest in the world. Although some writers, such as Henze (1994), are optimistic about Ethiopia's chances of economic rejuvenation, arguing that Ethiopia has the capacity to generate foreign exchange through the export of coffee, processed food, sugar, textiles and leather goods, it is also generally acknowledged that international assistance is critical in the process of redevelopment following the years of mismanagement under the previous regime. The generation of foreign currency through agricultural exports will not necessarily benefit those peasants and pastoralists who produce the goods, for, as Swift points out, production for export can be held accountable for many of Ethiopia's current problems:

> Capital-intensive export agriculture helped plunge the region into debt and soaked up resources – land and capital – needed for food production. In a way starvation itself has its roots in market logic. Food is a

commodity. And those who can't pay for it – wandering refugees who have already sold their last livestock or farmers without even devalued Sudanese pounds or Ethiopian birr – will have to do without. (Swift, 1992)

Peace makes possible a reordering of priorities: Mengistu spent more than 55 per cent of the national budget on defence, at a time when the country was burdened by food shortages, inflation and mounting debt (Christian Aid, 1992). As farmers are guaranteed land tenure, and with emergency relief being converted into development assistance in the form of fertilizer, improved seeds and tools, Henze believes that local farmers will be able to be self-sufficient in food within two or three years. He anticipates that much can be achieved through local effort, including the restoration of small farms, repair of roads and trails, and the improvement of land and water channels. Certainly the issue of land tenure is a critical one, and without security of land holding it is unlikely that there will be the incentive to make substantial improvements to the land.

The old state farms were almost always inefficient, and at meetings of local *kebelles* (official urban dwellers' associations) held in January 1994 throughout Ethiopia to discuss aspects of the constitution, the issue of land reform was high on the agenda. A visit to Kebelle 14 in Addis Ababa, an extremely poor community, revealed that among those present, land tenure was seen as a central issue, and was debated vigorously. It was of particular concern to the women, who had shown little inclination to engage in discussion of other issues, such as official languages, or the possibilities of presidential or parliamentary leadership. These urban people were also keen to debate the advantages and disadvantages of federal government and its implications for trade. It is probable that a number of them had migrated to the city once they were no longer able to sustain a livelihood on the land. The debate over the transfer from state to private ownership meant very little to these poor people, who are unlikely to be in a position to hold land for themselves; their primary concern was the introduction of laws which would guarantee the land rights of tenants and provide some sense of security and continuity, particularly for

women, who have had few if any such rights in the past. Some Ethiopians, such as the economist Befekadu Degefe, advocate a free market in land, but the government is unlikely to permit such a system for fear that desperate farmers will sell off their land and move to the cities (Swift, 1992).

The human rights and development agenda

Under the Mengistu regime arbitrary arrest, torture and extrajudicial execution were commonplace. During the 'red terror' of 1977–8 thousands of school and university students and former government officials 'disappeared' and were killed in secret on suspicion of opposition to the government. In Addis Ababa, Karchele, the central prison, and Maikelawi, the security detention centre, became synonymous with brutality, torture and death. In the same period there were also a large number of extrajudicial executions of political opponents, whose bodies were left in the street as a threat to others. In 1983 more than a million people were forcibly resettled from the northern highlands of Tigray and Wollo, and thousands are alleged to have died (Amnesty International, 1991b). The overthrow of the Mengistu government in 1991 brought a spirit of optimism and hope to both Ethiopia and Eritrea, and an end to the large-scale abuses of human rights of the previous seventeen years. Yet to ensure the long-term protection of human rights and to prevent the abuses of the past being repeated, it is clear the governments of both countries need actively to promote the principles of human rights to which they have made public commitments and ensure that appropriate procedures are introduced. As the Eritrean Paulos Tesfagiorgis argues, the achievement of human rights, democracy and development depends not only on the goodwill of people and governments in the emerging democracies but also on the support of the international community:

Overthrowing an 'ancien regime' is not enough to ensure a democratic future. The unequal distribution of power often survives the removal of old despots. This can delay or even prevent a smooth transition to people-directed development. The people of Eritrea and Ethiopia expect that independence and democracy will bring creative solutions to the problems of rural hunger and poverty as well as urban unemployment. If this does not happen popular dissatisfaction will grow. Governments, unable to implement their programs, become frustrated and defensive. Will they fall back on the old police methods to impose their will? Or rely on legal and democratic procedures?

It will take the combined weight of the international community to ensure respect for democratic rights and the development of a healthy civil society. But in countries as poor as those of the Horn this must also mean strong economic support to end hunger and give people hope in the future. For even governments with the best of intentions, like those of Ethiopia and Eritrea, could deny people's rights when faced with opposition. (Tesfagiorgis, 1992)

Although there was considerable optimism about the development of democracy as states gained independence in sub-Saharan Africa during the 1950s and 1960s, by the 1970s most of these new states were ruled by one-party or military regimes, often with the implicit or explicit support of Western governments. Human rights were invariably overlooked by those concerned with development or with development education, as it was fashionable to argue that authoritarian regimes were providing the necessary discipline for development. Consequently,

One-party rule and even military governments were considered to be choices with which rich, former colonial powers had no right to interfere ... To mention human rights and democracy in the context of the Third World could thus be construed as neocolonialist and paternalistic. The issue was made all the more difficult as, simultaneously, an American discourse of human rights was used as a cold war device to justify high arms expenditure and military intervention against nationalist movements, where these expressed communist sympathies. Given that development educators often felt sympathy for nationalist struggles against what was perceived as (neo)imperialism, only a bold and independent-minded Third World activist would feel comfortable placing human rights on the agenda. (Starkey, 1994, pp. 14–15)

Today, with the end of the Cold War, democracy and human rights are back on the development agenda. Western governments are no longer sup-porting dictators simply because they are anti-communist, and development aid is now frequently closely tied to the development of democratic structures. For example, Kenya was pushed towards multi-party elections in 1993 under the threat of and actual withdrawal of economic aid. Whereas the collapse of communism in Eastern Europe undermined the Marxist–Leninist model of development adopted by Mengistu, perhaps more significantly it was also clear to the Ethiopian people that it was failing them. The leaders of the EPRDF and the EPLF have shown themselves to be pragmatists and although, as opponents to the Mengistu regime, they also professed Marxist–Leninism, in power they have adopted an agenda which draws both on their socialist principles and on the concept of a market economy.

The EPRDF's commitment to democracy and human rights has generated considerable debate within Ethiopia, as was evidenced at the November 1992 human rights education workshop in Addis Ababa. The Minister of Education, Genet Zewdie, stressed the importance of self-determination for the Ethiopian people, pointing out that human rights had never before been experienced as a reality in Ethiopia. She argued that human rights are a fundamental basis upon which to build education for a democratic state. Nevertheless, as Tesfagiorgis has pointed out, even governments with the best of intentions may deny people's rights when faced with opposition. During the second half of 1992 the Transitional Government responded to opposition in a way which de Waal (1994) characterizes as 'reminiscent of an authoritarian regime, rather than one dedicated to democratic transition', culminating in violent repression of a student demonstration at Addis Ababa university at which at least seven students were killed when the police opened fire. Despite this tragedy, and the government's attempts to control opposition by undemocratic means, new political freedoms experienced by Ethiopians since May 1991 make it difficult for the EPRDF to adopt a more authoritarian stance.

Nevertheless, three years on from Ethiopia's first moves towards democracy, President Meles is arguing that Western-style multi-party democracy must wait. His argument is in some ways reminiscent of views expressed in the 1970s concerning the introduction of democratic processes in countries experiencing economic crisis:

> I believe many of those well-intentioned advocates of democracy in Africa are completely misguided. First of all they disassociate democracy from social and economic development. I don't think they can be disassociated – where there is social and economic decay, there is no room for democracy. When there is some hope then there is room for democracy. (BBC Radio 4, *File on Four*, 1994)

It is clear that in open elections the EPRDF would not be able to achieve a majority in Ethiopia. President Meles may be able to justify putting democracy on hold in a period of transition, but he is less likely to be able to secure long-term international support if he postpones it indefinitely. Although his policies of decentralization may prevent dictatorship, it would seem that for Ethiopia, as for other states, a solution must be found which guarantees the human rights of the people, including the right to development. Just as aid packages and loans from the World Bank and the IMF are now generally linked to indicators of democratic development so the United Nations has also made explicit the relationship between human rights, peace and development. In his 1992 statement *An Agenda for Peace*, UN Secretary-General Boutros Boutros-Ghali declares: 'Only a society of democratically protected human rights can offer the stability that can sustain development over time' (United Nations, 1992). This theme, with the consequent responsibilities of Western governments to respond to the needs of emerging democracies in Africa, is further developed in another UN statement:

> Time and again, all across Africa, helpful steps towards development have stopped because of instability. This cycle can be broken only through the growth of democratic practices ... Development aid must include support for the creation and strengthening of institutions of democracy. Democracy should be understood as the move towards better, more participatory government, perceived as such by the governed. Unless democracy takes root, violence, coups d'état, wars and general instability will recur, with an inevitable effect on socio-economic development. (Boutros-Ghali, 1992).

Ethnicity and democracy in Ethiopia

One indication of the ethnic and cultural diversity to be found in Ethiopia is that among a population of 55 million people some eighty languages are spoken. For many people in Ethiopia ethnic identity and loyalty is of greater significance than Ethiopian nationality. The Transitional Government of Ethiopia is facing increasing criticism from political opponents who are enjoying a degree of political freedom unknown in the past. In those areas of Ethiopia where resources are particularly scarce, ethnic conflict may actually be a fight for survival. Just as conflict and war may lead to famine, so famine and a scarcity of basic resources in the Horn has sometimes exacerbated ethnic divisions, as in the development of clan warfare over pasture and wells (de Waal, 1992).

Traditionally in Ethiopia the Amhara have formed the political élite and the majority Oromo people have generally been marginalized. The Transitional Government is dominated by the minority Tigrayans; the Oromo Liberation Front (OLF) has been ousted and 4,000 of its supporters imprisoned. Some members of other groups fear that the Tigrayans may merely be replacing the old Amhara leadership with their own. Taha Abdi, London-based spokesperson for the OLF, argues that the new Tigrayan leadership is more concerned with its own interests than with introducing democratic processes:

> Elections cannot be fair because there isn't freedom of movement for different parties in the country. There is only the government party which is the dominant party, that's running the show. The electoral process as a whole is dominated by this one party. In fact since 1991, we have a creeping one-party rule. So as long as this situation continues, we have the right to bear arms, to continue to resist. Resistance by the Oromo and the different peoples is a reaction to an oppressive system, to a one-party rule in the country ... Up until 1991 it was the Amhara political élite that was dominant. Now the Tigrayan political élite think it's their turn to govern Ethiopia the way they see fit – and they don't seem inclined to implement a real democratic process. (BBC Radio 4, *File on Four*, 1994)

In the case of the OLF the Transitional Government argues that it faces terrorist activity, opponents who are operating outside the law and who must be dealt with within the processes of law, but it is clear that it also faces a much broader issue in terms of the issue of ethnic identity and ethnic loyalty. Rather than try to play down ethnic divisions, the response has been to acknowledge and build upon people's sense of ethnic identity. In 1991 allocation of places in the country's Council of Representatives was effectively decided on ethnic lines. The country has been divided into nine ethnic regions, dismantling the centralized bureaucracy and replacing it with regional authorities. President Meles explains his policies:

> This ethnic issue, the issue of language, the issue of culture, the issue of identity, of the right of every citizen to decide what his identity is, that has been at the centre of politics in this country for at least thirty years. People have tried to wish it away – they have not succeeded ... So we might as well admit that they exist, admit that they are relevant, admit that they are important to people and take away the poison out of this difference ... I think that wishing away these differences, while in reality operating on that basis, has been the most backward form of political leadership in Africa. If people could truly and consistently wish away these differences, fine. But they don't actually. They pretend that they don't exist, whereas they operate on the basis of these differences. (BBC Radio, *File on Four*, 1994)

Since 1991 a policy of federalism has been promoted in Ethiopia, but is difficult to predict its effectiveness in meeting the needs of Ethiopians from various ethnic groups. The new regional authorities have considerable powers and responsibilities, including tax-raising, the determination of development priorities, and direct negotiation with external development agencies. Forced movement of people under the Mengistu regime and migration as a consequence of other factors, including war and famine, ensure that all the new regions are likely to include their own ethnic minorities. The smaller minorities will not in any case have their own regions. It remains to be seen whether regional government and regional participation will effectively resolve the issues of ethnic identity which this policy seeks to address, or whether old conflicts will resurface in new forms. The newly independent Eritrean state has a multi-cultural and multi-ethnic composition, but currently seems to be developing a common Eritrean identity and purpose while at the same time acknowledging cultural diversity. In Nigeria, the establishment of a federal state has not broken down ethnic consciousness or interethnic suspicion; in 1967–70 ethnic conflict resulted in the secession of Biafra and in civil war. Meles believes that by giving each region the right to secede from Ethiopia the government is pre-empting secessionist pressures. Faced with the day-to-day realities of government he expects the new regions to quickly realize that they are in fact interdependent. Whether a policy of federalization will resolve Ethiopia's ethnic conflicts and dissolve demands for secession or whether it will re-emphasize and strengthen old divisions and lead to the breakup of the old Ethiopian state are issues which remain strongly debated.

Human rights education workshop

The aims of the 1992 human rights education workshop in Addis Ababa were as follows:

1   to introduce the main international human rights instruments;
2   to provide some legal knowledge and understanding;
3   to explore how participants might effectively combine this knowledge with appropriate pedagogical skills and translate it into classroom practice to meet the needs of students (children, trainee teachers and law students); and
4   to explore how teaching for human rights might be incorporated into classroom materials.

Although the majority of participants were educators, there were also a small number of participants from the Ministry of Justice, all of whom had some legal training; their perspective was particularly valuable. In the process of planning the workshop the facilitators requested that a small number of teachers be invited as additional participants so that their perspectives could be taken into account and consideration given to the class-room realities.

The methodologies and structures adopted were very similar to those used in the International Training Centre on Human Rights and Peace Teaching (CIFEDHOP) annual summer school (Osler and Starkey, 1994), but since some of the participants were known to each other and attended as members of established teams, considerable emphasis was placed on collaborative planning. Since the facilitators were outsiders to Ethiopia with limited understanding of local conditions and cultures, the preliminary planning sessions with Ministry of Education officials and orientation visits to local schools were extremely important. Workshop activities were structured to allow participants to build upon their own experiences and specialist knowledge, and drew on a range of resources, including photographs, newspapers, training materials from Amnesty International and from a range of cultures and sources. Consideration was given to the fact that since the workshop was conducted in English all participants would be working in a foreign language, and activities were planned which allowed participants to work in the local languages of their choice.

One particular session which provoked much creative activity among participants was that using an issue of the Kenyan children's magazine *Pied Crow* on the rights of the child.[3] One of the strengths of this cartoon-format material is that it has been developed by a non-governmental organization to serve as a supplementary curriculum resource for teachers, and it reflects the concerns and everyday realities of Kenyan schoolchildren, raising development and human rights issues in an accessible way (Osler, 1993a, 1994; Ojwang, 1994). Participants were invited to look critically at the stories presented in the Kenyan materials which highlight the themes of protection, survival and development in the UN Convention on the Rights of the Child. They particularly welcomed the opportunity of using curriculum materials which had been produced in a neighbouring African country, and although the cultural and political context was clearly different, the materials did address certain issues on children's rights which

both countries shared. Working with copies of the UN Convention, they were then invited to write a story, cartoon strip or radio script which would highlight an aspect of children's rights for young people in Ethiopia. This proved to be a very fruitful exercise which drew on the participants' love of story-telling and particularly on the skills of those responsible for writing textbooks and producing schools radio and television broadcasts. Participants derived considerable pleasure in telling and listening to stories which drew both on folktales and on familiar and everyday experiences, and which highlighted some of Ethiopia's current problems, particularly those of child labour, street children and refugees. Despite the serious nature of the issues involved, most of the stories were full of humour and all contained positive messages for children about their rights.

Two other activities raised an important question for human rights educators. The first was an introductory 'Globingo' activity (Pike and Selby, 1988) in which participants were required to complete a simple grid by asking questions of each other, which on this occasion focused on the human rights experiences of their colleagues. The second was the presentation of a script which drew on the real-life story of a Latin American woman whose family had suffered human rights abuses at the hands of the government. One participant later told us that the part she took closely mirrored her own life story. Both activities allowed a number of participants to reflect on first-hand experiences of the denial of rights, but neither placed any individual in the position of revealing more about themselves than they chose. The question arises of how far human rights education, either in schools or in teacher workshops, should acknowledge or focus on human rights abuses.

Educators will generally wish to focus on the skills needed to promote human rights and the principles which underpin them, such as justice, equality, dignity, and reciprocity. Consideration needs to be given both to a historical perspective and to the future. Knowledge about the historical and continuing struggle for human rights is clearly critical, as the Council of Europe (1985) *Recommendation R (85) ... on Teaching and Learning about Human Rights in Schools* acknowledges. How then should we proceed when working with people who have recently experienced a denial of their rights? The members of Ethiopian non-governmental human rights organizations whom we met were primarily concerned with investigating and cataloguing the human rights abuses which had recently taken place in the country, and secondly with providing their members and the broader public with skills which would enable them to participate fully in a democracy. A human rights education programme clearly needs in the long term to focus on positive skills, experiences and knowledge about human rights that will enable people to continue in the ongoing process of working for justice and peace. Nevertheless, in a country where people have recently experienced gross abuses of their human rights, it may be necessary to face up to the immediate past, in order to ensure that justice is done and that such abuses will not be repeated. While emphasizing the positive values and skills which enable individuals and groups to claim their rights, human rights education programmes may need to develop ways of enabling people to come to terms with this recent history.

Ethiopian responses to human rights education

Participants were invited to evaluate the workshop by considering its strengths and weaknesses, alternative approaches, other issues they would like to have addressed and their further training needs. It was clear from the responses which we received that this was the first experience of human rights education for all those present, and they commented particularly on the new knowledge gained and on the participative methodologies used:

> The workshop is a success for all of us. This was the first I ever had in my life and I feel the programme was enough to inject knowledge. The methods were very interesting ones and were not boring. (Teacher educator)

> I like the method of presentation based on group activities. (Primary teacher educator)

> I appreciated the easy atmosphere that was created between the organizers and the rest of the participants. Also the simple mechanisms that were used during the workshop that make one understand the basic principles of human rights. (Legal specialist, Ministry of Justice)

> The workshop has become a landmark for me to realize human rights and to enrich my horizon of knowledge. Moreover, the experience shared with other participants and with the course coordinators is life-giving in itself and is very important. (History teacher)

> I valued the practical activities, the lively presentation. It is a self-learning process. (Curriculum specialist)

> I was impressed by two things in particular: first, the way we learned the articles of the Universal Declaration of Human Rights. If students are told to study such things a great many of them do not do it. But we learned well by matching them with pictures, etc. I also appreciated the harmony of presentation. At first I thought that you must come from the same home! (Guidance and counselling specialist, Distance Education Unit)

> The question of human rights education is the most important one in relation to the current situation of our country. The workshop has therefore given me important skills which I can use with my students in the future, particularly the materials and short stories which we have produced. (Teacher)

> I don't think there are other issues more important to me than human rights education. (Teacher)

Participants also highlighted a number of shortcomings which largely stem from the brevity of such a workshop and from the difficulties in maintaining a longer-term working relationship with trainers who are brought in from outside, particularly in a context in which participants lack a reliable postal service and do not have access to modern communication technologies. Many of the requests made implied a continuing programme of human rights education at both practical and theoretical levels, and participants stressed that as 'beginners' in this field they needed continued support. At the beginning of the workshop the Minister of Education pledged to set up a working party to incorporate human rights into the new civics curriculum, and a number of the participants expressed an interest in becoming involved in this initiative. Individuals also highlighted particular aspects of human rights education which they would have liked to have explored further, including women's rights, multicultural education and the political and potentially controversial nature of human rights education:

> The time was too short to treat such a broad subject. To be fair at least a week must be allocated. A small working group formed at the beginning might have been useful in drawing up a tentative plan of action in response to the Minister's demands. (Secretary-General of the Ethiopian National Agency for UNESCO)

> I want to know more about the controversial aspects of human rights which leads to antagonism between the people and the state, why the state tries to abuse human rights and why the state does not learn a lesson from the consequences of doing that. To know more there must be a continuity of this kind of programme, related to the practicalities, since human rights education is such a powerful tool. (Teacher)

> Issues such as unemployment, women and childcare are important points to include. (Technical and vocational education specialist)

> Continuation of the workshop should be considered. Any time delay with a follow-up will undermine the sustainability of the lesson started. This workshop is just an eye-opener and should not be seen as complete or finished. I strongly demand that this effort be continued. (Schools broadcasting specialist)

> We need to explore how human rights education can be made available to distance education students, since in our case we mostly rely on letters. (Guidance and counselling specialist, Distance Education Unit)

> There are many aspects of human rights education we might further explore, including multicultural education, dealing with social problems, dealing with economic development. (History teacher)

> We need to think about human rights education for parents. (Teacher)

> Further training on curriculum development should incorporate more human rights issues. (Primary teacher educator)

> I would like to apply human rights to a situational analysis of the world we live in. (Public Relations Officer, Ministry of Education)

> I would like further training on these same issues more than any other thing in the world because it is the most burning issue both in our case and throughout the Third World. (Teacher)

> I would like to explore the philosophical foundations of the principles of human rights. We also need further training on the comprehensive setting of human rights within a democratic system and further skills and techniques on developing innovative, decentralized and multicultural curricula. (Curriculum developer)

> I suggest that a member of the Carter Center should visit our country to further information on human rights education: in short, such workshops should go further into each region, whether they are administrative or autonomous. (Teacher educator)

It is clear from participants' comments that they recognized the importance of incorporating human rights across various curriculum areas and of addressing the needs of adult as well as school students. Teachers in particular outlined the importance of engaging the wider community in such an initiative. Their comments acknowledge the political nature of human rights education and the need for teachers to feel secure in tackling controversial or political questions. This is an issue which is likely to apply to teachers everywhere, as the Council of Europe suggestions for teaching and learning about human rights in schools make explicit:

> Human rights inevitably involve the domain of politics. Teaching about human rights should, therefore, always have international agreements and covenants as a point of reference, and teachers should take care to avoid imposing their personal convictions on their pupils and involving them in ideological struggles. (Council of Europe, 1985)

Nevertheless, teachers working in a country like Ethiopia, where until very recently such initiatives would have been unthinkable or might well have led to the arrest of the teacher concerned, may need further reassurances that their government is actively promoting these international agreements and covenants, which previously meant very little. Some participants stressed the need to explore in some detail the relationship between human rights education and democratic systems of government. One means of support and development for teachers may be through membership of a non-governmental organization concerned with human rights education.

The Ethiopian educators also recognized the relationship between human rights and social and economic development, relating it to such questions as unemployment, child labour, street children and migration. The last observation, from a teacher educator, is also a reminder of the immensity of the task of introducing human rights education into a country the size of Ethiopia, and of the importance of gaining the goodwill of local administrators and politicians in this task.

At the end of the workshop participants were invited to make plans and state what they would do to promote human rights education, in their various positions, with colleagues from the workshop and with others. In the short term many made commitments to reread the workshop materials, particularly the Universal Declaration of Human Rights (UDHR), and to talk to family members and friends about human rights and human rights education. A number made the point that to share this information with family members was new and exciting and that never before had they had the chance to consider their recent history within such a framework. Most stated they would hold orientation sessions, training or workshops for their colleagues on human rights education and as part of this that they would discuss how they might work together to implement UDHR in their society. As one inspector of schools expressed it, 'Whenever I make an inspection visit to schools I will help and encourage the teachers to share ideas about human rights with their students and I will advise them on how to introduce human rights education through classroom activities.' Other ideas for the promotion of human rights education included making posters for the workplace; demonstrating the teaching techniques they had encountered; publishing a summary of the workshop proceedings; introducing human rights concepts into legal awareness training programmes for rural women; writing articles for newspapers; setting up a children's human rights club at school; making applications for funding to development agencies; and reviewing human rights concepts in the curriculum and in the preparation of new textbooks. A teacher decided he would request that the school administration set aside a period of time once a month for human rights education activities across the school. Two participants pointed out the importance of working with both governmental and non-governmental organizations to develop strategies to promote human rights education. This is perhaps critical in a fast-changing political context when government commitment and priorities may change according to the degree of support that the government is receiving more generally. Many also stressed how the workshop had brought them into contact with colleagues working in related fields; for example, those concerned with schools broadcasting had had the opportunity to work closely with members of the curriculum institute, and felt that the workshop had enabled them to establish stronger working relationships which would enable the more effective support of the curriculum through schools broadcasting.

In 1993 a new Ethiopian education policy was issued which explicitly makes a commitment to human rights. A stated objective is to 'bring up citizens who respect human rights, stand for the well-being of the people, as well as for equality, justice and peace, endowed with democratic culture and discipline' (Education Policy Draft, June 1993, quoted in Ethio-Education Consultants, 1994).

Since the policy draft incorporating the concept of human rights was prepared, the Ethiopian government has issued a new education policy which includes a restructuring of education provision, lengthening primary education from six to eight years. The current structure is as follows:

pre-primary
primary education: grades 1–8
secondary education, first cycle: grades 9–10
secondary education, second cycle: grades 11–12
technical and vocational education: grade 10 + 3 years
tertiary education

In 1986–91, 38 per cent of children of primary school age were enrolled in school (UNICEF, 1994). This average figure disguises huge differences in school attendance between regions and between rural and urban populations. The effects of war and subsequent disruption of family life have accentuated these differences. A detailed study of 1,000 street children aged 7–17 in four Ethiopian towns found that 79.3 per cent had been enrolled in school for some period, despite that

Table 10.1 Topics in which human rights and development education might be addressed

Civics
Grades 4–8	The meaning of nationhood; culture; peace; ethics; government
Grades 9–12	Nation; culture; ethics; state and government

Geography
Grade 4	The geography of countries bordering Ethiopia
Grade 5	Africa (location, area, physical features); natural vegetation and wildlife; natural resources
Grade 6	World population; world economy: agriculture, mining, industry, trade, transport
Grade 9	People in different natural regions; interdependence between regions
Grade 10	Main industrial regions of the world; world trade, transportation and tourism; world population; world and regional organizations; the UN and its organs, systems, aims and objectives; the OAU and Arab League
Grade 11	Geography of Africa

History
Grade 4	The history of the peoples of Ethiopia and neighbouring countries
Grade 5	African history
Grade 6	The use of historical resources: archaeology, written documents, oral history/folk tales; primitive communal society; slave society; feudal society; capitalist society; socialist society
Grade 7	Ancient river valley civilizations; ancient Greek and Roman civilizations
Grade 8	The feudal system of Europe; Africa during the Middle Ages; the formation of the central governments of Europe; the Industrial Revolution in Europe and America; colonialism
Grade 9	The slave trade in Africa; characteristic features of European colonization; the French Revolution
Grade 10	Colonialism and its policies; World War I; the League of Nations; national liberation movements; World War II
Grade 11	Emergence of the Cold War; disintegration of the colonial system; forces of peace

Amharic
Grade 8	Culture and its influence on the development of a country
Grade 11	Cultural changes

English
Grade 10	Fund-raising for the displaced; community service; justice; admitting mistakes; apartheid
Grade 11	Destructive power of the neutron bomb

fact that one-third of all street children who had started school had dropped out, usually because of financial constraints. At the time of the study 48.5 per cent of children interviewed in Addis Ababa were attending school, 53 per cent of children in Bahir Dar, 37.5 per cent in Nazareth and 36.5 per cent in Mekele. Although the study found, not surprisingly, that street life interfered with school attendance, it also noted that

> many children would not have an opportunity to attend school if they didn't work on the streets. Within the school-appropriate age group, 7–15 years, 57 per cent of street boys and 68 per cent of street girls were attending school which probably compares favourably with community norms. (Veale and Azeb, 1993, p. xix)

While the Minister of Education made an explicit commitment at the 1992 workshop to incorporate human rights education into the civics curriculum, there are a number of topics within the prescribed curriculum for other subjects in which human rights and development education might be addressed (see Table 10.1). At primary level the curriculum includes both academic and vocational education: students study languages, science, social studies, mathematics, handicrafts, agriculture, arts, music, home economics and physical education. In the past primary education was through the medium of Amharic, but from the academic year 1992–93 students are instructed in one of eight local languages within their respective localities. Amharic is offered as a subject from grade 4 onwards and English is taught as a subject from grade 1. From grade 7 students are taught through the medium of English and a national examination takes place at the end of grade 8 which determines access to the first cycle of secondary education (Ethio-Education Consultants, 1994).

Teaching methodologies are also likely to determine the effectiveness of education for human rights and development:

> Democracy is best learned in a democratic setting where participation is encouraged, where views can be expressed openly and discussed, where there is freedom of expression for pupils and teachers, and where there is fairness and justice. An appropriate climate is, therefore, an essential complement to

effective learning about human rights. (Council of Europe, 1985, p. 4)

The teaching methods advocated in Ethiopian primary schools include 'problem solving, discovery methods, discussion, role play and traditional exercises' (Ethio-Education Consultants, 1994), but various factors may operate to prevent teachers from developing an open and participative classroom. Research by Harber (1990) on teaching in seventeen African countries indicated that these were likely to include the bureaucratic and authoritarian nature of whole-school organization; the wider political system in which teachers are unlikely to feel comfortable about exploring controversial issues and are unlikely to allow free discussion of political institutions, policies and personalities; shortage of teaching materials, very large classes, traditional forms of assessment; inappropriate textbooks; and poorly motivated and inadequately trained teachers. His findings were borne out by discussions with teachers in the Bahir Dar district, who pointed out that although they were interested in human rights education, they were uncertain about the commitment of their headteachers, and of the Ethiopian government, to such developments. They stressed that whereas non-governmental human rights organizations were being established in Addis Ababa, there were no similar developments in their area, and were reluctant to speak their minds in front of their colleagues and headteacher, preferring to contact us later by telephone and willing to discuss such issues openly only in the privacy of their homes.

Ethnicity, democracy and human rights education

Elsewhere in Africa there are a number of initiatives to promote human rights education. In Ghana and Nigeria programmes have been introduced into junior secondary schools and in the Gambia an International Centre for Human Rights

Education has been established (Osler, 1993b). Perhaps the greatest issue facing Ethiopia and the biggest threat to democracy is that of ethnic divisions and tensions. Although the Ethiopian government's response to this problem is somewhat unorthodox, this is clearly not an issue which is unique to Ethiopia, either in Africa or in the wider world. An examination of Ethiopian responses to education for human rights and development has revealed that there are some real difficulties in implementing such a programme, yet there is also evidence of an interest and commitment on the part of teachers to participate in such an initiative. Similarly, among those working at the Ministry of Education there is a recognition of the value of such an initiative in building a new, open and democratic political climate. Harber (1994) argues that if democratic political institutions are to be sustained in Africa then schools will need to educate for ethnic tolerance and mutual respect, recognizing that such an education will require not only direct consideration of such issues within the curriculum but changes in classroom and whole-school organization.

War has severely damaged Ethiopia's infrastructure, as was apparent in our visits to the provinces to explore the potential of the media to contribute to human rights education. A number of radio transmission stations have been destroyed, as have many of the listening stations where people would gather to listen to radio broadcasts at the beginning or end of a day's work. Nevertheless, people are committed to the process of peace and rebuilding, and one technician reported how people continue to bring him odd pieces of salvaged equipment in the hope that this might aid him in restoring a transmitter. In the formal school system, most secondary schools are equipped with a television, and some with a video recorder and, where appropriate, a generator, which permit the more flexible use of schools broadcasts. Primary schools tend to listen to the live transmission of radio programmes. These are invaluable aids to teachers and can also act as a means of in-service education to the teacher who is inadequately trained. We observed a number of lessons in primary and secondary schools in which both teacher and students responded most enthusiastically to schools broadcasts, answering questions put by the presenter and joining in songs and other interactive sequences. It would seem that there is tremendous potential in schools broadcasting for the introduction of development and human rights education to schools. Parents also might benefit from certain programmes if schools have the appropriate recording equipment. The Ministry of Education has a tremendous resource in its schools broadcasting personnel, who despite outdated and antiquated equipment show tremendous creativity. The human rights non-governmental organizations are committed to the idea of a media campaign to promote a culture of human rights and democracy, but lack the technical expertise required. If there is the political will, it would seem that joint action on the part of government personnel and non-governmental organizations might contribute to the government's stated aim of promoting a climate in which human rights and democracy might further develop. Resolving the key human rights issue of inter-ethnic tolerance and goodwill is crucial not only to democracy but also to the future existence of Ethiopia as a state.

Conclusion

Ethiopia faces a tremendous challenge in developing a political culture in which human rights, democracy and development can be realized. In particular the country needs to encourage inter-ethnic respect and tolerance. Education clearly has a considerable potential role to play in this process, both in supporting the development of a democratic political climate and in enabling people to participate fully in democratic processes and institutions. Clearly one priority must be universal primary education, but resources are also required to improve the quality of education through the continued training of teachers and the provision of appropriate classroom resources. If education is to contribute to the promotion of

human rights and development and promote inter-ethnic tolerance then attention will also need to be given to the development of classroom and whole-school practices which support rather than undermine democratic values.

Despite the legacy of war, which has undermined the level of educational provision in much of the country, Ethiopia has a tremendous resource in many of its teachers and senior educators, who, having experienced the neglect and abuse of human rights, are committed to human rights values and human rights education, recognizing the potential of such values in the future development of the country. Many are also quick to recognize the relationship between human rights and the social and economic development of the country.

The Ethiopian government and newly formed non-governmental human rights organizations have expressed a desire to promote human rights and democracy but the success of their initiatives is likely to depend on the renewed commitment of the international community. A genuine international commitment to human rights and democracy will require substantial investment to ensure the peaceful transition to democratic government, both through development aid that addresses the country's immediate economic development and through aid that makes a longer-term investment in education for human rights and development.

Notes

1 I wish to acknowledge Ellen Moore of Amnesty International USA Urgent Action Network, with whom I led the 1992 human rights education workshop, and Inge Estvad Petersen, radio and TV director for the Educational Department of the Danish Broadcasting Corporation, with whom I worked on the 1994 mission.
2 Jamal Benomar and Karin Ryan were the respective Carter Center representatives on these two missions. The views expressed in this chapter are my own, and do not necessarily represent those of the Carter Center.

3 *Pied Crow* magazine is available on subscription from CARE-Kenya, PO Box 43864, Nairobi, Kenya. Back copies may also be ordered.

References

Amnesty International (1991a) *Ethiopia and Eritrea: The Human Rights Agenda.* AFR 25/09/91, November. London: Amnesty International.

Amnesty International (1991b) *Ethiopia: End of an Era of Brutal Repression: A New Chance for Human Rights.* ARF 25/05/91, May. London: Amnesty International.

BBC Radio 4 (1994) *File on Four.* Report by Emily Buchanan, 7 June.

Boutros-Ghali, B. (1992) *Overcoming the Crisis in Development Cooperation.* Statement of the Secretary-General of the United Nations to the Conference on Global Development Cooperation, Carter Center, Atlanta, 4 December.

Christian Aid (1992) *Ethiopia: Emergency Sheet.* London: Christian Aid.

Council of Europe (1985) *Recommendation R (85) of the Committee of Ministers to Member States on Teaching and Learning about Human Rights in Schools.* Strasbourg: Council of Europe.

de Waal, A. (1992) Howitzer culture, *New Internationalist*, **238**, 26–7.

de Waal, A. (1994) Rethinking Ethiopia, in C. Gurdon (ed.), *The Horn of Africa.* London: UCL Press.

Ethio-Education Consultants (1994) *Education for International Understanding: The Case of Ethiopia.* Study prepared for the International Bureau of Education, 44th session of the International Conference on Education, Geneva, 3–8 October.

Harber, C. (1990) Education for critical consciousness? Curriculum and reality in African social studies education, *International Journal of Educational Development*, **10**(1), 27–36.

Harber, C. (1994) Ethnicity and education for democracy in sub-Saharan Africa, *International Journal of Educational Development*, **14**(3), 255–64.

Henze, P. (1994) The primacy of economics for the future of the Horn of Africa, in C. Gurdon (ed.), *The Horn of Africa.* London: UCL Press.

Ojwang, A. (1994) *Pied Crow* magazine in Kenya: a development education spice, in A. Osler (ed.), *Development Education: Global Perspectives in the Curriculum.* London: Cassell.

Osler, A. (1993a) Education for development and democracy in Kenya: a case study, *Educational Review*, **45**(2), 165–73.

Osler, A. (1993b) Teaching human rights, *Orbit*, **48**, 14.

Osler, A. (1994) Development education in a developing country: a study of curriculum innovation in primary schools, *Compare*, **24**(1), 79–92.

Osler, A. and Starkey, H. (1994) Fundamental issues in teacher education for human rights: a European perspective, *Journal of Moral Education*, **23**(3), 349–59.

Pike, G. and Selby, D. (1988) *Global Teacher, Global Learner.* London: Hodder & Stoughton.

Starkey, H. (1994) Development education and human rights education, in A. Osler (ed.), *Development Education: Global Perspectives in the Curriculum.* London: Cassell.

Swift, R. (1992) Horror and hope in the Horn, *New Internationalist*, **238**, 4–7.

Tesfagiorgis, P. (1992) Democratic elbow room, *New Internationalist*, **238**, 28.

UNICEF (1994) *The State of the World's Children.* Oxford: Oxford University Press.

United Nations (1992) *An Agenda for Peace.* Statement of the Secretary-General of the United Nations, A/47/277-S/24111. New York: UN.

Veale, A. and Azeb, A. (1993) *Study on Street Children in Four Selected Towns of Ethiopia.* Addis Ababa: Ministry of Labour and Social Affairs/UNICEF; Cork: University College.

11 Indigenous Language Rights and Education

STEPHEN MAY

When one significant section of the community burns with a sense of injustice, the rest of the community cannot safely pretend that there is no reason for their discontent. (Waitangi Tribunal, 1986, p. 46)

Introduction

The education of minorities,[1] in both 'developed' and 'developing' countries, is a complex and contentious issue. The long-established patterns of educational and social disadvantage for minority groups continue, in many cases unabated, despite a wide range of policy efforts. One has only to look to the alarming social and educational indices of many minority groups, across a range of nation-states, to confirm this general pattern of differential status and achievement.[2] As Stacy Churchill argues, in his analysis of educational policy towards minorities in OECD countries, policy-making must address its past and present failure to meet adequately the educational needs of many minority children. Moreover, if current policy is to achieve any significant change for minority groups, a thorough reappraisal of the education system, and its underlying assumptions, is required:

> Faced with a population whose goals may be different from the assumed goals of the 'majority' society, one must confront *de novo* all the issues, even the most fundamental, of what education is all about ... The minority issue is so powerful, emotionally, and socially, that the policy-making ground-rules are transformed. (Churchill, 1986, p. 21)

Such a transformation is not easy to accomplish. As Churchill elsewhere observes, 'coping with the needs of linguistic and cultural groups outside the majority group ... often poses a serious threat to the *status quo* both of school practice and public attitudes to education' (ibid., 33). A major point of contention that arises here is the degree of *differentiation* that should be accorded to minority education. To what extent should the delivery of minority education recognize separate cultural and language characteristics and how is this to be reconciled with maintaining the social cohesion of the wider society? Bullivant (1981) has described this central question as the 'pluralist dilemma'; a dilemma that is characterized, in his view, by the competing aims of 'civism' and 'pluralism'.

Until recently, debates about the pluralist dilemma within education have disproportionately favoured civism, or social cohesion, over pluralism. As such, education has been employed as a vehicle for *assimilating* minority groups as quickly as possible into the majority culture and language. Such assimilationist approaches to education have usually been characterized by the proscription of minority languages from schools. Via an advocacy of the *instrumental* value of education (those factors attributed to 'academic success'), minority cultural values and languages have been specifically devalued and/or have gone unrecognized in schooling. 'Getting ahead' for minorities has been assumed to involve the mastering of the majority culture and language at the expense of their own. It is ironic, then, that, despite its instrumental emphasis, assimilation has now come to be recognized by many as simply entrenching, rather than ameliorating, the social and cultural disadvantages of minority groups. Criticism has been levelled at the implicit, and often explicit, cultural hierarchy underpinning assimilation. This hierarchy regards minority languages and cultures as 'pre-modern', 'traditional' and 'regressive' and normalizes the majority culture and language as 'contemporary' – a view which equates modernization with 'westernization'.[3] The minority student is thus forced to choose between his or her (supposedly inadequate) cultural identity and the invariably Western culture of the school – a forced choice if ever there was one. As Howe (1992) argues, an education which requires minority children to dispense with their ethnic and/or cultural identities in this way is not necessarily an educational opportunity worth wanting.

A growing recognition of the problematic nature of assimilation has led some countries recently to adopt more pluralist approaches to the education of minorities. Thus, multicultural and bilingual approaches to education have been variously promoted by nation-states – particularly in the past twenty years – as more appropriate educational policies. A key tenet underlying most of these latter approaches is a concern with recognizing the cultural and (to a lesser extent) linguistic differences of minority groups within education. However, although this 'culturally pluralist' perspective can be regarded as an advance on an assimilationist stance, these programmes present their own particular difficulties, particularly in the degree to which they recognize and incorporate minority languages (see below). It is in this light that minority groups themselves have become increasingly vocal about the inadequacies of state-initiated attempts at delivering minority education, of whatever ilk. This has led, in some instances, to an advocacy of their own educational programmes – programmes which reflect and incorporate their particular cultural values and language and over which, crucially, they have a significant degree of control.[4] These developments have been most striking among indigenous minority groups – Māori, Sami (Lapps), Koori (Australian Aboriginal peoples) and Native Americans, for example. Indigenous peoples are perhaps the most socially and educationally marginalized of all minority groups.[5] Certainly, their cultural orientation and language(s) are seen to be most at odds with 'modern' society and thus the apparent choice between integrating into that society, and retaining their own cultural identity, is the most marked.[6] As Churchill summarizes it:

> The problems of indigenous peoples stand out as the most difficult and intractable faced by education today. Priority should be given to the study of their needs, *placing emphasis on their own role in defining the needs.* The tendency to deal with indigenous cultures in education as if their cultural base does not often depend upon a different language ... raises serious issues requiring study. *The relationship between language needs, indigenous cultures, and current schooling is very poorly known.* (Churchill, 1986, pp. 164–5; my emphases)

What follows in the remainder of this chapter is an attempt to explicate this 'relationship between language needs, indigenous cultures, and current schooling'. Because the recognition of language is often so central to the educational claims of indigenous minority groups, and so problematic to the majority, I want to begin with a discussion of the links between language, culture and education. From that, I will develop an argument for the recognition of indigenous language rights. My focus here on indigenous rights, rather than minority rights more generally, is intentional because, as Thornberry argues, although 'indigenous populations are frequently bracketed with minorities, there is a growing tendency to regard these groups ... as a separate issue in international and constitutional law' (1991, p. 6). Finally, I will illustrate the various interconnections outlined above in relation to Māori, the *tangata whenua* ('people of the land'; indigenous people) of Aotearoa/New Zealand.[7]

Language, culture and education

If any criticism can be levelled at previous educational policies towards minorities, even those that operate within a 'culturally pluralist' framework, it is their unwillingness to recognize the central link between language and culture. Fishman (1991) argues that language and culture are crucially linked in three key ways: indexically, symbolically, and in a part–whole fashion. First, a language associated with a particular culture 'is, at any time during which that linkage is still intact, best able to name the artifacts and to formulate or express the interests, values and world-views of that culture' (ibid, p. 20). In other words, no other language than the one most historically and intimately associated with a particular culture is able to express *as well* the particular artefacts and concerns of that culture. This is the indexical link between language and culture. Language and culture are also linked symbolically; that is, they come to stand for, or symbolically represent, the particular ethnic groups that speak them. The final aspect – the part–whole link – reflects the partial identity between a particular language and culture. Since so much of any culture is verbally constituted (its songs and prayers, its laws and proverbs, its philosophy and teachings, etc.), there are parts of every culture that are expressed, implemented and realized via the language with which that culture is most closely associated. Fishman argues that it is within this part/whole relationship that

> child socialization patterns come to be associated with a particular language, that cultural styles of interpersonal relations come to be associated with a particular language, that the ethical principles that undergird everyday life come to be associated with a particular language and that even material culture and aesthetic sensibilities come to be conventionally discussed and evaluated via figures of speech that are merely culturally (i.e. locally) rather than universally applicable. (Fishman, 1991, p. 24)

Given the obvious centrality of these linkages it may seem at first surprising that so few educational initiatives for minorities have made the respective minority languages their starting point. However, when one realizes that the omission or exclusion of a minority language from education and/or other domains of social life is primarily a political act, this becomes less surprising. Educations systems are not neutral and never have been. Rather, they reflect the particular 'cultural capital'

and 'linguistic capital' of the dominant group(s) within society (see Bourdieu, 1977, 1982, 1990a, 1990b; Bourdieu and Passeron, 1977, 1990).[8] Moreover, they are also a historical product, in many instances, of the linguistic uniformity and national homogeneity associated with the rise of nationalism and colonialism (Gellner, 1983; Smith, 1986; Anderson, 1993; and see below). Thus, minority-language education is particularly contentious exactly because it may necessitate changes, within a given nation-state, to the balance of wider power relations between ethnic groups and the languages which they speak.

Bearing this in mind, we have a useful commentary in Churchill's six-stage outline of the most common policy responses to the educational and language needs of minority groups. He suggests that the difference between the various stages is not always clear-cut, but attempts the following ranking (in ascending order) by the degree to which such policies recognize and incorporate minority culture and language:

- *Stage 1 (learning deficit)*: where the educational disadvantages faced by minority groups are associated with the use of the minority language. Accordingly, rapid transition to the majority language is advocated.

- *Stage 2 (socially linked learning deficit)*: sometimes but not always arrived at concurrently with Stage 1, this stage associates a minority group's educational disadvantage with family status. Additional supplementary programmes are promoted which emphasize adjustment to the majority society.

- *Stage 3 (learning deficit from social/cultural differences)*: most commonly associated with multicultural education, this stage assumes that minority educational disadvantage arises from the inability of the majority society – particularly the education system – to recognize, accept and view positively the minority culture. However, such acceptance does not usually include a commensurate recognition of the minority language.

- *Stage 4 (learning deficit from mother-tongue deprivation)*: though still linked to the notion of deficit, the need for support of the minority language is accepted, at least as a transitional measure. Accordingly, transitional bilingual education programmes are emphasized.

- *Stage 5 (private-use language maintenance)*: recognizes the right of minorities to maintain and develop their languages and cultures in private life to ensure these are not supplanted by the dominant culture and language. Using the minority language as the medium of instruction in schools is the most usual policy response here.
- *Stage 6 (language equality)*: the granting of full official status to the minority language. This would include separate language provision in a range of public institutions, including schools.

Churchill argues that Stages 1 to 4 all posit that the minority should seek the same social outcomes as the majority; that is, that the instrumental objectives of education, *as defined by the majority*, should be the same for both majority and minority groups. The premise is thus the integration of minority groups into majority society with minimal accommodation to minority goals. It is only as Stages 5 and 6 that objectives and outcomes also come to incorporate the *cultural values* of minority groups and, by so doing, begin to question the value of a monolingual society. Stage 5 recognizes, in addition to instrumental aims, the cultural value of retaining a minority language, at least in private domains. Stage 6 requires the greatest shift, with the majority group having to accommodate the minority group (and their language(s)) in all shared domains – a process which has been described elsewhere as *mutual accommodation* (Tharp, 1989; Nieto, 1992; May, 1994). From this analysis, Churchill concludes that, despite the noticeable policy advances in recent years, the delivery of minority education is still largely constrained to his first four stages. This might also well explain, at least to some degree, why differential social and educational outcomes for minority groups continue to persist. It would seem that much still needs to be accomplished if the transformation of our education systems, suggested by

Churchill, is to become a reality for minority groups.

Indigenous language rights

One of the key difficulties with recognizing minority language rights within education is that such recognition requires policy differentiation on the grounds of group association rather than on the basis of 'individual' rights alone. The apparent codification of *collective* rights in this way – resulting in the 'unequal' policy treatment of different cultural and language groups – is often seen as inimical to the individualistic and meritocratic tenets of liberal democracy. As Will Kymlicka observes, 'the near-universal response by liberals has been one of active hostility to minority rights ... schemes which single out minority cultures for special measures ... appear irremediably unjust, a disguise for creating or maintaining racial or ethnic privilege' (1989, p. 4). Accordingly, the liberal individualist position promotes an assimilationist ideal and has come to associate group-based oppression with assertions of difference (Young, 1993). Any deviation from the strict principle of individual rights is seen as the first step down the road to apartheid.

This position creates particular difficulties for indigenous minority groups whose status in many countries remains a highly complex legal and political issue. Historically, many indigenous peoples have been oppressed and/or marginalized by colonization. As a result, they have been undermined economically, culturally and politically, with ongoing, often disturbing, consequences for their individual and collective life chances, as reflected in current social and economic indices. In the process, they have also been denied the rights attributable to other citizens. Indeed, in some instances (as with the Koori in Australia), indigenous groups have only recently been granted full citizenship rights. Certainly, direct influence in policy decision-making – even over central issues such as the education of their children – has been extremely limited in most instances.

However, this pattern of qualified citizenship and societal marginalization has also been accompanied by some 'special privileges' and protection not afforded 'regular' citizens. Traditional systems of social order, including the right to limited forms of governmental autonomy (such as tribal or band government on Native American reservations) have been preserved in some cases in order to allow indigenous minorities to exercise some control over their traditional territories and ways of life (Churchill, 1986; Kymlicka, 1989).[9] Indigenous minority groups are consequently placed in a double bind. On the one hand, they find themselves in an extremely marginalized position within society and with little, if any, influence over the key policy decisions that affect them. On the other hand, what limited local autonomy is granted them is usually viewed with a good deal of suspicion, and often with outright opposition, because it may infringe on the individual rights of majority group members. 'We are all one people' or 'one law for all' are the catch-cries often heard here. A concern with equality and sameness overrides the principles of justice and difference (Squires, 1993). Differential provision, even if it is employed to redress past injustices, cannot be countenanced in liberal democracies, or so it seems.

This liberal antipathy to differential provision is particularly evident where minority language rights are concerned. As Fishman observes,

> Unlike 'human rights' which strike Western and Westernised intellectuals as fostering wider participation in general societal benefits and interactions, 'language rights' still are widely interpreted as 'regressive' since they would, most probably, prolong the existence of ethno-linguistic differences. The value of such differences and the right to value such differences have not yet generally been recognized by the modern Western sense of justice. (1991, p. 72)

Perhaps this is because the nation-state system, arising out of the nationalism of the past two centuries, is largely predicated on the development and maintenance of a *common* language and culture as a key identifier of (individual) citizenship (see Anderson, 1993; Gellner, 1983). Mass education has played a central role here in promoting the principle of 'one state, one culture', in which the boundaries of political and cultural communities are seen to coincide in the 'nation-state'. This coalescence – some would say elision – of the cultural and political community is expressed via the nation-state's supposed cultural and linguistic homogeneity. Moreover, this conception of the culturally and linguistically homogeneous nation-state is intrinsically tied to notions of modernity and 'progress'. Alternative ethnic, cultural and language identifications are thus, by definition, seen as regressive and pre-modern – none more so than those of indigenous minorities (see above).

But there is a problem here. Since most states are in fact *multinational* states – that is, containing at least two statistically and/or politically significant groups[10] – the ascription of individual citizenship rights must end up privileging members of the dominant group(s) within society. As Young argues, if particular ethnic groups 'have greater economic, political or social power, their group related experiences, points of view, or cultural assumptions will tend to become the norm, biasing the standards or procedures of achievement and inclusion that govern social, political and economic institutions' (1993, p. 132).[11] This is democracy by weight of numbers and it ends up being profoundly anti-democratic in its treatment of minority groups.

What is missing from the popular liberal conception of 'equal treatment for all' then is any notion of what Fishman (1991) calls 'cultural democracy' – the recognition of an *individual*'s right to retain his or her ethnic, cultural and language affiliations should these differ from the 'mainstream'. This moves the debate away from the problematic distinction between individual and collective rights to a reassessment of what individual citizenship rights within a liberal democracy might include. As Will Kymlicka (1989) has cogently argued, such rights should recognize the role of an individual's cultural community as a key 'context of choice' within which that person is situated and which he or she has the right to secure. This is consistent, he suggests, with previous accounts of liberalism and provides the basis by which differential rights for minority groups can be claimed.[12] These rights are based not on the exercise of choice alone but on the unequal *circumstances* facing indigenous groups. As Kymlicka observes, it must be recognized that members of indigenous (and other minority) cultures can face inequalities 'which are the product of their circumstances . . . not their choices or ambitions'. In contrast, dominant-group members rarely have to worry about the fate of their cultural structure in the choices they make. 'They get for free what [indigenous] people have to pay for: secure cultural membership' (Kymlicka, 1989, p. 190). Special political rights – including a central role for indigenous languages – can correct this inequality by ensuring that indigenous communities are as secure as non-indigenous ones.[13] Kymlicka concludes that such minority rights are neither favouritism nor ghettoization (both of which are commonly levelled criticisms). Rather, they 'help to ensure that the members of minority cultures have access to a secure cultural structure *from which to make such choices for themselves*, and thereby promote liberal equality' (ibid., p. 192; my emphasis). Nothing in this precludes cultural change and cultural adaptation; minority-group identity is not essentialized. Indigenous minority-group members continue to exercise their individual rights within their particular cultural and language milieux and, of course, contextually in relation to other cultural groups within a given society (see Young, 1993). The crucial element, however, is that members of the indigenous group are themselves able to retain a significant degree of control over this process – something which until now has mostly been the preserve of majority-group members.

Redefining the debate in this way is also consistent with current international law towards minorities, despite the long-standing reticence attached to a specific recognition of language rights. Article 27 of the International Covenant on Civil and Political Rights, for example, imposes a negative duty on nation-states with respect to minorities: 'minorities *shall not be denied* the right, in community with the other members of their group, to enjoy their own culture, to profess and practise

their own religion, or *to use their own language*' (my emphases). The words 'shall not be denied' could be read as imposing no obligation on a state to take positive action to protect those rights. However, an alternative and equally compelling view 'is that to recognize a right to use a minority language implies an obligation that the right be made effective' (Hastings, 1988, p. 19). This latter view is reinforced by the recent Universal Declaration of Linguistic Rights, adopted in Recife, Brazil, in October 1987 by the Association Internationale pour le Développement de la Communication Interculturelle (AIMAV), a UNESCO agency (see Fishman, 1991; Tollefson, 1991). AIMAV argued that explicit legal guarantees should be provided for the linguistic rights of individuals and groups, and called on the United Nations to endorse this position. These developments can also be linked directly to education. For example, Article 2(b) of the Convention Against Discrimination in Education – ratified on 12 February 1963 – specifically provides for the establishment or maintenance, for linguistic reasons, of separate schools, provided attendance is optional and the education is up to national standards. Moreover, Article 5 of this Convention recognizes the essential right of minorities to carry on their own educational activities and, in so doing, to use or teach in their own language. Although it subsequently qualifies this right, somewhat contradictorily, by making it conditional on a state's existing educational policies, and by ensuring it does not prejudice national sovereignty and the ability of minorities to participate in national life, the right to minority language education can nevertheless be established (Hastings, 1988).

Given all the above, it is my argument that indigenous minorities have a right both to an education in their own language and to a significant degree of control over the educational process itself as it affects their children. What follows is an account of recent developments in Māori education in Aotearoa/New Zealand, where this is beginning to occur. In the process, a long and debilitating history of colonization and marginalization for Māori is being contested, and Māori language and culture reasserted.

Social, economic and cultural disadvantage

In 1991, at the time of the last census, Māori in Aotearoa/New Zealand accounted for 14 per cent of the total population. They are a relatively youthful population group, with 59 per cent of Māori under the age of 25 years and 37 per cent aged less than 15 years. Thus, while accounting for only 14 per cent of the total population, young Māori represent 21 per cent of all primary (elementary) school students and 15 per cent of all secondary school students (Davies and Nicholl, 1993). As we shall see, the youthful age structure of the Māori population provides the potential for educational initiatives to have a major impact on the social, economic and educational status of Māori.

This status, however, has been, and continues to be, a considerable cause for concern in Aotearoa/New Zealand.[14] Like many other indigenous minority groups, Māori are over-represented in 'at risk' categories. Māori workers, for example, are heavily under-represented in high-income, high-skilled and growing sectors of the New Zealand economy. Conversely, they are over-represented in low-paid, low-skilled, declining occupations, and among beneficiaries and those not in paid employment (Manatū Māori, 1991). The emasculation of low-skilled and semi-skilled occupations over the last decade, as successive New Zealand governments have followed a New Right economic agenda, has resulted in a high level of unemployment for Māori: 24 per cent of all Māori over 15 years old compared with 11 per cent for the total population. Young Māori, in particular, have borne the brunt of the depressed labour market. In 1991, 43 per cent of all Māori teenagers (15–19 years) were unemployed. Moreover, given that 52 per cent of this group did not hold a school qualification, future employment prospects appear limited (Davies and Nicholl, 1993).

Some are suggesting, from this, the emergence of an increasing Māori underclass (Jarden, 1992; McLoughlin, 1993). When these economic statistics are linked to social and educational statistics for Māori this pattern seems to be confirmed.

Māori made up 45 per cent of the prison population and 30 per cent of all sole parents at the 1991 census. In 1991, 56 per cent of Māori aged between 15 and 59 years were receiving some form of income-support benefit and Māori were also proportionately over-represented on all other welfare benefits, except for the pension.[15] Combining these figures with educational status completes the picture of comparative disadvantage for Māori. Though increasing numbers of Māori have been completing school and pursuing tertiary education, particularly in the past decade (see below), 60 per cent of Māori aged over 15 still held no formal educational qualifications in 1991. This compared with 40 per cent for non-Māori. At the same time, Māori were nearly half as likely as the total population to hold a tertiary qualification (Davies and Nicholl, 1993). This low level of educational attainment is also a central explanatory variable for the current poor position of Māori in the labour market (Haines, 1989; Callister, 1989; Davies and Nicholl, 1993).

History, colonization and the Treaty of Waitangi

The present pattern of social, economic and cultural disadvantage for Māori is situated within a historical context of Pākehā (European) colonization of Aotearoa/New Zealand over the last two centuries.[16] This process of colonization, with one notable exception (see below), has closely followed the model outlined by Havighurst (1974; see also Hirsh, 1990):

1   tentative and cautious initial contacts, usually with an emphasis on trade rather than land settlement;
2   settlement and colonization by the 'Anglo' society and appropriation of land from the indigenous people;
3   resistance to this appropriation of land, leading to conflict and eventual defeat of the indigenous people;

4   retreat of the indigenous people to isolated strongholds and reduction of their population to its lowest number;

5   adoption of a policy of assimilation towards the remaining indigenous population, some of whom accept it;

6   eventual acceptance of assimilation as inadequate by both 'Anglos' and the indigenous people. Problems of socio-economic adjustment arise with the rapid increase of the indigenous population, urbanization and migration to the cities, and the growth of protest movements;

7   a move towards cultural pluralism, where members seek to live together in mutual understanding and cooperation yet maintaining a degree of cultural separation.

It is beyond the scope of this chapter to outline here in any detail the colonial history of Aotearoa/New Zealand (see Belich, 1986; Orange, 1987; Kawharu, 1989; Pearson, 1990; Sharp, 1990; Walker, 1990: Sinclair, 1993). However, it is important to examine briefly the one notable exception to the process of colonization described above: that is, the signing of Te Tiriti o Waitangi (the Treaty of Waitangi) on 6 February 1840. This treaty, agreed between Māori chiefs and the British Crown, attempted to establish the rights and responsibilities of both parties as a mutual framework by which colonization could proceed – an unusual event for its time. Captain Hobson, the Crown's representative, was instructed to obtain the surrender of Aotearoa/New Zealand as a sovereign state to the British Crown, but only by 'free and intelligent consent' of the 'natives'. In return, Māori tribes were to be guaranteed possession of 'their lands, their homes and all their treasured possessions (*taonga*)'.

There has since been considerable debate about whether the informed consent of Māori was ever obtained,[17] and the treaty was soon ignored in the subsequent quest for land.[18] Indeed, in 1877 Chief Justice Prendergast declared the treaty 'a simple nullity' – a legal view that was to hold sway until the 1980s. However, the significance of the treaty as the founding document of a bicultural Aotearoa/New Zealand has been re-established over the course of the past twenty years. A key influence in this re-emergence has been the Waitangi Tribunal. Originally set up in 1975, with limited powers to hear Māori grievances under the treaty, it was invested in 1984 with the retrospective power to settle Māori claims against the Crown, dating back to 1840. Within months huge land claims against the Crown had been lodged by *iwi* (tribes). By 1988 the number of these claims had reached 150, and by 1995 over 400 claims lodged with the tribunal were still outstanding. Waitangi Tribunal decisions over this intervening period have seen the Treaty of Waitangi reinvested with legal force in Aotearoa/New Zealand. Through its deliberations the tribunal has defined the treaty as 'the foundation of a developing social contract, not merely a historical document' (Sorrenson, 1989, p. 162). As Walker observes, the result is that the treaty has been transformed, in the space of just a few years, 'from "a simple nullity" to the level of a constitutional instrument in the renegotiation of the relationship between Māori and Pākehā in modern times' (1990, p. 266).[19]

Although many of the claims before the Waitangi Tribunal have had to do with expropriation of land under colonial rule, they have also, crucially, encompassed other 'non-material' possessions such as the Māori language. In the Māori language case of 1985–6, for example, the Waitangi Tribunal ruled that the Māori language could be regarded as a *taonga* (treasured possession) and therefore had a guaranteed right to protection under the terms of the treaty (Waitangi Tribunal, 1986). In its ruling, the tribunal defined the term 'guarantee' as 'more than merely leaving Māori people unhindered in their enjoyment of the language and culture'; it also required 'active steps' to be taken by the guarantor to ensure that Māori have and retain 'the full exclusive and undisturbed possession of their language and culture' (Waitangi Tribunal, 1986, p. 29). This is consistent with interpretations in international law, as discussed above, on the *active* right to minority language protection. However, the tribunal also found with respect to Māori-language education, an equality right in the Treaty *independent* of minority language rights (Hastings, 1988):

The promises in the Treaty of Waitangi of equality of education as in all other human rights are undeniable. Judged by the system's own standards Māori children are not being successfully taught, and for this reason alone, quite apart from the duty to protect the Māori language, the education system is being operated in breach of the Treaty. (Waitangi Tribunal, 1986, p. 51)

The tribunal's deliberations have contributed to, and been a product of, a recent political climate in Aotearoa/New Zealand that is more conducive than at any time since 1840 to recognizing its bicultural heritage and responsibilities. The result has been a time of rapid change, no more evidently than in the realms of language and education. In 1987, for example, the Māori Language Act was passed – recognizing, for the first time, Māori as an official language of Aotearoa/New Zealand.[20] The 1980s have also seen the rapid (and highly successful) emergence of Māori-medium language education. After well over a century of prejudice and proscription from Pākehā administrators, Māori language and culture are now being reasserted visibly within education. Moreover, this reassertion has come from Māori initially prepared to work outside the state education system until their language and educational needs, and *rights*, were recognized and acted upon. Gaining the right to education in an indigenous or minority language is as much a political battle as it is an educational one. The emergence (or, rather, re-emergence) of Māori-medium education in the 1980s is a case in point.

Māori language and education

From the beginnings of the state education system in Aotearoa/New Zealand in the 1860s–1870s, an assimilationist agenda was adopted towards Māori. Accordingly, the teaching of English was considered to be a central task of the school, and the Māori language was often regarded as the prime obstacle to the progress of Māori children (Benton, 1981). The result has been the marginalization of Māori, and *te reo Māori* (the Māori language), within the educational process. In particular, Māori have historically had very little meaningful influence in educational policy decision-making (G. Smith, 1990a). As Linda Tuhiwai Smith observes, schooling came to be seen as 'a primary instrument for taming and civilizing the natives and forging a nation which was connected at a concrete level with the historical and moral processes of Britain' (L. Smith, 1992a, p. 6). Ironically, in this process, Pākehā were not only to repudiate and replace Māori language and knowledge structures within education but were also to deny Māori full access to European knowledge and learning.

This was not always so. Prior to the arrival of Pākehā, Māori had practised a sophisticated and functional system of education based on an extensive network of oral tradition, and with its own rational and complex knowledge structure (G. Smith, 1989; Nepe, 1991). Moreover, upon European colonization, Māori actively sought to complement their own educational knowledge, and their long-established oral tradition, with 'Pākehā wisdom'. Largely for these reasons they turned to the early mission schools, which, though they taught only the standard subjects of the English school curriculum, did so through the medium of Māori. As a result, the period in which these schools were most influential – 1816 to the mid-1840s – saw a rapid spread of literacy among Māori. However, the 1840s saw a change to a much more overtly assimilationist policy towards Māori in education. State funding of mission schools was made dependent on English being the medium of instruction – a requirement that effectively ended Māori-medium teaching. This position was further formalized in 1867 when the state established a system of village day schools in Māori rural communities, ten years prior to the establishment of a parallel public system.[21]

The Native School system, as it came to be known, operated a modified public school curriculum, with a particular emphasis on health and hygiene. Initially, teachers were expected to have some knowledge of the Māori language, which was to be used as an aid in teaching English. However, by the turn of the century the Māori language had all but been banned from the precincts of the schools – a prohibition, often enforced by corporal punishment, that was to continue until the 1950s. This proscription of the Māori language was also to combine with a widely held view among Pākehā administrators concerning the unsuitability of Māori for 'mental labour'. A key objective of native schooling thus came to be the preparation of Māori for labouring-class status – an objective which was rationalized largely through racial ideologies (Simon, 1992). These education policies, along with those directed at land alienation, provide us with at least some explanation for the relative social and educational disadvantage of Māori today.

Language loss

Assimilationist policies in education have also contributed significantly to the rapid decline of the Māori language over the course of this century. This, despite the fact that the English-only policy of Native schools was not initially seen as in any way threatening the Māori language and culture, and was strongly supported by some Māori. Since the 1940s, however, there has been a growing concern among Māori about the state and status of the Māori language. In 1930, for example, a survey of children attending Native schools estimated that 96.6 per cent spoke only Māori at home. By 1960, only 26 per cent spoke Māori. The rapid urbanization of Māori since World War II has been a key factor in this language decline.[22] Although the Māori language had been excluded from the realms of the school for over a century, it had still been nurtured in the largely rural Māori communities. The effects of urbanization were to undermine both these communities and the language they spoke. By 1979 the Māori language had retreated to the point where language death was predicted (R. Benton, 1979; see also R. Benton, 1981, 1983, 1988; N. Benton, 1989).

With this growing realization came an increased advocacy of the need for change in educational policy towards Māori. New approaches to language and education were sought. Assimilation was replaced in the 1960s by a brief period of 'integration'. Heralded by the 1961 Hunn Report, integration aimed 'to combine (not fuse) the Māori and Pākehā elements to form one nation wherein Māori culture remains distinct' (see Hunn, 1961, pp. 14–16). Though an apparently laudable aim, integration proved little different in either theory or practice from its predecessor. It was less crude than assimilation in its conceptions of culture but a clear cultural hierarchy continued to underpin the model. Hunn, for example, clearly regarded those aspects of the Māori culture that were to 'remain distinct' as 'relics' of a tribal culture of which 'only the fittest elements (worthiest of preservation) have survived the onset of civilization'. Compared to this 'backward life in primitive conditions', he argued that 'pressure [should] be brought to bear on [Māori] to conform to ... the pākehā mode of life', which he equated with modernity and progress. This 'deficit' view simply reinforced the previous assimilationist agenda and resulted in the continued perception of Māori as an educational 'problem' (cf. Stages 1 and 2 of Churchill's typology).

In the face of mounting criticism from Māori, integration was replaced in the 1970s and 1980s by multicultural education. This latter approach – representing Stage 3 of Churchill's typology – came to be known as *taha Māori* (the Māori side). In what was, by now, an integrated state education system, it attempted to incorporate a specifically Māori dimension into the curriculum that was available to *all* pupils, Māori and non-Māori alike. As its official definition outlines, 'Taha Māori is the inclusion of *aspects of* Māori language and culture in the philosophy, organization and the content of the school ... It should be a normal part of the school climate with which all pupils should feel comfortable and at ease' (Department of Education, 1984a; my emphasis). The emphasis here was clearly on biculturalism, but this was also seen as a first step to the incorporation of other cultures within the curriculum along similar lines. As a related publication states, 'an effective approach to multicultural education *is through* bicultural education' (Department of Education, 1984b, p. 31; my emphasis). In this, *taha Māori* is consistent with many other multicultural education initiatives undertaken elsewhere (see May,

1994). However, *taha Māori* has also faced increasing criticism – particularly from Māori – for a number of key inadequacies.

First, the rationale for implementing *taha Māori* as a bicultural *stage* of multiculturalism is seen as incompatible with the terms of the Treaty of Waitangi. The view that all minority cultures should be recognized equally within Aotearoa/New Zealand has its attractions, but in practice it works very much in favour of the numerically dominant Pākehā group. Specifically, relegating Māori to the status of a single group among many (albeit a large and influential one) disadvantages Māori in two ways:

> it denies Māori people their equality as members of one among two (sets of) peoples, and it also tends to deny the divisions of Māoridom their separate status while exaggerating the status of other immigrant groups. In the end, Māori interests become peripheral, combined with other special problem areas. (Benton, 1988, p. 77)

Limiting biculturalism to support for 'aspects of Māori language and culture' within schools falls far short of the biculturalism that many Māori seek – a biculturalism concerned primarily with institutional transformation and social change. In this sense, multiculturalism can be seen as a useful ideology for *containing* the conflicts of ethnic groups within existing social relations rather than as the basis for any real power-sharing between Māori and Pākehā and, from that basis, other ethnic groups. Indeed, support for multiculturalism among some Pākehā arises less out of a valuing of diversity, or a concern for the interests of minority groups, than from a fear of the possible fulfilment of Māori bicultural aspirations (Simon, 1989).

Secondly, and relatedly, *taha Māori* has been criticized for its peripheral and selective treatment of Māori language and culture. In this sense, *taha Māori* conforms to what has elsewhere been termed as an 'ethnic additive' approach to multicultural education (see, for example, Gibson, 1984; Banks, 1988; Grant and Sleeter, 1989; May, 1994). Such an approach sees an 'ethnic' component tacked on to the existing monocultural curriculum – in this case, particular 'aspects of Māori language and culture'. Although the aim, in so doing, is to enhance the educational performance

of Māori children, multicultural education in this form actually does little, if anything, to change the cultural transmission of the dominant group within schooling. Moreover, with its emphasis on *lifestyles* rather than *life chances*, it fails to question or challenge existing social and cultural relations. As Bullivant argues, 'selections for the curriculum that encourage children from ethnic backgrounds to learn about their cultural heritage, languages, histories, customs and other aspects of their life-styles have little bearing on their equality of educational opportunity and life-chances' (1986, p. 42).

Multicultural education, in the form of *taha Māori*, is little different, then, from its predecessors in Māori educational policy. Language is not included beyond a token presence (and thus does nothing to redress language loss), and the control of policy remains firmly with members of the dominant Pākehā group. The very process of cultural 'selection' highlights this lack of control for Māori in educational decision-making. However well intentioned, cultural 'selection' is a paternalistic exercise which must, inevitably, reflect more the interests and concerns of Pākehā than those of Māori. This irony is illustrated by the conclusion of many Māori educationalists that the main beneficiaries of *taha Māori* have actually been Pākehā children (Irwin, 1988, 1989; Penetito, 1988; Smith, 1990b; see also Simon, 1986; Hirsh, 1990). As Graham Hingangaroa Smith argues,

> biculturalism as a curriculum thrust can be regarded as a 'two edged sword' for Māori aspirations. At one level the indigenising of Pākehā people needs to be supported, but at another level, it appropriates already limited resources away from the priority concern of Māori needs. (Smith, 1990b, p. 189)

Language reversal

None of the policies so far discussed have managed either to redress the educational disadvantages facing Māori or to reverse the rapid language loss in the Māori community. Indeed, it has been my argument that such policies have contributed significantly to both these phenomena. The results have been, on the one hand, the differential social and educational indices for Māori in Aotearoa/New Zealand and, on the other hand, the present linguistic homogeneity of Aotearoa/New Zealand. With regard to the latter, more than nine out of ten of Aotearoa/New Zealand's 3.5 million inhabitants are first-language speakers of English – a figure which makes it one of the most linguistically homogeneous in the world today. Even among those of Māori ancestry, only one in eight – 50,000 people in all – are first-language speakers, and the majority of these are middle-aged or older (R. Benton, 1981; N. Benton, 1989; Waite, 1992). However, two recent educational developments have begun to halt the process of language loss for Māori: first, the establishment of bilingual schools in the late 1970s; and second, and more significantly, the emergence of alternative Māori-medium (immersion) schools – initiated and administered by Māori – during the course of the 1980s. The latter movement, in particular, has combined with the wider political developments discussed above to spearhead the beginnings of what Christina Paulston has described as 'language reversal' – a process by which 'one of the languages of a state begins to move back into more prominent use' (1993, p. 281). In Aotearoa/New Zealand, this is particularly evidenced by what Paulston terms 'reversal of shift' where 'a language, which appears to be disappearing, has a renaissance and is saved from extinction by increased use' (ibid., p. 282).[23] In the process of this renaissance of the Māori language, the historical legacy of educational disadvantage for Māori is also finally beginning to be redressed.

The beginnings of this language reversal within education can be found in the early 1960s, when the Currie Commission included in its recommendations the teaching of Māori as an optional subject at secondary school level. This first tentative step to reintroduce *te reo Māori* into the school curriculum initiated a period of renewed debate on the merits of bilingual schooling in Aotearoa/New Zealand. It was to culminate, in 1977, with the first officially sanctioned English/Māori bilingual primary school at Ruatoki, one of the last predominantly Māori-speaking communities in the country.[24] Other schools were to follow – providing, primarily, a 'transition' approach to bilingualism (Stage 4 in Churchill's typology). By 1988, 20 such bilingual schools had been established, predominantly in Māori rural communities. In addition, 67 primary schools and 18 secondary schools by this time operated with at least some bilingual classes, catering for approximately 3,000 students (Benton, 1988; Hirsh, 1990). By 1991, however, this had risen rapidly to 251 primary schools and 54 secondary schools offering some form of bilingual education to 13,000 primary students and 2,500 secondary students respectively (Davies and Nicholl, 1993). Although these developments have been very encouraging, the rationales for bilingual programmes, and the degree to which they incorporate *te reo Māori* as medium of instruction, vary widely (Ohia, 1990; Hirsh, 1990; Jacques, 1991).[25] This degree of variability, as well as a continuing lack of both teaching and material resources for bilingual education, remains a cause for concern.

However, the development of these bilingual schools and bilingual programmes has been overshadowed by concurrent developments outside the state education system. Indeed, much of the growing enthusiasm for bilingual education within state schooling can be attributed to an independent movement for the establishment of Māori-medium pre-schools, Te Kōhanga Reo, instigated in 1982 by a small group of Māori parents. So successful has this movement been, in fact, that in the space of just over a decade it has changed the face of education in Aotearoa/New Zealand – affecting, in the process, all other levels of schooling.

Relative autonomy and community control: Te Kōhanga Reo and Kura Kaupapa Māori

Te Kōhanga Reo

Te Kōhanga Reo – meaning, literally, 'language nest' – was launched as a movement with the opening of its first centre on 13 April 1982. At the time of its inception, the continued survival of

Māori language and culture was still looking doubtful. As Kath Irwin observes:

> The proposed Te Kōhanga Reo movement, an initiative aimed at reviving traditional Māori knowledge and cultural practices, seemed like an impossible dream to some. Crucial elements which contributed to this doubt were a cultural base which was said to be too fragmented to support such an initiative, and a people whose alienation from this traditional base was considered to be such that they could no longer, nor would they wish to, take part in its reaffirmation. (Irwin, 1990, pp. 115–16)

And yet Te Kōhanga Reo has proved to be, by any comparative measure, a phenomenal success. In 1982, less than 30 per cent of Māori children aged 2–4 years participated in early-childhood (pre-school) education, compared with 41 per cent for non-Māori. By 1991, the Māori participation rate had risen to 53 per cent, largely as a result of Te Kōhanga Reo (Davies and Nicholl, 1993). Between 1983 and 1993, in fact, there has been a demonstrated growth rate in *kōhanga* student numbers of 250 per cent (O'Rourke, 1994). This has been matched by the proliferation of *kōhanga* around the country. After the initial centre had been established in April 1982, the number of *kōhanga* quickly rose to 54 by the end of that year. By August 1988 this had increased to 521 and by January 1993 to 802. In 1993, 49.2 per cent of all Māori children enrolled in early-childhood programmes – approximately 14,000 – were at a *kōhanga reo*.

The *kaupapa* (philosophy; set of objectives) of Te Kōhanga Reo can be summarized as follows (Sharples, 1988):

1 total immersion in *te reo Māori* at the *kōhanga reo*;
2 the imparting of Māori spiritual values and concepts to the children;
3 the teaching and involvement of the children in *tikanga Māori* (Māori customs);
4 the complete administration of each centre by the *whānau* (extended family; see below); and
5 the utilization of many traditional techniques of childcare and knowledge acquisition.

From this, three aspects can be highlighted as key organizing principles (see Kā'ai, 1990).

Te Reo
'*He kōrero Māori*' (speaking in Māori) is a central organizing principle of Te Kōhanga Reo. An environment where only Māori is spoken is seen as the best means by which 'language reversal' can be achieved. Only by this can the current dominance of English in almost every other domain in Aotearoa/New Zealand life be effectively contested. This accords with a 'maintenance' view of bilingualism (cf. Hakuta, 1986; Appel and Muysken, 1987; Romaine, 1989; Baker, 1988, 1993), as reflected in Stage 5 of Churchill's language policy typology. Culturally preferred styles of pedagogy, such as *teina/tuakana* roles (peer tutoring) and collaborative teaching and learning, also feature prominently in the ethos and practice of *kōhanga* (see Kā'ai, 1990; Metge, 1990; May, 1994 for a fuller discussion).

Whānau
Te Kōhanga Reo has been, from its inception, a parent-driven and resourced initiative based on *whānau* (extended family) principles.[26] *Kōhanga* are staffed by fluent Māori-speaking parents, grandparents and caregivers, often working in a voluntary capacity, and are supported by the wider *whānau* associated with the pre-school. *Whānau* may be constituted on traditional kinship grounds but have also come to include, in urban centres, a more generic concept in which criteria for affiliation have moved from kinship ties to commonality of interests and/or residence (Nepe, 1991). The significance of *kaumātua* (elders) is also highlighted in the *whānau* structure. *Kaumātua* are regarded as active participants in the educational process. They are used not just as repositories of knowledge but also as teachers who can model the language, and other forms of cultural practice and behaviour, to *kōhanga* children (L. Smith, 1989).

Mana motuhake (self-determination)
The central involvement of *whānau* in Te Kōhanga Reo has meant that Māori parents have been able to exert a significant degree of *local* control over the education of their children. The *whānau* approach is characterized by collective decision-

making and each *whānau* has autonomy within the *kaupapa* of the movement (Irwin, 1990). Meaningful choices can thus be made over what children should learn, how they should learn, and who should be involved in the learning (L. Smith, 1989). Individual *whānau* are also supported at a national level by the Kōhanga Reo Trust, which was established in the early 1980s to develop a nationally recognized syllabus for the purposes of gaining state funding. This latter objective was achieved in 1990. Prior to this, *kōhanga* had been almost entirely funded by *whānau* themselves. Although state funding presents some contradictions here (see below), the principle of 'relative autonomy' (G. Smith, 1990a, 1990b, 1992) remains a key feature of Te Kōhanga Reo.

Te Kōhanga Reo represents a major turning point for Māori perceptions and attitudes about education. Its success has also had a 'domino effect' on the provision of Māori-medium education at other levels of schooling as *kōhanga* graduates have worked their way through the school system over the course of the past fifteen years. This is particularly evident at the primary level with the development of bilingual schooling, already discussed, and the emergence of Kura Kaupapa Māori (see below). However, it is also now beginning to exert its influence on higher educational levels. For example, in 1993–4 two *whare kura* (Māori-medium secondary schools) were established and two *whare wānanga* (tertiary institutions) were formally recognized for funding purposes, with another awaiting approval (O'Rourke, 1994). However, it is to the primary-level *kura kaupapa Māori* (literally, 'Māori philosophy schools') that I wish finally to turn.

Kura Kaupapa Māori

The first *kura kaupapa Māori*, entirely privately funded, opened in February 1985. Five years of political advocacy by Māori followed before a pilot scheme of six *kura kaupapa Māori* was approved for state funding in 1990. With the success

of this scheme (see Reedy, 1992), rapid development has occurred. At the beginning of the 1994 school year, 28 *kura kaupapa Māori* had been established, catering for 1667 students (O'Rourke, 1994). The government has also since made a commitment for at least a further five *kura* to be approved each year.

The development of Kura Kaupapa Māori is largely attributable to the success of Te Kōhanga Reo and the increasing demand that it created for Māori-medium education at the primary level. The inability of the state education system to meet these demands effectively, beyond the limited options provided in bilingual programmes (see above), had led by the mid-1980s to the advocacy of Kura Kaupapa Māori as an alternative schooling option. A principal concern of *kōhanga* parents was to maintain the language gains made by their children.[27] Kura Kaupapa Māori, in adopting the same language and organizational principles as Te Kōhanga Reo, could continue to reinforce these language gains within a Māori cultural and language-medium environment. More broadly, the importance of 'relative autonomy' and 'community control' feature prominently in the advocacy of Kura Kaupapa Māori during the 1980s. Te Kōhanga Reo had served to politicize Māori parents with regard to the education of their children (L. Smith, 1989, 1992b; G. Smith, 1990b), and the advocacy of Kura Kaupapa was the natural extension of this.

In 1984, for example, the Māori Education Conference brought together Māori teachers, community leaders and educationalists from across the political spectrum to discuss the issues surrounding Māori 'underachievement' in education. The consensus from the conference was that only significant structural reform of the state education system could change the educational circumstances of Māori children. If this did not occur, the conference urged 'Māori withdrawal and the establishment of alternative schooling modelled on the principle of Kōhanga Reo'. In 1988, another *hui* (conference) produced the Mātawaia Declaration, which states:

> our children's needs cannot be met through a continuation of the present system of Pākehā control and veto of Māori aspirations for our children. It is time to

change. Time for us to take control of our own destinies. We believe this development is both necessary and timely.

These calls from Māori for greater autonomy, and structural change, within education were to coincide with the reorganization of the state education system in 1988–9. The reforms, outlined in the policy document *Tomorrow's Schools* (Lange, 1988), emphasized parental choice, devolution and local school management. Many of the changes which have resulted can be seen as problematic (see Codd *et al.*, 1990; Lauder and Wylie, 1990; Middleton *et al.*, 1990; Dale and Ozga, 1993), but the reforms did provide Māori with a platform to argue for separate recognition of Kura Kaupapa Māori. Initially, the government responsible for the reforms was reticent to apply its own rhetoric of local control to the Kura Kaupapa Māori case. However, after a considerable degree of prevarication, and as a result of consistent and effective lobbying by Māori, Kura Kaupapa Māori was eventually incorporated into the 1990 Education Amendment Act as a recognized (and state-funded) schooling alternative within the Aotearoa/New Zealand state education system.[28] The principles which have since come to characterize it can be summarized as follows (see G. Smith, 1992, pp. 20–3).

1 *Rangatiratanga* (relative autonomy principle). A greater autonomy over key decision-making in schooling has been attained in areas such as administration, curriculum, pedagogy and Māori aspirations.
2 *Taonga Tuku Iho* (cultural aspiration principle). In Kura Kaupapa Māori, to be Māori is taken for granted. The legitimacy of Māori language, culture and values is normalized.
3 *Ako Māori* (culturally preferred pedagogy). Culturally preferred forms of pedagogy are employed, such as peer tutoring and collaborative teaching and learning. These are used in conjunction with general schooling methods where appropriate.
4 *Kia Piki Ake i Ngā Raruraru o te Kainga* (mediation of socio-economic difficulties). Whereas Kura Kaupapa Māori (or education more generally) cannot, on its own, redress

the socio-economic difficulties faced by Māori, the collective support and involvement provided by the *whānau* structure can ameliorate some of its most debilitating effects.
5 *Whānau* (extended family principle). The *whānau* structure provides a support network for individual members and requires a reciprocal obligation on the part of these individuals to support and contribute to the collective aspirations of the group. It has been most successful in involving Māori parents in the administration of their children's schooling.
6 *Kaupapa* (philosophy principle). Kura Kaupapa Māori 'is concerned to teach a modern, up to date, relevant curriculum (within the national guidelines set by the state)' (Smith, 1990b, p. 194). The aim is not the forced choice of one culture and/or language over another but the provision of a distinctively Māori educational environment that is able to promote bilingualism and biculturalism effectively.

Conclusion

A number of caveats need to be outlined briefly in conclusion. First, I recognize (as do those directly involved in Māori-medium education) that education cannot compensate for society. As Irwin observes, if Māori-medium education was solely relied upon, with no other structural change, 'Māori children of the future would be bilingual, bicultural, and probably still mostly unemployed' (1990, p. 111). The developments in Māori-medium education thus need to be situated clearly within the much wider social, economic and political framework of change that has occurred in Aotearoa/New Zealand over the past twenty years. This has had, at its heart, the restoration of the Treaty of Waitangi to its central role in mediating Māori–Pākehā relations. Nevertheless, the development of Māori-medium schooling does provide us with a specific example of structural change within this broad process that has the *potential* to make a difference to the life chances of Māori children.[29]

Second, it is important to reiterate that these educational developments are neither separatist nor a simple retrenchment in the past. As Kymlicka has argued, nothing in the assertion of indigenous rights – or minority rights more generally – precludes the possibilities of cultural change and adaptation. The specific aim of Māori-medium education is, in fact, to accomplish this very process, *but on its own terms*. The crucial question then becomes one of control rather than retrenchment or rejection. Te Kōhanga Reo and Kura Kaupapa Māori provide the opportunity for Māori parents, working within national curriculum guidelines, to 'change the rules' that have previously excluded Māori language and culture from recognition as cultural and linguistic capital in schools. Māori knowledge and language competencies thus come to frame, but do not exclude, those of the dominant Pākehā group, and they are themselves the subject of negotiation and change. The stated outcomes of Kura Kaupapa Māori clearly highlight this process of mutual accommodation with their emphasis on bilingualism and biculturalism. As Graham Hingangaroa Smith argues, 'Kura Kaupapa Māori parents ... want for their children the ability to access the full range of societal opportunities' (1990b, p. 194). Moreover, Kura Kaupapa Māori remains only one option among many and, at this stage at least, still very much a minority one. For example, of all Māori students enrolled in the primary school system in 1991, 85 per cent were enrolled in mainstream programmes, 14 per cent in bilingual programmes of some kind, and less than 1 per cent in Kura Kaupapa Māori. Proponents of Kura Kaupapa argue that the crucial point is that Māori-medium education *is made available* to Māori (and non-Māori)[30] parents as a legitimate schooling choice, not that it is the answer to everything.

Third, the incorporation of Te Kōhanga Reo and Kura Kaupapa Māori into the state system does present some contradictions, particularly with regard to the notion of relative autonomy. Although state funding has underwritten these initiatives and, crucially, facilitated their expansion, there is an increasing possibility of state encroachment on what were originally local *whānau*-based initiatives. However, it would seem that the benefits of state involvement outweigh their disadvantages. In particular, the state education system is now beginning to address the critical shortage of material and teaching resources for Māori-medium schools, and for bilingual initiatives more broadly. This has already led to the rapid expansion of Māori/English bilingual training programmes within teacher education and a slow but growing expansion of Māori-language teaching material, both of which augur well for the long-term future of Māori-medium education. Incorporation within the national curriculum and assessment framework has also lent legitimacy to Māori-medium initiatives. This legitimacy has been reinforced by initial assessments which suggest that the academic progress of children in Kura Kaupapa is comparable to that of their mainstream peers, while providing the added advantage of bilingualism (Reedy, 1992; Hollings *et al.*, 1992).

There is still much to be accomplished, of that there is no doubt. However, Te Kōhanga Reo and Kura Kaupapa Māori represent, for the first time since 1840, a genuine educational alternative that meets the terms outlined in the Treaty of Waitangi of 'guaranteed [and active] protection' of Māori language and culture. The aims of Kōhanga Reo and Kura Kaupapa are also consistent with developments in international law concerning the educational rights of indigenous peoples. Moreover, they are contributing to Aotearoa/New Zealand's slow move towards a genuinely bilingual and bicultural society – Stage 6 of Churchill's typology. As Graham Hingangaroa Smith concludes:

> The advent of Te Kōhanga Reo and its politicizing effects on Māori parents has created a new interest and optimism in regard to Māori language and culture revival and survival. Kura Kaupapa Māori is a manifestation of [this] renewed Māori interest in schooling and education. The opportunity to capitalize on the potential of Kura Kaupapa Māori should not be lost in terms of dealing with the current schooling crisis [for Māori], in terms of meeting Māori needs and aspirations related to language and cultural survival, and in terms of building a fair and just New Zealand society in the future. (Smith, 1990b, p. 195)

Tera te haeata e takiri ana
mai i runga o Mata-te-ra.
The rays of the morning sun
strike a new dawn on the mountain.

Acknowledgement

I should like to thank Wally Penetito for his advice and comment on an earlier version of this chapter.

Notes

1 Although the term 'minorities' tends to draw attention to numerical size, its more important reference is to groups with few rights and privileges (see Byram, 1986; Tollefson, 1991). As such, I use it here and throughout this chapter to refer to groups with relatively less power, rights and privileges in relation to other, more dominant groups.

2 There are, admittedly, many inter- and intra-group differences evident among disadvantaged groups. However, this should not deflect us from acknowledging *the general pattern* of differential status and achievement apparent among minority groups; that is, that ethnic minorities tend to be *over-represented* in unfavourable social and educational indices in comparison to majority-group members.

3 The links between language and nationalism associate most 'national' languages with modernization in this way (see below). However, this is particularly evident in the case of English in its role as the current dominant world language.

4 This is not to suggest that minority groups have been unconcerned previously with the education of their children; quite the reverse. Rather, I wish to highlight the degree to which minority groups have been excluded in the past from shaping and influencing educational policy.

5 Drawing on Churchill (1986), three types of minority groups can be identified: 'indigenous minorities'; 'established minorities'; and 'new minorities'. 'New minorities' are recent migrants. 'Established' and 'indigenous' minorities are both minority groups which have long been established in their native countries. Established minorities (e.g. Welsh, francophone Canadians, Catalans) are

characterized by a lifestyle similar to that of the remainder of the national society, although sometimes falling behind in rate of evolution. As such, they are more likely to be able to lay claim to a right to conserve their identity and to back it with political might. Indigenous minorities are characterized by a 'traditional' culture which is often regarded as being at odds with that of the majority group. Given this, indigenous peoples are rarely in a position to assert their claims in the same ways. Although all these groups face racism, unequal social and cultural opportunities, and educational disadvantage, Churchill concludes that indigenous minorities are historically the most disadvantaged of the three.

6 John Ogbu's distinction between *voluntary* (immigrant) minorities and *involuntary* (caste-like) minorities provides a useful elaboration of this point (Ogbu, 1987; Gibson and Ogbu, 1991). Like Churchill, Ogbu argues that all minority groups are subject to racism and discrimination to some degree, and face cultural and language discontinuities in relation to schooling. However, for voluntary minorities these discontinuities are seen as *primary cultural/language differences*; that is, they existed prior to their immigration to the host country and are thus viewed as barriers to be overcome. As such, voluntary minorities are more likely to accommodate to the 'cultural model' of the majority group. In contrast, involuntary minorities – within which grouping Ogbu includes indigenous minorities – are characterized by a history of exploitation and/or subjugation *within* a particular country. Accordingly, involuntary minorities tend to develop a *secondary cultural system* in which cultural differences are viewed in light of that history, and in opposition to the majority group. Cultural and language differences thus come to serve a boundary maintenance function. They are seen as symbols of identity to be maintained rather than barriers to be overcome.

7 'Aotearoa' ('land of the long white cloud') is the name Māori have historically given to the country. 'New Zealand' derives from the Dutch origins of the explorer, Abel Tasman, the first European to sight the country. The joint use of Aotearoa/New Zealand highlights the bicultural nature of the country and is preferred by those 'New Zealanders' critical of the subsequent processes and effects of Pākehā (European) colonization (Bell, 1994; and see below).

8 Bourdieu highlights education's role in creating a 'unified linguistic market' which, linked with wider power relations, legitimates particular knowledge and language forms – usually those of the majority (ethnic) group – and devalues others – usually those of minorities. This helps to explain

why those whose cultural and linguistic capital corresponds with that of the school are not only initially advantaged but are also likely to have that advantage reinforced throughout their schooling. In contrast, disadvantaged groups are faced with knowledge and language discontinuities between home and school. These discontinuities, because they go unrecognized, tend also to be exacerbated over time.

9 Of course, protectionism in this form has also simply been used as a variant of assimilation. As Hartwig argues, concerning Māori in Aotearoa/New Zealand and Koori in Australia, 'whatever the differences between "amalgamationist" and "protectionist" strategies, the ultimate aim of the state for long periods in both countries was the disappearance of Aboriginal and Māori societies as distinguishable entities' (1978, p. 170, cited in Harker and McConnochie, 1985). Joshua Fishman is also particularly critical of this kind of 'protectionism'. As he argues, 'even in such settings indigenous populations are robbed of control of the natural resources that could constitute the economic bases of a more self-regulatory collective life and, therefore, robbed also of a possible avenue of cultural viability as well' (1991, p. 62).

10 Indeed, in 40 per cent of all states there are at least five or more such groups, and in nearly one-third of all states (31 per cent) the largest national group is not even the majority (Connor, 1993).

11 As Young observes, this analysis is equally applicable to gender and cultural minorities as well (see also Corson, 1993).

12 Kymlicka argues, for example, that this is consistent with Rawls's and Dworkin's previous analyses of liberalism and justice, which both *implicitly* recognize cultural membership as a primary good. The only reason they do not explicitly give it status as a ground for differential rights claims, he suggests, is because they accept uncritically the notion of the nation-state as politically and culturally coterminous (see above). If this assumption is dropped, cultural membership has to be explicitly recognized as a possible source of injustice and/or inequality – a point which earlier theorists of liberalism, like Hobhouse and Dewey, actually recognized.

13 Hastings argues, along similar lines, that the principles of 'equality' and 'non-discrimination' in international law must include 'protection of minorities' with respect to their language(s). This is because 'inequality does not result from differential treatment of persons who are different'. In fact, inequality may 'occur when persons who are different are treated in the same manner as everyone else' (1988, p. 13).

14 I am aware that any discussion of unfavourable social, economic and educational indices can, by its very nature, lend itself to a pathological conception. This has certainly been the case in many past analyses of Māori, for example. However, it is not my intention here. Rather, as Figueroa (1991) has argued, the argument should be moved away from a focus on the 'underachievement' or 'failure' of minority groups to a recognition that they are *unequally placed* within society, and its key institutions, thus addressing the cause rather than the symptom (see also Kymlicka's discussion of unequal circumstances). This is what I will attempt to do in what follows.

15 Of the Māori population, 4.3 per cent receive a pension compared with 17.1 per cent of non-Māori. McLoughlin (1993) argues that although some of this has to do with the young age structure of the Māori population, it is also because too few Māori live long enough. Health indicators here present a disturbing picture. Māori do not live, on average, as long as non-Māori. The immunization rates of Māori children – less than 60 per cent compared with 90 per cent for most other 'developed' countries – see Māori children suffer disproportionately from preventable diseases. Half of all Māori aged over 15 smoke (compared with about a quarter of the non-Māori population). This includes 45 per cent of men and 57 per cent of women, the latter figure having led to Māori women having one of the highest lung cancer rates in the world.

16 Prior to the arrival of the first Pākehā towards the end of the eighteenth century, Māori had been resident in Aotearoa/New Zealand for approximately 1,000 years. Their Polynesian ancestors had first settled around AD 800, towards the end of their Pacific ocean voyages of discovery and settlement that had begun in AD 200 (Walker, 1990). The Dutch explorer Abel Tasman was the first European to sight the country in 1642, but he received a hostile reception from the South Island tribes so it was not until the English sailor Captain James Cook 'discovered' the country again in 1769 that European settlement began.

17 Much of this has to do with the discrepancies between the official English-language version of the treaty and the Māori-language version which the chiefs actually signed. The treaty comprises three articles. In Article 1, for example, there is a distinction between the ceding of 'all the rights and powers of *Sovereignty*' in the English version – equating to the term *tino rangatiratanga*, or 'absolute chieftainship' in Māori – and the actual use in the Māori text of the lesser term *kāwanatanga*, or 'governorship'. In Article 2 this discrepancy is reinforced. In the official English version Māori are

granted 'exclusive and undisturbed possession of their Lands and Estates, Forestries, Fisheries and other properties which they may individually and collectively possess'. In the Māori translation this becomes 'the absolute chieftainship [*tino rangatiratanga*] of their lands, of their homes and all their treasured possessions'. Thus, the chiefs are likely to have understood Article 2 as confirming their own sovereign rights in return for a limited concession (granted in Article 1) of Pākehā 'governorship'. Article 3 – the least contentious – extends to Māori the rights of British citizens, although the Māori version talks again of governance, rather than sovereignty, reinforcing the previous emphases (see Orange, 1987; Kawharu, 1989; Walker, 1990).

18 After an initial period of relative stability and prosperity, land wars in the 1860s were initiated against Māori tribes by the settler government (established in 1852) in an attempt to expropriate Māori land for the rapidly growing numbers of Pākehā settlers. When this proved inconclusive, the government resorted to legislation which transformed communally owned Māori land into individual titles – as in English law – in order to expedite the further sale of the land. This proved so successful that by the turn of the century almost all New Zealand territory was in European hands. Concomitantly, the Pākehā population had risen from 1,000 in 1838 to 770,000 by 1900 while the Māori population had fallen from an estimated 100,000–200,000 at the time of European settlement to the nadir of 45,549 in 1900; in effect, a 75 per cent population collapse of Māori over the course of the nineteenth century (Stannard, 1989; Walker, 1990). As Claudia Orange concludes, 'In many respects New Zealand, in spite of the treaty, has been merely a variation in the colonial domination of indigenous races [*sic*]' (1987, p. 5).

19 The emphasis on biculturalism, rather than multiculturalism, in Aotearoa/New Zealand is intentional. It is not that these two concepts are seen as mutually exclusive – although opponents of biculturalism, it can be argued, do tend to see it this way (see below) – it is rather that the Treaty of Waitangi requires the country's bicultural and bilingual commitments to be attended to first, *and in their own right*, before any subsequent move to multiculturalism. Multiculturalism in Aotearoa/New Zealand cannot occur without first addressing our bicultural commitments.

20 This legal recognition of the language is still somewhat limited. In particular, the right to use or to demand the use of Māori in the public domain does not extend beyond the oral use of the language in courts of law and some quasi-legal tribunals (Benton, 1988). More positively, the Act did provide for the establishment of a Māori Language Commission, Te Taura Whiri i te Reo Māori. Closely modelled on the Irish Bord na Gaeilge, the Commission's role is to monitor and promote the use of the language, although its staff and resources are also limited. A recent draft National Languages Policy has continued these positive developments by highlighting, as its top priority, the reversal of the decline in the Māori language (Waite, 1992).

21 This parallel arrangement was to continue until the dissolution of the Native School system in 1969.

22 Prior to World War II less than 10 per cent of Māori had lived in cities or smaller urban centres. By 1981, 79 per cent of Māori lived in urban areas (N. Benton, 1989).

23 Paulston distinguishes 'language reversal' from two other frequently used terms: 'language revival', where a language that has no native speakers left is revived as a medium of communication (e.g. Hebrew); and 'language revitalization', where an attempt is made to expand the domains of a particular language (e.g. Finnish, Irish). Language reversal is further separated into three types by Paulston: 'legal reversal', where a shift in political power results in the legal acceptance of a previously illegal language (e.g. Catalan in Spain); 'reversal of shift' (Māori); and 'rebound of an exoglossic language', where an adopted rather than indigenous language becomes the language of the state (e.g. Swahili in Tanzania).

24 Ironically, the Currie Commission may well not have wished this development as it was also clearly ambivalent about any greater role for the Māori language in the educational process (Benton, 1981). It certainly did not envisage the development of Māori/English bilingualism in schools (Hirsh, 1990). As the Commission states, the school 'is not, nor can it ever be the prime agency in conserving the Māori cultural heritage'. This is, of course, true to a point. However, it begs a question – if the school clearly performs this function, at least to some degree, for Pākehā children, why cannot it do so also for Māori? (Harker, 1980; Benton, 1987).

25 Monte Ohia (1990) argues that the usual rationales for establishing bilingual programmes, particularly in secondary schools, involve 'improving' the behaviour of Māori students and their attitudes to schools. Hirsh observes that the programmes he observed in his review of bilingual education ranged from total immersion 'to programmes where instructions were given in Māori but where English was the main medium. The programmes also varied considerably in the amount of Māori used during the day – in some cases so little that it would be

difficult to describe the programme as bilingual, while in no way denying that a Māori perspective had a strong presence' (1990, p. 48).

26 The traditional *whānau* arrangement includes grandparents, relatives and other children but the concept of *whānau* also incorporates values of *aroha* (love), *manaaki* (caring, sharing and empathy) and *wairua* (spirituality). All these elements, and the reciprocal commitments they entail, shape the educational activities of *kōhanga*.

27 Indications were that these were being rapidly lost by *kōhanga* children upon their transfer to local primary schools. Such was the concern of some parents that they kept their children in *kōhanga* for an additional year until a primary Māori-medium option could be found.

28 Initially, the government argued that a *kura kaupapa* was a 'special character' school under the new legislation – the same category as given to Catholic schools that had previously been integrated into the state system. Māori argued, however, that *kura kaupapa* could not be equated with an existing school category in this way (Benton, 1987; Sharples, 1988). Another option, the provision for a group of twenty-one or more parents to opt out of the state system, was also rejected. Proponents of Kura Kaupapa argued that this option was envisaged as a strictly limited one since the rationale provided for it in *Tomorrow's Schools* clearly states that 'the establishment of a new institution will only be as a last resort' (Lange, 1988, p. 77). Moreover, the approval of such schools would remain at the behest of the state education authorities. As Pita Sharples argues, 'the "opt-out" option exists as a remedial device and does not promote Kura Kaupapa Māori as a *bona fide* option in the school system with full and equal rights with state schools' (cited in G. Smith, 1989, p. 35). In contrast, Sharples, and other leading Māori educationalists, argued that Kura Kaupapa should be provided *as of right* as a genuine alternative within the state system for those parents who wished it – a position that was eventually to win the day.

29 Although significant gaps between the educational performance of Māori and non-Māori remain, these disparities are slowly beginning to be reversed. Retention rates for Māori in secondary education, for example, have improved markedly over the course of the 1980s. Between 1981 and 1991, the proportion of Māori who remained in school until the sixth form (16 years) more than doubled from 24 to 55 per cent. There have also recently been substantial increases in Māori participation in the tertiary sector. Between 1986 and 1991, for example, there was a fourfold increase in the number of Māori enrolled in tertiary education, with Māori making up 7 per cent of all tertiary students in 1991 (Davies and Nicholl, 1993).

30 In 1991, 8 per cent of children in Te Kōhanga Reo were non-Māori (Davies and Nicholl, 1993).

References

Anderson, B. (1993) *Imagined Communities: Reflections on the Origin and Spread of Nationalism*, 2nd edn. London: Verso.

Appel, R. and Muysken, P. (1987) *Language Contact and Bilingualism*. London: Edward Arnold.

Baker, C. (1988) *Key Issues in Bilingualism and Bilingual Education*. Clevedon: Multilingual Matters.

Baker, C. (1993) *Foundations of Bilingual Education and Bilingualism*. Clevedon: Multilingual Matters.

Banks, J. (1988) *Multiethnic Education: Theory and Practice*, 2nd edn. Newton, MA: Allyn & Bacon.

Belich, J. (1986) *The New Zealand Wars*. Auckland: Auckland University Press.

Bell, A. (1994) New Zealand or Aotearoa? The battle for nationhood in the English curriculum, *Curriculum Studies*, **2**, 171–88.

Benton, N. (1989) Education, language decline and language revitalization: the case of Māori in New Zealand, *Language and Education: An International Journal*, **3**, 65–82.

Benton, R. (1979) *Who Speaks Māori in New Zealand*. Wellington: New Zealand Council for Educational Research.

Benton, R. (1981) *The Flight of the Amokura: Oceanic Languages and Formal Education in the South Pacific*. Wellington: New Zealand Council for Educational Research.

Benton, R. (1983) *The NZCER Māori Language Survey*. Wellington: New Zealand Council for Educational Research.

Benton, R. (1987) Fairness in Māori education: a review of research and information, in *Report of the Royal Commission on Social Policy*, vol. 3. Wellington: Government Printer, pp. 287–404.

Benton, R. (1988) The Māori language in New Zealand education, *Language, Culture and Curriculum*, **1**, 75–83.

Bourdieu, P. (1977) The economy of linguistic exchanges, *Social Science Information*, **16**, 645–68.

Bourdieu, P. (1982) *Ce que parler veut dire: l'économie des échanges linguistiques*. Paris: Arthème Fayard.

Bourdieu, P. (1990a) *In Other Words: Essays towards a Reflexive Sociology*. Cambridge: Polity Press.

Bourdieu, P. (1990b) *The Logic of Practice*. Cambridge: Polity Press.

Bourdieu, P. and Passeron, J. (1977) *Reproduction in Education, Society and Culture*. London: Sage.

Bourdieu, P. and Passeron, J. (1990) *Reproduction in Education, Society and Culture*, 2nd edn. London: Sage.

Bullivant, B. (1981) *The Pluralist Dilemma in Education: Six Cases Studies*. Sydney: Allen & Unwin.

Bullivant, B. (1986) Towards radical multiculturalism: resolving tensions in curriculum and educational planning, in S. Modgil, G. Verma, K. Mallick and C. Modgil (eds), *Multicultural Education: The Interminable Debate*. London: Falmer Press, pp. 33–47.

Byram, M. (1986) Schools in ethnolinguistic minorities, *Journal of Multilingual and Multicultural Development*, 7, 97–106.

Callister, P. (1989) *Implications for Māori Development, Economic and Sectoral Trends to 1997*. Wellington: New Zealand Planning Council.

Churchill, S. (1986) *The Education of Linguistic and Cultural Minorities in the OECD Countries*. Clevedon: Multilingual Matters.

Codd, J., Harker, R. and Nash, R. (eds) (1990) *Political Issues in New Zealand Education*, 2nd edn. Palmerston North: Dunmore Press.

Connor, W. (1993) Beyond reason: the nature of the ethnonational bond. *Ethnic and Racial Studies*, 16, 374–89.

Corson, D. (1993) *Language, Minority Education and Gender*. Clevedon: Multilingual Matters.

Dale, R. and Ozga, J. (1993) Two hemispheres – both New Right? 1980s education reform in New Zealand and England and Wales, in B. Lingard, J. Knight and P. Porter (eds), *Schooling Reform in Hard Times*. London: Falmer Press, pp. 63–87.

Davies, L. and Nicholl, K. (1993) *Te Māori i roto i ngā Mahi Whakaakoranga* [*Māori Education: A Statistical Profile of the Position of Māori across the New Zealand Education System*]. Wellington: Ministry of Education.

Department of Education (1984a) *Taha Māori: Suggestions for Getting Started*. Wellington: Department of Education.

Department of Education (1984b) *A Review of the Core Curriculum for Schools*. Wellington: Department of Education.

Figueroa, P. (1991) *Education and the Social Construction of 'Race'*. London: Routledge.

Fishman, J. (1991) *Reversing Language Shift: Theoretical and Empirical Foundations of Assistance to Threatened Languages*. Clevedon: Multilingual Matters.

Gellner, E. (1983) *Nations and Nationalism*. Oxford: Blackwell.

Gibson, M. (1984) Approaches to multicultural education in the United States: some concepts and assumptions, *Anthropology and Education Quarterly*, 15, 94–119.

Gibson, M. and Ogbu, J. (eds) (1991) *Minority Status and Schooling: A Comparative Study of Immigrant and Involuntary Minorities*. New York: Garland Publishing.

Grant, C. and Sleeter, C. (1989) *Turning on Learning: Five Approaches for Multicultural Teaching Plans for Race, Class, Gender and Disability*. Columbus: Merrill.

Haines, L. (1989) *Work Today: Employment Trends to 1989*. Wellington: New Zealand Planning Council.

Hakuta, K. (1986) *Mirror of Language: The Debate on Bilingualism*. New York: Basic Books.

Harker, R. (1980) Research on the education of Māori children, in *Research in Education in New Zealand: The State of the Art*. Wellington: NZARE/Delta, pp. 42–72.

Harker, R. and McConnochie, K. (1985) *Education as Cultural Artifact: Studies in Māori and Aboriginal Education*. Palmerston North: Dunmore Press.

Hastings, W. (1988) *The Right to an Education in Māori: The Case from International Law*. Wellington: Victoria University Press.

Havighurst, R. (1974) *Anthropology and Cultural Pluralism. Three Case Studies: Australia, New Zealand, United States of America*. Wellington: New Zealand Council for Educational Research.

Hirsh, W. (1990) *A Report on Issues and Factors Relating to Māori Achievement in the Education System*. Wellington: Ministry of Education.

Hollings, M., Jeffries, R. and McArdell, P. (1992) *Assessment in Kura Kaupapa Māori and Māori Language Immersion Programmes: A Report to the Ministry of Education*. Wellington: Ministry of Education.

Howe, K. (1992) Liberal democracy, equal opportunity, and the challenge of multiculturalism, *American Educational Research Journal*, 29, 455–70.

Hunn, J. (1961) *Report on the Department of Māori Affairs*. Wellington: Government Printer.

Irwin, K. (1988) Racism and education, in W. Hirsh and R. Scott (eds), *Getting It Right: Aspects of Ethnicity and Equity in New Zealand Education*. Auckland: Office of the Race Relations Conciliator, pp. 49–60.

Irwin, K. (1989) Multicultural education: the New Zealand response, *New Zealand Journal of Educational Studies*, 24, 3–18.

Irwin, K. (1990) The politics of Kōhanga Reo, in S. Middleton, J. Codd and A. Jones (eds), *New Zealand Education Policy Today: Critical Perspectives*. Wellington: Allen & Unwin, pp. 110–20.

Jacques, K. (1991) Community contexts of Māori–

170 *Stephen May*

English bilingual education: a study of six South
Island primary school programmes. Unpublished
Ph.D. dissertation, University of Canterbury,
Christchurch.

Jarden, K. (1992) Education: making a Māori underclass, *Race, Gender, Class*, **13**, 20–25.

Kā'ai, T. (1990) Te Hiringa Taketake: Mai i Te Kōhanga
Reo ki te kura. Māori pedagogy: Te Kōhanga Reo
and the transition to school. Unpublished M.Phil.
thesis, University of Auckland, Auckland.

Kawharu, I. (ed.) (1989) *Waitangi: Māori and Pākehā
Perspectives of the Treaty of Waitangi*. Auckland:
Oxford University Press.

Kymlicka, W. (1989) *Liberalism, Community and Culture*. Oxford: Clarendon Press.

Lange, D. (1988) *Tomorrow's Schools: The Reform of
Education Administration in New Zealand*. Wellington: Government Printer.

Lauder, H. and Wylie, C. (eds) (1990) *Towards Successful Schooling*. London: Falmer Press.

McLoughlin, D. (1993) The Māori burden, *North and
South*, November, 60–71.

Manatū Māori (1991) *Māori and Work: The Position of
Māori in the New Zealand Labour Market*. Wellington: Economic Development Unit, Manatu Māori.

May, S. (1994) *Making Multicultural Education Work*.
Clevedon/Toronto: Multilingual Matters/OISE Press

Metge, J. (1990) *Te Kōhao o te Ngira: Culture and Learning*. Wellington: Learning Media, Ministry of Education.

Middleton, S., Codd, J. and Jones, A. (eds) (1990) *New
Zealand Education Policy Today: Critical Perspectives*. Wellington: Allen & Unwin.

Nepe, T. (1991) Te Toi Huarewa Tipuna. Kaupapa
Māori: An educational intervention system. Unpublished MA thesis, University of Auckland, Auckland.

Nieto, S. (1992) *Affirming Diversity: The Sociopolitical
Context of Multicultural Education*. New York:
Longman.

Ogbu, J. (1987) Variability in minority school performance: a problem in search of an explanation, *Anthropology and Education Quarterly*, **18**, 312–34.

Ohia, M. (1990) The unresolved conflict and debate: an
overview of bilingual education in New Zealand secondary schools, *SAME Papers*, 111–32.

Orange, C. (1987) *The Treaty of Waitangi*. Wellington:
Allen & Unwin.

O'Rourke, M. (1994) Revitalisation of the Māori language, *New Zealand Education Gazette*, **73**, 1–3.

Paulston, C. (1993) Language regenesis: a conceptual
overview of language revival, revitalisation and re-
versal, *Journal of Multilingual and Multicultural De-*velopment*, **14**, 275–86.

Pearson, D. (1990) *A Dream Deferred: The Origins of
Ethnic Conflict in New Zealand*. Wellington: Allen &
Unwin.

Penetito, W. (1988) Māori education for a just society, in
Report of the Royal Commission on Social Policy,
vol. 4. Wellington: Government Printer, pp. 89–114.

Reedy, T. (1992) *Kura Kaupapa Māori Research and
Development Project: Final Report*. Wellington: Ministry of Education.

Romaine, S. (1989) *Bilingualism*. Oxford: Basil Blackwell.

Sharp, A. (1990) *Justice and the Māori: Māori Claims in
New Zealand Political Argument in the 1980s*. Auckland: Oxford University Press.

Sharples, P. (1988) *Kura Kaupapa Māori: Recommendations for Policy*. Auckland: Te Kura o Hoani Waititi
Marae.

Simon, J. (1986) *Ideology in the Schooling of Māori
Children*. Delta Research Monograph 7. Palmerston
North: Education Department, Massey University.

Simon, J. (1989) Aspirations and ideology: biculturalism
and multiculturalism in New Zealand education,
Sites, **18**, 23–34.

Simon, J. (1992). State schooling for Māori: the control of
access to knowledge. Paper presented to the AARE/
NZARE Joint Conference, Deakin University, Geelong, Australia, November.

Sinclair, K. (ed.) (1993) *The Oxford Illustrated History of
New Zealand*. Oxford: Oxford University Press.

Smith, A. (1986) *The Ethnic Origin of Nations*. Oxford:
Basil Blackwell.

Smith, G. (1989) Kura Kaupapa Māori: innovation and
policy development in Māori education, *Access*, **8**,
26–43.

Smith, G. (1990a) The politics of reforming Māori education: the transforming potential of Kura Kaupapa
Māori, in H. Lauder and C. Wylie (eds), *Towards
Successful Schooling*. London: Falmer Press, pp.
73–87.

Smith, G. (1990b) Taha Māori: Pākehā capture, in J.
Codd, R. Harker and R. Nash (eds), *Political Issues in
New Zealand Education*, 2nd edn. Palmerston North:
Dunmore Press, pp. 183–97.

Smith, G. (1992) Tane-Nui-A-Rangi's legacy: propping
up the sky. Kaupapa Māori as resistance and intervention. Paper presented to the AARE/NZARE Joint
Conference, Deakin University, Geelong, Australia,
November.

Smith, L. (1989) Te Reo Māori: Māori language and the
struggle to survive, *Access*, **8**, 3–9.

Smith, L. (1992a) Ko Taku Ko Ta Te Māori: the dilemma
of a Māori academic. Paper presented to the AARE/

NZARE Joint Conference, Deakin University, Geelong, Australia, November.

Smith, L. (1992b). Kura Kaupapa and the implications for curriculum, in G. McCulloch (ed.), *The School Curriculum in New Zealand: History, Theory, Policy and Practice*. Palmerston North: Dunmore Press, pp. 219–31.

Sorrenson, M. (1989) Towards a radical reinterpretation of New Zealand history: the role of the Waitangi Tribunal, in I. Kawharu (ed.), *Waitangi: Māori and Pākeha Perspectives of the Treaty of Waitangi*. Auckland: Oxford University Press, pp. 158–78.

Squires, J. (ed.) (1993) *Principled Positions: Postmodernism and the Rediscovery of Value*. London: Lawrence & Wishart.

Stannard, D. (1989) *Before the Horror*. Honolulu: University of Hawaii Press.

Tharp, R. (1989) Psychocultural variables and constants: effects on teaching and learning in schools, *American Psychologist*, **44**, 349–59.

Thornberry, P. (1991) *Minorities and Human Rights Law*. London: Minority Rights Group.

Tollefson, J. (1991) *Planning Language, Planning Inequality: Language Policy in the Community*. London: Longman.

Waitangi Tribunal (1986) *Findings of the Waitangi Tribunal Relating to Te Reo Māori and a Claim Lodged by Huirangi Waikerepuru and Ngā Kaiwhakapumau i te Reo Incorporated Society (Wellington Board of Māori Language)*. Wellington: Government Printer.

Waite, J. (1992) *Aoteareo: Speaking for Ourselves*. Wellington: Learning Media, Ministry of Education.

Walker, R. (1990) *Ka Whawhai Tonu Matou: Struggle without End*. Auckland: Penguin.

Young, I. (1993) Together in difference: transforming the logic of group political conflict, in J. Squires (ed.), *Principled Positions: Postmodernism and the Rediscovery of Value*. London: Lawrence & Wishart, pp. 121–50.

12 Human Rights Education and Intercultural Relations: Lessons for Development Educators

MICHELINE C. REY-VON ALLMEN

The challenge of education in the contemporary changing world

As the century draws to its close, the globe is racked by major changes, sometimes planned and sometimes unexpected, affecting all sectors and aspects of social life. Yet even given the enormity and rapidity of those changes, it may well be that the most essential changes have yet to come: those concerned with human rights and social relationships on a world stage.

One of the major gaps in current thinking about development education is the relative absence of considerations of interdependence and the need for an intercultural concept of development education that can be attentive to human rights. True, it is difficult to think in terms of interdependence, solidarity, mutual responsibility and social integration[1] in the context of societies which have lived through colonialism and imperialism and which continue to oscillate between, on the one hand, an acute claim to the validity of their own specific culture and, on the other hand, the negation of difference, irrespective of the individual. Recent events such as the fall of the Berlin Wall did not produce responses to many of the hopes which it evoked, but rather gave way to ethnic conflicts and economic tensions.

In contemporary societies, which have been made increasingly multicultural through the phenomenon of migration and where migration has sharpened interethnic relations, which in any case are as old as the human race, all humans share their similarities as much as their differences. This recognition of the objective reality of commonality, however, has not prevented the rise of racism and ethnic cleansing. That is because the twentieth century has adopted an egocentric, linear and monocultural 'logic'. Because of this way of thinking, even when plurality has been taken account of, differences have been hierarchized or marginalized. For each person the priority which counted remained self-interest, conceived in terms of personal autonomy and the short term. The world remained divided into more and less developed regions, and what carried weight as a priority was overdevelopment of the former. Development of the 'Third World' was subordinate and accessory.

But, in spite of this aberration, the survival of our planet compels us to come to terms with the interdependence of all the elements of nature, human groups and individuals the world over. More and more people are taking account of this process and beginning to generate new paradigms of human action and relationship. Against this background, if we seek to construct a viable world order, which can include those who are rich and powerful as well as those nations which are poor and weak, we have to pass from the logic of 'mono' to the logic of 'inter'. To accept otherness and interdependence, to accept that others may be right at the same time as oneself, to base one's behaviour and choices on mutual responsibility and human solidarity would indeed represent a Copernican revolution in the modes of thought of most people (even of those involved in development education), as in the logic of government, social organization and international relations.

And yet, nothing less than such a revolution is needed if the planet is not to be complicit in its own destruction. If the world does indeed begin to take cognizance of the inappropriate nature of its ideological foundations and begin to search for new conceptual tools and for new paradigms of behaviour and action, a new challenge will face education, especially development education. It is a challenge which demands an intercultural approach, offering a new opportunity for education to enrol in an logic of 'inter', which recognizes interdependence and promotes a socially sustainable development based on social integration, mutual responsibility, human solidarity and human rights.

Towards an education based on solidarity and mutual responsibility: conceptual and terminological refinements

More and more the demand is being heard for an education which recognizes interdependence and local and international solidarity. Increasingly, such voices call attention to the moral bankruptcy of the rich calling for their own human rights while at the same time, by their economic or cultural actions, denying those same human rights to disadvantaged or deprived people in their own countries and to those who live in the developing world. Insofar as these demands arise from different contexts and processes, the words may differ, but the demands are similar. Let us look at some of the expressions which have been raised by intergovernmental, international and European organizations and member agencies of the United Nations family.

The United Nations Educational, Scientific and Cultural Organization (UNESCO) uses the expression *international education* in making reference to the Recommendation Concerning Education for International Understanding, Co-operation and

Peace and Education Relating to Human Rights and Fundamental Freedoms (UNESCO, 1974). Such an education should develop a sense of social responsibility and of solidarity with less privileged groups and encourage respect for the principle of equality in daily behaviour. It should also contribute to the development of qualities, aptitudes and competencies which enable the individual to attain a critical consciousness of national and international problems. It should further international understanding and reinforce world peace and the struggle against colonialism and neocolonialism in all their forms, as also all forms of racism, of fascism and apartheid, and all ideologies which inspire national or racial hatred.

Human rights education rests on the principles which form the basis of the United Nations Charter, the Universal Declaration of Human Rights and other international and regional covenants and agreements on human rights. The Universal Declaration of Human Rights, adopted unanimously by the United Nations General Assembly in 1948, is now recognized as one of the most important international baseline documents for regulating the rights and responsibilities of humankind. Many countries have adopted parts of its wording and values in their constitutions, particularly the many countries which have become independent since the end of World War II. The declaration also recognizes children as in need of special care and attention (Article 25), and declares in Article 26: 'Everyone has the right to education. Education shall be free, at least in the elementary and fundamental stages. Elementary education shall be compulsory' (United Nations Center for Human Rights, 1988).

This and successive instruments aimed at defining and elaborating human rights and fundamental freedom require equal importance to be placed on economic, social, cultural and political rights, as well as the rights of individuals and collectivities. They demand the indivisibility of all human rights. The promotion of such rights must necessarily include a struggle against racism and racial discrimination, xenophobia and all other forms of intolerance, the protection of national, ethnic, religious and linguistic minorities and the rights of migrant workers and their families. It must include equality in fundamental rights, for example in the equalization of the condition of women, the promotion of the rights of the child and the fight against torture and 'disappearances', and the rights of handicapped persons.

For example, the Declaration of the Rights of the Child, adopted by the General Assembly in November 1959, gave official and explicit recognition to the human rights of children. This declaration specifically addresses children's rights and has become a *sine qua non* to guide private and public action in the interest of children since its publication. Principle 7 states:

> The child is entitled to receive education, which shall be free and compulsory, at least in the elementary stages. He shall be given an education which will promote his general culture, and enable him, on the basis of equal opportunity, to develop his individual judgment, and his sense of moral and social responsibility, and to become a useful member of society. (United Nations, 1960, p. 192)

And in Principle 5 the declaration states: 'The child who is physically, mentally or socially handicapped shall be given the special treatment, education and care required by his particular condition' (ibid., p. 199).

Further, and following ten years of preparations, the Convention on the Rights of the Child was adopted by the United Nations General Assembly in November 1989. The convention goes further than the declaration by making states which accept the convention legally accountable for their actions towards children and by representing a commitment to the future. More than seventy countries signed the convention and thus 'recognize the right of the child to education ... on the basis of equal opportunity' (United Nations Center for Human Rights, 1990, p. 23). Those that signed also recognized the right of disabled children to 'enjoy a full and decent life' (ibid., p. 21) and the state's obligation to provide for the special needs of the disabled.

Development educators need to take account of a number of precursor traditions in their efforts to make their work more attentive to the principle of interdependence (in which is included the concepts of mutuality and reciprocity), social integration (which includes the idea of social solidarity with the poor) and human rights (which implies the responsibility not only for one's own human rights but also for those of others). A development education for the twenty-first century needs to be centrally focused on education for human rights, which includes a concern with peace and the development of democracy and social justice, as envisaged in the international and regional instruments on human rights, in order to evoke an understanding and realization which will reinforce them. It is also concerned with the elimination of illiteracy and the orientation of education towards the full blossoming of each individual, as well as respect for human rights and fundamental liberties.

In its turn, *education for democracy* underlines the fact that democratic values are needed for the effective exercise of human rights. Nor is it just a matter of content, for the educational process itself should be democratic, aimed at participation and conceived in such a way as to permit individual and civic societies to improve the quality of life.

Education for citizenship is another expression related to education for democracy. No major education project funded by the major multilateral agencies has included in its components a commitment to education for citizenship. Yet the skills, attitudes and knowledge which define the rights and duties of an individual participating within a political collectivity are critical to social and political cohesion as well as to economic development. Thus, education for citizenship or for multiple citizenship (some people speak of 'world citizenship') has to take into account different levels of local, national, regional (continental) and international aspects of human activity in society as well as its different dimensions: social, political, cultural and economic (see the argument for different levels of citizenship education developed in Lynch (1993)). On that basis, civic education deploys all the educational practices and subject matters which are aimed at the transmission and acquisition of individual and social rules of life, subject to democratic regulation according to the rule of law and human rights. But education for citizenship is not only about critical knowledge, reflective attitudes and interpersonal skills, not least of conflict resolution and social problem-solving; it is also at the same time about critical reflection on the role of these rules and norms in the social life of the school, its processes, procedures, content and pedagogy (see Lynch, 1991).

Clearly, education for citizenship does not exist in that explicit way in all school systems, but appears under different labels, such as moral education, political education, social and family education. None the less, common concerns and areas of content can be identified. Among such convergences is the one which bases political systems on human rights and which affirms the need for an education for human rights. Even if civic education was originally contained within a perspective aimed at legitimating and justifying the different political forms of the nation-state, it is not possible to contain it within that dimension today. The demands of international cooperation, the increasing migration of humankind and of good and bad ideas, and the necessity of mutual responsibility require a critical mode of thinking and constant reference to universal principles (Council of Europe, 1993).

Education for peace has the aim of constructing on the basis of universal human values respect for life, for freedom, for solidarity, for tolerance, for human rights and for equality between men and women (Unesco, 1993a). But it is also concerned with facilitating the learning of communication skills and of sociacy, or the ability to live in communities, as well as the ability to negotiate and resolve conflicts peacefully and creatively, but above all non-violently. Education for peace must include a dimension of education for disarmament which emphasizes the interrelations among disarmament, on the one hand, and peace and international security, friendly cooperation among states and human rights, and economic and social progress on the other. It should include the right of each person to refuse to participate in military service for reasons of conscientious objection, as well as the right to oppose the obligation to wage war or to kill. It invites reflection of the problems posed by the arms race and its costs, and it encourages the development of a public opinion favourable to disarmament. In the family, education for disarmament could suppress the purchase of war toys, so as to encourage the child to develop attitudes supportive of peaceful conflict resolution (UNESCO, 1980).

In the context of the proclamation of 1995 as the Year of Tolerance, UNESCO wanted to give a new meaning to the word 'tolerance', promulgating the notion that our ability to appreciate others is the ethical basis of peace, of security and of intercultural dialogue. In *education for tolerance*, what is at stake is first, tolerance as a basic attitude to be set in the minds of all, but secondly, dispositions for social and political functioning which govern and form links between human beings, between history and the present, between states, between governments and the governed, between the majority and the minority, between the citizen and the non-citizen. Such questions are translated into the realm of international law, social institutions, justice, education, culture and communication. The point of convergence of all these aspects is in the essential issue of an ethic of shared responsibility (UNESCO, 1993b).

Development education aims to evoke in children and young people such attitudes as world solidarity, peace, tolerance, social justice and environmental awareness. It should also help them to clarify their own human rights and to identify with the human rights of others. The knowledge and competencies thus acquired should permit them to promote these values and to bring about a change in their lives and the lives of their community, as much at the local as at the world level. What is needed is for teachers and young people to be enlightened over a range of issues, from traditional school subject matter to the big international questions, but drawing on five international themes (Guerrero, 1993):

1 interdependence; that is, the involvement of the world and its inhabitants in a fragile equilibrium;
2 images and perceptions; that is, the way in which one regards oneself and others – stereotypes and egocentric attitudes, and how to avoid them;
3 conflict: the nature of conflict and how to resolve it; the diversity of expressions of peace and how to sustain them;

4   social justice; that is, the behaviours, structures and systems which favour or inhibit the real participation of each person in the life of society; and

5   change and the future; that is, gaining an understanding of how actions today will influence the future and learning how to envisage different future scenarios.

Environment education aims to change the vision that we have of the world and to teach about the relationships which are woven into the ecological systems between humankind and nature. Such an education underlines the fact that education for sustainable development is intrinsically linked to environmental education. On the one hand, development needs to be ecologically sustainable; on the other, it also needs to ensure the long-term involvement of members of the community. For this to happen, each person has to have the feeling that he or she is really participating in the life of the collectivity (United Nations Children's Fund, 1993).

Intercultural education is concerned with a more global reflection, having two dimensions. At the level of reality, of objective and scientific description, it is an invitation to take account of the dynamic released by communication, regional and transcontinental migration, to recognize the reality which fashions communities and on the basis of which they transform themselves. All life, all interaction is dynamic, each culture is mixed and we are all migrants and all of mixed heritage. That is a truism; however, it is not easy either to take account of these exchanges and these transformations or to accept them. Taking that as its point of departure, intercultural approach invites us to make sure that these interactions lead to mutual respect and to the enrichment of socially integrated and mutually responsible communities, rather than reinforcing dominance and rejection. 'Intercultural', by giving full value to the prefix 'inter', implies interaction, exchange, opening up, reciprocity, interdependence, solidarity. In addition, the root word 'culture' is given its full meaning: recognition of values, of lifestyles, of symbolic representations that are used as refer-

ences by human beings, individuals and groups in their relations with others and in their apprehension of the world; recognition of the interactions which intervene at the same time in the multiple registers of a single culture, as between different cultures across space and time (Rey, 1986, 1996).

Thus, 'intercultural' signifies at the same time:

1   the recognition of the diversity of representations, references and values, for our societies are all pluri- or multicultural;

2   dialogue, exchange and interaction among these diverse representations and references;

3   above all, dialogue and exchange among persons and groups, whose references are diverse, multiple and often shared;

4   reciprocal questioning concerning egocentric visions and ethnocentric perceptions of the world and of human relations;

5   dynamism and dialectical relationships, changes real and potential in time and space, for with communication cultures and identities are transformed and each individual participates in several.

Consequently, intercultural education has to be seen as a strategy:

1   to question our convictions, of self or society, whether they are egocentric, sociocentric or ethnocentric, and our monocultural norms;

2   to transform the stereotypical images and representations and to overcome the prejudices which generate judgements and actions;

3   to transform and diversify the relationships of power and to give equal rights to those groups and individuals who are undervalued, with regard either to their competencies, cultural references or means of expression;

4   to favour the opening up, the recognition of complexity of existing relationships, as much between cultures, social classes, institutions, streams of education, academic subject matter, scientific objects, etc. as between human beings of all ages, languages, ethnic groups, cultures and religions;

5   to teach and develop skills of negotiation and communication between individuals, groups

and communities, to ensure that they are positive for all parties;

6   to articulate the responsibilities which accrue to each person with regard to local and national communities, as also with regard to the international community.

Even if these various expressions and notions have specific accents and approach problems from a particular point of view, they intersect and contribute to the presentation of the same totality. In consequence they are not devoid of redundancy. The problem is accentuated by the fact that these preoccupations are advanced by nebulous groups of movements, conveyed at national and international levels by such organizations as NGOs, religious movements and diverse agencies within society, which tend at the same time to awaken awareness and to elaborate strategies, methodological tools and pedagogical materials to favour this awareness. These movements, often anchored in local history, recognize themselves by means of key words which sum up their projects: multicultural education, anti-racist education, education for world citizenship, education for nonviolent conflict resolution, world or global education, peace education, etc. If these diverse tendencies were in origin juxtaposed, not to mention rivals, each of them is now designing projects taking into account many dimensions, and consequently the interactions are multiplying.

The expression 'education for human rights' has a tendency to recapitulate (that is, to sum up and take the lead of) these different perspectives and to be used in a generic manner. As a matter of fact, on 1 January 1995 the United Nations declared the opening of the decade of human rights. Nevertheless, such an education will have to be clearly intercultural, for the interpretation of human rights does not always avoid ethnocentrism. Further, international instruments on human rights are marked by the eras which have produced them, and they need the critical spirit and the contribution of citizens of both today and tomorrow to make them real, to achieve them, and to develop them. In this sense, *intercultural education is the inevitable pathway to any human rights education which attempts to overtake ethnocen-*

trism, as well as education for development which emphasizes social integration and solidarity.

Intercultural education: a perspective for all ages and contexts

Human rights education, solidarity and development concern everyone, from early childhood to adulthood. They concern all forms of education, in school and out of school, formal and nonformal, and all types of training, whether general educational or lifelong education, or oriented towards profession skill enhancement or emancipation and social participation. Often human rights education has been limited to secondary education. Perhaps the reason is that it is with an adolescent audience used to studying that formal education is easiest and succeeds best. But it is precisely those young people who are the most disadvantaged who should merit most attention. For this reason, it needs emphasizing that intercultural education is not solely for future professionals and intellectuals, but for all members of the community. Equally, such an education is not restricted to cognitive education; it commences with early childhood. From the earliest age, a child has need of mediation from its parents, brothers and sisters, teachers, etc. – to help it interpret reality and to develop, to construct its knowledge and personality. An interpretation of reality which is oriented towards human rights and understanding of others is thus of importance for the child's development and its integration into community life. But the education of adults should not be neglected. Particular attention should be paid to those whose profession specifically puts them into contact with others and those whose professional situation may lead them to violate human rights. They need to be informed of those rights and of their responsibility for avoiding and preventing abuse.

One way to combat breaches of human rights is to educate marginalized, deprived people and populations which have been made vulnerable. It is a matter of affording them all the protection necessary, to let them speak and to give them education, so that they can effectively demand their rights. One might think of young girls and women who live in countries and communities where tradition marginalizes them, of working children, children in war zones, who know only the human rights of which they are deprived and which they demand, young deprived people in the suburbs, minority populations, linguistic, ethnic or religious displaced persons, exiles and migrants. In the struggle against sexism, attention needs to be given not only to girls' education, but also to the education of boys and the transformation of the sexist behaviour of men towards women, which are needed in order that the education of girls and women can be effective.

The role of informal education is important, because it is often better able to respond with subtlety to the needs of deprived populations, to recognize their qualities and to draw out their competencies. It is not always necessary for development educators to take responsibility for the education of such people. The need may rather be to recognize and to legitimate the means of education and training that they choose and give them support. In rural areas, for example, local women's organizations, sometimes linked to international organizations, are a powerful means of education for democratic life and emancipation.

One important difficulty, when one speaks of educational perspectives, resides in the immense disparity of educational situations. Clearly, projects cannot be the same in situations of extreme poverty as in situations of abundance. Indeed, there is a kind of naivety in speaking of educational methods which are more or less sophisticated when certain regions lack even the most elementary resources, and are subject to poverty and disaster. But an education for social integration and solidarity can at least underline the shared responsibility of the international community, stating precisely the principles and orientations, which are adaptable to different contexts, as well as proposing the conceptual, methodological and educational tools required. The following sections are intended to recapitulate the main directions formulated by the different agencies which are concerned with human rights education, intercultural relations and development.

Towards an intercultural development education

This chapter has argued that development educators need to be more attentive in their work to a number of precursor traditions, including that represented by the term 'intercultural education'. For brevity's sake we refer, in the rest of the chapter, to such an education as 'intercultural development education'. Such an education for human rights, for intercultural relations and for development education demands a preparation with at least two dimensions, which are symbiotically linked: conceptual and cognitive knowledge learning, on the one hand, and experiential learning on the other. The first dimension, which may actually come second in the process of learning, has the aim of equipping the learners, according to their level of learning, with the conceptual tools to apprehend reality and interpret the signals which they receive, in order to master these elements. It is important that any information is presented in the most objective way possible from multiple points of view, in order to enable the learners to achieve a certain distance from their daily experience, to move beyond partial and parochial viewpoints based on prejudice so as to place themselves in and communicate with a diverse world of knowledge and points of view.

The experiential dimension places education firmly within the context of the life being lived, integrating the knowledge and concepts with relational and affective dimensions. Together, these dimensions seek to mobilize the whole personality and potentialities of the learner to achieve a balanced and harmonious development which may help the learner to be accessible to others. The learner learns to perceive and master the complexity of emotions which are at stake in social relations in an intercultural context, to exercise respect for persons, while appreciating the potential for mutual enrichment in such encounters, and to act in cooperation with others. Equally, individuals need to develop those attitudes of moral autonomy and courage which will enable the individual to stand out from the crowd, to stand up for what is right, even when others may be against it. This latter is important if the lessons of civic education in totalitarian states are to be learned, as well as when the rights and the dignity of the poorest and of the socially deprived people have to be protected against the excessive requirements of local or international economic powers.

Related to the knowledge dimension of an intercultural development education, the objectives may be articulated through the medium of an individual subject or through all the normal school subjects, or simply allowed to permeate, because all the objectives may be designed and delivered in such a way as to foster tolerance, human rights, international understanding and human development, whether they are based on natural science, social science or domestic science, whether they are linguistic or literary, artistic, religious, mathematical, informatic or technological. All may be located within an everyday context which invites students to reflect on contemporary issues and conflicts, including those where competing rights are at stake.

In some countries, it is in the context of a subject called civics that issues of human rights are encountered. Local and national political institutions are considered, as well as the process of democracy in the context of national legislation. This needs to be done in an international context, for even though the presentation has to be measured to the level of development of the individual, that does not mean that the presentation has to be restrictive and ethnocentric. Such studies should evoke concepts such as justice, equality, liberty, peace, dignity, the rule of law and democracy. That requires engagement with the appropriate regional and international human rights instruments, simplified or presented through drama, case study, film or stories if necessary, but in any case including economic, social and cultural rights, as well as civil and political rights, seen in the context of their interdependence and indivisibility. Such a consideration would include the violation of human rights as well as the efforts

made in each region for combating such abuses and the strategies suggested for doing so.

Of course, there can be no such education which does not contain a dimension of critical reflexivity, for the debate which is democracy implies that the individual exercises his or her freedom of opinion, in order to assume the values of responsible citizenship. It has been observed that some teachers reject the political dimension in teaching for human rights because they have been required to remain neutral or to act in conformity with the official or majority viewpoint (Harwood, 1986). As a consequence they are afraid to influence their pupils. This demands a difficult skill from teachers, namely the ability to lead debate, to make available as a resource person all necessary elements, many of which may be formulated by the pupils themselves, and to invite them to exercise their critical faculties, using human rights as their point of reference. For this they must have the confidence of the education authorities, the parents and the community, so that this liberty of expression and learning for social responsibility may be nurtured and protected. For without this confidence and the security which it endows, the efforts of the teachers will be in vain and the exercise of citizenship fictitious and unfertile.

Of course, intercultural development education may draw on history, which is a reconstruction of social events and relationships from the past which have been deemed worthy of record, a symbolic representation of the past seen against contemporary knowledge. This link between the past and the present can provide pupils with a springboard to show that they may influence which future actually occurs. History has usually been taught in a restricted manner, partial and limited to military and political aspects, and often national(istic) or regional. This has to be changed. Pupils need to acquire a broader sense of history. For this, a reconstruction of history is needed, a rethink in the context of the contemporary world, which can see each locality and region as the product of historical forces, where there have always been interaction and interdependence. Such an exercise may be useful in identifying the prejudices, ethnocentric judgements, sexism, racism and partiality inherent within current interpretations (in school books, newspapers, mass media, etc.) which have hindered an objective view of international and intercultural relations. Of course such an approach could also be generated with materials from other subject areas used to provoke the critical questioning of the pupils. New technologies may be used for similar goals, and already in some countries media and computer studies are subjects within the curriculum that may contribute to similar goals of objectification, gaining of distance and prejudice reduction.

Sciences may also contribute to the development of intercultural approaches to intercultural development education, which may identify the differing approaches in different cultures, as well as combating the abuse of scientific knowledge in order to infringe human rights or justify violence and war (UNESCO, 1991).

Equally, languages and language awareness may be a particularly efficacious means of developing intercultural awareness and responsibility, in view of the joy of discovery which children take in communication with children of other languages and cultures. Too often, early learning of languages is restricted to the children of the privileged or those who appear most gifted, when all children may profit.

The school is not only a place for the acquisition of knowledge. It is also, and *par excellence*, a place of life experience, social integration, mutual acceptance and responsibility. Furthermore, all knowledge is mediated by communication and is dependent on the quality of educational relationships and pedagogical approaches adopted. Thus the role of the school and classroom in promoting the goals identified above through their climate, their structure and relationships is important. Children need to learn to be themselves attentive to human rights, with their schoolmates and with the community. That is a two-way street of movement of receiving and sharing with human acceptance for all, for to be accepted is the *sine qua non* condition to being accepting. The aim is a rich and diverse culture of acceptance and learning within which pupils come to feel comfortable with diversity, where friendships and mutual understanding can grow within a context of human similarity and difference, and where pupils and teachers respect each other and each other's human rights in all their actions. It is particularly important that teachers and the managers of the school make the effort to make all their educational practices conform with such a climate, for pupils are sensitive to any divergence between the spoken rule and the practised rule.

The preparation of educational personnel for intercultural development education

Sometimes teachers have to dispose what others propose. But an intercultural development education cannot rest on the obedience and submission of teachers (no more than of pupils). Rather they are asked to be creative, and their creativity has to be nourished with conceptual and methodological tools, grounded in human rights. Thus, their education, initial and in-service, has to be democratically structured, so as to permit them to try out diverse forms of communication, of expression, of responsibility and autonomy, which may assist them in developing their critical faculties. Such a training should favour cooperation over competition, offering those in training the opportunity to live human rights and to denounce their infringement. For this, the support of the educational authorities and of the teacher trainers will be imperative. Diverse modes of communication and participation, such as simulation and role-playing, workshops, seminars, discussions and debates, as well as the more usual pedagogies are called for. Project work, research, interviews, class newspapers, story-telling, theatre, marionettes, debates, case studies, and the use of authentic documents, newspaper cuttings, photographs, slides, TV clips, and films, may provide opportunities for participation and self-realization; the process itself may be as important as or more important than any product.

Such approaches do not demand a *tabula rasa*, but rather the identification of that which exists and is conducive to the achievement of the goals of intercultural development education. At all costs such teaching–learning approaches should be participatory and active. Cooperative group work has to help underprivileged pupils to participate efficiently and obtain recognition. Because learning is dependent on prestige, the children whose abilities are most recognized will be the most willing to get involved and to learn. Thus a more positive participation by less prestigious pupils may contribute to the levelling of inequalities.[2] The quality of communication is vital in such encounters. Skills of listening, of expressing (through verbal and non-verbal means) the reasons for miscommunication, the rites of interaction (which differ from culture to culture), the importance of face-saving, etc. have to be learned, experienced and discussed (metacommunication).

Indispensable to such an approach is a democratic school management which can promote human rights and social responsibilities in school. Here, openness to the outside is as important as the opening up inside the school. The involvement of members of the community from different cultural groups, the utilization of community resources, such as libraries and museums, participation in cultural and artistic events in the locality, musical events, sports events, festivals of food, twinning of schools, inter-school correspondence, collaboration with local organizations, study visits and field trips, association with the UNESCO schools projects, celebration of feasts and festivals, especially those concerned with human rights suggested by the United Nations, etc., can all contribute to an intercultural development education which can sensitize children to their rights and their responsibilities.

What about the evaluation of educational outcomes? In schools, often it is the fact learned, the essay written or the artefact produced which is the object of assessment. In project work in developing countries, it is often the rate of disbursement, the loans repaid or the number of classrooms constructed which are the criteria for praise or censure. Yet these are only the operants to achieve the purpose of intercultural development education. What has to be evaluated is the improvement of human relations and communication, of human well-being and justice, in order to build relations between persons and nations based on mutual respect, understanding and human rights.

A shared responsibility

Responsibility to develop an intercultural development education cannot be borne solely by the educational institutions and the teachers. It has to be shared by all the groups making up the community, not forgetting the media and research. The interdependences and mutual responsibilities constitute fundamental realities, principles and perspectives which have to underlie the organization of the whole social life and educational activity. They are decisive in the decisions and choices to be made, the activities to be proposed as well as the modalities of negotiation to be adopted to achieve the goals. They are concerned with educational and linguistic policy, educational legislation, the organization of the life of the school and the relations between girls and boys, the choice of educational priorities, the subject matters taught and the criteria for the assessment of skills and behaviours, the training of teachers and their relations with parents and with the community, and finally international relations.

We are all concerned in two ways: it is important that in our own professional context we are aware of and committed to the protection of human rights, for there is no point in demanding of education the adoption of orientations which are not taken seriously elsewhere. Equally, it is important that we lend our assistance to the educational authorities to take decisions which favour intercultural education. The mass media, for example, could encourage a spirit of tolerance in public opinion rather than one of violence. As for research, in all disciplines, it could offer a deeper knowledge and understanding of the interdependence of human beings and their environment and of the interactions which fashion international and multicultural reality.

Solidarity and mutual responsibility do not concern only the local or the national community.

They concern also international relations, especially the relations between North and South, West and East, the centre and the periphery. Human rights and social justice are indivisible. We cannot demand them for ourselves and deny them to others. We cannot demand economic and social well-being or cultural and religious recognition for ourselves at the cost of the economic and social well-being or of cultural and religious denial of others, and claim to be living a just life, based on human rights. It is important that children in school in the 'North', learn the cost to the 'South' of their affluence. It is important that development educators working in both industrialized and developing nations base their actions on ethical principles such as those set out in international instruments of human rights.

However, let us remember that these sets of principles remain instruments (which may be misused, ethnocentrically interpreted or called upon only when we seek to impose our views on others). It is also the shared responsibility of people all over the world (not only from the North, the West or the 'centre') to use them as tools towards social justice, peace and intercultural understanding, locally and throughout the world. It is our common and mutual responsibility to assume a critical approach of the way human rights are interpreted and used, and to educate the new generations in such a way that they are willing and able to improve and develop them – because there is no hope for any sustainable development if it is not rooted in a critical and dynamic 'logic of inter', in an education for human rights built upon the conviction that intercultural cooperation and understanding can overcome ethnocentrisms and unilateral powers.

Notes

1 It is interesting to note that the World Summit for Social Development (WSSD) in Copenhagen in March 1995 shared these concerns, and that these issues were strongly underlined by 'The Copenhagen alternative declaration of March 8 1995' (in *NGO News*, an NGO Forum supplement).

2 The role of cooperative group work in reducing prejudice is covered by Lynch (1987).

References

Council of Europe (1993) *Civic Education, Teaching about Society and the Transmission of Values*. Strasbourg: Council of Europe (57th Donaueschingen Seminar).

Guerrero, A. (1993) UNICEF: politique d'éducation au développement, *L'Indépendant*, **8**, 93.

Harwood, D. (1986) To advocate or to education? What role should the primary teacher adopt in political education? *Education*, **14**(1), 51–7.

Lynch, J. (1987) *Prejudice Reduction and the Schools*. London: Cassell/New York: Nichols.

Lynch, J. (1991) *Multicultural Education in a Global Society*. London: Falmer Press.

Lynch, J. (1993) *Education for Citizenship in a Multicultural Society*. London: Cassell.

Rey, M. (1986) *Training Teachers in Intercultural Education?* Strasbourg: Council of Europe.

Rey, M. (1996) D'une logique mono à une logique de l'inter, in *Pistes pour une éducation interculturelle et solidaire* (Cahiers de la section des sciences de l'éducation, no. 19). Geneva: Université.

UNESCO (1974) *Recommendation Concerning Education for International Understanding, Co-operation and Peace and Education Relating to Human Rights and Fundamental Freedoms*. Paris: UNESCO.

UNESCO (1980) *Rapport du Congrès mondial de l'Unesco sur l'éducation pour le désarmement*. Paris: UNESCO.

UNESCO (1991) The Seville Statement on violence preparing the ground for the constructing of peace, disseminated by decision of the General Conference of Unesco at its 25th session, Paris, 16 November 1989, ed. with commentary by D. Adams.

UNESCO (1993a) *Programme d'action pour promouvoir une culture de paix*. Paris: UNESCO.

UNESCO (1993b) *Presentation of the Director-General of Unesco to the Istanbul Meeting of Experts on the Problems of Tolerance*. Paris: UNESCO.

United Nations (1960) Declaration of the Rights of the Child, in *Yearbook of the United Nations 1959*. New York: UN Office of Public Information, pp. 192–9.

United Nations Center for Human Rights (1988) *The International Bill of Human Rights*. Human Rights Fact Sheet 2. Geneva: UN.

United Nations Center for Human Rights (1990) *The Rights of the Child*. Human Rights Fact Sheet 10. Geneva: UN.

United Nations Children's Fund (1993) *EDEV News*, **4**, 2.

Part Four

Innovation, Change and Evaluation

13 The Life Cycle of an Innovation: Implications for Implementation in Education

FRED CHAMBERS

The value of models of innovation

Innovation in education, an apparently simple concept, in practice is difficult and problematical. If it were not, then the difficulties that those introducing innovations meet would have been conquered long ago. The evidence is to the contrary: many texts on innovation stress the problems met (Rogers and Shoemaker, 1971; Nisbet, 1974; House, 1979; Fullan, 1991; Rudduck, 1991; Smyth and van der Vegt, 1993; Sparkes, 1989, 1990). Anything that helps to provide a clearer picture of the process of innovation, and helps us understand the cause of various problems, has value. To this end, in this chapter a model of the process of innovation will be developed.

Models are intended to simplify complex situations without making them simplistic. A good model has several values. It demonstrates essential aspects of the reality. It can help clarify a complex concept (Wilson, 1984; Checkland, 1981). It helps to ensure that the 'secret' mental models we carry in our heads are open to others, thus permitting informed discussion (Forrester, 1981). It permits manipulation. A good model will bring explanatory powers as well as descriptive powers. Finally, a model (even if it is not an accurate model) will provoke discussion.

The pattern within innovations that we are to discuss here has been identified in many innovations in the field of education. However, because of the constraints of space only one will be considered here, that of the introduction of a new primary syllabus within an education system. A further example of the same pattern of innovation

from an entirely different field of study, credit legislation, will also be considered to show a possible universality. Thus, we will consider two apparently unrelated innovations and identify within each the same pattern of development. This pattern has been identified in many other innovations in various fields. An explanation will be put forward for the phenomenon, and the not inconsiderable implications for all concerned with innovation in education will be discussed.

Examples of innovations

Kurikulum Baru Sekolah Rendah – The New Primary School Curriculum

In the late 1970s the Malaysian Ministry of Education redesigned the entire primary school syllabus, the new version being called KBSR (Kurikulum Baru Sekolah Rendah – the New Primary School Syllabus). This was a major undertaking involving a new philosophy, a new syllabus in all subjects, new materials and new methodologies.

In the period that followed, several smaller innovations were introduced, within the framework of the large-scale innovation, to improve it in various ways. For instance, within the KBSR curriculum the English-language teaching syllabus had undergone major changes. Many teachers in primary schools, particularly rural ones, did not have the language competence to teach the new syllabus or an understanding of the new methodology

Figure 13.1 Large-scale innovation (KBSR) being improved by a small-scale, incremental innovation (RuPEP)

and teaching techniques. This was particularly apparent in the eastern state of Malaysia, Sabah, on the northern tip of the island of Borneo. A high proportion of remote schools in the mountainous jungle-covered terrain, with little contact with the English-speaking world, meant that many teachers were not equipped to teach the new language. To meet this need a further supporting innovation, the Sabah Rural Primary English Programme (RuPEP), was introduced with the intent of supporting the English teachers in the remote primary schools. The large-scale innovation of KBSR was being supported by a small-scale innovation, RuPEP.

By the early 1990s KBSR had become inappropriate, for various reasons we will investigate later. As a result, a new primary curriculum, also called KBSR but this time standing for Kurikulum *Bersapadu* Sekolah Rendah (the *Mixed* Primary Curriculum), was introduced. So, over a period of some fifteen years or so a curriculum had been born, developed, become dated and eventually expired.

Australian credit laws

In the early 1980s, in several Australian states it was decided that legislation was needed to control the conditions under which loans and various other credit arrangements were made by various organizations concerned with lending money. In the face of considerable initial resistance from those who considered it unnecessary or intrusive the Credit Act 1984 was passed. This required,

among other things, those who provided loans to be registered and to meet certain conditions.

Almost from the moment it became law, the Act needed amendment because of conflicts of law with both state and federal legislation which had not been identified previously. Such problems were met by various means: by regulation, by executive order and by amending acts. By the early 1990s, for various reasons to be considered below, the existing laws were no longer adequate and a new statute is being drafted to replace the 1984 version. Correction through amending legislation is no longer sufficiently effective and a new statute rationalizing and improving upon existing legislation is required. Again, over a period of ten or so years, a piece of legislation had been born, developed, become inappropriate and eventually expired, being eventually replaced by a new statute.

Identifying the cycle

In both these cases of innovation from widely differing fields, a similar pattern occurring over a period of time can be seen. Initial large-scale innovations were followed by several years of smaller innovations that occurred within the framework of the initial innovation. It is this 'large-followed-by-many-small-followed-by-large' pattern of innovations that I intend to investigate.

This is a pattern suggested by Weick (1984). Basing his thoughts on Hollander's (1965) study of innovation in the rayon industry, Weick argues that small-scale innovations can be more effective than large-scale innovations. It is his suggestion that it was

> a possibility . . . that minor innovations were dependent on preceding major innovations. Ten to fifteen years after a major innovation the number of minor changes that were improvements was close to zero (Hollander 1965: 205–6). Small alterations in techniques can improve productivity for some time after a major function but these improvements may not go on indefinitely. (Weick, 1984, p. 43)

Hollander's and Weick's accounts, therefore, sug-

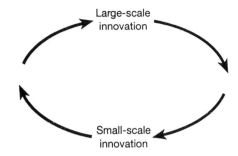

Figure 13.2 The cyclic nature of innovations

gest a pattern similar to that shown in Figure 13.2 with large-scale innovations being introduced, then refined through smaller innovations before being replaced by new, large innovations as the system becomes dated and inappropriate because of changing conditions.

However, I suggest that a finer pattern can be differentiated where the nature and quality of the small-scale innovations following a large-scale innovation change over time. It is this pattern that I wish to investigate, refine and consider.

The cycle of innovation

We begin our consideration at the point where a new, large-scale innovation has been introduced as the previous system has become so unproductive or inappropriate that, as in the case of the Malaysian school curriculum or the Australian credit legislation, a major innovation is required to recover the situation.

With such large-scale innovations it is not surprising that immediately after implementation many problems are found that had not been envisaged. Things go wrong as those concerned try to implement new systems that they are not familiar with and for which they do not, as in the case of the English-language teachers in rural Sabah, have command of appropriate skills; systems develop unforeseen problems. Often at this point many involved in the innovation despair, and there is a desire to return to the 'old, proven way'. To do so, however, is not acceptable for various reasons. Too much money and prestige have been invested in the new system, and in any event, when rose-

tinted spectacles are removed the old ways are seen not to have been adequate. As a result, the obvious course of action is to correct or improve the existing system by a number of smaller 'amending' innovations.

Small amending innovations

Small amending innovations occur predominantly in the period immediately after a large-scale innovation. They serve the function of correcting problems which for various reasons had not been identified prior to the implementation of the large-scale innovation or which are caused directly by its implementation.

In the case of the Malaysian primary curriculum, RuPEP, the supporting English-language teacher development programme already referred to was such an example. In the case of the Australian credit law, among other things the Act proved to be unduly onerous for some credit providers, and in some cases unfair. As a result, changes (small 'amending' innovations) had to be made by regulation, in this case the Credit Regulation (1984).

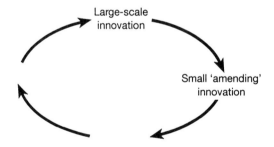

Figure 13.3 Small 'amending' innovations in the innovation cycle

As these 'small amending innovations' occur in a period of considerable disruption, and are correcting evident problems, they are likely to have considerable impact and provide the perception that small innovations are very effective. In the case of the successful RuPEP programme, for example, its success is possible because the small innovations are improving a relatively chaotic situation brought about by a large-scale innovation. This is not a criticism of large-scale innovation. In the nature of things, during such major events there will inevitably develop problems that cannot be foreseen.

However, as time passes, the number of problems caused by the initial introduction of the large-scale innovation decrease. Those involved become more experienced with the new systems, and as the major problems are identified appropriate solutions are found. Eventually the system that was new is now in place and working well, and the possible 'amending' innovations have been implemented.

Small 'refining' innovations

With a relatively satisfactory macro-system now in place and functioning, incremental adjustments to the system are still desirable but the emphasis of their intent moves. Rather than being motivated by problems caused by the initial large-scale innovation they are now more concerned with attempts to improve and refine the system that is in place. These improvements may either come from genuine 'new ideas' intended to advance the status quo by refinement, or be motivated by changes in the surrounding conditions that demand adjustment in the system.

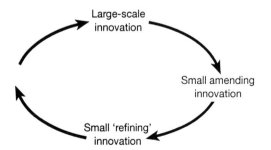

Figure 13.4 Small 'refining' innovations in the innovation cycle

For instance, in the Malaysian context, some time after the introduction of KBSR the work of various educationalists on 'process writing' was identified as useful and pertinent to the primary curriculum. Within the general framework of KBSR, materials to develop process writing skills were written, as a new innovation, and primary teachers trained in their use. During the same period, innovatory work on the teaching of 'thinking skills', which had not existed in any sophisticated form when KBSR was being devised, was also evolved. A programme to introduce these into the curriculum was also developed. In the case of the Australian credit laws, in the phase of 'refining' innovations the opportunity was taken to extend the legislation to cover a wider field of transaction than had originally been identified as appropriate.

Typically, in each case, the nature and purpose of the incremental changes had changed as compared with stage 1. In that period, small, incremental innovations were intended to correct basic flaws in the wider system that had not, for one reason or another, been identified at the introduction of the innovation. In stage 2 the innovations are concerned with incremental improvements to refine the system, either from 'new thoughts' developing within the specific part of the education system or to meet new developments in the wider system.

Small 'resuscitating' innovations

Over a period of time, however, the general external conditions in the wider system, of which the education system is only part, continue to change. The system that had been appropriate swiftly or slowly, depending on the circumstances, becomes dated and inappropriate. Small, incremental innovations continue to be implemented to prop up the system, and at first these may be sufficient. Eventually, however, the system becomes so weak that all these innovations are doing is maintaining a largely ineffective and inappropriate system – rather like a doctor giving resuscitation to someone who is going to die anyway – and thus only staving off the inevitable. By this time, the small innovations are ineffective and what is required is not corrective small innovations but a new, major, large-scale innovation ... and hence we have come full circle.

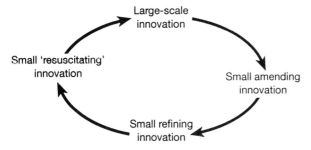

Figure 13.5 Small 'resuscitating' innovations in the innovation cycle

In the case of the education example, the full cycle is identified with the period from the introduction of the Kurikulum Baru Sekolah Rendah to the introduction of the new curriculum, the Kurikulum Bersapadu Sekolah Rendah. In the case of the non-educational example it is represented by the cycle from the introduction of the Credit Act (1984) to the introduction of the new Credit Bill which is currently being drafted.

The period of the innovation cycle

Hollander (1965) mentions a period of ten to fifteen years for this cycle to occur in the rayon industry. The period for the KBSR curriculum would seem to fall within a similar time-scale. Likewise, the Credit Act fits within a similar framework. However, it is unwise to presume that this is some kind of constant, and it may vary, within and between fields, for various reasons.

First, innovations have been identified as being caused by dysfunctional stress in the system, which has to be met (Haynes, 1990). Possible causes of the stress have been identified by Levin (1976) as:

1 natural catastrophe such as earthquake or flood;
2 external forces such as new technology, values, immigration or war;
3 internal contradictions such as indigenous change in technology or the development of

new values internally.

These, clearly, cannot be constrained to fifteen-year periods. Any system can become inappropriate. When that occurs is dependent upon conditions that may change gradually or catastrophically so that there may be a very rapid degeneration through the cycle. The events of the late 1980s in the Eastern-bloc countries very rapidly brought out a crisis for change in many subsystems. These were too great for small innovations to cope with successfully, and have resulted in rapid, holistic changes in the education system, including the primary education system.

Second, what is seen as constituting a large-scale, holistic innovation is relative. What is a holistic innovation to one particular school may be only a minor perturbation in the wider view of a Ministry of Education. Therefore, if there are contrasting views as to what constitutes a large-scale, holistic innovation then there will be contrasting views as to what is the natural period of such changes.

Third, not all innovations complete the full cycle. Some innovations may never experience the refining period. For instance, innovations can move directly from 'amending' innovations to 'resuscitating' innovations for various reasons. The original large-scale innovation might be so badly planned that it tends to collapse into 'resuscitating' innovations. Or the same kind of collapse may be brought about by drastically changing external circumstances that never permit the stage to be reached where 'refining' innovations can occur.

An example of this can be seen in the Malagasy education system. In 1978, as a result of major political changes, a new Education Act, commonly referred to as 78–040, came into force, bringing significant innovations. By 1984 further relatively minor, amending innovations to the syllabus were introduced by a further Act. However, after this, for political reasons the education system largely fossilized, and the natural development of further amending or improving innovations was not permitted. By 1990, it was obvious that the existing education system was inadequate and close to collapse. There were limited attempts to introduce

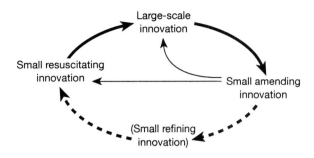

Figure 13.6   Major problem limiting 'The natural process of innovation' leading to an incomplete cycle

resuscitating innovations such as CRESSED (Crédit Réinforcement du Section Éducatif), an in-service support programme. In 1991, however, the inadequacy of the existing system was acknowledged, and moves towards a totally new Education Act began. In this case, for particular reasons, namely restraint on any kind of change because of political dogma, several stages of the normal cycle were minimized in the manner demonstrated in Figure 13.6.

Another example of the cycle being incomplete may be found in the study of the management of a language-teaching organization (Colledge, 1995). After the introduction of a large, holistic innovation, a new manager was brought in. After identifying the problems, as part of a 'new-broom' syndrome the manager, rather than introducing amending innovations to correct the relatively tractable problems from the original large innovation, introduced a new, large-scale holistic innovation (and as a result of this lack of timeliness met severe problems).

The completed cycle of innovations

The relatively simple cycle of innovation expressed in Figure 13.1 can now be more fully specified, as in Figure 13.5.

In summary, holistic innovations inevitably cause problems, if only because of their size. These problems require further 'amending' innovations. When the situation is relatively stable, further improvements can be made through 'refining' innovations. Eventually, however, the whole system becomes dated. Innovations aimed at 're-

suscitating' the innovation may succeed for a while but eventually a new holistic innovation is required.

Some implications for education practice from the model

Let us presume that the model is correct in principle. The question then arises, 'So what?' I have already outlined some of the advantages of using models but the most immediate gain may be if the model provides insights that explain various phenomena that we see occurring in day-to-day practice in education innovations. The model provided above does this in respect of at least five common observations in innovation implementation.

Large versus small innovations

The size of any innovation is a key issue for implementers. The desire is to maximize the impact of the innovation by making it as large as possible (Berman and McLaughlin, 1977). At the same time it must remain 'manageable' and not so large as to be so unwieldy that it fails during implementation (Weick, 1984).

Typically, advantages and disadvantages of large- and small-scale innovations can be perceived and summarized as in Table 13.1 and 13.2.

If both large-scale and small-scale innovations have advantages and disadvantages, the question remains, where does the overall advantage lie? Which, on balance, is superior? Weick (1984) appears to argue in favour of small-scale innovations on the grounds that they are much more likely to be capable of being implemented. Berman and McLaughlin (1977) appear to favour large-scale innovations on the grounds that whereas large-scale innovations are likely to be less successfully implemented than small ones (presumably for the

Table 13.1 Advantages and disadvantages of small-scale innovations

Advantages	Disadvantages
Manageable	Limited impact
Flexible	Slower to achieve impact
Tend to reduce resistance	May lose impetus
Less risk of unintended consequences	May be considered 'not worth the effort'
Can create confidence through success	

Table 13.2 Advantages and disadvantages of large-scale innovations

Advantages	Disadvantages
Swift to have major impact	Can provoke greater resistance
Can meet a 'window of opportunity'	Have the potential for major unintended consequences
Meet a need for urgency	Tend to be less flexible
Suit R & D models of innovation in hierarchical organizations	Require more management skills
Present a *fait accompli* in competitive fields	Complex, therefore more difficult to control
Highly visible	

reasons outlined above), it is large innovations that have most impact on practice. (Whether the impact is positive or negative is an open question!)

The answer provided by this model is clear. Neither has an inherent advantage. Small-scale innovations are likely to appear successful if they are 'amending innovations' following a major innovation and they can provide rapid solutions to pressing problems, or if they are refining innovations seen as genuine improvements on an essentially sound system. Small innovations will not be effective if they are resuscitating innovations, placed within a situation that is essentially unsound and which is demanding systemic change.

The argument put forward by Weick (1984) in favour of small innovations is true, therefore, only in certain conditions. The position of those who favour large-scale innovation is equally context-dependent. Large-scale innovations may well have more impact on practice; that may be true virtually by definition. But whether it is the most efficient and effective way to bring about an impact, and whether that impact is beneficial or otherwise, is again contingent on the conditions.

Always to favour either large or small-scale innovation *in principle* faces many obvious impracticalities, as recounted by Colledge (1995).

The iterative nature of amending innovations

The second implication in practice relates to the iterative nature of amending innovations. If we return to the model, we have already noted that smaller amending innovations come out of larger, holistic innovations. But amending innovations are likely to suffer from problems similar to those faced by larger, holistic innovations. That is, they themselves may contain certain problems that need amending and thus in turn generate their own 'amending' innovations. An example may help to clarify. We have already noted how KBSR as a large, holistic innovation led to the development of RuPEP as an amending innovation. In turn RuPEP faced certain problems. For instance, initially it was conceived that the education officers conducting the programme would be based in large educational centres and travel to the rural districts to deliver the programme. This proved very difficult, and was adjusted by the further innovation of placing English Language Officers in rural centres for the duration of the project. The original amending innovation was thus itself amended by a further 'amending amending' innovation (referred to in future, for brevity's sake, as an AA innovation).

The process is iterative and universal. The new AA innovations are likely, in turn, to require amendments (AAA innovations! – though this iteration does not proceed *ad infinitum*, for reasons we will consider below). The result is that one major innovation is likely to cause an 'explosion' of further innovations. This is the second practical implication of this model. It means that innovations do not occur in neat, orderly, linear streams. Rather, one major innovation, particularly if not well conceived, is likely to lead to a whole constellation of amending innovations which in turn lead to further innovations.

Figure 13.7 Amending innovations developing further amending innovations

This phenomenon can be seen within the current British education system, where government measures arising from the Education Reform Act 1988 have resulted in so many amending innovations that a moratorium on innovation had to be called.

Those who are the recipients of such a battery of innovations are likely quickly to suffer from confusion and lack of certainty, which constitute the familiar syndrome of 'innovation fatigue', an effect noted by Hutchinson (1993). Hutchinson quotes Glover, who in 1990 referred to 'initiative overload', and Wallace, who in 1991 talked of 'chaotic conditions'.

Innovation and the nature of change

The third practical implication of the model is its ability to explain change. Any theory of innovation needs to have built within it a theory of change.

Change can be interpreted in various ways. Frequently writers do not clearly distinguish between innovation and change. Many use the terminology interchangeably. A writer (for instance, Havelock, 1973), may refer to 'innovations' but then refer to 'agents of change' rather than 'agents of innovation'. Rudduck (1991) uses 'innovation' to refer to the planned process, and 'change' to refer to the result of the innovation, so that there may be innovation with change (successful innovation) and innovation without change (unsuccessful innovation).

If we try to tease apart these different uses of terminology a relatively simple pattern emerges. First, though 'change' can refer to the effect of an innovation on the systems it is applied to, it is better to make a distinction by referring to this as 'impact'. Hence the impact of the RuPEP programme was to improve the quality of teaching of English-language teachers.

A second common distinction, as in White (1988) and Nicholls (1983), is to consider that innovation is planned whereas change is unplanned developments occurring naturally over time; '*Change* can occur spontaneously and does not involve conscious planning or intention. *Innovation* is defined as *deliberate* alteration – intention is a crucial element' (White, 1988, p. 114).

Although the choice of terminology to describe these two phenomena may be arbitrary, the events themselves are clearly distinguishable. Some new events are planned and can be called *innovations*, whereas others appear self-generating and can be referred to simply as *change*.

Such descriptions, however, fail to explain the cause of change.

If we return to the model of innovation outlined above we are able to distinguish a possible explanation. We can perceive that change – unplanned, marginal adjustments – can occur in two ways. First, any innovation of any scope can have adjustments made in an *ad hoc* manner at its margins by individuals or groups. These do not warrant the term 'innovation' as they are of a relatively minor nature. For instance, they may be a local influence rather than applying to the whole geographical area of the innovation. Second, within the model presented, changes will occur at the end of a line of amending innovations as the amendments to amendments become so small, with such restricted impact, that they can no longer be considered as innovations.

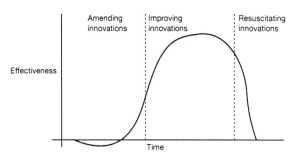

Figure 13.9 Time/effectiveness pattern in incrementally adjusted large-scale innovations

Figure 13.8 The relationship between innovation and change

The pattern of effectiveness of large-scale innovations

The fourth phenomenon on which this model may cast a light is related to the pattern of effectiveness of innovations. Innovations, as we noted above, are rarely accepted when first introduced and resistance is common at this stage. However, provided there is a certain robustness in the system, innovations are often eventually accepted. Partly this can be explained through 'routinization' – individuals eventually accepting power-coercively introduced systems. However, it can also be explained because the innovation is amended and improved to make it acceptable through the system of incremental adjustments we have been considering.

Thus, in effect, people accept the innovation because it is now working, whereas they originally rejected it because it did not work.

The 'ineffectiveness' of evaluation

There is considerable evidence that the results of evaluation are largely ignored and ineffective innovations permitted to continue (Cronbach, 1982; Cook and Shadish, 1986; Kushner and MacDonald, 1987; McLaughlin, 1985; Rog and Bick-

man, 1984). This can be explained as human perversity, stupidity or cupidity. However, such consistent perversity concerning apparently dysfunctional activities may deserve further consideration. It is fairly clear that evaluations of large-scale innovations carried out in the early stages of the innovation are likely to identify major problems. However, those responsible for managing innovations recognize (intuitively!) that current problems do not necessarily preclude eventual success. The very purpose of the evaluation, if it is formative in nature, is to provide information that can be used to develop amending and refining incremental innovations that will move the larger innovation to the successful stage. Of course, this need not necessarily happen. Innovations can, and do, fail, and one reason why they may continue is that possibly no one can think of a better alternative. The identification, however, of a 'difficult' innovation should not automatically provide grounds for ceasing to support the innovation. Rather it should be used as information to develop amending innovations.

Conclusion

I believe that models of innovation such as the one presented here provide a useful way of conceptualizing aspects of the process of innovation and change in education, with all the advantages of any model. The model developed here emphasizes:

1 the cyclic nature of innovation;
2 the nature of various types of small innovation including amending, improving and resuscitating innovations;
3 the relationship of the relative impact of large- and small-scale innovations to the point in the innovation cycle where the innovation occurs;
4 the iterative nature of innovation; and
5 the distinction, and the causal relationship, between innovation and change.

In particular, in relation to the realities of innovation, the model helps to explain:

1 why both large and small innovations can appear to be more or less effective, but any argument as to which are inherently better is largely specious;
2 why particular features of both large- and small-scale innovations can appear to be both an advantage and a disadvantage;
3 the way in which innovation 'breeds' innovation with the potential for badly planned innovations to cause innovation overload and fatigue for all involved;
4 the patterns of effectiveness of large- and small-scale innovations; and
5 the apparent lack of effectiveness of evaluation.

References

Berman, P. and McLaughlin, M. (1977) *Federal Programs Supporting Educational Change:* vol. VII, *Factors Affecting Implementation and Continuation.* Santa Monica, CA: Rand Corporation.

Colledge, S. (1995) Introducing a new EAP syllabus. Unpublished MA work, Chichester Institute of Higher Education.

Checkland, P. (1981) *Systems Thinking, Systems Practice.* Chichester: Wiley.

Cook, T. D. and Shadish, W. R. Jr (1986) Program evaluation: the worldly science, in *Evaluation Studies Review Annual.* vol. 11. Newbury Park: Sage Publications.

Forrester, J. W. (1981) Understanding the counter-intuitive behaviour of social systems, in Open Systems Group (ed.), *Systems Behaviour*, 3rd edn. London: Paul Chapman.

Fullan, M. (1991) *The New Meaning of Educational Change.* London: Cassell.

Havelock, R. G. (1973) *The Change Agents' Guide to Innovation in Education.* Englewood Cliffs, NJ: Educational Technology Publications.

Haynes, M. E. (1990) *Project Management.* London: Kogan Page.

Hollander, S. (1965) *The Sources of Increased Efficiency: A Study of Du Pont Rayon Plants.* Cambridge, MA: MIT Press.

House, E. R. (1979) *The Politics of Educational Innovation*, Berkeley, CA: McCutchan Publishing.

Hutchinson, B. (1993) The effective, reflective school: visions and pipe dreams in development planning, *Education Management and Administration*, **21**(1), 4–18.

Kushner, S. and MacDonald, B. (1987) The limitations of program evaluation, in R. Murphy and H. Torrance (eds), *Evaluating Education: Issues and Methods.* Milton Keynes: Open University Press.

Levin, H. (1976) Educational reform: its meaning, in M. Carnoy and H. Levin (eds), *The Limits of Educational Reform.* New York: McKay.

McLaughlin, M. W. (1985) Implementation realities and evaluation design, in R. Lance-Shortland and M. M. Mark (eds), *Social Science and Social Policy.* Newbury Park: Sage Publications, pp. 96–120.

Nicholls, A. (1983) *Managing Education Innovations.* London: Allen & Unwin.

Nisbet, J. (1974) Innovation: bandwagon or hearse? in A. Harris, M. Lawn and W. Prescott (eds), *Curriculum Innovation*, Milton Keynes: Open University Press.

Rog, D. J. and Bickman, L. (1984) The feedback research approach to evaluation: a method to increase evaluation utility, in D. S. Cordray and M. W. Lipsey, *Evaluation Studies Review Annual*, vol. 11. Newbury Park: Sage Publications, pp. 306–12.

Rogers, E. M and Shoemaker, E. F. (1971) *Communication of Innovations: A Cross-cultural Approach*, 2nd edn. London: Macmillan.

Rudduck, J. (1991) *Innovation and Design: Developing Involvement and Understanding.* Milton Keynes: Open University Press.

Smyth, L. F. and van der Vegt, R. (1993) Innovation in schools: some dilemmas of implementation, *Education Management and Administration*, **21**(2), 115–22.

Sparkes, A. C. (1989) Towards an understanding of the personal cost and rewards in teacher initiated innovation, *Education Management and Administration*, **17**, 100–8.

Sparkes, A. C. (1990) Power domination and

resistance in the process of teacher initiated innovation, *Research Papers in Education*, **5**(2), 153–78.

Weick, K. E. (1984) Small wins: redefining the scale of social problems, *American Psychologist*, **39**, 40–9.

White, R. V. (1988) *The ELT Curriculum: Design, Innovation and Management*. Oxford: Blackwell.

Wilson, B. (1984) *Systems: Concepts, Methodologies and Applications*. Chichester: Wiley.

14 The Tension between Evaluation for Learning and Evaluation for Accountability

PHILLIP HUGHES

Early in this century the medical educator William Oser wrote concerning examinations, 'At their best, a means to an end; at the worst the end itself. They may be the best part of an education or the worst. They may be its very essence or its ruin' (Oser, 1913). What Oser wrote about examinations is true of the whole field of evaluation.

Evaluation is a powerful aspect of education, and unavoidably so. It will inevitably have an impact, it is only the nature of that impact that we can influence. Molière's central character in *Le Bourgeois Gentilhomme*, M. Jourdain, was delighted to be told by his tutor the difference between poetry and prose and thus to discover that, all his life, he had been speaking prose. We are similarly involved in evaluation. It is a normal and unavoidable part of our lives, but we somehow fail to make our thinking explicit and to analyse its elements. Yet there are vital issues involved even in the day-to-day occurrences of evaluation that we need to resolve.

The way in which we assess student achievement is a vital aspect of the way we define the curriculum. The most explicit statements of what we believe to be important in the curriculum appear in the process of student assessment. This is not simply because it becomes the focus of student attention but because it is for teachers and others the definition of what schools see to be valuable.

Two distinct approaches exist, perhaps in competition, perhaps complementarily.

1   Political accountability and community support and understanding of what schools are doing both require that achievement standards be assessed and reported in meaningful terms. In this approach, assessment is used for monitoring and accountability in state or national systems, for example in terms of nationwide testing of student achievements in core areas of the curriculum. To do such testing in ways that are reliable and valid and still remain understandable to the public and to politicians is not an easy task.

2   In approaches that integrate assessment with learning, students' everyday work is used for continuous assessment rather than assessment's depending on formal examinations or standardized tests. These approaches include records of student achievements, portfolios, practical tests and school-based feedback to help define objectives and to encourage learners to take responsibility for their learning.

These two approaches are considered in detail in a conference paper edited by Nisbet, 'Relating pupil assessment and evaluation to teaching and learning' (Nisbet, 1994), where he comments that the first approach has resulted from pressure by politicians, parents and administrators, whereas the second is favoured by the professionals in education. He continues to discuss the possibility of doing both, given that both have merit, but concludes that the 'high-stakes' accountability procedures will soon come to dominate the 'low-stakes' learning-related student assessment. He continues:

> A more constructive resolution of the conflict between the two uses of assessment, the 'accountability' use and the 'institutional' use, is to seek to combine both within a single system of assessment. This implies designing national testing to provide for

national monitoring. Hence, we are distinguishing two levels in the use of assessment in education: assessment of the system and assessment of the process. (Nisbet, 1994, p. 168)

This is a very constructive suggestion in a situation where the pressures from both points of view are very strong. Nisbet himself asks whether these two approaches are compatible or irreconcilable.

A similar issue is raised by Stephen Kemmis in a paper in which he reported on a collision of views on evaluation evident at a national evaluation conference:

> a collision between views of evaluation as (in some sense) a process of gathering information for bureaucratic–administrative decision-making, on the one hand, and evaluation for a more generally educative purpose, on the other. Some here are interested only in one view, and some only in the other; some believe that the two can be reconciled in a more liberal eclectic and pragmatic view of education, and some that the two are permanently and essentially in opposition. Those who take the oppositional view see evaluation for bureaucratic administrative decision-making and evaluation for participant education as contrary poles in an opposition between conflicting interests in the modern state. I take this dialectical view. (Kemmis, 1989, p. 63)

The idea that there are two conflicting views has underpinned strongly contested debate on the conceptualization of evaluation and its practice. However, it is worth considering whether that conflict is a necessary one, as Kemmis implies, or whether some resolution is possible, as Nisbet believes.

Patterns of the past

Much of the hostile feeling in education concerning the ill-effects of some forms of evaluation dates back to the 'payment by results' patterns of the last century. This general approach followed from the Newcastle Commission in Britain. At that period, schools operated very much as independent institutions, developing their own programmes, appointing their own teachers and having no links with one another or with any central body, except

for receiving grants. It was the receipt of these funds which was to provide the lever for change.

The Newcastle Commission, which reported in 1861, represents an early attempt to use evaluation to change learning patterns. The commission was set up in order to raise the standards of achievement in the basic subjects. It reached the following conclusion:

> There is only one way of achieving this result, which is to institute a searching examination by competent authorities of every child in every school to which grants are to be paid, with the view of ascertaining whether these indispensable elements of knowledge are thoroughly acquired, and to make the prospects and position of the teacher dependent, to a considerable extent, on the results of this examination. (Newcastle Commission, 1861, p. 101)

The report of this commission led to the institution in England of the 'payment-by-results' system, which was to last forty years in formal terms but whose effects are still apparent. The examinations in the schools were conducted by inspectors, who tested in a very limited area of computation and also with one problem. The grants were paid on the basis of the number of pupils attaining a pass mark, which could be achieved through the computation area only. The consequences were disastrous: the already limited teaching became narrower still, concentrating on the rote learning of simple number facts and ignoring any applications. There was no encouragement for higher achievement and thus the main effort was spent on cramming the weaker children to get a pass mark and neglecting the needs of the average and more able pupils. The effects were thus quite the reverse of the intentions, contributing to very limited achievement coupled with a lasting distaste for learning. It contributed also towards a lasting heritage of mistrust between teachers and inspectors: the attitude of British teachers and teacher unions in the 1990s to efforts to develop testing programmes in the basic skills areas still shows the negative attitudes to widespread testing first generated by an example such as the Newcastle Commission.

In contrast, one of the first examples of curriculum evaluation on a wide scale was that carried out by J. M. Rice in 1892 in the United States, where he was asked to report on the standards of spelling in American schools. He visited thirty-six major American cities, talked with 1,200 teachers and had testing programmes implemented for 33,000 students. As a result of this, he was able to indicate that standards in spelling bore no relationship to the time spent by teachers in teaching spelling by the drill method then common. This was a different type of operation altogether from payment by results, because what Rice was attempting to do was establish what connections there were between particular approaches and the level of achievement in a particular area. Although this was an external approach, it was done with the cooperation of teachers in an issue they felt to be important.

The major early development of evaluation in education came with the work of people like Binet, Thorndyke, Galton and others in the psychometric tradition, which dominated the scene for the first half of the twentieth century and led to the development of group and individual tests of intelligence and to standardized tests. The first application of evaluation into the curriculum area came with Ralph Tyler's evaluation in 1942 of an eight-year study, reported in Smith and Tyler (1942). This was the first project to extend from strict psychometric measures to look at the full range of observations of pupil performance. The report was interesting in two senses. First, it established a pattern for evaluation which is still most influential, the pattern which specified statements of purpose, clarified in a variety of ways, statements of teaching methods, statements of pupil activities and statements of outcome which were used as part of the evaluation theme. Second, in an attempt to give a complete picture Tyler used a variety of records including pupil performance, sociograms, interviews, pupil diaries and case studies. Almost all the sorts of information which we would currently suggest as relevant were used in one way or another. But that was not typical of the forms of evaluation used at that time – nor is it typical of the way people describe Tyler today, because he is often used as an arch-example of the limited evaluator, which misrepresents the way he actually operated.

An important extension of Tyler's work was by Bloom, Krathwohl and others (Bloom *et al.*, 1956) in their attempt to provide means of obtaining more valid measures by specifying objectives in a more precise and consistent way and by indicating levels of complexity in a way that could be communicated to different groups. Their work in this regard had a significant and continuing impact on evaluation and on curriculum design. We find quite early in the American scene, emanating particularly from the University of Illinois, including writers such as Cronbach (1963) and Hastings (1969), the view that the psychometric model was only one way of looking at the evaluation of situations and particularly of people's operations, and suggesting that sociology, history and anthropology offer a number of other relevant patterns. This concept was developed further by Robert Stake (Stake, 1967), also of the University of Illinois, who stressed both the formal and the informal aspects of evaluation and introduced the concept of evaluation as portrayal, particularly through the use of case studies.

A further major development came with Michael Scriven's (1967) 'goal-free evaluation'. This approach deliberately kept consideration of goals by the evaluator out of the early stages of evaluation in order to allow the evaluator to view the total processes more objectively. Scriven's approach was implemented through his use of a product checklist which replaces consideration of the goals with an analysis of needs. Scriven also introduced the concepts of 'formative' and 'summative' evaluation, which refer to evaluation used during and at the end of a process, respectively. The former is directed to assisting teaching and learning, the latter towards making a final judgement of achievement.

A further need for extension was pointed out by Stufflebeam *et al.* (1971), who developed the context/impact/process/product (CIPP) model as an approach which included an evaluation of the objectives themselves as well as the degree of their achievement.

Evaluation in education in the United States has often been unfairly caricatured as being restricted to the paradigm of the psychometric approach and a behaviourist model, and evaluation in the

United Kingdom has been typified as using humanistic and process-oriented approaches. Neither stereotype is accurate. The American situation is much more diverse, as has been shown, and, despite all that has been written about it in the UK, evaluation is strongly product oriented, with a dominant practice still being the conduct of examinations at the end of secondary education.

In the UK, an important development in evaluation in 1976 was the setting up of the Assessment of Performance Unit (APU) by the Department of Education and Science. The terms of reference of the APU were 'to promote the development of methods of assessing and monitoring the achievement of children at school and to seek to identify the incidence of underachievement'. Its four tasks were:

- to identify and appraise existing instruments and methods of assessment which may be relevant for these purposes
- to sponsor the creation of new instruments and techniques for assessment having regard to statistical and sampling methods
- to promote the conduct of assessment in co-operation with local education authorities and teachers
- to identify significant differences of achievement related to the circumstances in which children learn, including the incidence of underachievement, and to make the findings available to those concerned with resource allocation within the appropriate Department, local education authorities and schools. (Department of Education and Science, 1977, p. 14)

Within the APU, working groups were set up for seven areas of the curriculum. The working groups were quite specifically not related to particular areas of the school curriculum, even in those cases where there were school subjects of similar names. For example, science was regarded as a term describing particular ways of thinking about and tackling problems rather than as a particular school subject or group of subjects. Not all the working groups developed published charters but a general pattern of policy became clear. Assessment was to be based on a small number of key

areas, each concerned with one important and distinct facet of the basic skills and attitudes that pupils should develop. For example, the science group looked at criteria under five headings: observation, generalization, explanation and enquiry, component skills, and attitudes.

Note that the APU itself designed its work in order that there should not be comparisons made between particular schools and particular pupils. The methods of light sampling defined by the APU ensured this. However, the work of the APU was seen by many people working in evaluation in England and Wales as a very considerable threat to a more constructive use of evaluation. They saw the APU, in spite of good intentions, as capable of being used for political ends, and the mention in the terms of reference of the use of information by those who distribute resources did little to allay this fear. It is interesting to compare this situation to that which has arisen in the USA in states such as Michigan, and which is reported by Jerome T. Murphy and David K. Cohen (1974). They stressed the difficulties that arise from the uncritical use of assessment measures which make comparisons between schools and which are then proposed as the basis for the allocation of resources.

Many of the initiatives in evaluation in Britain in this period were based on the type of conflict perceived by Kemmis, the use of evaluation as a political instrument by government. A strong alternative approach developed. A key paper in the British evaluation scene was a publication by Parlett and Hamilton (1972), 'Evaluation as illumination.' Parlett and Hamilton distinguished what they described as the traditional 'agricultural paradigm' of evaluation, and their own preferred form, the 'social anthropology paradigm'. The approach depends heavily on participant observation and on the ethnographic fieldwork of social anthropology. Concerned by a comparative lack of success of many large curriculum projects both in the USA and the UK and feeling that the classical model of evaluation was inadequate, they developed an approach which shows distinct similarities to the concepts put forward by Stake (1973) of evaluation as portrayal. Parlett and Hamilton used 'triangulation' as a key element of their three-stage approach: first, an overall study to identify significant features; second, the selection of a number of such features for more intensive inquiry; and third, the attempt at 'explanation' through seeking general principles underlying the organization of such a programme. The concept of 'triangulation' relates to the use of a number of different perspectives on a particular incident, in order to develop a more inclusive and revealing picture.

The Parlett and Hamilton paper was closely followed by a conference at Churchill College, Cambridge, in December 1972 which, though not able to reach agreement on all issues, published a statement indicating some major shifts in concern. These were as follows:

1   [We believed] that the traditional methods of evaluation had paid too little attention to the whole educational process in a particular milieu and too much attention to those changes in a student's behaviour which could be measured;

2   that the educational research climate had underestimated the gap between school problems and conventional research issues;

3   that curriculum evaluation should be responsive to the requirements of different audiences, illuminative of complex organizational processes, and relevant to both public and professional decisions about education. (Macdonald and Parlett, 1973, p. 23)

The work of Parlett and Hamilton on illuminative evaluation was paralleled by work focusing on case studies, including that of Barry Macdonald, the evaluator in the Humanities Curriculum Project. In this project, carried out in 1971, he made a quite deliberate and carefully considered move away from a psychometric approach to a style relying on methods usually associated with historical and anthropological research: for example, observation, interviewing and documentation. In addition, Macdonald redefined the idea of audience. He aimed his work at decision-makers of various kinds, the sponsors (the Schools Council and Nuffield Foundation), the employing authority, the schools and the examination boards.

Macdonald began to see evaluation in terms of supplying answers to questions that would be asked by the consumers or decision-makers. However, he realized that even this was too restrictive, since such a view assumed that questions could be specified in advance, whereas he felt that many questions would arise only during the process of the evaluation itself. Consequently he adopted a very ambitious combination of traditional and non-traditional methods – so ambitious, in fact, that his work was never finished.

A major development in the evaluation field is the growth in the use of the case study. First recommended in education by Stake (1973), it has now become a very widely used approach. Although lacking easy generalizability, it can offer a 'conviction of reality' through its clear descriptions of actual situations. Its full potential remains to be realized.

The logical extension of these approaches was in the movement in England and Wales on profiles and records of achievement. This movement was seen specifically as an alternative to the past:

> After more than a hundred years of external-exam dominated certification procedures, education seems to be on the brink of an assessment revolution. Two schemes that have attracted particular interest as alternatives to the exam system are pupil profiles and records of achievement. This interest has been officially endorsed by the 1984 government policy statement for England and Wales declaring that all school leavers should be given a record of achievement by the end of the decade. (Broadfoot, 1986, p. 2)

Here again, we see the identification of the conflict between the two evaluation approaches. Broadfoot clearly envisages the conflict as being resolved by the move towards the more school-based emphasis, taking into account the recent thinking on evaluation in the UK. That conclusion was to prove to be mistaken in view of later events.

Significant evaluation decisions of the present

Since the activity in thinking on evaluation in the 1970s and early 1980s there has been a pause in development. Instead, the running has been taken over at a different level, by politicians in particular. It is possible to trace similar patterns of political intervention in education in Australia, England and Wales, and the USA. Because the process is further advanced in England and Wales through the Education Reform Act 1988 (ERA 88), the British situation will be analysed briefly to indicate the nature of the intervention.

ERA 88 provides detailed legislation for a national curriculum as one aspect of the most significant legislation on education in England and Wales since the Education Act 1944. The inclusion in the legislation of the idea of a national curriculum is, at first sight, surprising. It is surprising because the rest of the legislation has a different emphasis. It is surprising, also, because of the long-established practice in England and Wales that the curriculum should be determined by the schools themselves rather than be determined centrally, and especially when that central determination is by political action.

The section of the legislation on the National Curriculum listed ten foundation subjects to be taken by all pupils during their period of compulsory education: English, mathematics, science, a modern foreign language (in secondary schools), technology, history, geography, art, music and physical education. The 'core' subjects among these would be English, maths and science, with the majority of time at the primary level being devoted to these. The draft legislation indicated that secondary schools would devote 30 to 40 per cent of their time to the three core subjects and 80 to 90 per cent of the time in years 4 and 5 to the foundation subjects. Themes such as information technology and health education would have to be taught through the foundation subjects. In the event, the legislation did not include the time specification, with the Minister indicating in the House that such precise specification was irrelevant and that it was 'up to schools, heads and local authorities to deliver the national curriculum and bring children up to the level of attainment targets' (report in the *Guardian*, 21 November 1989).

The Attainment Targets were specified for students at the ages of 7, 11, 14 and 16, initially in the core subjects, with an extension envisaged later for the other foundation subjects except for art,

music and physical education, where there would be 'guidelines' only. The achievement of these attainment targets would be assessed through national tests at the four levels. In addition, and with some apparent inconsistency, it was indicated that Records of Achievement, previously seen as an alternative to a formal assessment process, should be introduced nationally.

Although these elements of foundation and core subjects, and of clearly specified assessments, differ from the established practice of many years, the concept is not a new feature on the British scene. One of the papers in a publication called *The National Curriculum* pointed out that much the same pattern had existed much earlier:

> Thus in essence the proposed national curriculum, in so far as it is expressed in terms of core and foundation subjects, appears as a reassertion of the basic grammar school curriculum devised at the beginning of the twentieth century by such men as Robert Morant and James Headlam. The curriculum was thus subordinated to the demands of a test procedure which was itself employed to justify a reduction in educational expenditure, although this latter aim was expressed in terms of securing value for money. (Lawton and Chitty, 1988, p. 23)

These aspects, however, of a specified set of subjects and of well-defined assessment tasks, had seemed to be very much part of a superseded past. The concept of a legislated national curriculum is not a new feature on the world scene. There are many countries where national legislation on the curriculum is the normal way of operating, for example, China, Thailand, Korea, Malaysia, the Philippines, Papua New Guinea. Yet the UK's tradition of leaving curriculum issues to the schools was so long-standing and apparently firmly based that a change through legislation to this pattern of definition was surprising. The change, though dramatic, was not sudden, but was based on a particular philosophical position and on a carefully defined political strategy. In December 1986 Kenneth Baker, then Secretary of State, chose an Independent Television programme to announce that a third Thatcher government would legislate for a 'national core curriculum' with specific objectives whose achievement would be assessed at three different age levels. The serious intent behind this announcement was made quite clear by Mr Baker at the January 1987 Society of Education Officers Conference:

> I believe that, at least as far as England is concerned, we should now move quickly to a national curriculum ... the changes I envisage are radical and far-reaching and may therefore, be unwelcome ... But I believe profoundly that professional educators will do a disservice to the cause of education, and to the nation, if they entrench themselves in a defence of the *status quo.* (Department of Education and Science, 1987)

The origins of this particular version of a national curriculum are not entirely clear. When it appeared in the legislation after the announcement by Mr Baker, it was part of a more general package, including the right of open enrolment for students, provision for schools to opt out of local authority control into grant-maintained status, and devolution of financial management to the school. These three elements, stressing the importance of the local school as a decision-making centre and the value of parental choice, are in contrast with the other element; the national curriculum provides a uniform pattern for all state primary and secondary schools, although it leaves independent schools free to make their own choice.

Kenneth Baker claimed that although the National Curriculum was his idea, it was consistent with earlier thinking, including that of the Callaghan Labour government: 'The national curriculum is not a change of direction, but the natural next stage in what has been a process of evolution' (*The Times Educational Supplement*, 25 September 1987). It is true that both the Department of Education and Science (DES) and Her Majesty's Inspectorate (HMI) had been pressing in different ways for a curriculum change. The Department of Education and Science view appeared in the Labour government Green Paper *Education in Schools* (Department of Education and Science, 1977a), the Conservative government policy statement *Better Schools* (Department of Education and Science, 1985) and in detail in *A Framework for the School Curriculum* (Department of Education and Science, 1980), which pressed for a centrally prescribed curriculum with specified core

subjects with allocated amounts of time. The HMI view, which was summed up in the paper *Towards a Statement of Entitlement* (Her Majesty's Inspectorate, 1981), argued that the Department of Education and Science view was too instrumental in nature and instead proposed a common curriculum based on students' right of access, with a liberal education rationale which indicated the need for students to be involved in particular areas of experience, rather than specified subjects.

There was, however, a quite separate strand of influence on the Conservative government from groups within the party, such as the Conservative Philosophy Group, involving people such as Margaret Thatcher, Roger Scruton and Rhodes Boyson, and the Centre for Policy Studies, established by Sir Keith Joseph in 1974. Also included were separate but related groups such as the Black Paper Group, the Critical Quarterly Society, and the Hillgate Group. Broadly, this strand was strongly critical of teachers and educational administrators, seeing them as preventing the need for rigour in education and as pressing towards left-wing political ends. Typical of the criticism were Oliver Letwin's remarks:

> Excellence became unfashionable in the sixties with disastrous results. It came to be regarded as a dirty word representing a dirty concept. As a result, the attempt to excel all but disappeared, to be replaced by a dispiriting and soul-destroying mediocrity. Mr Baker is attempting to reinstate the excellent – and about time too ... Only among the cognoscenti – still infected with the ideas of the sixties – is there still a continuing resistance ... it is something we have to face before we can hope to overcome it. Mr Baker's tests will serve the purpose admirably: we have to pray that that the layman will triumph over the inbred, decadent cognoscenti. (*The Times Education Supplement*, 25 September 1987)

For this group, the first three elements of the legislation were much more palatable than the idea of a national curriculum. For them, curriculum, as with the other elements, should be a matter of choice, determined by 'market forces', in this case as shown by where students chose to attend. This would imply that schools should offer quite different programmes of teaching, as part of market competition. Dennis O'Keeffe, who was associated with Roger Scruton of the Conservative Philosophy Group and the Hillgate Group, wrote:

> All the economic successes since 1979 have come from shifting power to the consumer and trusting markets to do the rest ... The Government should have considered financial changes, such as tax relief, which would allow more parents effective rights of exit from the system: this would create competition and generate efficiency. The Government believes in capitalism. Why then does it favour coercive education? The surest advantage of markets is that they cannot be controlled politically. (*The Times Educational Supplement*, 18 September 1987)

Why, then, was the apparently inconsistent idea of a national curriculum included in the legislation? Janet Maw in an article on national curriculum policy gave the following explanation:

> two factors appear salient in evaluating curriculum policy changes. The first was simply political expediency, the need for an 'issue' around which to rally support during the election campaign ... with no 'Falklands factor' to hand, education was tailor-made as an issue because the teachers' action and the activities of a small number of Labour LEAs allowed the Conservatives to launch a populist appeal on the slogans of 'standards' and 'choice'. In relation to the education package as a whole – opting out, budget devolution, and open enrolment – the national curriculum was central in enabling the Conservatives to claim a genuine concern for education, to deny that they were neglecting the many in favour of the few. This can be seen as the main reason for *having* a national curriculum, in opposition to the privatizing, differentiating tendencies of the rest of the package ... The second factor that appears to be important is that the Education Reform Act in its present form is the result of ideological conflict, not *between* politicians [and] bureaucrats, but ideological conflict *within* the political Right in general. (Lawton and Chitty, 1988, pp. 60–1)

What seems clear is that the idea of a national curriculum was an attractive political option, not because of the support of educators, but because it was attractive to the wider public, particularly to parents. To them it seemed attractive because of the apparent clarity as to what was to be taught and because it promised regular reports on students' achievements on a comparable basis. It seemed attractive, too, because it was seen as affirming the power of parents as against the perceived arrogance of educators.

Again the conflict in methodological approaches is made manifest, in this situation in England and Wales and in similar moves in the USA and Australia. Even more, however, those of us in education need to ask ourselves whether the stances on both sides of the conflict are not making it sharper than is necessary. In particular, if we are to avoid the worst excesses of a politically dominated approach, we may need to be more sensitive ourselves to the diversity of the legitimate 'participants' in educational evaluation.

Where do we go from here?

It is clear that the perception of the conflict between the two styles of evaluation is in fact reflected in current practice. Evaluation may be used by participants to improve their understanding of a situation and their ability to deal with it. This is a positive experience for the participants and may lead to improvements in the situation itself, although the latter is not a necessary result. Evaluation may also be used by external people, to determine the effectiveness of a process (or institution) as measured against certain defined goals and to determine the efficiency of the various actors and activities in the achievement of the goals. The conflict perceived by Kemmis comes from the negative reactions of the actors in this situation as they see the evaluation activities and, particularly, the judgements as a threat to them. These negative reactions, if sufficiently strong and if organized to obtain wide support, can be successful in either halting the evaluation or preventing the implementation of its findings.

Do we therefore make the assumption that what Kemmis calls 'evaluation for bureaucratic–administrative decision-making' should not proceed because of this likelihood of conflict? Kemmis seems to hold this view:

> In accepting this framework for evaluation, we tacitly take a position in the age-old opposition between the interests of the state and those of civil society – the society of people as members of social classes, communities and informal groups. It is possible to reject the view that evaluation is a matter for the state alone,

and, on the contrary, to take the view that people as members of communities, as part of civil society, also have rights to know and that evaluation can be arranged in support of their rights to know. (Kemmis, 1989, p. 65)

Although there is an important point here, the distinctions made are too absolute. The black-and-white classification of 'the state' on one hand, and 'civil society' on the other, is simplistic. The action of the state may, in fact, be on behalf of elements of the civil society, those 'social classes, communities and informal groups' who have 'their rights to know'. Indeed, it is possible that the rights to know of various groups in our society are being restricted by the concept that evaluation for participant education is the only legitimate use of evaluation. This is not the view held by Kemmis, but it is a view commonly held, and based on the distinction made by Kemmis. We need to challenge the argument itself because of its widespread use to isolate schools from their particular communities and from the wider society.

We have seen in recent years a substantial loss of esteem by schools and a parallel loss of status (and salary relativity) by teachers. This is a very different situation from that which existed in the 1950s and the 1960s, when there was general agreement on the value of education and the major problems were to deal with shortages of teachers and of buildings which hindered the work of schools. In Australia the end of the 1960s saw a potent alliance between teachers, teacher unions and professional bodies, parents, education systems and politicians to make education a national priority. The alliance played a part in the 1972 national election which brought the Whitlam government to power. This was followed by a large increase in funding and the establishment of bodies such as the Schools Commission and the Curriculum Development Centre, which saw their task as working not only with education systems but with schools and teachers and with parents and parent organizations.

The economic stringency of the mid- and late 1970s following dismissal of the Whitlam government saw a gradual loosening of the powerful alliance that had developed, the beginning of the

loss of esteem of schools and the elimination of any policy bodies in education capable of offering policy advice on an independent basis. The 1980s saw a consolidation of this process, proceeding quite independently of the political colour of governments to a stage where education systems are discredited as policy advocates for education and have been the subject of such severe and repeated restructuring that they are demoralized and ineffective. A reduction in central powers had been the hope of many people for Australian education but the effective dismantling of the education departments did not achieve a reduction but merely a displacement in central powers, which now rest in the hands of politicians and political advisers at both state and federal levels. In theory, this has been accompanied by a devolution of authority to the school level, but so far this devolution has been more in principle than reality. The schools are indeed on their own in facing criticism and they no longer have the broad support of effective systems, nor have they been able to rebuild the partnerships with parents which are so important to their effectiveness, their community standing and their political status.

What has all this to do with education policies?

We have seen that in England and Wales ERA 88 included legislation for a National Curriculum involving very elaborate assessment procedures, largely because it was politically attractive rather than because of its consistency with other aspects of the Act. It was politically attractive because parents felt closed out of the schools and, in particular, felt deprived of the sort of information they wished to have. At a recent National Conference of Australian Educators, David Hargreaves (1990), a well-informed analyst of the English scene, said that parents had indicated their very strong wish to have three sorts of knowledge, in the following order of priority:

1 Parents wish to know the achievements of their children relative to the age-group.
2 Parents wish to know the strengths and weaknesses of their children's school, relative to other schools.

3   Parents (and the wider community) wish to know of rises and declines in student achievement generally.

Yet this is the sort of knowledge which teachers generally have felt unwilling to give, ostensibly because of the same sort of argument as that advanced by Kemmis: that evaluation is for the benefit of the participants, as part of an educative and developmental process.

That argument, and its subsequent result, has contributed greatly to the loss of standing of schools, particularly of public-sector schools. We now have a climate in which a number of misapprehensions are identified by critics of education and given repeated coverage in the media. These include the following:

1   Achievements in literacy and numeracy have declined.
2   Students prefer soft options to serious study.
3   Students are rude and undisciplined.
4   Teachers are left-wing radicals, concerned mostly with such subjects as peace studies and sex education.
5   Teachers are naive and poorly educated, with little knowledge of or sympathy for the world of work.
6   Schools are attempting to solve all social problems.
7   Schools make no difference to students' achievements, they merely confirm the differences established by social background.

Although we may resist the uninformed and often contradictory nature of much of this criticism, those of us in education must take some of the blame for its wide circulation and acceptance. In particular, the view that evaluation in education is essentially to help teachers is to blame. This is the version of the Kemmis case which is popular in schools and which is justified by a simplified view of the distinction between two views of evaluation: evaluation for the state and evaluation for civil society. With respect to schools, the elements of civil society have frequently been taken as the teachers, and clearly they are a vital part of it. But so too are students and parents, and a range of other interest groups. It is justifiable to take students as being the primary interest group, rather than teachers, for it is their learning which is the essential reason for schools. Yet even as we acknowledge this, the importance of giving appropriate information to parents becomes obvious because of their role in effective student learning. Further thought indicates the value of other groups having wider and more accurate knowledge of the schools. These include employer groups, who very often hold strong views about student performance, views which may not match the facts.

There is a very real challenge for schools, regardless of particular evaluation requirements of the state, to define broadly but accurately their own participant groups, involving always teachers, students and parents, with other groups included as is appropriate. The worst excesses of state demands on education have normally arisen where schools have turned inwards and ceased to provide information of the type and in the mode relevant to the particular interest groups.

References

Bloom, B. J. *et al.* (1956) *Taxonomy of Education Objectives: Cognitive Domain.* New York: David Mackay.

Broadfoot, P. (1986) *Profiles and Records of Achievement.* London: Holt, Rinehart & Winston.

Cronbach, L. (1963) Course improvement through evaluation, *Teachers College Record,* **33**, 71–84.

Department of Education and Science (1977) *Education in Schools: A Consultative Document.* London: HMSO.

Department of Education and Science (1980) *A Framework for the School Curriculum.* London: HMSO.

Department of Education and Science (1985) *Better Schools.* London: HMSO.

Department of Education and Science (1987) Kenneth Baker calls for curriculum for pupils of all abilities, Press Release 22/87, 23 January.

Hargreaves, D. (1990) Keynote Address to National Conference of Australian Educators, Australian Council for Educational Administration, Hobart.

Hastings, T. (1969) Kith and kin of education measures, *Journal of Education Measurement,* **6**, 127–30.

Her Majesty's Inspectorate (1981) *Towards a Statement of Entitlement.* London: Department of Education and Science.

Kemmis, S. (1989) Self evaluation in the context of program evaluation, *Evaluation Journal of Australasia*, **2**(1), 59–66.

Lawton, D. and Chitty, C. (1988) *The National Curriculum.* Bedford Way series. Institute of Education, University of London.

Macdonald, R. and Parlett, V. (1973) Rethinking evaluation, *Cambridge Journal of Education*, **3**, 16–27.

Murphy, J. T. and Cohen, D. K. (1974) Accountability in education: the Michigan experience, *Public Interest*, **36** (Summer), 83–104.

Newcastle Commission (1861) *Report of the Commissioners Appointed to Inquire into the State of Popular Education in England* (the Newcastle Commission). London: HMSO.

Nisbet, J. (1994) Relating pupil assessment and evaluation to teaching and learning, in P. W. Hughes (ed.), *The Curriculum Redefined: Schooling for the 21st Century.* Paris: OECD.

Oser, Sir W. (1913) Examinations, examiners and examinees. *The Lancet*, **16**, 14–23.

Parlett, Y. and Hamilton, Y. (1972) Evaluation as illumination, in D. Towney (ed.), *Curriculum Evaluation Today.* Schools Council Research Studies. London: Macmillan, p. 48–57.

Scriven, M. (1967) Methodology of evaluation, in R. Tyler *et al.* (eds), *Perspectives of Curriculum Evaluation.* AERA Monograph Series on Curriculum Evaluation, no. 1. Chicago: Rand McNally.

Smith, L. and Tyler, R. (1942) *Appraising and Recording Student Progress.* New York: Harper & Row.

Stake, R. E. (1967) The countenance of educational evaluation, *Teachers College Record*, **68**, 1–17.

Stake, R. E. (1973), Program evaluation, particularly responsive evaluation. Paper presented at Conference on New Trends in Evaluation, Göteborg, Sweden, October.

Stufflebeam, D. *et al.* (1971) *Educational Evaluation and Decision-Making*, Itasca, IL: Peacock for Phi Delta Kappan National Study Committee on Evaluation.

15 Educational Assessment: Its Role in Improving the Efficiency of Primary Education in Developing Countries

LÉO LAROCHE

Introduction

All societies must face major upheaval, caused by changes observed during the past decades in several fields of human activity. The twentieth century has been full of important transformations in the political, cultural, scientific, social and technological fields. All of this has had significant repercussions on the way people live and on the way they prepare to fully undertake their role in society. Education has been identified as having an important role to play in ensuring an effective adaptation to these changes. That is why most Western countries have made important modifications to their education systems, especially during the second half of the twentieth century. These reforms have targeted the different components of the school systems: study programmes, personnel training, teaching material, planning or developing schools and learning assessment. Additional resources have been granted to permit greater school attendance. These resources have proved to be a good investment, as much for the society as for the individuals involved.

Developing countries cannot escape this problem of a society affected by major changes in various fields. The image of the world as a big village is more and more a reality. Information circulates in all directions, and new technologies are becoming more easily accessible. Some see that as a promise of improvement in standards of living. Leaders of a number of developing countries are increasingly placing education at the centre of reforms under-taken to meet the needs of those changes identified as being essential for ensuring the development or improvement of the people's standard of living. That is why important changes have been made to the school system of several countries. While drawing their inspiration from the main contemporary trends in educational organization, the co-ordinators wish to set up measures adapted to their specific context.

When planning activities to be conducted in their school system, the coordinators must choose measures that are most likely to bring about the desired changes. Which modifications should be chosen in view of the expected advantages and the available resources? How does one take into account the current practices acquired from diverse sources? The organization of educational reforms should rely on measures already in place; it is not a question of making a clean sweep of everything that already exists, but rather of introducing new measures more likely to adapt the system to new realities.

That is why assessment is often found at the centre of measures organized to modify a school system. Frequently, assessment is the first action undertaken in order to gain a better description of the situation, the most objective description possible. Then it will be easier to choose actions adapted to reality. When the authorities are organizing measures included in a plan for changes in educational matters, appropriate assessment actions will confirm or invalidate the pertinence of current activities and will thus facilitate essential changes in orientation. Furthermore, resorting to assessment will often be an occasion for those persons involved in their organization to gain a wider awareness of the different parts of an education system. An assessment activity conducted with rigour can reveal the different elements of the system, underscoring the interrelationship that develops between the aspects that some people would be tempted to isolate in order better to demonstrate their strategic importance.

This chapter deals with learning assessment as a means of establishing a diagnosis of the functioning of a school system and as a mechanism for decision-making purposes. Conducting an assessment is an occasion to examine the different elements of an education system. Many people must be involved in order to establish an accurate picture of the situation. Conducting an assessment demands the use of proven techniques if one wants to have rigorous data that will be useful for making enlightened decisions. After having made some general comments on education assessment, I will illustrate my remarks using assessment activities conducted in a school milieu. An illustration of learning assessment activities recently conducted in a developing country will be supplied in detail. Two types of assessment activity will be favoured: first, a mechanism (a sample-based assessment) that permits the examination of the system's results regarding student achievements is examined; second, and dealt with more briefly, is a more specific look at the learning assessment activities done by each student attending the schools.

Learning assessment

It is not my intention to present a complete treatise on the place of assessment in an education system. Numerous works have already covered the subject adequately. However, it seems relevant to recall certain concepts connected to any assessment process before presenting scenarios of conducting assessment activities in developing countries. My comments will be grouped in relation to the roles likely to be filled by assessment, the objectives usually used and, finally, the conditions, all the while favouring the realization of the assessment in a given milieu. This section will be concluded by the presentation of a typology of learning assessment.

Role and subjects

The resources given to the school system will probably not increase significantly during the next few years. This is a tendency that will be observed in most countries and, in particular, in developing countries. We all know that striking needs exist in numerous other social sectors, such as in health. Coordinators of the different education systems must do everything possible to do better with the same resources, and sometimes with fewer. In other words, productivity must be increased. Not only is it important to ensure that more children attend school, but these same children must acquire skills, as much cultural as professional, that will be useful for becoming active members of society. An appropriate assessment mechanism can supply useful information to the personnel working in a school system. Indeed, one of the most widely recognized functions of any mechanism of learning assessment is that related to the production of data that will be useful for making decisions. Information thus made available will facilitate the follow-up activities for ensuring an operation favourable to achieving objectives. Sometimes, certain assessment activities will be more oriented towards establishing a diagnostic; identifying the main problems will thus help the personnel of the system to choose strategies adapted to the situation. Sometimes, data made available by an assessment will be used instead to make a report; this is done to find out whether the resources given to education produce the expected results. It is evident that the global context must be considered here when making such a judgement.

Furthermore, conducting an assessment in a school environment is usually an occasion for making the people assigned to such an operation aware of the importance of the different elements of the system. The simple fact of starting an assessment mechanism permits the personnel to develop an awareness of the different facets of the system and to perceive clearly the close connections that exist between the complementary elements. For the past few years, we have been witnessing the specialization of tasks in all sectors of activities. This tendency is also seen in education. The result of such an orientation is the availability of competent human resources to carry out specific tasks. However, there is the risk of compartmentalization. Conducting an assessment requires the participation of personnel coming from different sectors of the school organization: curriculum, instructional material, pedagogical methods, training and upgrading for teachers, organizing classrooms. The personnel called to play a role in conducting an assessment rapidly come to clearly perceive the different elements as being part of the same system pursuing the same general objectives. This awareness of the complexity of the academic institution permits a better emphasis of the priorities to choose if the improvement of the services offered is desired.

Thus, there can be several objectives when organizing an assessment process: making decisions, follow-up, accountability, diagnosis, improving services. This list could be completed according to circumstances particular to a given milieu. The subjects of assessment can also be very diverse. They are frequently classified in relation to the following three components: resources, process and results. When one is dealing with learning assessment, examining the results is the main interest. Thus, we wish to scrutinize the achievement of the objectives targeted by the school system. However, this kind of mechanism will have to be able to relate the results obtained to the available resources as well as to the administrative and pedagogical practices used by the milieu. Such a relationship of the different components of the system will permit better identification of the conditions favourable to achieving the objectives of the school system.

That is why several developing countries have set up measures to provide schooling for the greatest number of children possible, and it is true that more young people attend school — mainly elementary school. For certain countries, there is an almost dramatic increase in the rate of school attendance. This is almost always accompanied by a lack of resources of all kinds: classrooms, teaching material and competent personnel. Furthermore, the curriculum is not always updated to account for new realities. Even if more young people attend school, one may wonder whether the training received under such conditions meets the needs. A rigorous assessment mechanism can supply information that will help the coordinators to choose the best strategies for a particular context.

Conditions to respect

Using rigorous learning assessment mechanisms permits better administration of the school system by supplying, among other things, valid information for making decisions. However, such procedures must respect certain implementation conditions. Some of these conditions are recalled here by relating the comments to the more specific context of developing countries.

Setting up an assessment activity of an education system concerns a multitude of participants: personnel working in the schools themselves, students, parents, general public, employment sectors. In short, education concerns everyone. Therefore, evaluation in education should have a global design. One should be able to establish links between different elements that are often interconnected. Furthermore, the mechanism used should make it easier to describe the system. That is how preparing indicators can inform the people concerned and be useful when making decisions. This objective description should deal with the diverse components of the system and permit links between the different elements examined to be established. Also, it would be appropriate to use the most durable characteristics of the system as the subject for analysis. Often one is tempted to include aspects connected to the situation. It is sometimes necessary to examine points associated with precise events. However, the more permanent aspects of the education system should be given more importance. This will make it possible to establish, more easily and in a more rigorous manner, comparisons in time or in relation to different subsectors of the system. Thus, it will be possible to make reports that will establish comparisons in relation to several plans: longitudinal, spatial, sectorial.

When one is organizing an assessment mechanism or executing the different operations required for its development, it is desirable to obtain the participation of people from different parts of the system, so that, those not associated with the process are not left feeling insecure, and so as to ensure that the information collected is as complete as possible; incomplete information might invalidate certain conclusions. It is important to obtain the collaboration of the political and administrative coordinators of the system as well as the persons connected with conducting the educational activities in the chosen schools. To do that, a feeling of trust among the different partners concerned must be established from the outset. Comprehensive information about the targeted goals of this kind of assessment activity should permit the different participants to be well acquainted with these goals. Too often, a lack of information creates mistrust and, by this very fact, decreases the collaboration between the personnel working on the different operations connected with the setting up of an assessment mechanism.

As has been briefly mentioned above, resources at the disposition of education systems are becoming more and more limited, especially in developing countries. The coordinators must use their imagination to do more, or at least as much, with fewer resources. Assessment is often used to identify the priorities to favour or to detect the problems that should be corrected first. When choosing an assessment mechanism among the strategies liable to improve a situation, some people tend to believe that the results obtained from such an assessment operation will solve most of the identified problems. They risk being very disappointed at the end of the planned operations. This is all the more likely to be so if very limited resources are granted for ensuring the different operations required to conduct an assessment activitiy. Too

often, a team is given a defined mandate without even having the minimal resources needed for executing the planned tasks. Every day, such a team may even have to 'defend' the resources initially provided by the coordinators of the school system. Even if the importance of the resources in question is minimal in relation to those necessary for conducting the whole education system, the persons assigned to the operations connected with executing an assessment activity are often at a disadvantage because of the overnumerous administrative procedures provided to guarantee the allocation of these resources. It often happens that activities fall behind schedule because it is impossible to have the resources at the proper time even though they were planned. When one is assessing learning, a delay of a few weeks in completing certain activities can compromise the entire operation, or at least defer its completion significantly. The resources provided for executing the assessment operation must be available at the desired time; furthermore, it is important to provide adaptable administrative mechanisms to ensure optimal allocation of the required resources.

New technologies are being introduced in all sectors of activity and education is no exception. Developing countries must make the 'technological change of direction' in order to be more efficient, doing more with fewer resources. However, it is important that the introduction of new technologies be done with particular care. Rejecting current practices and blindly replacing them by new ones is not the way to proceed. A good balance of old and new must be found that will permit the participants in the system to perform the planned operations better so as to reach the fixed objectives. All sectors of the educational system are affected by the introduction of new technologies. This fact should be taken into consideration when assessing. In this way, the chosen assessment subjects will reflect the current reality. The coordinators of the assessment will have to modify their mechanism accordingly to take into consideration the changing reality. Furthermore, the method of conducting the assessment will be influenced by the introduction of new technologies that have been made available. For example, the presence of microcomputers in all sectors of human activity profoundly modifies a number of practices. The domain of educational evaluation does not escape this problem. New technologies for data processing have recently appeared. It is important that developing countries make this technological change of direction in order to improve both the rigour of the assessment mechanisms set up and the efficiency of the operations conducted. However, the introduction of new technologies can make the operations more complex. Simplicity should be emphasized, otherwise one risks having difficulty in using the results of the assessment. As was mentioned above, assessment concerns everyone in the school system. It is important that the data collected during an assessment be understandable to those concerned. Thus, the coordinators for conducting an assessment activity must be in a position to introduce new techniques of data processing for the purpose of being more effective and rigorous. However, they must consider the people who will use the collected results in order for the operation to be really useful.

None the less, the assessment coordinators must not fear to introduce new methods of operating made available by technological developments. These changes in methods should be accompanied by training activities in order to help people use these new practices. In certain milieux, it may be tempting to resort to external resources for conducting activities using new technological tools. Proceeding in this way may give the illusion of a more efficient and less troublesome method of conducting the operations. None the less, there is a risk of creating a dependence on external resources. It is much wiser to provide strategies that permit the transferring of competence. If resources outside the school system – be it national or international expertise – must be used, the local coordinators of the assessment mechanism must be closely associated with them. One must be aware, then, that certain operations will take more time to be completed since it will be necessary to provide activities of sensitizing, upgrading and training. However, in the long run there will be tangible benefits to such a strategy of introducing new working methods because the appropriation of these technologies by the internal resources of the organization will permit a more general and less costly use of them.

Typology

It may be practical to group together the different assessment activities in a school system in relation to major functions. Examining the assessment activities conducted in a given milieu, however, underscores the interrelationships that develop or should develop between several activities conducted at different times and by different persons. For this presentation, the following three categories of learning assessment activities will be considered: assessment for purposes of certification of studies; classroom assessment; and assessment of the results obtained by the education system. The first two assessment types are more familiar to the general public. The mechanisms that are found in these two assessment categories are also widely present in all school systems. This is not the case for the assessment of the general functioning of the system. Setting up this kind of mechanism demands resources that are not always available. It also requires resorting to techniques that have not necessarily been mastered by the personnel concerned. In quite a detailed manner, a scenario will be presented for setting up this kind of mechanism for assessing the general functioning of a school system such as is measured by the degree to which objectives connected with student learning are attained.

Certain assessment activities must be conducted in all educational systems: for example, learning assessment for the purpose of certification of studies, student promotion, or selection of candidates for training activities. The question here is not one of knowing whether this type of assessment should be present in a school system, but rather, of knowing whether the mechanisms already present are rigorous enough. When decisions about the orientation of the students are made using information obtained by a learning assessment procedure, the equity of these decisions must be assured. Existing systems are often difficult to modify. Little by little, working methods have been established and, usually, an administrative structure has been set up. Over a period of time, current practices have been accepted by the different participants of the system. Even if it is recognized that there are deficiencies in a learning assessment system that can play an important role in the personal and professional orientation of the students, it is likely that few measures will be undertaken to change the practices.

Another important sector affected by learning assessment is that of classroom assessment conducted by the teaching personnel. These are mechanisms set up to show the degree to which the students master concepts or skills. Such information is useful, as much for the teacher as for the students, in order to adjust practices accordingly. To be effective, this type of 'formative' assessment must be done using techniques and tools adapted to the various contexts of the school environment. For this, a working procedure exists that the personnel must acquire. In several developing countries, the majority of the teachers possess only partial knowledge of the most appropriate assessment techniques for adapting teaching to the situation. If it is wished to change the conduct of teacher in relation to classroom assessment practices, it is necessary to provide significant resources. A number of people, often scattered over a vast territory, must be reached. Furthermore, the knowledge level in this domain may vary considerably from one individual to another, thus requiring the planning of adaptable sensitizing strategies.

Other assessment actions can supply information about the general functioning of the school system or the functioning of any of its sectors of activity. These are often periodic operations conducted at moments that are considered to be strategic by one or another coordinator of the system. Administrative concerns are often the subject of an investigation of such assessments. The results measured in relation to mastery of knowledge or skill are rarely targeted by such assessment mechanisms of the functioning of the education system. We will see further on that setting up such a procedure can help bring about an improvement in the whole system.

In the remainder of the chapter, different aspects connected with learning assessment in developing countries will be examined using illustrations drawn from projects conducted recently or in process of being conducted. Although I have been associated with a number of assessment projects carried out internationally, I will limit my remarks to an assessment project that has been taking place since 1992 in Benin in West Africa. Thus, it will be possible to touch upon the different parts associated with an educational assessment operation, and underscore the major steps that should not be ignored when setting up a rigorous assessment mechanism. I will also point out the importance of associating different people working in the education system with one or another phase in the development of such an undertaking. My remarks will deal mainly with the assessment of the general functioning of the system. I think it is useful to use a detailed example of this form of assessment, one little used in developing countries. However, I will comment on the issues at stake in classroom assessment and certification of studies. These conditions are often a prerequisite to setting up educational services of quality and a means of promoting respect for equity.

An important step: clarifying objectives

Before one sets up a set of measures connected with learning assessment, it is important to do some serious planning. This activity should be accomplished with the collaboration of personnel working in most, if not in all, sectors of the school system. This kind of strategy facilitates contacts between the different sectors of the educational system and also gives the opportunity to underscore the links that are established. The preparation of a plan of action should thus demand the participation of a variety of people working in the system. It is desirable to obtain the collaboration of high-level coordinators as well as personnel more directly connected to the operations taking place in an assessment mechanism.

When analysing the requests by the developing countries for exterior aid, the sponsors usually demand the preparation of plans of action that will demonstrate the links to be established between different measures. Furthermore, such a measure helps in establishing priorities to take into account available resources as well as favoured objectives. Such an exercise was carried out in 1992 in Benin (Debeauvais, 1993). This planning operation targeted the whole school system. Several plans of action were proposed thanks to the collaboration of the Beninese coordinators working in the education system. International consultants joined the procedures. Fourteen plans of action were developed dealing with four main sectors of the educational activity:

1 pedagogy;
2 planning;
3 institutional reform; and
4 mobilization of resources and participation of the public.

In relation to the 'pedagogy' sector, four plans of action were defined. They target the following domains:

1 curriculum;
2 instructional material;
3 teacher training; and
4 learning assessment and student orientation.

When the plans of action were being prepared, it appeared evident that numerous links exist between the different measures proposed to improve the quality of the services supplied by the system. This observation is more verifiable for plans sharing the same sector of activity than for those linked to the pedagogical part of the reform that the country plans to undertake.

The plan of action for learning assessment and student orientation prepared in Benin is structured around three main programmes of activities: a deeper understanding of the strengths and weaknesses of the school system; a more effective assessment of the students during the course of their training; and a more equitable system of certification of studies. To illustrate this, here is a concise presentation of each of these programmes.

The first set of proposed measures permitted the defining of an institutional framework and some mechanisms aimed at producing the sort of graduates needed by the cultural, economic and social environment. This examination of the coherence between the school results and the socio-economic context is done to appraise the progress of the education system in general as well as the performance of the students. A sample-based assessment mechanism focusing on the results was used. This sample-based mechanism is presented later in the chapter.

The second set of activities led to the development of an assessment programme so that the students' progress during their school years could be followed better. It aims essentially at the assessment of students during their education and their academic orientation with particular emphasis on follow-up and orientation of students in difficulty. This part of the plan of action on assessment thus affects all the teachers working in the school system. Many of them need to have their skills upgraded. Professional training is often deficient in many sectors of teaching, as is shown by many current practices in classrooms. Changes of this kind demand the contribution of significant resources in view of the great number of teachers to be reached. The activities required to update the competence of the teachers prior to conducting learning assessment more effectively should take into account strategies adopted in a comprehensive plan of training and upgrading of the personnel.

The last set of activities of the plan of action on assessment developed in Benin deals with the certification of elementary school completion and the selection of candidates for secondary school. This part of the assessment programme deals specifically with the government examinations. A critical study will be made of the tools and methods currently in use in this African country for assessment at the end of a study cycle. It is hoped that the situation can be improved and that new tools and methods can create a more rigorous mechanism better able to meet the needs of the individual as well as the society.

A great deal of work has been necessary in order to finalize a plan of action for learning assessment that is acceptable to the different participants of the system. Conducting this activity clearly showed the close links that exist between the different sectors of the education system. The coordinators had to specify, for each measure chosen, the targeted objectives, the actions to undertake, the tasks to complete, the resources needed and the division of the responsibilities. Furthermore, it was necessary to quantify the resources in order to establish the costs connected with each task. Finally, a schedule was established that had to take into account the activities decided upon in the other plans of action, in particular those having to do with the teaching sector. When examining this planning, one cannot help but wonder about the feasibility of certain measures. In fact, it is obvious that certain activities will require optimal conditions in order to be completed as planned. This is unfortunately not the situation that prevails in a number of developing countries. Certain parts of such a plan of action thus become goals to target, an ideal to strive for that must be revised in due course.

System assessment

A number of developing countries believe that a nation-wide assessment of the academic performance of the students is likely to supply precious information for their educational policies. Such data can, in fact, bring necessary light to the decision-making process dealing with planning, development and implementation of programmes intended to provide education for young people. This kind of rigorous mechanism can help the better management of the education system, using reliable data. This does not mean measuring the individual performance of the students or teaching personnel, but rather assessing the performance of the system and supplying pertinent indicators about its state of health. Having this information will make it easier to provide the appropriate corrective measures. Setting up such a mechanism demands the participation of a number of people involved in the system, and the

assurance that certain steps will be respected. Finally, introducing a sample-based assessment will require that the personnel master new techniques if, on the one hand, reliable data are to be obtained and, on the other hand, the results are to be used judiciously.

The following paragraphs illustrate the establishment of this kind of mechanism in a developing country. My remarks are structured around the following points:

1   conducting activities prior to setting up an assessment mechanism;
2   developing national expertise in the domains connected with conducting sample-based assessment;
3   field-testing the process to make corrections that are needed before generalizing the operation;
4   conducting required activities to collect information needed to evaluate the system;
5   analysing the collected data and distributing the observed results; and
6   choosing the follow-up work for the operation, taking into account the information made available.

Preliminary activities

Before a start is made on the different activities required to ensure the assessment of the students' performance on a national level, it is essential to define the objectives targeted by such a mechanism. An assessment operation is often perceived as a threat by the school personnel. Certain data-collecting activities may be considered as an interference into teachers' professional life. Tensions may arise among the coordinators of the system as well as among the teachers or even the students. Therefore, particular attention must be given to clarifying the objectives pursued by such an undertaking.

Furthermore, the subjects targeted by this kind of assessment procedure should be well-defined. Experience shows that the coordinators of the education system often have difficulty in defining priorities when choosing the subject of the first assessment. They frequently want to assess everything at the same time. Thus, they run the risk of imposing an impossible mission on themselves. It is wiser to be modest, especially when implementing such a mechanism. Sometimes it is difficult to foresee accurately the different tasks that will have to be accomplished when assessing a school subject at a single teaching level. On the other hand, certain subjects are more difficult to assess: assessment techniques and the materials for data collection are sometimes less available for these teaching subjects. In such a case, it is better to start in subjects that can be assessed more relatively. In spite of everything, the difficulties encountered are surprising even if the operation is dealing with a more limited number of subjects considered to be 'easy' to assess. It is also important to establish a realistic timetable for the running of an assessment activity of student performance on the national level. At least two years is needed to complete all the operations. One must keep in mind that certain activities will take place according to the school timetable. A delay of a few weeks in carrying out certain tasks may oblige the coordinators to postpone the remaining operations by several months or even by a complete year.

Resorting to resources outside the education system may be necessary when establishing the plan of operations. The personnel in service do not necessarily possess the required knowledge to draft enlightened plans for the activities taking place in an assessment mechanism. Sometimes, international specialists in the field must be called in. Examining current practices and available resources with an outside specialist can make one clearly aware of the state of the situation. This method is likely to be carried out in a more objective manner if persons outside the system are associated with it. In that case, the mandate that is entrusted to such human resources should be well-defined so that the plans established respect the particular context of the country. An exemplary plan of action could be drafted and still be of no use because it is not sufficiently adapted to the situation.

Local expertise

In a number of places, conducting a sample-based assessment operation is entrusted to external resources. It is true that proceeding in this way can guarantee greater credibility of the results obtained. Thus, one will opt for this strategy when it is necessary to establish control, mainly administrative control, of the functioning of the system, functioning that is believed to be inappropriate or inefficient. However, a number of assessment operations of school systems are conducted in certain developing countries using external resources almost exclusively. In these cases, the techniques used are not mastered by the country's own personnel and the schedules do not permit the holding of training activities that would make it possible for the resources concerned within the school system to acquire this knowledge. Thus, there is a risk that links of 'dependence' may be created with the external expertise; there is a tendency to resort again to the outside resources when a new assessment operation is needed. The cycle of dependence could easily last indefinitely if the methods of operating are not modified by associating the personnel working in the school system more closely with them.

To correct the situation, the decision has to be made to use a sufficient number of the country's own resource persons of an appropriate quality; one must be particularly aware that the first cycle of assessment done by nationals of the country could easily take more time. However, the benefits drawn from an activity conducted in this way will surpass the simple production of a report of the situation as analysed. The persons associated in that way will have become familiar with the assessment method. They will master new techniques that may be used in other situations, and they will have had the possibility to examine correctly the links between the different sectors of school life.

However, favourable conditions must be planned so that an assessment operation conducted under the responsibility of nationals of the country may be successful. Outside expertise should probably be used during the organizational stage.

Such resources will bring the information needed for conducting a rigorous activity benefiting from the use of tested technologies. However, it is important that the introduction of new methods take into account the particular context of the assessed milieu. Sometimes it is necessary to adapt the strategies to be able to conduct a similar operation at another occasion. Practices often have to be adapted to the reality of the country if one wishes to integrate assessment into the current operations of the system. However, this should not be done by diminishing the rigour of the procedures.

To implement this technological transfer, training activities for the local personnel will have to be planned. It will be wise to do this upgrading in a concrete manner. It is often more effective to learn while actually doing activities that are part of an assessment mechanism. Thus, the outside expertise can accompany the process at strategic moments, leaving the country's nationals the job of carrying out the different operations. In this case, the possibility of errors must be accepted, and certain operations will have to be redone. None the less, learning done in this way proves to be effective if enough time is devoted to it. The personnel concerned must possess the required motivation throughout the entire course of such an operation. For that, the school coordinators should find incentives that are likely to encourage the participation of the personnel when required.

Pilot test

Learning assessment implies resorting to tested techniques and to materials usually not available in many developing countries. Remember that we are not talking about assessing the students individually to make decisions as to their orientation in the school system or to attest their academic achievements. Instead, a sample-based assessment mechanism permits decisions about the general performance of the system. The intention is to identify the strengths and the weaknesses of the system and to detect the factors liable to be connected to the performance of the students. The

techniques used to establish this kind of diagnosis must be adapted to the context, and it is important that the personnel master them. A pilot test of the mechanism is necessary if one wishes to have a procedure adapted to the situation, while at the same time respecting the standards required to guarantee the desired rigour. Unfortunately, some people tend to believe that these are superfluous activities that can be sacrificed to obtain more rapid results on the state of functioning of the system.

A first series of activities should thus permit the country's own personnel to acquire the necessary knowledge for carrying out the coming operations. The concepts connected with preparing the required materials for this form of assessment must be mastered. Holding workshops for people working in the school system is an appropriate strategy. Forming a multidisciplinary team associated with the setting up of such a mechanism will permit the identification of the human resources needed for pursuing the activities. Undoubtedly, it will be necessary to bring in outside experts as associates, especially when starting the process.

Developing the materials should rapidly mobilize the personnel. In the first place, it is important to define the assessment subjects connected with the goals chosen for the operation. It is wise to establish a table of specifications for each subject that will point out the weighting to give to each dimension that will be assessed. Apparently, it is not the current custom to do this kind of planning of the subject to be assessed before preparing the required materials. On the other hand, these materials provided must not only permit a decision to be reached about the performance of the students, but also allow potential problems to be identified in order to improve the situation. The test used must facilitate such an identification of the difficulties met by the students. Furthermore, using supplementary questionnaires will make it possible to examine the more or less close connections to be established with certain contextual variables.

Conducting a pilot test of the materials in a limited number of schools is essential. As well as allowing the quality of the materials to be tested, this kind of exercise supplies information about the procedures used. To be useful, field testing should be done under conditions similar to those that will exist for the final administration of the mechanism. Thus, the coordinators must plan the entire set of activities that will be conducted at the time of administering the assessment. This involves, among other things, planning the following tasks:

1   preparing the materials in accordance with the table of specifications previously defined;
2   developing information documents about the mechanism;
3   creating administrative instructions to ensure procedural standardization;
4   preparing, marking and coding guides for the students' answers to the tests;
5   choosing appropriate techniques for data entry and file preparation that will be used when compiling statistics; and
6   adopting control mechanisms to ensure quality of the data collected and rigour in conducting the operation.

Clearly, this is an ambitious undertaking, especially when the personnel who are assigned to it do not always have all the relevant knowledge and when the required technical resources must be set up during the implementation of the mechanism. For example, data processing is an aspect that demands the introduction of new technologies in the organization. Several possibilities exist. However, attention to the particular context of the system is important when choosing the tools to use for realizing the different technical operations required by the implementation of such a mechanism. As an example, the coordinators of a sample-based assessment conducted in Benin chose the microcomputer to execute the different tasks of data entry and data processing. The software EduStat[1] was chosen to assist the personnel in these different operations of entering data, setting up required files, selecting necessary samples and compiling statistics from the information collected.

A serious pilot test thus demands the devoting of significant resources. The time usually required will cover a complete school year. Those are conditions to be respected if one wishes to have a rigorous mechanism that will supply useful information to the system coordinators.

Administration

The pilot test described above permits a better preparation of the activities that must be completed in order to ensure the rigorous administration of the assessment mechanism. A study of the statistics produced will supply useful information to finalize the materials to be used. A review of the problems met during the field testing will facilitate the coordinators' task when setting the rules to use for the administration of the mechanism.

A number of operations will have to be completed. Material, financial, as well as human resources will have to be made use of if the success of the enterprise is to be ensured. One of the tasks that should be started right away is that connected with setting up the sample that will be used to conduct the research. We know that a sample must respect certain criteria if we wish to generalize from the results observed among the students contacted. Sometimes it is difficult to acquire exhaustive information about a population that is the focus of the assessment. It will then be necessary to consider this when interpreting the results.

The administration of materials that permit learning assessment requires the collaboration of the administrative and teaching personnel. It is also suitable to provide favourable conditions for the students so that they perform realistically. It should be noted here that this form of assessment is uncommon in the school systems of many developing countries. The operation can create stress for the teachers as well as the students. It is important to plan information strategies to minimize the negative effects of it. This does not mean 'tricking' the students, but rather establishing the most objective possible assessment of the level of student performance.

The information collected using this kind of assessment mechanism must be reliable. The school coordinators as well as the general public must not doubt the exactness of the results obtained. It is also wise to provide quality control mechanisms throughout the course of the operation. When the results are published, some people will undoubtedly question the rigour of the activities conducted in the schools. It will be wise to provide quality control procedures in the form of structured visits to a sample of schools participating in the study.

Data analysis

After the information has been collected in the chosen milieu, a series of operations is used to make a careful examination in order to describe the situation studied and to draw the essential conclusions. A number of technical tasks will have to be undertaken to obtain data that will then be processed to establish the syntheses needed for the preparation of the reports. These could have different forms depending on the public sectors targeted.

Conducting a sample-based assessment requires the participation of numerous resources. Preparing the plan for distributing the results is a very important activity if one wishes to benefit from all the possible effects of such a project. For example, the distribution of these results must take place as rapidly as possible after administering the mechanism. When planning the operation, it is important then to plan the form of the reports that will be produced after having studied and analysed the numerous data collected, in relation to the public targets that one wishes to reach. When preparing the assessment activity, a plan may be drawn up indicating the content of these publications. Moreover, during the course of the operation, it is possible to prepare reports on the way the study is conducted, the objectives pursued and the materials used. Knowing that such reports are to be written about the results obtained helps in planning the human resources that will have to be assigned to preparing them.

Four types of reports can be identified, aimed at different sectors of the public concerned. The first report could be the 'official report' of the assessment. This document would be intended first and foremost for the coordinators of the school system. It should contain enough information for readers to understand the general functioning of the operation. Importance should be placed on the presentation of the results obtained as well as on their interpretation.

The second report could be presented as a synthesis of the results observed. It would be intended for all principals (headteachers) and teachers within the education system. Emphasis must be placed on the presentation of the results, the connections with certain contextual variables and the follow-up to be given to the pedagogical plan in the light of the results observed. This report should not exceed twenty pages and should be written in an understandable manner in the language of the personnel working in the schools. The content of the first report presented above should be used as basic material to prepare it.

Another report, intended for the general public, could take the form of a leaflet. It should be distributed to the parents of the students and to the general public. As well as explaining the operation as a whole, the main findings could be summarized. The language used should be very accessible to the targeted public, and if possible and appropriate, it could even be translated into some national languages.

The last document, more technical, could take the form of an archive of the operation. This document, printed in a very limited number, would be intended for the coordinators of the project and would constitute the record of it. It would contain all the documents produced during the administration of the project (materials, reports of the workshops or seminars, list of people associated with the project, list of sample schools, complete statistical reports). It would be a voluminous document that explained in detail the different activities that took place during the exercise. This will make it easier to conduct the operation again at another time or for other subjects. During the operations, the documents should be collected as available before they are no longer easily accessible.

Follow-up work

The decision to undertake an assessment activity is usually justified by the desire to obtain reliable information in order to make better choices. As was shown above, the procedure demands time and varied resources. Thus, it is important to draw all the benefits expected from this kind of operation. The examination of several assessment activities conducted in various school environments does not always indicate such an optimal use of the results. Major changes could have taken place in the system since the assessment activity was started. Consequently, the priorities chosen by the personnel must often be adjusted. On top of all that, it is possible that the persons who initiated the assessment project are no longer coordinators of the same activities in the system when the results are distributed.

Thus, it is important to make the results available very rapidly after collecting the data. The first sample-based assessment activity in a school system demands a rather long period of time. The personnel must acquire the necessary expertise and provide themselves with the required tools. However, particular attention must be given to the distribution of the results. That is why it is essential to supply the affected personnel with reports written in an accessible language. The fact must be taken into consideration that these publications are not usually intended for assessment specialists, but rather for people who will have decisions to make in one or another sector of the educational activity. The results obtained by a learning assessment activity must facilitate this decision-making process.

Student assessment

The preceding section presented learning assessment conducted on representative samples of the school population. A form of activities such as this makes useful information available for the coordinators who must make choices in order to improve the services offered, or else adjust their aim concerning the objectives to be reached. The impacts of an assessment conducted using samples concern more the school system in its entirety than any sector of activity. If this type of operation is very useful for the general management of an education system, it is not the mechanism currently most used by those working in the system. Assessments of the learning achieved by each of the students attending the schools have a very widespread use. When we speak of learning assessment, we think first of all of the assessment activities done in the classroom by the teachers. We also think of the tests or year-end examinations for certification of studies or for selecting candidates suitable for study at a higher level.

We know the problems, often major ones, connected with these assessment activities. They are usually connected, on the one hand, with the often deficient knowledge on the part of the people carrying out the assessment and, on the other hand, with the dependence of the educational activity on a curriculum that does not always meet the needs of the individual and society. I shall deal concisely with the issues at stake in learning assessment such as is practised in the classroom and the mechanisms set up for certification of studies or for selecting candidates for training activities.

Classroom assessment

Several forms of assessment take place every day in each class. The teacher must check the progress made by the students in the different subjects making up the programme. In this way, practice can be better adjusted to reality. Furthermore, the results of the classroom assessment inform the students themselves about their degree of learning. The parents are also interested in having information about their child's mastery of the school subjects. To be effective, this kind of information mechanism on individual performance should respect certain criteria. The teachers who administer such assessment forms must have appropriate tools and prerequisite knowledge.

Classroom assessment can have several forms depending on the goals aimed at. It may be homework that the teacher will mark afterwards. It may also be lessons that the teacher gives the students at the beginning of the day. These tests can often take the form of oral questioning. The primary goal of these exercises should be to inform the teacher about the degree to which the lessons in class have been learned. This information will permit teachers to adjust their teaching strategies accordingly. The results of these assessments, conducted almost daily, make it easier to identify students having difficulties. The teachers then can adapt their teaching to meet the various needs of the students in the class. It is sometimes difficult to offer such personalized services in the schools in developing countries in view of the large size of most of the classes.

It happens frequently that this assessment, which should be used to adjust the teaching to the particular context of a group of students, is used instead for administrative ends. In such circumstances, 'formative' assessment becomes 'summative' assessment. Proceeding in this way can lead to repercussions in the manner of teaching used in the classroom. The students are left to believe that they cannot make mistakes because all these 'assessments' will be taken into account to establish a final mark that will certify a pass or failure. Such confusion in the role filled by assessment during the learning process can influence the teaching used in the classroom.

Furthermore, too often the assessment done in class calls only upon skills connected with memorizing. This is the easiest taxonomic level to assess. However, one should not be satisfied with this category of assessment subjects if the education system is to reach the designated objectives. For that, it will be necessary to provide assessment tools capable of supplying information on the degree of mastery of a variety of skills.

If classroom assessment is to fill its true role of learning support, adapted materials and a good deal of expertise are required. Teachers working in developing countries unfortunately do not possess all the necessary skills. Most of them repeat practices that they themselves knew when they attended elementary school. It should also be noted that the curriculum available in some milieux is not very explicit as to the targeted objectives. And what can be said about the material conditions that exist in the classes or about the almost nonexistent teaching materials? All these factors make the task of the teacher, who is very often confronted with overcrowded classes, very difficult.

In spite of the rather unfavourable conditions, it is still possible to do better provided that one possesses a minimum of knowledge about the specific methods of assessment. It is important to provide the minimum conditions needed for certain assessments to take place. Also, holding sensitizing activities for measurement and evaluation in education could become an important lever in changing current practices in the classes. A systematic reflection on classroom assessment usually results in the adoption of new methods. Time and resources must be devoted to that since it is a matter of reaching each teacher. Setting up a plan for upgrading the school personnel should be an important part of dealing with learning assessment in the classroom.

Certification of studies and student selection

One of the most visible activities of learning assessment conducted by the school is that connected with certification of studies. This end-of-studies or end-of-school-year assessment plays a very important social role: to attest that the students have reached specific learning objectives. This recognition of studies carried out in accordance with set standards must, however, be able to count on rigorous procedures in order to be credible. The importance of giving equity to this kind of mechanism must be pointed out: the results of this assessment play an important role in the personal life of the particular individuals in relation to their professional orientation. The assessment should not create harmful injustices for the individual as well as the society.

Examining the mechanisms set up in some of the schools to certify the studies completed by the students reveals a number of problems that can harm this assessment activity. This is very often an operation that demands significant resources and that is held at the end of each school year in developing countries. Preparing examinations, distributing and collecting materials, correcting the tests and processing the data collected demand almost miraculous feats in some milieux. Material conditions are not always favorable: the different people concerned must be very inventive to succeed in conducting the activities in an acceptable manner. Even so, the value of the attestations, certificates and diplomas issued by the school can often be questionable.

Here also, questions can be raised concerning the materials used to carry out this assessment function. Too often the examinations used do not completely cover the subject to be assessed. Just as for the other forms of assessment presented above, techniques exist that are adapted to summative assessment. The coordinators of these operations do not always master them. On the other hand, it is often very difficult to introduce changes in a mechanism that remains impenetrable, secret and rather withdrawn into itself. Introducing new methods sometimes proves to be the only way to give credibility to this activity.

Furthermore, the examinations held for choosing the candidates for specialized education or for secondary school or higher education do not always identify the students most likely to undertake such studies. The drop-out and failure rate are sometimes very high. This kind of predictive assessment also possesses specifics that must be mastered. Collaboration is essential, especially between teaching levels, when planning the mechanism that will supply the information needed for choosing the students who meet the selection criteria already established.

Conclusion

In the space available, it was not possible to discuss all the facets of learning assessment. However, the issues mentioned help to make clear the important role that appropriate assessment mechanisms can fill. This is clearly verified in developing countries that have decided to give particular attention to this part of teaching. Thus, the introduction of new assessment mechanisms or the examination of those that exist supplies the opportunity to question all the components of the education system.

However, to conduct the learning assessment well and to respect the numerous goals targeted by this function, the personnel concerned must possess the appropriate techniques and tools, and sufficient competence. The coordinators for personnel upgrading must find activities liable to interest many people at an acceptable cost. That is a great challenge.

A number of learning mechanisms supply indicators about the general functioning of the educational activity in a given country. A set of indicators like that should deal with the different facets of the school scene. It is desirable to have information about the results of the system and not only data about chosen resources. We often neglect to collect reliable data that will permit us to pass judgement on the achievement of the objectives pursued by the school institution. Data about the performance levels of the students permit us to assess the results of the educational policies set up. Such information makes possible comparisons between the standing of different systems, and makes it possible to examine the changes that have taken place in the course of time. The first preoccupation motivates some countries to conduct common assessment activities. There are a number of advantages in doing this, such as the sharing of expertise, cost reduction and information exchange. As for the second preoccupation of establishing longitudinal comparisons of the results, care must be taken to set up procedures that will permit such links to be established.

supplies consulting services in education on the international, national and local levels.

Note

1 EduStat™ is developed and supported by EDUCAN Inc. (560 St-Laurent West, suite 106, Longueuil, Quebec, Canada J4H 3X3), a private Canadian firm that

Reference

Debeauvais, M. (1993) L'éducation de base pour tous, trois ans après Jomtien, *Diagonales*, **27** (July), 39–41.

16 The Role of Evaluation in Large-scale Educational Interventions: Lessons from the Andhra Pradesh Primary Education Project

HARRY TORRANCE, COLIN LACEY
AND BARRY COOPER

Introduction

The so-called Jomtien Declaration, produced as a result of the World Conference on Education for All held in Jomtien, Thailand, in 1990, re-emphasized the need to universalize access to education while also focusing attention on the quality of educational provision and the importance of producing significant learning outcomes, rather than simply encouraging enrolment, retention and the mechanistic completion of certification requirements (cf. Little *et al.*, 1994). A number of commentators have subsequently commented on the changing policy options facing various donor agencies and non-governmental organizations (NGOs), and the different agendas for development which seem to be emerging. Thus, for example, Kenneth King (1992) has noted the move away from small-scale 'enclave projects' towards much more ambitious attempts by donors to engage with national and local policy-making processes and locate funded interventions in the context of locally identified needs and priorities, the better to try to ensure sustainability. This begs questions of how the process of engagement is conceptualized and operationalized, and how information about implementation is gathered and made use of. David Archer (1994) has noted the dangers for NGOs of being drawn into large-scale substitution activities – filling the gaps left by uneven and inadequate state provision – and argued for NGOs sustaining their role as innovators

and advocates in the face of such pressure for long-term engagement and sustainability. The corollary of such an 'arm's length' approach, however, is that NGOs 'must document their work more rigorously than in the past in order to feed policy debates and influence major players' (Archer, 1994 p. 223).

These debates are particularly pertinent to developments at the present time in India, from where our data for this chapter are drawn. There are currently a number of major educational interventions in India at various stages of development. Together they will involve key agencies (the ODA, the World Bank, the European Union) in spending and/or lending something in excess of $500 million over the next several years. The Government of India (GOI) has responded to this opportunity and to previous criticisms of top-down administration by developing a new, devolved administrative framework, the District Primary Education Programme (DPEP; see Government of India, n.d.), which is attempting both to integrate various interventions into an overall planning process and to locate that process at local level. Thus districts (i.e. administrative units within the individual states which make up India's national federal structure) are drawing up plans for local educational improvement in conjunction with appraisal missions by donors, and these in turn are being coordinated at state and national level.

These developments are extremely significant and there is a new spirit of optimism among GOI officials and the staff of donor agencies that substantial progress will be made in tackling India's obdurate educational problems concerning enrolment, retention and literacy (Government of India, 1993).

Our experience of the Andhra Pradesh Primary Education Project (APPEP; see Ravi and Rao, 1994) as consultants to its evaluation leads us to share the general feeling of cautious optimism and to believe that well-planned large-scale interventions *can* succeed, though whether or not they will depends on many factors. There are a number of cautions and lessons to be learned from past experience that need to be remembered and related to future plans. We have already noted Archer's (1994) argument that the concept of sustainability needs to be re-examined, with NGOs in particular being wary of being drawn into long-term substitution activities. There are parallels here with the roles to be played by donor agencies in the developments described above; clearly, sustainability will be jeopardized if expenditure is inflated without learning about what is most effective and without concomitant planning for the future replacement of specific financial inputs. Archer goes on to describe the NGO role as that of low-cost innovators who could feed soundly based evaluations to policy-makers. His argument also contains relevant advice for international donors collaborating with GOI and state governments within DPEP. If competent evaluations are not carried out, lessons will not be learned and policy-making will not benefit from the substantial sums being spent – a matter of particular concern not only to those states not yet included in DPEP, which are unlikely to be funded to the extent of those first involved, but also to the national government and the donor agencies themselves.

Caroline Dyer's perceptive analysis of Operation Blackboard (OBB) takes these warnings a step further (Dyer, 1994). Dyer outlines how OBB was conceived as a straightforward, large-scale national programme designed to deliver basic educational inputs – buildings, equipment and teachers – across the country, in an effort to provide minimum levels of educational provision. Its major elements, the provision of at least two classrooms and separate toilet facilities for boys and girls, the

provision of at least two teachers (one a woman) and the provision of essential pedagogic material from blackboards to toys and games, seemed so obviously valid and relevant to GOI's educational aspirations that no pilot schemes or evaluations were ever carried out. Dyer's study in Gujarat shows that in the absence of such feasibility studies the scheme was unrealistically structured in terms of both time and finance. The programme broke down at local level because the monitoring system had little relevance for effective management and ignored structural problems which occurred between the levels of government: all-India, state and district. In addition, the innovation itself, a blanket one-shot remedy, was seen as irrelevant to the needs of many local communities and in some cases actually disrupted rational local planning based on local priorities. Dyer concludes that 'policy-makers still pay scant regard to the actual process of education in schools', and also that 'the nature of the bureaucracy ... does not focus on and incorporate as part of the implementation process an adequate assessment of the outcome and impact of decisions made and actions taken throughout the multiple levels of government' (1994, p. 252).

This last example suggests some general features of large-scale educational innovations which derive from agreements between relatively small élites at the apex of large administrative/government structures, which we shall discuss in more detail before presenting aspects of the APPEP evaluation itself.

The political life cycle of projects

Large-scale educational projects have a recognizable and characteristic life cycle. It is perhaps helpful to describe this cycle as a series of stages of development.

In order to get support for a large-scale project it is important to employ a strong, relatively simple idea that appears to provide the answer to a long-standing social or educational problem. Unfortunately, in reality, the problem analysis implied by this simple scenario rarely holds in practice. Politicians and administrators favour relatively rigid, resource-oriented solutions that are politically expedient and administratively non-complex (for example, the provision of 'inputs', as with OBB), but these 'traditional' approaches to educational development are clearly inadequate to the focus on quality adopted by Jomtien. They are also unlikely to succeed even on their own terms since the 'obvious relevance' of the solution – which is a strongly held belief at the centre – may not be accepted at all at the periphery. In addition, there often exist complex political structures in which local and regional interests are not seen to be at one with national interests. Within those structures there may be powerful individuals who will seek to obstruct new developments simply because they are supported by other, rival individuals. Notwithstanding these real difficulties, however, at this stage the project needs a facilitator (change agent) who keeps the message simple, strong and untainted by likely complexities and potential disasters.

The early history of APPEP, a state-wide project which comprised building provision, the training of teachers in activity-based pedagogy and some provision of enhanced classroom resources, was fraught with these kinds of difficulty. The project was fortunate in having a field manager who was experienced in education, believed in the project, understood some of the complexities and realized that the training and continuing human resource development aspect of the project would be more important than the building programme. However, in the initial stages this potential flexibility within the project's strategies was given a low profile and some of APPEP's supporters saw it as a school building programme whereas others saw it as a teacher training programme.

If a project comes through the early stages of national committees and/or international negotiation, it emerges with something of a fanfare, some promotional spin and, most importantly, flush with cash. This is not to imply that it will actually have sufficient resources to accomplish its aims, or that funds will reach their destination. Indeed, there can be occasions when projects have more money than the local infrastructure can absorb; it

simply cannot be spent quickly enough, and this may even lead to competition between donors for the limited local supply of competent personnel (Hoppers, 1994). A new project will, however, have the consequence that centrally there will be money for project-related appointments, activities and initiatives. Enthusiasm and organizational and operational skills are a priority at this stage. However, if no one insists on evaluation at this point then the pioneering spirit that prevails within the project, and the imperative to implementation, will not identify it as a priority.

The APPEP project was fortunate in being situated in one state within India. Its inception was therefore seen as a victory for the state government of Andhra Pradesh (GAP), and the project was taken on enthusiastically by state authorities. In addition, the funding agency, the Overseas Development Administration (ODA), had insisted on a pilot scheme and an evaluation before the major tranche of cash for the state-wide project would be released. The British Council (BC) field management also had a strong belief in evaluation and at an early stage appointed an evaluator, Sri Shridar Rao, with a UK consultancy back-up.

Education is a diffuse, and therefore always difficult to evaluate, process – the more so where projects take seriously aspirations to improve the quality of educational experiences. As a large state or national project develops it is likely to be increasingly beset by a coalition of opposition interests ranging from local or national political groupings to proponents of rival educational doctrines. If criticism is met simply with denial or counter-statements, it will not be long before support for the project begins to crumble. It is relatively simple to highlight examples of mistakes, poor administration and lack of take-up. Unless a well-grounded general picture is also available, isolated problems and anecdotal evidence can begin to define the project. There will be new, simple, strong ideas for solving long-standing educational problems so that even educational reformers will have some reason for leaving a flagging idea in order to begin again with a new project, with new vigour and new promise. Thus can a culture of cyclical project generation be generated – 'the seduction of the novel', as Hoppers (1994, p. 184)

Table 16.1 The training cascade as planned

Year in which trained	District group I (9 districts)	District group II (8 districts)	District group III (6 districts)	Whether trained at time of Main Survey 1 (late 1991)	Whether trained at time of Main Survey 2 (late 1992)	Whether trained at time of Main Survey 3 (late 1993)
1989–90	1st 20%			Yes	Yes	Yes
1990–91	2nd 20%	1st 20%		Yes	Yes	Yes
1991–92	3rd 20%	2nd 20%	1st 20%	No	Yes	Yes
1992–93	4th 20%	3rd 20%	2nd 20%	No	No	Yes
1993–94	5th 20%	4th 20%	3rd 20%	No	No	No
1994–95		5th 20%	4th 20%	No	No	No
1995–96			5th 20%	No	No	No

has termed it – in which new cash is injected and new careers are launched.

At all stages of its development APPEP has had a project management that has listened to and often responded to evaluation reports at a formal and informal level. To some extent this was due to fortunate choices of director and to some extent to the insistence of the ODA inspections and the BC field management. As the project has developed, and the need for change and new components of the project became apparent and were promoted by the BC field management, the relationship between the Indian project management, the BC field management and the evaluation has become operationally closer, giving rise, *de facto*, to a form of process management. This developing scenario represents an alternative to the culture of cyclical project generation. Instead, the project evaluation reports at regular intervals during the development of the project, thus arming the management with hard evidence of achievements and failures. Shortcomings are reported in time for remedial action, the project strengthened, and criticism anticipated, tempered by evidence and thus politically contained. In learning from our experience of APPEP, we are suggesting that projects be conceptualized in the beginning as less of a blueprint, more as a process, with active management based on sound evaluative evidence allowing the project to change and adapt to new knowledge about its implementation and outcomes.

However, before developing this argument further, we will discuss the evaluation in more detail, beginning first with a brief account of APPEP. For more detail the reader should consult earlier papers (Lacey *et al.*, 1993; Cooper *et al.*, 1996). This discussion will inevitably be illustrative in nature, but will serve to indicate how the evaluation has tried to combine technical quality with relevance to decision-makers.

APPEP and its evaluation: an overview

The project is attempting to introduce a range of 'active' primary school teaching methods into all the primary schools in the twenty-three districts of Andhra Pradesh. It aims to accomplish this by including every primary school teacher in the state in a rolling programme of in-service training and materials distribution to schools. This involves a total of approximately 50,000 schools and 130,000 teachers over the period 1989–96. Beginning in 1989–90 in nine districts, it was planned to train 20 per cent of the schools each year. The introduction of training into the remaining districts was staggered, as set out in Table 16.1.

The six APPEP principles around which training is organized are:

1   the development of activity-based learning;
2   the use of practical work;
3   the use of small-group work as well as whole-class teaching;
4   the recognition of individual differences in learning;
5   the use of the local environment for teaching materials and as a teaching context; and

Table 16.2 Planned numbers of schools in sample

	Untrained	Recently trained	Trained between 1 and 2 years	Trained more than 2 years	Total
Main Survey 1 (1991)	276	224[a]			500
Main Survey 2 (1992)	133	276	224		633
Main survey 3 (1993)	26[b]	133	276	224	659

[a] This group has always included a small number of schools which had received their training earlier than this as part of a pilot project.
[b] These schools were introduced as part of the Assessment Run, to be described later.

6 the display of children's work and the creation of an interesting classroom environment.

Alongside this training programme there has also been a programme of building provision. Extra classrooms have been provided for a proportion of schools, and in some, improved accommodation has been provided in order that these schools may function as Teacher Centres (for further details see Ravi and Rao, 1994).

Given the complexity of both the project and its evaluation, it will be necessary to discuss selected elements of the latter in turn. An initial overview may help the reader. The evaluation has included as its major feature successive annual large-scale sample surveys which have collected data from headteachers, teachers, parents and pupils, as well as classroom observation data and data from routine testing carried out in the schools. It has also carried out case studies, undertaken evaluation of the training courses, and, more recently, added an assessment study based on locally produced test items more oriented to the project's pedagogic aims than the traditional tests produced by teachers. We will discuss aspects of this design and its results, beginning with a description of the sample for the series of annual Main Surveys.

Main Survey sample

Given the size of the project, the assumptions about evaluation in the local culture and the expectations of the funding agents, it was clear from the beginning of our involvement that the design of the evaluation would include a large-scale survey.

Initially, some local stakeholders wanted this to involve all schools. Eventually it was agreed that a relatively small percentage of schools would be surveyed in order to allow the collection of good-quality data. The stratified random sample was designed with a number of criteria in mind (for details see Lacey *et al.*, 1993). First of all, it was designed in order to ensure coverage of trained and non-trained schools, with and without new buildings, and with and without Teacher Centre status. Second, it was further stratified to cover schools across the range of urban, semi-urban, rural and tribal locations. In the first Main Survey (late 1991), which followed a pilot involving some 130 schools, the sample consisted of 500 schools, of which, according to the implementation plans, 224 should have been trained at the time of the survey. The trained and untrained schools were subsequently found to be well matched on such variables as parental literacy (see Cooper *et al.*, 1996).

This design initially allowed comparisons of trained and untrained schools. As the survey was repeated in subsequent years it also allowed the progress of the project to be followed and issues of sustainability to be explored. To allow a greater range of comparisons, further untrained schools were added in subsequent Main Surveys. By Main Survey 3 (late 1993) the comparison groups set out in Table 16.2 were available.

Modelling project outcomes

One difficulty for the evaluation concerned the wide range of outcomes desired from the project by various stakeholders. As we have noted earlier,

Figure 16.1   The heuristic model

for some the project was primarily concerned to change classroom pedagogy via a programme of teacher training, leading to improved learning outcomes. For others this was only one part of a programme aiming to increase the enrolment and retention of pupils, especially those from disadvantaged groups (tribal children, and girls in particular). As a result of the range of demands it was clear that the evaluation would have to collect a wide range of data but also that it would have to develop some theoretical understanding of the ways in which these various outcomes might interact in practice. In the absence of such understanding, there was likely to be a rapid disillusionment with the programme. For this reason, the consultants, in conjunction with the local Evaluation Cell, developed a heuristic model to indicate how the various features of the project might be expected to interact over time (see Figure 16.1). The model arranges the inputs and hoped-for outcomes in a sequence which represents a prediction of the order in which events are likely to happen. For instance, although it is clear that implementa-

tion must occur before such direct effects as changed classroom practice could be observed, it does not follow that improved classroom practice in line with the APPEP principles will occur. Implementation is a necessary but not sufficient condition. This was an important message to get across to some audiences. In addition, by predicting three orders of effect, the model injected a time dimension into the consideration of effects. We hoped that the model would replace *ad hoc* explanations and rhetoric with a framework for interpreting possible results and their possible significance in a sequence of events. By making the model public we were attempting to focus the discussion so that emerging evidence could be interpreted within a shared framework of understanding of how the project might develop in practice.

The construction of the model also revealed some potential shortcomings in the design logic of the APPEP innovation. The model represents this logic as a series of sequential steps. It therefore gives the impression that an improvement in one element could without any complication feed into the educational process and produce better outcomes downstream. An improvement in 'direct effects' would therefore produce better first-order, second-order and third-order outcomes (bearing in mind the necessary but not sufficient condition, outlined earlier). However, any consideration of possible outcomes reveals potentially complex interactions in which positive effects in some factors could have negative effects on others. For example, a sequence of effects causing an increase in enrolment might well produce larger classes of pupils and overcrowding in classrooms, thus making it more difficult for teachers to sustain the innovation. Likewise, an increase in the number of marginal[1] pupils attending and staying on at school, and perhaps suffering from more crowding and less effective teaching as a direct result, could easily cause a decrease in average test scores recorded at the end of the year (for a more detailed discussion of the model and these issues, see Cooper *et al.*, 1996). It might also cause some flight to the private sector on the part of wealthier families.

Table 16.3 Percentage of teachers trained in 619 schools at Main Survey 2 (late 1992)

School's formal position according to training plans	Percentage of teachers trained				
	0	0.1–49.9	50–99.9	100	Totals
Untrained	123	7	2	0	132
Recently trained	10	22	39	192	263
Trained more than a year	27	29	47	121	224
Total numbers of schools	160	58	88	313	619

Issues of validity

It is well known that good-quality data are difficult to obtain in the context of developing countries (e.g. Chapman and Boothroyd, 1988). India is no exception, and data on enrolment are an especially difficult area (Chattopadhyay *et al.*, 1994; Jangira, 1994; Kurian, 1983). The tendency to provide data in line with official requirements and expectations is a particular problem. For this reason the evaluation was designed to allow data collection from a variety of sources in order to allow triangulation of various types to be used. The consultants also encouraged the use of a variety of analytic strategies to counter the tendency of participants in the project to exaggerate the degree of implementation (see Lacey *et al.*, 1993, for an example).

A related problem concerned the tendency of some observers of the project to assume that, if a school had been formally included in the training programme, then first, training had indeed occurred, and second, the trained teachers remained in the school. In fact, some slippage in the training programme, along with some transfer of trained teachers, led to a much more complex scenario, as shown in Table 16.3. It can be seen that in Main Survey 2, of the schools which should have been trained for more than one year, only 121 of the 224 had a full complement of trained teachers. It became very important to develop an understanding of the implications of this distribution for the evaluation of the project.

This problem could, of course, be referred back to and interrogated in the context of the heuristic model. Thus, in some schools the training component of the project had not in fact been implemented. However, for the majority of the schools which should have been trained it was the next stage of the model that posed the greatest challenge to the evaluation. How were we to ascertain the extent of classroom implementation of project principles, especially given the tendency to exaggeration? We decided to develop a variety of indices of project implementation.

Before we describe the range of data collected for this purpose, it is important to note the human resources available to the evaluation. In each of the twenty-three districts within the state of Andhra Pradesh four members of staff of the District Institutes of Education and Training (DIET lecturers) had some of their working time allocated to the evaluation. They worked under the direction of the seven members of the APPEP Evaluation Cell in Hyderabad, with which we have a consultancy relationship. Training in data collection was given to the DIET staff by the Evaluation Cell, occasionally with our involvement.

Indices of project implementation: direct effects

It was clear that if we were to collect data which would be of real value it would be necessary to collect them from a variety of sources, by a variety of means. It certainly would not be adequate to rely on headteachers' and teachers' self-reports of their practice. Furthermore, we would want to be in a position to develop a variety of indices of implementation for use in analyses of the survey data. For this reason a wide range of questionnaire and interview schedules were developed, alongside a schedule for classroom observation (see Lacey *et al.*, 1993; Cooper *et al.*, 1996). Among other data, these schedules collected background information on the school and its community, basic enrolment and attendance data, routine test scores, and teachers' accounts of their practice and their response to the APPEP training. Schedules for pupils and parents were included in order to

Table 16.4   Triangulation of data on group work

Pupils report groupwork or not	School's *APPEPness* value	
	Below-average *APPEPness*	Above-average *APPEPness*
No	527 (77.2%)	163 (29.0%)
Yes	156 (22.8%)	399 (71.0%)
Total	683 (100%)	562 (100%)

allow triangulation of the data obtained from the school itself. A variety of indices of the implementation of project principles were developed, some based on teachers' self-report data and some on the classroom observation data. The observation indices were designed to measure the degree to which the classroom practice represented the implementation of APPEP principles. The self-report and observation indices, which correlated significantly with one another, have been combined into an overall index of project implementation that has come to be called *APPEPness* (for a full description, see Cooper *et al.*, 1996).

It is perhaps worth giving one example of the way in which triangulation has been used to throw light on the adequacy of measures of implementation such as *APPEPness*. Table 16.4 shows the response of pupils to a question which asked them whether they sometimes worked in groups in their classroom, broken down in terms of each school's *APPEPness* value. The pupils' responses are collected by the DIET lecturer, not the teachers themselves. These are data from Main Survey 2 (late 1992). It can be seen that there is a distinct difference between the distributions of responses in the two cases. In schools with above-average *APPEPness* scores, 71 per cent of pupils report group work, whereas in schools with below-average *APPEPness* scores, only 23 per cent do so. Thus *APPEPness* seems to be measuring something real. This measure was also found to be correlated with pupils' enjoyment of school (Cooper *et al.*, 1996). The existence of adequate summary measures of implementation made a variety of evaluative analyses available to the project management.

First-, second- and third-order outcomes

Such measures having been used to establish that the project was leading to real change in classroom teaching in at least a proportion of schools (Lacey *et al.*, 1993; Cooper *et al.*, 1996), the next task for the evaluation became the exploration of any effects of these changes in such areas as enrolment and attendance, and pupils' learning.

It became clear early on that data on enrolment, as reported from the headteachers, were neither reliable nor valid (see also Chattopadhyay *et al.*, 1994; Jangira, 1994; Kurian, 1983). We know, for example, from case studies carried out for the evaluation that children are often marked as enrolled in the village's state school though they are in fact attending a local private school. Such problems have made analysis of this area fraught with difficulties. However, the evaluation has also had access to alternative data, in particular data on the children actually in the school on one day during the period of the Main Survey each year (as well as the marked attendance in the register for that day). These data, collected by the DIET staff member visiting the school, are regarded as more valid and, although obviously subject to substantial random variation at a school level, should prove relatively reliable when used in analyses of grouped schools. Given the limitations of space, we will present just one example of the use of these data, in conjunction with our *APPEPness* measure, to explore the effect of private schools on attendance in the state schools in our sample.[2]

Attendance

There was a question in Main Survey 3 (late 1993) to ascertain whether the schools in our survey were experiencing competition from a local unrecognized private school. This was used, in conjunction with the attendance data (i.e. children counted present), to develop Table 16.5 which shows the attendance data over three years for the schools which had been

Table 16.5 Aggregate attendance as counted on the day of visit in three main surveys, as affected by the presence of an unrecognized private school in the locality of the survey school at Main Survey 3

	Competing unrecognized private school?		Competing unrecognized private school?	
	No	Yes	No	Yes
Late 1991:	Percentage change 1991–3[a]			
Main Survey 1 (boys)	16,943	17,695	Boys: 1.45	−5.85
Main Survey 1 (girls)	12,479	14,757	Girls: 8.72	−1.06
Main Survey 1 (total)	29,422	32,452	Total: 4.53	−3.67
Late 1992:				
Main Survey 2 (boys)	16,747	16,827		
Main Survey 2 (girls)	12,886	14,383		
Main Survey 2 (total)	29,633	31,210		
Late 1993:				
Main Survey 3 (boys)	17,189	16,660		
Main Survey 3 (girls)	13,567	14,600		
Main Survey 3 (total)	30,756	31,260		
Number of schools	298	199		

[a] The figure of 1.45%, for example, is obtained thus: 100 × (17,189 − 16,943)/16,943.

in Main Survey 1. The 1991–3 change data make it clear that there is an apparent effect due to unrecognized private schools; state-sector project schools seem to be losing pupils to these schools. What if project implementation, as measured by *APPEPness*, is brought into the analysis? The results are shown in Table 16.6. It can be seen that there are apparent effects due both to the competition of an unrecognized private school and to project implementation. In both cases – that is, with and without competition from local unrecognized private schools – the group of schools with higher *APPEPness* scores also have the better rates of change in attendance between 1991 and 1993. This is one of a number of findings that suggest the project is making a real difference in the schools. Another set of findings concern pupil achievement, to which we will now turn.

Pupil achievement

The evaluation has been investigating and using assessment data in three main ways:

1   investigating current classroom practice through questions in the Main Surveys;
2   collecting routine annual exam scores through the Main Surveys; and
3   developing Common Achievement Tests to be used with a subsample of schools involved in the Main Surveys.

In respect of current classroom assessment practice, it was considered important to gather evidence of this because the principles of APPEP insisted on a much more active approach to teaching and learning in the classroom, and there was a concern that traditional assessment methods might impede such developments. Successive Main Surveys have indicated that teachers do not use a wide range of assessment methods and would like more included on classroom assessment in the in-service training programmes. New material has now been developed by the Central Project Human Resource Development (HRD) Cell for use in the training courses. This is just one example of the way in which the evaluation has been able to provide formative feedback for project development.

A key question which the evaluation faced was how best to try to gather evidence with regard to learning outcomes. Although APPEP was not initially designed to raise achievement this became one of a number of outcomes that some stakeholders expected to be produced by more active classroom teaching and learning methods. As the heuristic model makes clear, we hypothesized that changes in achievement were not likely to be identified immediately, and might well involve identifying different (broader) learning outcomes (second-order outcomes) as well as better learning outcomes (third-order outcomes).

An immediate source of data was routine exam scores, which are recorded annually by schools. We decided to collect a sample of Class 3 and Class 5 student scores as part of the Main Survey work in order to monitor what impact, if any, APPEP had

Table 16.6 Aggregate attendance as counted on the day of visit in three main surveys, by the presence of an unrecognized private school in the locality of the survey school at Main Survey 3 and *APPEPness* (i.e. project implementation)

	Competing unrecognized private school?					Competing unrecognized private school?			
	No	No	Yes	Yes		No	No	Yes	Yes
Main Survey 2 *(APPEPness)*	Lower	Higher	Lower	Higher		Lower	Higher	Lower	Higher
Late 1991:						Percentage change 1991–3			
Main Survey 1 (boys)	8,392	7,206	9,603	7,735	Boys:	1.35	2.01	−9.06	−1.75
Main Survey 1 (girls)	6,168	5,309	7,568	6,721	Girls:	6.99	11.85	−4.66	2.22
Main Survey 1 (total)	14,560	12,515	17,171	14,456	Total:	3.74	6.18	−7.12	0.10
Late 1992:									
Main Survey 2 (boys)	8,376	7,143	8,930	7,575					
Main Survey 2 (girls)	6,337	5,531	7,131	6,698					
Main Survey 2 (total)	14,713	12,674	16,061	14,273					
Late 1993:									
Main Survey 3 (boys)	8,505	7,351	8,733	7,600					
Main Survey 3 (girls)	6,599	5,938	7,215	6,870					
Main Survey 3 (total)	15,104	13,289	15,948	14,470					
Number of schools	161	114	100	90					

on them. We did not anticipate a major impact, certainly not in the short term, but the evaluation needed to be able to answer questions about such routine achievement scores if asked. It would also be important to investigate unusual patterns of scores if they occurred. This would be another part of the formative feedback that the evaluation could provide to the project.

Calculating means and distributions on the data collected demonstrates normal distributions of scores across all subjects in both Class 3 and Class 5, with mean scores usually being in the mid to high forties out 100 (Lacey *et al.*, 1995). This suggests that teachers are norm-referencing when marking and indeed are marking quite severely. We have also noted a correlation between higher scores and higher levels of recorded parental literacy.[3] This is to be expected from what we know of previous research on student achievement and is important to take into account when making claims about the effects of schooling, and APPEP in particular. This also demonstrates the importance of being able to link such outcome data to other survey data relating to school and socio-economic effects so that the impact of the project can be attributed with more confidence. In fact the Main Survey 3 data suggest that the trend in routine tests scores over time is favourable to APPEP

but is conflated with other effects such as levels of parental literacy (Cooper *et al.*, 1994). Thus we can say that APPEP has not depressed routine scores – quite the reverse, they are improving – but this improvement cannot be attributed to APPEP alone.

However, although it is important to monitor the system as it operates currently, routine exam scores by themselves do not give us very reliable data on achievement. The tests are largely set and marked by teachers themselves (though some are obtained from agencies for administration and marking by teachers within the school), and thus the scores are not directly comparable – the same test is not being used across schools. Furthermore, the tests are traditional paper-and-pencil tests of recall of knowledge; they do not assess any of the wider learning outcomes in which APPEP is interested: better understanding, interpretation and application of knowledge, for example. For this reason we have also collaborated with the development of new common achievement tests by the Evaluation Cell for use in a subsample of Main Survey schools.

These tests comprise four subject-specific achievement tests for Class 5 students, linked to the Class 5 curriculum and nationally recommended Minimum Levels of Learning (in maths, language, i.e. Telugu, environmental studies 1 and environmental studies 2). They have also been trialled in schools to ascertain how teachers and students reacted to them, how long they took in practice, how feasible it was to include practical activities, and so on. They have been considerably simplified during this process since it was found that more ambitious attempts to include practical and group activities could not be managed at school level.

The test design now comprises Part A and Part B, in each subject, with Part A designed to test traditional recall of knowledge and Part B to test understanding and interpretation (Lacey *et al.*, 1995). It was hypothesized that APPEP students would do at least as well as a control group on Part A and better on Part B. The tests are administered in the subsample of schools by DIET lecturers who have been trained at central workshops run by the Evaluation Cell. They are also marked by the DIET lecturers under instructions from the Evaluation Cell and the scripts and mark sheets are then sent to the Cell for processing. A subsample are re-marked centrally to check on marking standards across the DIET lecturers.

The first full run of the Common Achievement Tests took place in February and March 1994, following previous trials and a small pilot in 1993. A comparison of those schools which were un-trained according to administrative plans and ac-tually had no trained teachers with those APPEP schools which were longest trained according to plans and actually had 100 per cent trained teach-ers showed that the latter group had higher mean scores in every case (i.e. four subjects by boys/girls by Part A/Part B); thus students in APPEP schools were doing better on Part A as well as Part B of the tests (Lacey *et al.*, 1995). More important still, further analysis revealed that the higher-scoring schools had *lower* reported levels of parental liter-acy; that is, APPEP schools had achieved higher scores despite having lower literacy levels. This is the most powerful evidence to date of APPEP's having a positive impact on student achievement, though it will be important to see whether such results are repeated in the 1995 Assessment Run linked to Main Survey 4, when the same instru-ments and procedures will be used, with minor alterations to safeguard the integrity of the tests.

Conclusion: learning from the APPEP evaluation

We have been able to describe only very selec-tively some of the results of the evaluation of APPEP. The examples have been chosen to illus-trate such critical features as adequate sampling, the use of control variables, triangulation and so on. Generally, it can be seen that the evaluation has been able to establish an annual routine of data collection and a set of analytic approaches which have allowed it to respond to a wide variety of the questions and concerns of decision-makers. In this concluding section of the chapter, we wish to discuss what can be learned from this experi-ence.

The APPEP evaluation did not limit itself to presenting results descriptively; it also extended its role to their interpretation, drawing on the heuristic model developed for this purpose. As a result, it has played an important part in the man-agement of the project. Without it the field man-agement team would have found it much more difficult to demonstrate the project's successes and explain its apparent failures. It has succeeded in providing formative evaluation to what has in-creasingly been seen as a process rather than a blueprint project. This function was particularly important after the initial phase of the project.

The heuristic model was used to explain why the project did not immediately deliver learning gains or better enrolment figures. Using the data analysis techniques that we have described in con-junction with the model, it was possible to show that after the first year of the evaluation, and allow-ing for exaggeration, some 30 to 40 per cent of teachers were actually implementing the main ele-ments of the project in the classroom and only in 30 per cent of project schools was the project not being implemented at all. In addition, pupils en-joyed the new approaches. In the second year it was possible to point to more progress. The phe-nomenon of pupil enjoyment continued. Inter-views with parents confirmed that the new methods encouraged their children and that ef-fects spilled over into the community. Most im-portantly, it could be shown that where schools had 100 per cent trained teachers and were implementing the project, third-order effects were beginning to emerge. Furthermore, it was possible to point to shortcomings in the training programmes along with the effects of non-implementation and teacher mobility. By the third year of the evaluation the sustained effects of the innovation had produced a more marked effect on third-order outcomes. It was now possible to show that the APPEP pedagogy had positive effects on attendance and attainment. The evaluation design has therefore allowed both sustainability and development to be assessed. The developing picture of project progress described enabled funding to be maintained and the project to be developed.

Partly as a consequence of insights from the evaluation, several new project components have been launched during 1994. These include the introduction of new textbooks and readers in the language area, the strengthening of the Teacher Centre component of APPEP, and the development of the social and community side of the project in order to enhance the participation of girls and tribal children.

For an evaluation to contribute successfully in this manner to the development of a project in a developing country context, teamwork is required across a wide range of professional, managerial and cultural boundaries. Technical competence, local knowledge and an understanding of what information is relevant and useful to decision-makers have to be brought together to create an evaluation which will be seen as legitimate and relevant by key stakeholders. What lessons can be learned from APPEP's attempt to achieve this?

We must stress that the process of evaluation has not always been straightforward. First of all, there are local cultural barriers to the open examination of practice for the purposes of evaluation. We had to insist on introducing, in order to protect both the local evaluators and the evaluated, various procedural norms. We stressed the importance of being open to the results of enquiry and criticism, as well as the need for confidentiality in order to protect teachers and others involved in the evaluation. Even so, there have been continuing difficulties in this area. A greater problem, however, concerns the skills and understanding required to carry out a fruitful evaluation.

Members of the Evaluation Cell in Hyderabad, brought together from a variety of professional backgrounds, have found themselves, to some extent, learning on the job. They brought a variety of academic skills, as well as local knowledge, to their task, but they lacked experience of evaluation *per se*. In particular, they had little experience of advanced analysis of survey data, they lacked experience in report-writing, and they had no experience of case study work. Five members of the Cell have received training in the UK at various points during the evaluation, but inevitably the time devoted to this was restricted by the need for them to be in post managing the process of data collection, data entry and preliminary analysis, as well as by an official requirement that courses should not be longer than three months. In addition, there has been an inevitable loss of skills from the Cell as a result of staff mobility and career advancement. As we write, there are two members of the Cell waiting for training in their designated area of expertise.

As the evaluation proceeded, it became clear that the Cell itself would not be immediately ready, in spite of the training received, to undertake more advanced analysis of the data, nor to produce useful reports without considerable support. The BC field management responded flexibly to this problem. Contracts with the consultants have included time for data analysis in the UK, and this feature, coupled with visits to Hyderabad and well-developed working relations with the Evaluation Cell, have made possible a division of labour which has both successfully delivered the evaluation and contributed to local capacity-building.

Nevertheless, one important lesson for future projects such as DPEP is clear. The identification and training of local evaluators must occur very early in the project cycle if later problems, including those of dependence on outside support, are to be avoided. Such training should be substantial and wide-ranging. In addition, it will be important to put in place a recognizable career avenue for evaluators in order that their skills, once developed, can be retained to produce a critical mass of expertise where they are needed. This will be an essential requirement for sustainable development.

In the case of APPEP, it was decided by the field management that the desire for a technically competent evaluation outweighed any ideological preferences for a purely local evaluation. In fact, throughout the career of APPEP so far, the role of the BC field management has been of critical importance. APPEP has been fortunate in having a field management that has been able to make realistic demands of the evaluation, to respond to criticism and to hold a dialogue with the evaluators that takes on board the technical strengths and the limitations of findings. Gradually, the role of facilitator or animateur has become less dominant, with the field management team moving from being the carrier of a strong, simple message to being the interpreter of sound technical information from the evaluation about the progress of the project.

These elements, coupled with the dedication and competence of the central project team (HRD Cell), have combined to produce a successful project. However, the culture of cyclical project generation is not experienced in dealing with success. One of its fundamental assumptions is that previous projects have failed and that, apart from the one or two strong, simple ideas which propel the new generation of projects, there is little need to inspect the past for successful practices and modes of organization.

DPEP has its 'strong, relatively simple ideas' which derive in some measure from the failure of Operation Blackboard. Operation Blackboard was a highly centralized, resource-based programme which was imposed from the centre without much regard to local conditions and needs. Most of its failures have been blamed on these features and DPEP is consequently highly devolved, based on local (that is, district-level) plans. However, in the process of devolving resources and functions without relinquishing overall central government control, DPEP is in danger of cutting out vital intermediary state functions in the name of local responsiveness.

APPEP has not yet been a powerful influence in shaping the administrative and evaluation structures within DPEP. Yet it would appear there are some important lessons to be learned. If DPEP and, indeed, other similar post-Jomtien projects are to benefit from the APPEP experience, it will be necessary to ensure:

1   the technical competence of the evaluation;
2   a flexible attitude to buying in outside expertise when it is necessary;
3   a close association between evaluation findings and management decisions at the state as well as the district level;
4   rigorous and relevant training programmes to ensure the upgrading and sustainability of state-level evaluation cells; and
5   career structures at the district, state and central government levels that ensure retention and development of trained personnel.

The culture of failed project/cyclical development can be held at bay and a new virtuous cycle of successful project development can be substituted. We are optimistic that in India, DPEP is well placed to make this change. However, it will require that key decision-makers within DPEP learn the lessons from APPEP and graft them carefully on to the developing DPEP structures.

Acknowledgements

We wish to acknowledge the contribution of Project personnel in Hyderabad to our thinking on these issues. We would also like to acknowledge the support of the British Council, which is funding the Evaluation Consultancy, and the help and advice given to us by British Council Field Officers and Managers in India, particularly Dr Tony Davison, Dr K. N. Rao and, previously, Mr David Theobald. However, the views expressed in the chapter are those of the authors, and should not be attributed to either the ODA or the British Council.

Notes

1 By marginal we mean to refer, for example, to those students from illiterate families who would not previously have attended school.

2　Given the limitations of space, we will not discuss the complexities of the enrolment data in this paper.

3　It must be noted that the evaluation had access only to a school-level measure of parental literacy, a factor which obviously limited the modes of analysis available in this area.

References

Archer, D. (1994) The changing roles of non-governmental organizations in the field of education (in the context of changing relationships with the state), *International Journal of Educational Development*, **14**(3), 223–32.

Chapman, D. W. and Boothroyd, R. A. (1988) Threats to data quality in developing country settings, *Comparative Education Review*, **32**(4), 416–29.

Chattopadhyay, R., Chaudhuri, S. and NagiReddy, V. (1994) *The Status of Primary Education in Assam: A Project Sponsored by UNICEF Calcutta*. Calcutta: Indian Institute of Management.

Cooper, B., Lacey, C. and Torrance, H. (1994) *Technical Report for Main Survey 3 of the APPEP Evaluation*. Manchester: British Council/Overseas Development Administration.

Cooper, B., Lacey, C. and Torrance, H. (1996) Making sense of large scale evaluation data: the case of the Andhra Pradesh Primary Education Project, *International Journal of Educational Development*, **16**(2), 125–40.

Dyer, C. (1994) Education and the state: policy implementation in India's federal polity, *International Journal of Educational Development*, **14**(3), 241–53.

Government of India (1993) *Education for All: The Indian Scene*. New Delhi: Department of Education, Ministry of Human Resource Development.

Government of India (n.d.) *The District Primary Education Programme*. New Delhi: Government of India, Ministry of Human Resource Development.

Hoppers, W. (1994) Learning the lessons: a thematic review of project experiences, in A. Little, W. Hoppers and R. Gardner (eds), *Beyond Jomtien: Implementing Primary Education for All*. London: Macmillan, pp. 163–86.

Jangira, N. K. (1994) *Learning Achievement of Primary School Children in Reading and Mathematics: A Synthesis Report*. New Delhi: National Council of Educational Research and Training.

King, K. (1992) The external agenda of aid in internal educational reform, *International Journal of Educational Development*, **12**(4), 257–63.

Kurian, J. (1983) *Elementary Education in India: Myth, Reality, Alternative?* New Delhi: Vikas Publishing House PVT Ltd.

Lacey, C., Cooper, B. and Torrance, H. (1993) Evaluating the Andhra Pradesh Primary Education Project: problems of design and analysis, *British Educational Research Journal*, **19**(5), 535–54.

Lacey, C., Cooper, B. and Torrance, H. (1995) *Report on DPEP Evaluation Workshop – Delhi – January 1995*. Manchester: British Council/Overseas Development Administration.

Little, A., Hoppers, W. and Gardner, R. (eds) (1994) *Beyond Jomtien: Implementing Primary Education for All*. London: Macmillan.

Ravi, Y. and Rao, S. (1994) The Andhra Pradesh Primary Education Project, in A. Little, W. Hoppers and R. Gardner (eds), *Beyond Jomtien: Implementing Primary Education for All*. London: Macmillan, pp. 20–44.

Conclusion:
Education and Development: Towards a New Development Relationship[1]

JAMES LYNCH

This series is dedicated to the achievement of a key area of public policy for developing countries: universal primary education, and its form, content, process and financing, expeditiously, cost-effectively and with personal and social outcomes of high quality. It bases its case on the right to education of every individual as an entitlement grounded in human rights, as enshrined in the 1948 Universal Declaration of Human Rights and reaffirmed in other international instruments and covenants, including at the 1990 World Conference on Education for All and at the commencement of the United Nations Decade for Human Rights Education in December 1994.[2] At least at the primary level, education must be free, and the entitlement must cover girls, children with special educational needs, and the children of minority, itinerant and indigenous peoples. It is linked to collateral fundamental human rights to basic health care and adequate nutrition.

In the first section of this volume a number of economic and financial concerns surrounding this commitment have been addressed. While recognizing the need for a stable, political, institutional and macro-economic setting for sustainable development, Chapter 1 by Fernando Reimers examines the nature of the impact of structural adjustment on the education sector in several countries in the context of the increasingly austere economic climate of the 1980s. In comparing adjusting and non-adjusting countries, Reimers argues that there is nothing automatic in the response of adjusting countries, but rather that the diversity of policy responses of countries within the same re-

gion suggests that the impact, together with failures and missed opportunities consequent on such policies, is the result of choices made by sovereign states, albeit in dialogue with country teams of certain international agencies. Those missed opportunities can never be recouped. National policy élites and international agencies must accept responsibility for those missed opportunities to protect education, even to give it a more prominent role in the policy dialogue. They must learn from that failure. The arguments of this chapter endorse those adumbrated in the introductory chapter to this volume. There, the need for safety nets and checks and balances was underlined and the attachment of 'social covenants' to all adjustment programmes advocated, in order to protect specified essential social expenditures, and particularly primary education. Additionally, an updating of the United Nations 20/20 initiative was proposed, without which major social targets, such as universal free primary education, cannot be achieved.[3]

The second chapter, by Robert Smith, critically examines a number of aspects of the educational policy of arguably the most important, powerful and influential of these agencies, the World Bank. In spite of recent developments to the contrary, Smith argues that the style of development of the Bank is positivistic, technicist, non-participatory and intellectually restricted in its choice of paradigms. In a principled and positive way, Smith seeks to expose the weaknesses inherent in the assumptions, values and epistemologies which characterize the World Bank's approach to educational policy-making. In particular, the unproblematic view of education projected by the Bank's policy declarations, as well as the language used to convey those meanings and its 'parochial' choice of supporting evidence, is argued to reflect an almost exclusively instrumental in-house view of education.

The use of paradigms generated in the United States as a basis for policies in developing countries is criticized as typifying the one-dimensional Western, industrialized 'bank' view of education, leading to an arguably faulty view of the relationship between schooling and economic development. This situation would perhaps be less critical in an open market for development assistance, were it not for the fact that there is a substantial convergence in aid agency approaches. Many bilaterals link their aid policies to those of the Bank, which expects ready-made solutions, quick and obvious returns with short-term successful outcomes, expressed in explicit and quantifiable terms. This process is argued to be supported by an incestuous relationship to research to support policy-making and proposition.

As argued in the introductory chapter to this volume, international development as dispensed by the major agencies can only support social and economic development in poor countries; it cannot replace that commitment and the political will on the part of the country itself. It is important that the macro-policies of the major agencies fully espouse local ownership and self-determination as critical factors in fundamental development, so that the involvement of local communities is more potent and more meaningful for them. This is a joint responsibility which necessitates a greater equality of communication in the policy dialogue, as well as a deeper and more balanced partnership. The series advocates, therefore, the local, national and international responsibility of communities, governments and agencies to secure the means for all children to enjoy their human rights, based on a full recognition of the value and epistemological contribution of the borrowers at national and local levels and the full measure in grant form of the promised contributions from the industrialized countries.[4]

The subsequent chapter, by Clem Tisdell, considers some of the stock-in-trade economic methods of international financial agencies and notes the limitations of the methods. In particular, the concept of social returns to education stemming from the human capital approach is noted as being relatively restricted compared to the concept of social return used in welfare economics. Again, echoing the chapter by Smith, the limitations of relying on estimates of enhanced earnings as indicators of returns on education are outlined and the potential for consequent conflict between equity and efficiency is discussed, although it is argued that equity considerations reinforce the argument for giving universal primary education a high priority. The chapter sounds a note of warning about the declining access to primary education in Africa and the increasing numbers of children worldwide without any primary education, at the same time as donor weariness among governments towards funding primary education is increasing – and, perhaps, their capacity is decreasing.

Although, as argued by both Smith and Tisdell, there are other important personal and social 'yields' on investment in primary education, 'rate of return to education' studies (Schultz, 1961; Bowman, 1980) from different countries seem to indicate that the estimated rates of return are typically more than 10 per cent and that the highest rates of return are on investment on the lowest level of formal education (Psacharopoulos, 1985). According to this evidence, primary education has a direct and positive effect not only on economic development, but also on productivity, as well as on life chances, health, nutrition and the rate of population increase. In addition to the greater economic returns which investments in primary education yield, they appear also to contribute to greater equity (United Nations, Children's Fund, 1991), as well as to social development and nation-building (Lockheed and Verspoor, 1992). Yet in comparative terms, primary education continues to receive a low priority and status, with nations in the developing world investing many times more per capita on higher education than on primary and basic education. Military spending in many developing countries still exceeds expenditure on health, nutrition and education combined.

Associated with the note of warning sounded by Tisdell on the harsher economic climate for the support of primary education is the rising recognition of the many world environmental crises. As a contribution to the matching of human desires and ecological realities to achieve sustainable development, an art still very immature, Chapter 4 by Mark Burch advances the argument for a more holistic perspective on the human–environment relationship. In particular, it argues that education for sustainable livelihood affords an alternative paradigm to the established paradigms of education for economic and technical growth, as espoused by the major aid agencies. The latter aims to transmit the information and culture needed to manipulate ecosystems, so as to respond adequately to sometimes artificially stimulated human desires. The former aims to transform consciousness so as to fulfil human needs in harmony with ecosystems. The chapter endorses the argument of this series that the horrific impact on natural resource depletion, the environment, and social structures of current growth paradigms highlights the need to draw economic policies to the bar of a more rigorous environmental and social accountability in the greater common interest.

That greater common interest includes all domains of human experience interactively – cultural, social (including economic and environmental) and in essence. The issue is the paradigm we use to make sense of our social reality and how we strive for our own satisfaction and improvement and those of humankind: a paradigm of selfish utilitarianism, of individualistic, rationalistic materialism, which recognizes no higher-order morality than self-interest and the most efficient allocation of resources; or one which recognizes human beings as deeply normative, affective members of social collectivities, sustained by their relationships in community, finding their satisfaction and the human norms for their judgements in caring as much about others as in pursuing their own narrow social or economic self-interest? As Etzioni (1988) has argued, we are now in the middle of a paradigm struggle in response to that

question. The old individualistic, utilitarian, neo-classical paradigm is no longer adequate to the needs of a world with rapidly changing economic, social, cultural and economic problems. The Burch chapter argues that an alternative community-focused, environmentally wise paradigm is needed which can take account of individual human rights and responsibilities.

One country where decades of civil strife have seriously damaged both the environment and primary education is Mozambique. In her chapter, Jean Anderson outlines a contemporary initiative developed jointly by the UNICEF country strategy team, the Mozambique Ministry of Education and a team from the College of St Mark and St John in the United Kingdom. As part of that strategy, the college is providing training for a vanguard cadre of senior and middle-ranking planners and managers, charged with leading the EFA development. The approach, involving sessions in the UK and in Mozambique, together with relevant research undertaken by participants, is advanced as an alternative and innovatory model of technical assistance, susceptible to adoption in other partnership relationships between industrialized and developing countries seeking to achieve universal primary education. The chapter thus raises again not only the debate about how to achieve education for all (EFA), but the debate about present and future relations between industrialized and developing countries, which will provide an essential context to their partnership in pursuit of education for all. It makes a modest contribution to an appraisal of those relationships, and, picking up the critique of the growth and 'dependence paradigms' of development levied by Burch, advances the case of the series for a new 'covenant of interdependence'.

Echoing the criticisms of several of the contributors to Part One of this volume, Part Two picks up the theme of the parameters and paradigms which may be utilized in the conceptualization of policies for the achievement of EFA. As argued in the introduction to this volume, many development educators are unaware of the underlying values and epistemologies which silently guide their judgements and decisions about education in developing countries. Addressing this problem, the chapter by Fernando Reimers which commences Part Two argues that the traditional approach to educational planning is limited by its non-participatory nature. Picking up a theme introduced by Smith earlier in the volume, the chapter advances an alternative, participatory policy dialogue to achieve organizational learning in ministries of education.

Using El Salvador as an example, the chapter describes a case in which a participatory methodology was used in the aftermath of the twelve-year civil war. The methodology was used to carry out an education sector assessment to identify the principal problems facing the education system and to discuss options for reform. The process involved extensive participation by a number of organizations, as well as intensive dialogue with an advisory group which included representatives from political associations and groups. The chapter proposes that, given the nature of the problems faced by planners, processes of communicating and negotiating competing views are more conducive to organizational learning than are technical planning processes that purport to provide answers to highly placed decision-makers.

Once again, the cherished assumptions and ideologies of development, according to the usual 'Northern' paradigms and knowledge monopolies, are found wanting. For new strategies and new human relationships to develop, innovation at both the conceptual and operational levels is required and no one intellectual methodology suffices. Projects such as the one described, which have manifested thinking and action 'outside the box', reinforce the need for a new, more participatory partnership of policy dialogue which critiques existing strategies and tactics, provides alternative and relevant institutional learning, and achieves goals of greater equity within systems and institutions.

Presaging the major preoccupation of Volume 2 with diversity and gender equity, Chapter 7 by Lynn Davies focuses on an important and neglected aspect of such a participatory style of policy dialogue, namely the extent to which school management facilitates or inhibits the preparation of girls for such participation. Examining the connections between the organization of schooling and equity outcomes, she poses the question of

how management policy impacts on equity considerations in the school and how management affects the social outcomes of schooling, particularly in terms of later female participation in politics and decision-making. She asserts that the power relations and authority structures and styles are a potent part of the hidden curriculum of any educational institution. Just as structural adjustment policies have a disproportionate impact on women (Gordon, 1994), so indeed democratic or authoritarian school styles of organization and management, both formal and informal, appear to have a differential impact on male and female students.

The chapter traces through the relationship among democratic schooling, equity, self-esteem and empowerment, quoting examples of facilitatory approaches sanctioned by states. The words 'empowerment' and 'participation' are critiqued, in the one case because of the word's suggestion of patronage, and in the other arguing that participation and learning to participate are less important than how participation takes place. Taking up one of the major permeative themes of the series, Davies argues that greater gender equity will come not from a sharper focus on women and girls, but from the struggle which has respect for the equal rights of all and is solicitous of diversity. For this a democratic apprenticeship within a democratic schooling is essential. The chapter raises fundamental issues concerning the contribution of a more democratic education for greater equity to economic and broader social and political development. Davies thus seeks to identify the means and the implications for school management of the Jomtien Action Framework, which states that education for women and girls 'should be designed to eliminate the social and cultural barriers, which have discouraged or even excluded women and girls from the benefits of regular education programmes, as well as to promote equal opportunities in all aspects of their lives' (World Conference on Education for All, 1990, p. 62).

Chapter 8 by Kenneth King, although presented in a relatively unproblematic way, raises the major dual issue of the international knowledge industry, a General Motors conglomerate of knowledge production and dissemination which controls and influences through knowledge the distribution of life chances and the quality of life. He defines the increasing difficulties faced by institutions in developing countries in providing the resources which would give access to new knowledge and the growing technological gap between knowledge-weak and knowledge-strong societies. Of course knowledge exchange has to be seen as part and parcel of the economic exchange between 'North' and 'South', with the major epistemic communities in the industrialized countries charging a high price for entry to the club. How to free developing countries from such knowledge bondage is extremely problematic, given that it is the institutions in the 'North' that define the rules of the game. They largely bracket out local knowledge, culture and communications systems, and have a vested interest in continued knowledge dependence. Once again the issue of unequal interdependence is posed, this time in epistemological rather than economic terms.

The final chapter in Part Two retrieves this issue of interdependence. Carol Kochhar locks on to the issue of how to develop greater independence, or at least to reduce dependence. She argues that there is a linkage between economic dependence and educational dependence. In many cases aid has entailed long-term dependence, has done little to spur the economy and has not promoted the full participation of those affected by decisions, the so-called beneficiaries. Both aid agencies and academic institutions have played a part in evoking educational dependence. Reducing that dependence requires strategic investment in human resource development, to bring about social stability and self-determination. Universal primary education is critical to the achievement of those goals. The chapter includes examples of innovative approaches to promote independence, arguing that dependency theory is important for development educators because of the burden imposed by dependence and the potential benefits of promoting self-reliance.

Kochhar thus reiterates a point made in the World Bank documents provided for the World Summit for Social Development, organized in Copenhagen in March 1995. There it was argued that whereas 'sound economic policies and a well-functioning labour market were essential for economic growth, they remained insufficient without investments in human capital' (World Bank, 1995, p. xi). Human capital was defined as knowledge, skills and good health, seen as prerequisites for productive employment, informed and active citizenship and a better quality of life (ibid.). Investments in universal primary education in particular were argued to have been instrumental in bringing about the East Asian 'miracles' and were advocated to boost the economic growth of the poorest countries. Four priorities for investment were seen as crucial for development: basic education; girls' education; cost-effective health services; and early childhood development (ibid., p. 45).

The third part of the volume focuses more sharply on human rights and the need to call policies to the bar of a human rights accountability. The chapter by Audrey Osler trenchantly identifies the difficulty of operationalizing such an approach where respect for human rights has not reigned before. Picking up the issue of the need for an informed and active citizenry, Osler's chapter considers some of the difficulties in operationalizing an education for human rights in a context where the most gross abuse of human rights has held sway for many years, and where political uncertainty and economic crisis still predominate. Echoing one of the major concerns of this series, namely that for mutuality and reciprocity in education, Osler identifies a number of initiatives for the development of a context, content and process where human rights are recognized and respected by government, groups and individuals. She identifies the contribution of such an education to the development of political freedom and democracy.

Addressing the issue of cultural diversity and its implications for education, Stephen May's chapter addresses the specific issue of human rights, as reflected in language policies. The varying degrees to which language rights are recognized and incorporated within state education policy are examined. Based on a critical analysis of policy development and drawing on recent developments in international law and a number of key tenets of liberal democracy, an argument is advanced for indigenous language rights in education. Drawing on a new, more culturally sensitive interpretation of the Treaty of Waitangi, an innovative and highly successful model of such an education which draws on community involvement and local control is provided by the emergence of Maori-language schools. The argument of the chapter is that the injustice of one section of the community is the concern of all. Thus, May's chapter refines the focus on EFA, asserting that the basic right of all the world's citizens, contained in the International Declaration of Human Rights, to education at least at the primary level must include a right to a quality education expressive of the child's culture and appropriate to particular national, local and personal needs, or it is meaningless.

Continuing the theme of human rights education, the chapter by Micheline Rey-von Allmen highlights the theme of interdependence of humans and the dependence of humans on their ecosystem. On the basis of her work in intercultural relations, she argues the need for an education based on solidarity and mutual responsibility. She cites a number of international instruments which support her vision of a world accepting greater independence. Education must develop the concept of environmentally and economically sustainable development, responsible world economic and political co-citizenship and an appreciation of the responsibility for shaping and sharing a new global community, with new norms of relationship. The chapter advances the case for a development education which is interculturally sensitive, critically reflexive, grounded in human rights, and accepting of democratic process.

Like Davies, and projecting a response to the identified needs and difficulties identified by Osler in introducing human rights education in Ethiopia, Rey-von Allmen argues the need for a democratic school management which can promote human rights and social responsibility in the school as a prerequisite to any concept of sustainable development. The development of an appropriate universal primary and basic education of high quality, seen as both process and product, can be a major means to change the relationship

between North and South towards greater emphasis on what she terms the 'inter'. At the same time, intercultural development education can be a means for the construction of new and healthier, non-exploitative relationships at institutional, national and international levels, where interests above self-interest are seen as valid and desirable, to the benefit of all humanity. Once again her contribution highlights the shared responsibility of industrialized countries for the poverty and deprivation of developing countries and for the restricted life chances of their populations, caused at least in part by the economic and cultural dominance–submission relationship between North and South.

The final part of this volume raises some of the major issues surrounding innovation, change and evaluation. Using examples from a number of fields of study, including education, but drawing particularly on the introduction of a new syllabus into primary education in Malaysia, the chapter by Fred Chambers tries to establish a typical pattern where the function of innovation is different at different stages. Each of these stages has different and distinct functions. The implications of such a patterning for innovations in education are considered, as well as the iterative nature of innovations and the relationship between innovation and change. He sounds a warning note about the way in which ineffective innovations are allowed to continue because evaluations are ignored and therefore remain ineffective. The model proposed poses once again the question of what educational approaches can be developed which are efficient and cost-effective, more relevant and tailor-made for the problems of each nation, and what is the best cultural and economic fit.

Picking up the challenge on behalf of evaluation, the chapter by Phillip Hughes seeks to identify two competing types of evaluation according to their objective, whether for learning or for accountability. The first is an essential part of effective teaching and learning, the second looms increasingly large in the demand from the public for value for money. Illuminative evaluation, based on ethnographic fieldwork as in social anthropology, is adumbrated, and the demands for assessment, inherent in the UK's Education Reform

Act of 1988, are identified. Evaluation is seen as providing information demanded by interest groups within a democratic society. In resisting demands for such information, schools have damaged themselves and teachers their professional esteem in the eyes of the public. The lessons for developing countries are clear and relate to earlier contributions to this first volume. Schools need to be more open in their provision of essential and legitimate information to parents and the community. Quality schooling within a democracy implies no less.

Léo Laroche seeks in his chapter to focus the role of assessment more sharply on to developing countries. He argues that any educational reform should include an integral and important role for evaluation, in order to ensure the success of the operation. Such evaluation may address several objectives including verifying the fit between the services offered and the socio-economic context; certificating and attributing diplomas; evaluating the scholastic progress of students; selecting the best candidates for the different programmes offered; monitoring study programme implementation and material usage; and measuring the satisfaction of the beneficiaries. Laroche illustrates these with examples of methods used in developing countries, indicating the circumambient preconditions necessary for an effective evaluation, including the training of educational personnel; rigorous design; and mechanisms for controlling the quality of data.

The final contribution to the volume looks at the role of evaluation in large-scale interventions through the example of the Andhra Pradesh Primary Education Project. The new structural arrangements attempt to avoid top-down administration and to locate the process at local level. The characteristics of large-scale innovations which rest on agreements among relatively small élites at the apex of large administrative structures are noted. Attention is drawn to the need to ensure the technical competence of any evaluation, a flexible attitude to buying in expertise from outside the project, a close association of evaluation findings and management decisions, rigorous and relevant training, and procedures for the retention and professional development of trained personnel.

In an interdisciplinary and cross-sectoral way, this first volume has sought to set out the major concerns of the series, while at the same time making a distinctive contribution to the issue of the means whereby universal primary education may be achieved and the goals which should be addressed in that odyssey. Those goals include of course the central importance of human resource development and especially basic education for the creation of the human capital indispensable to productive social development and political stability. They should embrace the importance of responding to the special needs of women and girls, the impaired and situationally disadvantaged, linking that entitlement to a further package of entitlements in basic health care and nutrition. Education for all should be one of the major means to pull the majority out of the slough of poverty and ignorance, providing for the generation of income-earning opportunities, the encouragement of entrepreneurship and wealth creation, and a balance between the role of government and the private sector. It must seek to maintain or construct the social capital implicit in communitarian traditions as a basis for economic development[5] and to nurture nation-building, while fostering innovation and competitiveness. It needs to be coupled with sound macro-economic policies, including a social covenant to protect the poor, and with a long-term commitment to technical training, capital investment, new technologies and continuing education (Porter, 1990).

The volume raises a number of issues about the underlying values and presuppositions, aims and strategies, and evaluation of current development education in an attempt to identify new parameters, theoretical insights and approaches. Several major themes which run through all volumes have been introduced: gender equity; inclusive schooling; a universal package of entitlements for all children based in fundamental human rights; economic, social and cultural mutuality between developed and developing countries; environmental sustainability; and financial equity, community involvement, democratic participation and educational development seen as fundamental human resource development for economic progress.

It argues for a new 'Charter of Relationships' between developed and developing countries at both macro and micro levels, based on a more mutual and reciprocal relationship of interdependence. At the micro level, a new, more child-centred and culturally responsive model of the education 'enterprise' has been advanced. New definitions of what constitutes good and effective education and how it is monitored and evaluated are suggested. Its aim has been to contribute to the forging of a fundamental paradigm change in values and a new course of action in the field of education congruent with human rights, in order to achieve a new and more financially equitable and humanly just relationship between developed and developing countries for the benefit of all. Succeeding volumes take up the challenges set by this one in substantiating further the characteristics of those new relationships.

Notes

1 This concluding chapter draws on some of the material in my book *Education and Development: A Human Rights Analysis* (Cassell, 1997).
2 The decade was formally proposed by the Director-General of UNESCO, Federico Mayor, at the 1993 World Conference on Human Rights in Vienna. In October 1994 the UNESCO International Conference on Education adopted a framework recommending learning for peace, human rights and anti-racism.
3 The UN 20/20 initiative suggests that at least 20 per cent of government budgets and at least 20 per cent of aid agencies' programmes be devoted to basic social services.
4 The current target is 0.7 per cent of gross national product to be allocated to development assistance by the industrialized countries.
5 A recent treatment of the importance of the relation between this social capital and economic success is given by Fukuyama (1995).

References

Bowman, M. J. (1980) Education and economic growth: an overview, in T. King (ed.), *Education and Income: A Background Study for the World Development Report, 1980*. World Bank Working Paper 402. Washington, DC: World Bank, pp. 1–71.
Etzioni, A. (1988) *The Moral Dimension: Towards a New Economics*. New York: Free Press of Glencoe.
Fukuyama, F. (1995) *Trust: The Social Virtues and the Creation of Prosperity*. New York: Free Press of Glencoe.
Gordon, R. (1994) Education policy and gender in Zimbabwe, *Gender and Education*, 6(2), 131–41.
Lockheed, M. and Verspoor, A. (1992) *Improving Primary Education in Developing Countries*. New York: Oxford University Press.
Porter, M. H. (1990) *The Competitive Advantage of Nations*. New York: Free Press of Glencoe.
Psacharopoulos, G. (1985) Returns to education: a further international update and implications, *Journal of Human Resources*, 20, 584–604.
Schultz, G. W. (1961) Investment in human capital, *American Economic Review*, 51, 1–17.
United Nations Children's Fund (1991) *The State of the World's Children*. New York: Oxford University Press.
World Bank (1995) *Advancing Social Development*. Washington, DC: World Bank.
World Conference on Education for All (1990) *Meeting Basic Learning Needs: Final Report*. New York: WCEFA.

Name Index

Subject Index

academic institutions
  and economic dependence   111, 112–13
  and educational dependence   118–22, 127, 243
accountability
  environmental   xii
  evaluation for   198–207
  human rights   x
active citizenship   x
adult literacy programmes   91, 92
Afghanistan   108
Africa   83, 92
  assessment project in Benin (West Africa)   214–16
  children with disabilities   107
  political changes   xiii
  reducing educational dependence   119
  see also individual countries; sub-Saharan Africa
aid agencies   x, xi, 104–28, 240, 241
  bilateral and multilateral   xix–xx
  and educational dependence   117–27, 243
  failure to achieve goals   105–13
  intersectoral approach   104–5
AID (Agency for International Development)   107, 119
AIMAV, Universal Declaration of Linguistic Rights   154
Amnesty International   136, 137, 141
Andhra Pradesh Primary Education Project (APPEP, India)   52, 226–38, 245
  attendance   232–3
  Evaluation Cell   236
  Main Survey sample   229
  modelling project outcomes   229–31
  outcomes   232
  principles of   228–9
  pupil achievement   233–5
  validity issues   231
APU (Assessment of Performance Unit, UK)   201
Asia
  children with disabilities   107
  educational expenditure   9, 10, 11, 12, 13
  numbers of university students   6
  per capita income   6
  political changes   xiii
  returns on investment in education   36
  see also individual countries
assessment   209–24, 245
  accountability and learning   198–207
  administration   219–20
  certification of studies   222–3

data analysis   220
  formative   214, 222
  learning assessment   210–14
  pilot tests   218–19
  social anthropology paradigm of   201
  student assessment   221–3
  summative   222
  system assessment   216–21
  types of   213–14
  see also evaluation
Australia
  credit laws   188, 189, 191
  education policies   206
  Koori people   152
authentic development   116
authoritarianism, and patriarchy   87–90, 242

backward mapping   28–30
biculturalism, and Māori education   159, 164
bilateral agencies, values, epistemologies and paradigms of   xix–xx
bilingual schools, and Māori education   160
Botswana   85–6, 88
Brazil   70, 91, 94
Bretton Woods institutions   xv
Britain
  Education Reform Act (1988)   194, 203, 206, 245
  evaluation in education   199, 200–1
  National Curriculum   83, 203–5, 206
  Newcastle Commission   199
  Overseas Development Administration (ODA)   25, 29
British Council (BC)   227, 228
bureaucracy, and gender   85–7
business groups, economic aid by   113
business–education partnerships   124

capacity-building   52–3
  and educational development   121, 126
  in Mozambique   53–62
CAPS (Central American Peace Scholarship) programme   120
CD-ROMs, and educational research   98, 99
change, and innovation   194
'Charter of Relationships'   xxiv, 246
child-centred philosophy   127
children's rights   141, 175, 240
Chile   53
China   83, 203

ethnicity – *continued*
  and patriarchy 90
European Bank for Reconstruction and Development xiv
evaluation 225–38, 245
  APPEP (India) 228–37, 245
  case studies 202
  CIPP model 200
  formative and summative 200
  goal-free 200
  for learning and accountability 198–207
  significant decisions on 202–5
  triangulation method of 201–2
examinations 223
expenditure *see* educational expenditure
experiential learning, and intercultural development education 179–80

federalization, in Ethiopia 140
FEPADE (Business Foundation for Educational Development, El Salvador) 72, 73, 74, 75, 77
financial strategies x, xi
  see also educational expenditure
financing education 9–14
flags of convenience ix, xi
Ford Foundation Committee 118
formative assessment 214

Gambia 146
gender
  and aid projects 112
  and democratic schooling 82–95, 242
    mixed or single-sex 92
  and discourse 84–90
  and educational development 127
  and returns on investment in education 38
  see also girls; women
Ghana 94, 146
girls
  education of x, xviii, xx, xxi, 179, 242
  and human rights 179
  see also gender; women
GNP (gross national product), and education expenditure 5–6, 9–11, 13, 40
goal-free evaluation 200
government institutions, and aid projects 111–12
Guatemala 52

higher education, World Bank paper on (1995) 24–5
HIID (Harvard Institute for International Development) 71, 72, 73, 74, 76–7, 78
Hillgate Group 205
history, and intercultural development education 180–1
HMI (Her Majesty's Inspectorate) 204
home conditions, and educational opportunities 7–9
human capital investment xvi
  in primary education 34–42, 243
human resource development xviii–xix
human rights ix, x, xxiii, 239
  abuse of xiv–xv, 135, 136, 142
  children's rights 141, 175, 240
  and development 115–16
  education 243
    in Ethiopia 135–48, 244
    and intercultural relations 173–83, 243–4
    political dimension of 180
  and institutional violence 88
  organizations 123
Humanities Curriculum Project 202

IIEP (International Institute for Educational Planning) 61
illiteracy 5, 106
impairments, children with 106–7
incomes
  and investment in primary education 35, 37
  per capita 6, 8
India 83, 92–3, 225
  Andhra Pradesh Primary Education Project (APPEP) 52, 226–38
  DPEP (District Primary Education Programme) 225, 226, 236, 237
  Government of 225–6
  OBB (Operation Blackboard) 226, 227, 237
indigenous language rights 149–69, 244
  Māoris 154–65
'innovation fatigue' 194
innovations 187–96, 244
  amending 193–4
  and education practice 192–5
  effective patterns in large-scale 195
  evaluations of 195
  examples of 187–8
  large v. small 192–3
  and the nature of change 194
  small amending 189–90
  small 'refining' 190
  small 'resuscitating' 190–1
  value models of 187
Institute of Advanced Projects 119–20
institutional violence 88
Inter-American Development Bank 67, 77, 117
intercultural education 177–83, 243–4
International Council of Voluntary Agencies xvi
International Covenant on Civil and Political Rights 154
International Declaration of Human Rights xviii
international education 174
International Monetary Fund (IMF) 3, 39–40, 109
international organizations, and research dissemination 101
investment, in primary education xvii, 34–42, 240–1

Japan 70
Jomtien Conference on Education for All (1990) xiv, xvi, xviii, 3, 4, 7, 225, 227, 239
  and capacity–building 52, 53, 54

Kenya 53, 138, 141
Korea 70, 88, 203